Legal Secretary's Encyclopedic Dictionary

THIRD EDITION

Legal Secretary's Encyclopedic Dictionary

THIRD EDITION

By The Prentice-Hall Editorial Staff

Revised by

Mary A. De Vries

Prentice-Hall, Inc.   Englewood Cliffs, New Jersey

Prentice-Hall International, Inc., *London*
Prentice-Hall of Australia, Pty. Ltd., *Sydney*
Prentice-Hall of Canada, Ltd., *Toronto*
Prentice-Hall of India Private Ltd., *New Delhi*
Prentice-Hall of Japan, Inc., *Tokyo*
Prentice-Hall of Southeast Asia Pte. Ltd., *Singapore*
Whitehall Books, Ltd., *Wellington, New Zealand*

Library of Congress Cataloging in Publication Data
Main entry under title:

Legal secretary's encyclopedic dictionary.

 1. Legal secretaries—United States—Handbooks,
manuals, etc. I. De Vries, Mary Ann. II. Prentice-Hall, Inc.
KF319.L36 1981   349.73'024651   81-8700
                     347.30024651   AACR2

ISBN 0-13-528869-X

Printed in the United States of America

A Word from the Reviser
On the Increased Practical Value
This Edition Offers . . .

I remember one of the first times I discussed legal secretarial duties in depth with legal secretaries, researchers, and attorneys. That was more than a decade ago. Some years later, while preparing a book for legal secretaries, I again probed the matter of legal secretaryship. Things had changed—that much was certain. Now, while preparing this third revised edition of *Legal Secretary's Encyclopedic Dictionary (LSED),* I have had another opportunity to work with legal secretaries, attorneys, and other law-office personnel. Once again, I have learned how much things have changed in the legal community. This time, the change seems to be more dramatic. It encompasses not only recent changes in the law and related legal procedures but impressive changes in legal secretaries themselves and the responsibilities they assume.

The legal secretary of the 1980s has a broader legal vocabulary; she has a greater understanding of legal procedures—in the law office, in the courtroom, and generally wherever legal matters are handled; she has stronger skills to use in preparing legal documents, assisting in legal research, and processing all kinds of legal writing; and she has assumed a more important role in representing her office in public and client relations. In short, today's legal secretary is a well-educated, well-informed, and highly skilled professional—greatly respected and admired by co-workers, clients, and everyone she meets.

Since previous editions of *LSED* have served legal secretaries so well, it has been a challenge to make this revised edition even more useful to the professional legal secretary of the current decade. Bringing the many entries up to date was essential, of course. Today, more than ever, you need current information to stay well informed. But you also need additional practical information about legal procedures to handle your duties quickly and expertly; more definitions of commonly used legal terms to enrich your vocabulary; and quick, easy-to-follow guidelines to enhance your typing, filing, and other office skills.

5

To make this revised edition fit the expanding role of today's legal secretary, we have reviewed and completely updated each entry from the previous edition, adding valuable new information in many cases to make the entries more useful. The entry on *accounting,* for instance, now explains the use of modern legal accounting methods such as numerical coding.

In previous editions, numerous general secretarial entries were mixed throughout the legal entries. To sharpen the focus on the legal information, which is of primary concern to you, we have reorganized and regrouped the miscellaneous general entries into a few major categories: Correspondence, Filing, Mail, Manuscript, Printing, Punctuation, Reminders, Telegraph, Telephone, Travel, Type Face, and Typing.

As a legal secretary, you must constantly strive to recognize and understand the wide range of legal terminology you hear each day in the law office. To help you expand your vocabulary, we have added more than 140 essential new terms, for example:

> abstract of record •dominant estate • false arrest • hung jury • interroga-
> tories • long-arm statutes • palimony • promissory estoppel • reversible
> error • sub-chapter S corporation • tender • unjust enrichment • vested •
> words of art

Moreover, we have expanded the information in many previous entries to give you a broader source of legal data. For instance, the entry *Statute of Limitation* now includes a detailed table showing the statutes of limitations in number of years for each of the fifty states.

The legal secretary's role is not the only thing that has been changing dramatically. Some practices and procedures have been revised too. More legal documents are now prepared on 8½- by 11-inch paper, for example; photocopies rather than carbon copies are preferred in many offices for some file copies or additional copies; legal backs are no longer mandatory in certain situations. All of these changes in practice and procedure are reflected in each revised and updated entry.

The best features of the previous editions have been retained, however. The entries in this revised edition, for instance, still contain the easy-to-follow, step-by-step instructions for preparing and processing all kinds of legal papers. They still contain the many sample forms that illustrate firsthand how a properly prepared document really looks. In other words, this revised edition still fully lives up to the term *encyclopedic dictionary*. It defines, describes, explains, instructs, and illustrates.

Every conceivable area of law is covered, from real estate to taxes to wills. Similarly, every imaginable document is described—both court and noncourt papers, legal forms and certificates of all kinds, including the applicable captions, clauses, signature lines, and so forth. Also included are entries about litigation and appeals and other court actions; about legal research, citations, bookkeeping, and legal correspondence; about business organization, corporations, and trusts; about legal ethics and contacts with clients; and much more. It's all there, with entries arranged in alphabetical order; many of the entries have cross-references to other terms that provide additional or related information. No book, of course, can provide all of the exceptions that are peculiar to individual states and specific jurisdictions. Therefore, the careful legal secretary will always double-check in her own jurisdiction and state for any particular requirements concerning size of paper, form of citation, and other matters that may differ from general practices and procedures described in this book.

In every possible way, this third edition of *LSED* has been expanded, updated, and substantially improved to meet the changing needs of legal secretaries in the 1980s. You might say that both—the book and the legal secretaries—have changed significantly in recent years. You might also say that the two are made for each other: as one of today's well-informed, highly skilled professional legal secretaries, you can expect to receive substantial rewards from making this book one of your closest companions.

Mary A. De Vries

Acknowledgments

This third edition of *Legal Secretary's Encyclopedic Dictionary* was largely inspired and revised with the help of a remarkable team of legal experts. In particular, I want to acknowledge the contributions of David L. Osmon, attorney at law, Osmon, Wilber & Strother; Judy Strother, law student, University of Arkansas School of Law; and Mary Ross and Janice Reed, legal secretaries, Osmon, Wilber & Strother. I also appreciated the help of Lane Strother and others at Osmon, Wilber & Strother, and I am grateful for the research assistance we received through the use of facilities at the University of Arkansas School of Law.

Before a single entry was written for this third edition, David Osmon, Judy Strother, Mary Ross, and Janice Reed carefully reviewed all entries in the previous edition and submitted detailed recommendations for corrections and other improvements. In addition, they provided basic information for more than 140 new entries. A major portion of the extensive research for this third edition was undertaken by Judy Strother. All new and revised information was reviewed and improved further by David Osmon. Together this amazing team of talented professionals checked and double-checked the facts and figures that were eventually organized and refined for publication.

I want to thank the firm of Osmon, Wilber & Strother and the outstanding individuals who participated in this project. I am also grateful to the many persons and organizations throughout the country who answered questions, supplied published forms and materials, and offered suggestions on ways to make this third revised edition especially valuable to legal secretaries everywhere.

Abandonment. A knowing relinquishment of one's right or claim to property without any intent to again gain title or possession in the future. Abandonment includes both the intent to abandon and the act of abandonment. Abandonment of leased premises does not relieve the lessee of liability for rent. See also DESERTION.

Abduction. The offense of taking away a wife or child by FRAUD or open violence. The most frequent type of abduction is the carrying away of a female to force her to marry or, with her consent, for the purpose of marriage even though she cannot legally marry without the consent of her parents. The crime also includes such conduct as enticing children away from their parents and enticing females for the purpose of sexual intercourse or prostitution. See KIDNAPPING.

Abeyance. A condition in which the ownership of REAL PROPERTY or PERSONAL PROPERTY is undetermined; a state of affairs being incomplete or undetermined.

Abrogation. The annulment or repeal of a law or obligation by an authoritative act. For example, the COMMON LAW is abrogated by statute.

Abstract Company. A business enterprise whose main function is to search land records and to make a summary of the material parts of every recorded instrument affecting the title to a particular tract of land. The summary is called an ABSTRACT OF TITLE. See also LAND DESCRIPTION.

Abstract of Record. A short, abbreviated form of the case as found in the court file. Abstracts of record are used as a means to bring before an appellate court an abbreviated, accurate, and authentic history of all proceedings in the case that took place in a lower court.

Abstract of Title. Evidence of TITLE to REAL PROPERTY. An abstract is a condensed history of the ownership of or rights in a particular tract of land. It consists of a summary of the material parts of every recorded instrument affecting the title. It begins with a description of the land covered by the abstract and then shows the original government grant and all subsequent deeds, mortgages, releases, wills, judgments, mechanics' liens, FORECLOSURE proceedings, tax sales, and other matters affecting title.

Of course, only a summary of these items is shown. For example, a deed is summarized as shown on the following page.

JASON MORRIS AND EDNA MORRIS, HIS WIFE to WILLIAM BROWNE	WARRANTY DEED Dated June 16, 1912 Ack. June 19, 1912 Rec. June 21, 1912 Transfer Tax Consideration Witnesses Bk. 35, page 38

Conveys a large plot of land including the premises under examination.

The abstract concludes with the abstractor's certificate. This discloses what records the abstractor has or has not examined. For example, if the abstractor certifies that he or she has made no search of federal court proceedings affecting the property, it will be necessary to write to the Clerk of the District Court, who will supply the search for a small charge.

Abstract companies, lawyers, and public officials prepare abstracts. (See ABSTRACT COMPANY.) Abstract companies do by far the greatest portion of the abstracting, except in a few states where there are no abstract companies.

A CONTRACT OF SALE, often called a purchase and sale agreement, frequently provides that the seller shall furnish an abstract of title. This usually means that he or she will give the purchaser an abstract of title certified immediately before the closing of the sale. The original abstract is sent to the abstract company and the company *recertifies* its accuracy and brings it down to date.

Paying the abstractor. When abstract continuations are typed in the law office, the secretary should keep a close record of the continuations so the abstractor may be paid. An arrangement should be made with the abstractor as to how often he or she is to be paid, for example, once a week or the first of the month. A simple method is to use a 3- by 5-inch card with columns for debit, credit, and balance. Frequently, however, payment is included as part of the closing costs and is thus handled immediately after the completion of the real estate transaction.

Number and filing continuations- When continuations are typed in the law office, or when title opinions are given on abstracts, a numbering system should be used to facilitate filing the continuations and/or title opinions and retrieving them. This can be done by the use of 3- by 5-inch index cards.

When the real estate is subdivided real estate or is part of an addition to a city or township, type at the top of the card the name of the subdivision or the addition, and beneath it type each continuation or opinion according to block and lot number. In the case of rural real estate, set up a separate card for each section showing the section, township, and range in numerical sequence. Then, for example, to determine if a continuation or an opinion has been done on the NW¼ NW¼ of Section 3, Township 20 North, Range 5 West of the 5th Principal Meridian, you simply go to the card on that section, township, and range, and any continuations or opinions will be noted there by reference to the file where they are kept. The actual copies of the continuations or opinions should thus be maintained in separate files with only a cross-reference on the index card.

Some index systems are set up under the owners' names. However, since real estate has become such a marketable commodity, in many areas the ownership of real estate changes so rapidly that it is sometimes difficult to keep ownership records updated. Also, simply by checking the current opinion or continuation, you can determine the ownership of the property.

Acceleration Clause. An essential statement contained in a CONTRACT evidencing a debt (as in MORTGAGE, PROMISSORY NOTE, or INSTALLMENT CONTRACT), which provides that the entire debt becomes due and payable immediately when some condition of the contract is breached. The acceleration may be automatic when the breach occurs or it may require an unequivocal election to accelerate. Notice of such intent to accelerate must be given to the obligor.

Without this clause, the mortgagee or seller would have to sue for the amount of each payment as it becomes due, or wait until the entire debt matures. For example, the *acceleration clause* in a MORTGAGE contract might read: *That the whole of said principal sum shall become due after default in the payment of any installment of principal or of interest for ___ days, or after default in the payment of any tax, water rate, or as-*sessment for ___ *days, after notice and demand.*

Acceptance. See CONTRACTS.

Accessory. One who, after the commission of a FELONY, helps the felon to avoid or escape arrest, prosecution, or punishment with knowledge of the offender's wrongful act or liability for such act. The one who aids is known as an *accessory after the fact,* and the felon who is aided is known as the *principal.* One who aids or encourages the felony but is too far away to participate in it is an *accessory before the fact.* See also ACCOMPLICE; AIDING AND ABETTING.

Accommodation Maker (Party). One who signs a note or other obligation as a favor without compensation. The accommodation maker, as surety, remains liable for the note but receives no consideration. The accommodation maker obligates himself or herself to guarantee the debt of the accommodated party.

Accomplice. One who has taken part with the one accused in perpetration of, or in preparation for, a crime, with intent to assist in the crime. Whether or not a person is classified as an accomplice is important, since many states have statutes forbidding conviction when the only incriminating evidence is that given by an accomplice. See ACCESSORY; AIDING AND ABETTING.

Accord and Satisfaction. Payment of money, or other consideration, usually less than the amount owed, to discharge an obligation or debt. The parties must have actually or impliedly agreed that the payment of the smaller sum will discharge the debt. It is an equitable remedy that must be pled as a bar to recovery in a subsequent lawsuit.

Accounting Records for the Lawyer. 1. *Business.* Books of account must be kept regularly and accurately in a law office. Also, a monthly profit and loss statement should be prepared and evaluated so the law office can determine, on a month to month basis, the amount of profit, the percentage of net profit to gross incomes, and other areas important for accurate evaluation of the business entity.

In most small offices, the principal secretary is also the bookkeeper. A basic bookkeeping course would be most helpful to the legal secretary who handles this task. Basically, it is essential that all receipts and all expenditures be recorded so at the end of the accounting period, whether it be monthly, quarterly, semiannually, or annually, an accurate statement of account (sometimes called "profit and loss statement") can be prepared.

A coding system for both receipts and disbursements is helpful. For instance, for receipts, probate income could be coded 101, real estate income 102, personal injury income 103, income tax income 104, trial income 105, bankruptcy income 106, and so on. Expenses could be coded as utilities 501, legal supplies 502, janitorial supplies 503, rent 504, travel 505, auto 506, and so on.

When income in any form is received, it should be entered in a receipt book, coded, and, if desired, credited to the producing attorney by initial, alphabetical designation, or number designation. In many offices, an attorney's compensation is based upon his gross production, and it is therefore necessary to credit the attorney who produced the income. These receipt records are, from time to time, compared with the bank deposits so it can be determined that all money received was properly deposited in the business account.

In the payment of expenses, it is useful to make the code designation of the expenditure on the stub of the check. Then, at the end of the accounting period, the amount of each check can be entered in a columnar journal and, after all entries are made, each column can be totaled and these totals used to prepare a statement of account. It is very important that the business recover costs it has advanced on behalf of a customer or client. Therefore, when payment is made that represents a cost advanced for a customer or client, that expense should be posted immediately to the client's account.

Complete billing and posting systems can be purchased from several sources. Although they may at first appear to be expensive, they will more than pay for themselves as an accurate method of keeping up with time and expenses. Many offices now use computers to prepare their statement of account at the end of the accounting period. This is simply done by setting up the code designation on the computer. The posting is then done daily, weekly, or perhaps monthly. Once each receipt and expenditure is properly coded into the computer, the computer will total all columns and show the net profit or loss for the accounting period. The computer can be used to handle the entire accounting system with each attorney in the office having a code designation, each account having a code designation, and each type of service having a code designation. Thus, when the code for the attorney, the client, the type of service, and the charge therefor are all coded into the computer, the computer will automatically post and maintain the account until the account is ready for billing, at which time all the information necessary for the final statement can be retrieved from the computer.

Trust accounts. The attorney should maintain a trust account for depositing funds belonging to others. These trust accounts can be used to close real estate transactions, to handle court costs, or to make alimony payments. It is unethical for an attorney to deposit trust funds in personal or business accounts. Secretaries who handle trust money should be extremely careful with records and disburse the funds only at the direction of the attorney who is responsible, lest the attorney be accused of mishandling the funds. Secretaries who assist in maintaining trust accounts should be extremely careful also to avoid overdisbursements on any account. Therefore, each individual account balance should be maintained at all times, and any disbursement from an individual's trust fund should be debited to that individual's account immediately upon disbursement.

2. Personal. Although the size of the lawyer's estate might not justify a formal set of books, every lawyer must keep a record of income and expenditures for tax purposes, if for no other reason. Frequently, the secretary maintains these records. Three broad classes of records are usually kept:

1. Records of what the lawyer owns, such as stocks, bonds, and real estate.
2. Records that must be kept for income and other tax purposes.
3. Records of living expenses that are not deductible under the income tax law, in addition to records for other purposes.

A columnar book, or journal, supported by detailed records of income-producing property, is adequate. Columnar books are available in single or double pages with from two to thirty-six money columns and additional columns for date, for number and amount of checks, and for an explanation of the item being entered in the journal.

Separate columns should be allotted to income and to expenditures. There should be a separate column for each source of recurring income and a miscellaneous column for nonrecurring items. Because of the special tax treatment accorded stock dividends, it is important that dividends be kept separate from other income.

A separate column should be allotted to each class of deductible expenses that recur frequently. Deductible items that occur only occasionally may be entered in an *Other Deductions* column and analyzed at the end of the year for the lawyer's federal income tax return. Nondeductible expenditures may be kept in a *Nondeductible Expenses* column unless the lawyer wants to know what a particular class of expenses has cost. In that case, a separate column is allotted to each class of expenses in which the lawyer is interested. The lawyer may want a record of one or more of the following expenses:

1. House expenses, if the lawyer owns the home he or she lives in. This includes expenditures for repairs, replacements, decoration, outside painting, grounds, and the like. Taxes and mortgage interest are deductible expenses.

2. Wages paid to employees. These records must be kept for SOCIAL SECURITY TAX purposes and for filing an information return required by the government. Also, in some localities an employer of one or more domestic employees must pay state unemployment and disability insurance taxes on their wages.

3. Life insurance and other premiums. The cost can be determined from the INSURANCE records.

4. Education of children.

5. Clothes.

6. Recreation, including expenses incurred at country clubs and other social clubs.

7. Money spent in support of a dependent.

8. Travel, other than in connection with business. A record of business travel expenditures must be kept for income tax purposes. (See EXPENSE ACCOUNT.)

9. Automobile expenses, other than in connection with business. A record of business automobile expenses must be kept for income tax purposes.

10. Membership dues, other than those that are deductible.

11. Hobbies, such as expenditures on greenhouses, raising chickens, keeping stables, and the like.

12. Gifts.

Acknowledgment. In law, the act by which a person who signs a legal instrument goes before an authorized officer, such as a NOTARY PUBLIC, and declares that he or she executed the instrument. The notary public signs what is called the *certificate of acknowledgment.* The function of the certificate of acknowledgment is twofold: It entitles the instrument to be recorded or filed and it authorizes the instrument to be given in evidence without further proof of its execution.

Laws governing acknowledgments. Most states, under the Uniform Acknowledgment Act, require the acknowledgment of an instrument before it can be recorded or filed. In those states that have adopted the Uniform Acknowledgment Act the laws governing the use of acknowledgments and their form are similar. Otherwise the law varies with the state, and each state's statutes must be adhered to strictly. A basic principle of law governing acknowledgments is that *the law of the state where the instrument is recorded or used governs*—not the law of the state where the instrument is executed. For example, an instrument prepared in a New York office to be recorded in Florida will use the form and wording that follow the Florida statutes, although the certificate will show that the acknowledgment was made in New York. An instrument sent to Florida to be signed and returned for recording in New York will follow the New York laws governing the certificate of acknowledgment, although it will show that the acknowledgment was made in Florida.

The lawyer usually dictates, or makes available to the secretary, a form of the acknowledgment he wants used. Figures 1 to 3 show how various acknowledgments may be typed. The illustrations are not meant to be copied word for word, but serve merely as examples.

Essentials of an acknowledgment. Although acknowledgments vary with the state, they all have certain basic essentials. These are:

1. *Venue.* An acknowledgment always begins with a recital of the venue, that is, the name of the state and county in which the acknowledgment is made. In Kentucky, Massachusetts, Pennsylvania, and Virginia, the venue recites the name of the *commonwealth* instead of the *state;* in Louisiana, the *parish* instead of the *county.* Type the statement of the venue in solid caps, bracket it, and follow with *ss.,* the abbreviation for *scilicet.* The abbreviation may be caps or small letters. Like most abbreviations, it is followed by a period. Technically, a colon should also follow because scilicet means "to wit," but few law offices observe this technicality.

2. *Date of acknowledgment.* An acknowledgment always recites the date on which the acknowledgment is made. When you type the certificate of acknowledgment, leave blank spaces for the day of the month and also for the name of the month if you are preparing the instrument near the end of the month. Although a client is supposed to sign and acknowledge an instrument on the 30th of April, he or she might not get into the office until the 1st day of May. The date of the acknowledgment does not necessarily coincide with the date of the instrument, but the date of an acknowledgment must *never* precede the date the instrument was signed.

3. *Designation of person making acknowledgment.* The name of the person making the acknowledgment always appears in the certificate. Type it in solid caps. If the person making the acknowledgment is making it in a capacity other than that of an individual, that capacity is also stated, but not in solid caps. For example, when a person makes an acknowledgment as secretary of a corporation, the designation is written, ". . . EDWARD WILLIAMS, secretary of Royal Matches, Inc., . . ." The person who makes the acknowledgment does not sign the certificate.

4. *Signature and designation of officer taking acknowledgment.* The officer who takes an acknowledgment signs the certificate. In typing the certificate, type a blank line for his or her signature four spaces beneath the body of the certificate. Type the officer's title underneath the line. In many states the certificate also recites the name and full title of the officer taking the acknowledgment. If you do not know who is to take the acknowledgment, leave a blank space long enough for the average name to be inserted in handwriting.

5. *Date of expiration of commission.* Many states require that an acknowledgment taken by a notary public show the date of the expiration of his or her commission. On acknowledgments to be used in those states, type "My commission expires. . . . . . ., 19 . . ." two spaces below the signature. Notaries usually have a rubber stamp showing the expiration date of their commission, and the typed line is not necessary except as a reminder that the date of expiration must appear on the certificate.

6. *Notary's seal.* In almost all cases the certificate of acknowledgment must also bear the notary's seal, especially if the instrument is acknowledged outside the state where it is to be recorded. See NOTARY'S SEAL.

STATE OF ALABAMA)
                   : ss.
COUNTY OF FRANKLIN)

     I, JOAN ELLIS, a notary public in and for the said state and county, duly commissioned and sworn, hereby certify that JOHN P. JONES, and MARY P. JONES, his wife, who are to me personally known, this day appeared before me personally, and severally acknowledged that they signed, sealed, and delivered the foregoing deed for the purposes therein stated. The said MARY P. JONES, wife of said JOHN P. JONES, being duly examined by me, separate and apart from her said husband, did declare that she signed, sealed, and delivered the said deed freely and voluntarily, and without compulsion by her said husband, with intention to renounce and convey all dower or other right, title, and interest in the property thereby conveyed, for the uses and purposes therein stated.

     IN WITNESS WHEREOF, I have hereunto set my hand and official seal this 30th day of April, 19—.

_____
                     Notary Public

Acknowledgment: Figure 1.
*Certificate of acknowledgment by
husband and wife—separate examination.*

Acquittal. 1. *Contracts.* A release, absolution, or discharge from an obligation, liability, or engagement.

2. *Crimes.* The legal and formal certification of the innocence of a person who has been charged with crime; a deliverance or setting free of a person from a charge of guilt.

Additur. The power of a judge to increase the amount of an inadequate award of money in a jury verdict. The DAMAGES are increased, with the consent of the defendant, as condition for the denial of plaintiff's motion for a new trial on the grounds that the damages awarded are inadequate. Additur is usually proposed in informal, off-the-record discussion between the judge and counsel for both sides.

Additur, as well as REMITTIUR, is an effective means of giving a just award without the expense and trouble of a new trial.

STATE OF KANSAS   )
                     : ss.
COUNTY OF JOHNSON)

      I hereby certify that on this day before me, an officer duly authorized in the state aforesaid and in the county aforesaid to take acknowledgments, personally appeared ROY SMITH and FRANK PARKER, to me known and known to be the persons described in and who executed the foregoing instrument as president and secretary, respectively, of Henderson Company, Inc., a corporation named therein, and severally acknowledged before me that they executed the same as such officers, in the name of and for and on behalf of the said corporation.

      IN WITNESS WHEREOF, I have hereunto set my hand and affixed my official seal this   day of September, 19—.

                            —————————————————
                                  Notary Public

              My commission expires

Acknowledgment: Figure 2.
*Certificate of acknowledgment by
corporation—two officers.*

Ademption. The failure of a *specific legacy* (see LEGACY) because the subject matter no longer belongs to the testator's estate at his death. See also ADVANCEMENT.

Adjective Law. See SUBSTANTIVE LAW.

Adjuster. One who settles an insurance claim. The adjuster determines the amount of loss and makes an agreement with the insured for a settlement.

Adjustment of Charges and Income (Real Estate). Upon a sale of REAL PROPERTY, an equitable apportionment, or proration, between seller and purchaser of the charges against the property to be conveyed and of any income produced by the property.

Date of adjustment. In many instances, adjustments are made as of the

```
STATE OF NEW YORK    )
                      :  ss.
COUNTY OF YATES      )


        On this         day of              , 19—, before me, Diane
Watson, notary public in and for said county and state, personally
appeared Phillip T. Owens, known to me to be one of the partners of the
partnership that executed the within instrument, and acknowledged to
me that such partnership executed the same.



                     _____
                     Notary Public in and for said
                          County and State
```

Acknowledgment: Figure 3.
*Certificate of acknowledgment by
partnership.*

day immediately preceding the day on which TITLE is closed; that is, the purchaser bears the charges and receives the income beginning with and including the day on which title passes to him or her. The CONTRACT OF SALE may, however, fix some earlier date of adjustment. If the date for CLOSING TITLE is postponed, the consent to adjournment may indicate a new date of adjustment.

Items adjusted. The following are generally apportioned between purchaser and seller:

1. *Taxes.* These include county, town, city, village, and school taxes. The basis for adjustment depends upon local custom and the agreement of the parties. As to taxes paid for the year for which they are levied and in which title is closed, seller is generally entitled to an amount representing the unexpired portion of that year. When taxes have not yet been paid for the year, they should be paid out of the proceeds at closing or, if not yet payable, should be credited to the buyer.

2. *Water charges.* These include both municipal and private water charges.

3. *Insurance premiums.* These include fire, plate glass, rent, boiler, and other similar insurance. Liability and compensation insurance premiums are generally not apportioned; the purchaser obtains such insurance on his or her own account immediately upon taking title.

4. *Interest on mortgages.* Interest is adjusted from the date of the last payment.

5. *Rents.* In the case of rents collected by the seller for the month in which title is closed, the purchaser is entitled to that portion representing the unexpired part of the month. If rents that have become due have not been paid at the date of closing, the purchaser may give to the seller written assurance, in the form of a letter, that upon receipt of the rent, the

purchaser will turn over to the seller the portion to which the seller is entitled.

The contract of sale may enumerate the items to be adjusted. Other items not mentioned, for example, fuel on hand, prepayments on service contracts, and the like, may also be prorated according to local practice. If payment due on the closing is to be made by certified check, the purchaser should bring to the closing a check for the approximate amount and sufficient *cash* to cover adjustments.

Method of calculating adjustments. For the purpose of simplification, many local real estate boards recommend the practice of computing by a 360-day method, rather than a 365-day method. Each month represents 1/12 of the annual charge, and each day 1/30 of the monthly charge. When the period for which computation is made is more than one month, the time is computed by full months and by the actual number of days in excess of such full months. For example, the period between March 15 and June 3 is 2 months (April and May) and 20 days (17 days in March and 3 days in June).

Examples of calculation of adjustments. Following are some examples of calculations of adjustments. For the purpose of the examples, assume that title closes June 8, 19___.

1. *Tax adjustment.* Taxes in the locality are payable semiannually, April 1 and October 1. The seller paid taxes on April 1 for the preceding 6-month period. During the current 6-month period, the seller is responsible for taxes from April 1 to, but not including, June 8, the closing date. He would have to allow the buyer the amount of the taxes for that period—2 months (April and May) and 7

days. Assuming that the taxes for the 6-month period amount to $1,500, the taxes for one month are $250 ($1,500 ÷ 6), for one day, $8.33 1/3 ($250 ÷ 30). An adjustment of $558.33 is made in favor of the purchaser [2 × $250 + (7 × $8.33 1/3)].

2. *Interest adjustment.* Suppose there is a mortgage of $24,000 on the property, with interest at 10 percent payable quarterly on 15th of December, March, June, and September. When title closed on June 8, interest had been paid to but not including March 15. The purchaser is entitled to an allowance for interest from and including March 15 through June 7, or for a period of 2 months (April and May) and 24 days (17 days in March, 7 days in June). The interest on $24,000 at 10 percent per annum is $200 per month, $6.66 2/3 per day ($200 ÷ 30). The interest for 2 months, 24 days is $400 (2 × $200) + $159.98 (24 × $6.66 2/3). An adjustment of $359.98 is made in favor of the purchaser.

3. *Insurance adjustment.* Suppose there is a fire policy on the property that was paid one year in advance. The expiration date of the policy is August 1, 1983. The seller is therefore entitled to an adjustment of insurance for 61 days (June 8, 1980, the date of closing, to August 1, 1980, the renewal date for the insurance policy). The premium is $360 per year, $30 per month, or $1 per day. An adjustment of $61 is made in favor of the seller.

4. *Rent adjustment.* The seller had collected the rents in advance for the month of June. They amounted to $5,000. The purchaser is entitled to an adjustment for the period from and including June 8 through June 30, or 23

21

days. Since June has only 30 days, the rent per day is $5,000 ÷ 30, or $166.66 2/3 per day. The purchaser is entitled to an adjustment of $3,833.33 (23 × $166.66-2/3). If there is more than one tenant, the rent for each must be prorated separately, unless the rents had all been collected for the same period.

Administrative Law. The rules and regulations framed by an administrative body created by a state legislature or by Congress to carry out a specific statute. For example, the federal income tax law is administered by the Internal Revenue Service, which issues regulations and rules that have the weight of law as long as they keep within the scope of the income tax statute. Frequently such regulations interpret in a specific way the legislature's general intent when it enacted the statute. Thus, administrative bodies, which are primarily executive in nature, may also have powers that resemble legislative or judicial authority.

Administrator. See LETTERS OF ADMINISTRATION.

Admiralty. A court empowered to enforce maritime law and exercise JURISDICTION over a maritime CONTRACT, TORT, and certain maritime crimes. Admiralty jurisdiction is placed by the Constitution within the federal judicial system, although state and federal common law courts can and do enforce most maritime rights. Only a federal court can enforce a MARITIME LIEN, however. There is no requirement of diversity of citizenship or of a minimum amount of monies involved as there is in federal civil cases. Federal admiralty courts may hear all such cases involving waters that are navigable in foreign or INTERSTATE COMMERCE. Whether a particular water is navigable is a question of fact of which the courts may take JUDICIAL NOTICE, but should the point be in doubt, evidence may be introduced and considered.

Admiralty has developed its own procedure and terminology, and attorneys in this field (see PROCTOR) generally insist that its peculiar customs be followed. The secretary who works for a lawyer specializing in admiralty, therefore; must be aware of terms that are unique in admiralty. See CITATION (Admiralty Proceeding); LIBEL AND SLANDER; (in Admiralty Practice); RESPONDENT; CLAIMANT; PETITION. An example of a verified libel and answer (corresponding to the complaint and answer in a common law proceeding) demonstrating the correct form and terminology to be used follows. The cause of action involves the alleged damage of goods aboard ship. (See figures 1 to 4).

See also MARITIME LIEN; CHARTER-PARTY; GENERAL AVERAGE LOSS; SALVAGE.

Admissible Evidence. Evidence that a trial court may receive in deciding the case. Various rules determine whether evidence may be admitted. The judge may properly receive only admissible evidence and need not allow all of it to be introduced.

Admission to the Bar. The status that allows a person to practice law

LIBEL

TO THE HONORABLE THE JUDGES OF THE UNITED STATES DISTRICT COURT
FOR THE SOUTHERN DISTRICT OF NEW YORK

The libel and complaint of A-1 IMPORTING COMPANY against the Steamship TEMPEST, her engines, boilers, etc., and FRY SHIPPING COMPANY, in a cause of contract, civil and maritime, alleges upon information and belief, and respectfully shows to this Honorable Court, as follows:

FIRST: At all times hereinafter mentioned, libelant was, and now is, a corporation organized and existing under and by virtue of the laws of the State of New York, with an office and place of business at 500 Fifth Avenue, in the City and State of New York.

SECOND: At all times hereinafter mentioned, the Steamship TEMPEST was, and now is, a general merchant ship engaged in the common carriage of goods by water for hire and is now or will be during the pendency of this action within this District and subject to and within the jurisdiction of the Honorable Court.

THIRD: At all times hereinafter mentioned, FRY SHIPPING COMPANY was, and now is, a corporation organized and existing under and by virtue of the laws of the Republic of Liberia, with an office and place of business at 50 Water Street, City and State of New York.

FOURTH: On or about June 15, 19—, at London, England, John Doe, Inc., as shipper, delivered to the respondent and to the Steamship TEMPEST a shipment consisting of 50 cartons of linen in good order and condition, and the respondents then and there accepted the said merchandise so delivered to them and in consideration of the payment of certain freight charges, paid or agreed to be paid, agreed to transport said merchandise as a common carrier of the Port of New York, and there deliver the same in like good order and condition as when shipped to shipper's order, notify A-1 Importing Company, in accordance with the valid terms and conditions of its bill of lading No. 42 dated June 15, 19—, at London issued that date by the duly authorized agent of the respondent and the Steamship TEMPEST.

FIFTH: Thereafter the respondent loaded the said merchandise on board the Steamship TEMPEST, and the said vessel having the said merchandise on board, sailed from the Port of London and subsequently arrived at the Port of New York where the TEMPEST and the respondent failed to deliver the merchandise in the same like order and condition as when received by the respondent, but on the contrary, delivered it crushed and damaged and contaminated by water and other substances unknown to libelant.

SIXTH: At all said times, libelant was the ultimate consignee of the merchandise and brings this action not only on its own behalf but on behalf of and for the benefit of all parties who may become interested, as their respective interests may ultimately appear.

SEVENTH: Libelant and said other parties have duly complied with all valid obligations and conditions of the aforesaid contract of carriage on their respective parts to be performed.

EIGHTH: By reason of the premises, libelant and said other parties have sustained damages in the amount of $15,000, as nearly as the same can now be estimated, no part of which has been paid although duly demanded.

NINTH: All and singular premises are true and within the admiralty and maritime jurisdiction of the United States and of this Honorable Court.

WHEREFORE, libelants pray:

1. That process in due form of law, according to the course and practice of this Honorable Court in causes of Admiralty and Maritime jurisdiction, may issue against the respondent FRY

(continued on following page)

(continued from preceding page)

SHIPPING COMPANY, and that the said respondent be cited to appear and answer, all and singular, the matters aforesaid.

2. That process in due form of law, according to the course and practice of this Honorable Court in causes of Admiralty and Maritime jurisdiction, may issue against the Steamship TEMPEST, her engines, etc., and that all persons claiming any interest in the said vessel be cited to appear and answer, all and singular, the matters aforesaid.

3. That this Honorable Court may adjudge and decree that the said respondent pay to libelant its damages as aforesaid, together with interest and costs and that the Steamship TEMPEST be condemned and sold to pay the same.

4. Libelant may have such other and further relief in the premises as in law and justice it may be entitled to receive.

> WINSTON & SILLS
> Proctors for Libelant
> Office & P.O. Address
> 11 John Street
> New York, New York 10001

Admiralty: Figure 1. *Illustration of libel and complaint.*

VERIFICATION

STATE OF NEW YORK ⎫
⎬ ss.:
COUNTY OF NEW YORK ⎭

MICHAEL R. HALL, being duly sworn, deposes and says:

That he is the Vice President of A-1 IMPORTING COMPANY, the libelant herein.

That he has read the foregoing libel and knows the contents thereof and the same is true of his own knowledge except as to matters therein stated to be alleged upon information and belief, and as to those matters he believes them to be true.

That the reason why this verification is made by deponent and not by libelant is that libelant is a corporation and depondent is an officer thereof.

That the sources of deponent's information and the grounds of his belief are reports made to him by employees, and libelant's records.

....

Sworn to before me this
day of August, 19...

Admiralty: Figure 2. *Example of verification of libelant.*

ANSWER

TO THE HONORABLE THE JUDGES OF THE UNITED STATES DISTRICT COURT FOR THE SOUTHERN DISTRICT OF NEW YORK

The answer of respondent FRY SHIPPING COMPANY to the libel of A-1 IMPORTING COMPANY, in an alleged cause of contract, civil and maritime, alleges upon information and belief, as follows:

FIRST: It denies knowledge or information sufficient to form a belief as to the allegations of article First of the libel.

SECOND: It admits that the Steamship TEMPEST was and is a general merchant ship engaged in the common carriage of goods by water for hire, denies that it is now within this district and subject to and within the jurisdiction of this Honorable Court and denies knowledge or information sufficient to form a belief as to its future whereabouts.

THIRD: It admits the allegations of article Third of the libel.

FOURTH: It admits that at London, England on or about June 15, 19— it received from John Doe, Inc., a shipment consisting of 50 cartons, contents and condition of contents unknown to it, for transportation to the Port of New York for an agreed freight, and delivery there as ordered by the shipper, in accordance with and subject to the terms, conditions and exceptions of its bill of lading No. 42 dated June 15, 1977, issued to and accepted by the said shipper at London by respondent's duly authorized agent. Except as above admitted, respondent denies the allegations of article Fourth of the libel.

FIFTH: It admits that the shipment referred to in article Fourth herein was loaded on board the TEMPEST and carried by it from London to New York where it was delivered in accordance with the terms of the aforementioned bill of lading, which constituted the contract of carriage. Except as herein admitted, it denies the allegations of article Fifth of the libel.

SIXTH: It denies knowledge or information sufficient to form a belief as to the allegations of article Sixth of the libel.

SEVENTH: It denies the allegations of article Seventh of the libel.

EIGHTH: It admits demand and non-payment and denies the remaining allegations of article Eighth of the libel.

NINTH: It admits the admiralty and maritime jurisdiction of the United States and of this Honorable Court and denies the remaining allegations of article Ninth of the complaint.

TENTH: Further answering, respondent alleges that the 50 cartons referred to in the libel were received at London and transported subject to the terms, conditions and exceptions of bill of lading referred to in article Fourth of the libel, conditions and exceptions of bill of lading referred to in article Fourth of the libel, which constituted the contract of carriage, and in accordance with the Carriage of Goods by Sea Act.

The following exception was noted on the face of the said bill of lading:

"CARTONS WATER-STAINED BUT
APPARENTLY DRY"

The said Carriage of Goods by Sea Act provided in part as follows:

"Sec. 3 (6) ***," In any event the carrier and the ship shall be discharged from all liability in respect of loss or damage unless suit is brought within one year after delivery of the goods or the date when the goods should have been delivered.***."

"Sec. 4 (2). Neither the carrier nor the ship shall be responsible for loss or damage arising or resulting from—

(continued on following page)

(continued from preceding page)

(i) Act or omission of the shipper or owner of the goods, his agent or representative;

* * *

(n) Insufficiency of packing;

* * *

(q) Any other cause arising without the actual fault and privity of the carrier and without the fault or neglect of the agents or servants of the carrier***."

Any damage sustained by the shipment occurred before it was delivered to the respondent, and respondent is not liable.

Suit was not brought against respondent within one year after delivery of the goods, and respondent is not liable.

Any loss or damage to the shipment which occurred while it was in respondent's custody was the result of one or more causes excepted in the Carriage of Goods by Sea Act, and respondent is not liable.

All and singular the premises are true.

WHEREFORE, respondent prays that the libel herein be dismissed with costs.

MILES AND SHARPE
Proctors for Respondent
26 Broadway
New York, N.Y. 10001

Admiralty: Figure 3. *Illustration of answer of respondent.*

VERIFICATION

SOUTHERN DISTRICT OF NEW YORK } ss.:

COUNTY OF NEW YORK

EVAN C. SHARPE, being duly sworn, says:

I am one of the proctors for the respondent herein. I have the foregoing answer and know the contents thereof, and the same is true to the best of my knowledge, information and belief. The sources of my knowledge or information are communications received from the respondent and an examination of the papers relating to the matter in suit. The reason why this verification is not made by respondent is that the said respondent is a foreign corporation.

. . . .

Sworn to before me this
        day of August, 19—

Admiralty: Figure 4. *Example of verification for respondent.*

within a state. Each state has its own requirements for admission to the bar. In every state, the requirements include these four factors: academic training, legal training, moral character, and belief in and loyalty to the form of the United States Goverment.

In almost all states the applicant for admission to the bar must take an examination even though he or she is a graduate of law school. Admission to practice in one state does not license the attorney to practice in another state. The attorney must comply with the rules which that state has for admission of an "attorney applicant." However, almost all of the states will admit an attorney from another state without examination after the attorney has practiced for a specified time, provided he or she meets other requirements. A few states require the attorney applicant to take an examination.

License to practice in one or more states does not admit the lawyer to practice in federal courts. To be admitted to practice in the United States Supreme Court, an attorney must have practiced three years in the highest court in his or her state or territory. A member of the bar moves the attorney's admission in open court. Requirements for admission to the federal courts of appeals and district courts vary with the circuit and the district.

An attorney may obtain special permission to argue a particular case before a court in which the attorney is not licensed to practice. This often happens in criminal cases when the accused wants a nationally famous criminal lawyer to represent him or her in the state in which the accused is to be tried.

Adoption. The taking and receiving as one's own that to which one bore no proper relation, colorable or otherwise. The act of taking another's child into one's own family, treating the child as one's own, and giving the child all the rights and duties of one's own child. Adoptions are made legal by making application to the probate court for the right to adopt. Adoptions are usually very secret and in the case of infants, the adoptive parents do not usually know the original surname of the infant they are adopting. The secretary should be very careful never to divulge information to the adoptive parents. See figures 1 and 2.

Adultery. The conscious act of sexual intercourse between a married person and a person other than his or her legal spouse. Adultery is grounds for DIVORCE in every state in this country.

Ad Valorem Tax. A tax or duty based on the value of property. In contrast, a *specific* tax is levied as a fixed sum on each article of class, without regard to its value. (See DUTY.)

Advancement (Inheritance). A payment given to an HEIR by a person who does not intend to leave a WILL (see INTESTATE). One makes the payment with the intention that it substitute for the share of one's estate that such heir would ordinarily receive under the laws of intestacy.

Advancement does not apply where there is a will, unless the will expressly so provides. The maker of a will may refer

27

IN THE COURT OF COMMON PLEAS, DADE COUNTY, FLORIDA
PROBATE DIVISION

IN THE MATTER OF THE ADOPTION OF
EVAN SAMUEL WRIGHT   Case No. _____

PETITION FOR ADOPTION

The undersigned, Joseph S. Wright and Pauline O. Wright represent to the Court that they are husband and wife and they respectfully petition the Court for permission to adopt as their own child, Evan Samuel Crane, and to have the name of said child changed to Evan Samuel Wright.

Your petitioners represent to the Court that the following is a correct statement concerning the petitioner, the child and the child's custody:

PETITIONERS

NAME:	Joseph S. Wright
ADDRESS:	3013 Hardesty Place West, Miami, Florida 33156
DATE & PLACE OF BIRTH:	November 18, 1943 Gainesville, Florida
NAME:	Pauline O. Wright
ADDRESS:	3013 Hardesty Place West, Miami, Florida 33156
DATE & PLACE OF BIRTH:	October 9, 1945 Orlando, Florida
DATE & PLACE OF MARRIAGE:	April 1, 1966 Orlando, Florida
RELATIONSHIP TO CHILD:	None

CHILD

NAME:	Evan Samuel Crane
ADDRESS:	3013 Hardesty Place West, Miami, Florida 33156
DATE & PLACE OF BIRTH:	March 7, 1965 Hialeah, Dade County, Florida
PROPERTY:	None

(continued on following page)

(continued from preceding page)

The following information is given to determine the persons or person whose consent to said adoption is required to be obtained pursuant to R. C. 3107.06; are required to be notified of the filing to the Petition for Adoption pursuant to R. C. 3107.08.

The child is in the permanent custody of the Dade County Children Services Board, a certified organization.

The said child is living in the home of the petitioners herein and was placed in said home on the 1st day of November, 1974, for purposes of adoption by the Dade County Children Services Board.

A certified copy of the child's birth certificate is attached herewith.

Your petitioners represent that they are possessed of sufficient means and ability to properly maintain and educate the said child.

Your petitioners hereby waive notice of any hearing on the petition filed in this cause pursuant to the provisions of Sec. 2101.28 of the Florida Revised Code. Your petitioners further waive notice of any investigation made or report submitted, or availability for examination of the contents of any reports hereafter submitted, by the next friend of said child appointed by the Court in this case.

WHEREFORE, your petitioners pray that upon the final hearing in this cause, they may be permitted by order of Court to adopt Evan Samuel Crane and that the name of said child be changed to Evan Samuel Wright, all in accordance with Chapter 3107 of the Florida Revised Code, pertaining to adoptions.

_____
Joseph S. Wright

_____
Pauline O. Wright

STATE OF FLORIDA, COUNTY OF DADE, SS:

The undersigned, the petitioners in the foregoing petition for adoption, being first duly sworn, say that the statements contained in the foregoing petition are true, as they verily believe.

_____
Joseph S. Wright

_____
Pauline O. Wright

Sworn to before me and subscribed in my presence this 15th day of May, 19—.

_____
Notary Public

Adoption: Figure 1. *Sample*
Petition for adoption.

IN THE COURT OF COMMON PLEAS, DADE COUNTY, FLORIDA
PROBATE DIVISION

IN THE MATTER OF THE ADOPTION OF:
EVAN SAMUEL WRIGHT   Case No. _____

<u>FINAL DECREE OF ADOPTION</u>

    This day this cause came on to be heard on the petition for adoption and change of name of Evan Samuel Wright and the evidence. The Court, being fully advised according to law, is of the opinion that the facts stated in the petition are true; that the petitioners, Joseph S. Wright and Pauline O. Wright, husband and wife, residing at 3013 Hardesty Place West, Miami, Florida 33156, are of good moral character and of reputable standing in the community, and have ability and means properly to care for, rear, and educate said child by them sought to be adopted, according to law in this proceeding; and that the best interest of said child would be promoted by such adoption.

    Further, the Court finds that such child is suitable for adoption, and is satisfied that all the statutory provisions relative to adoption have been complied with; that the child is in the permanent custody of the Dade County Children Services Board, a certified agency, which has answered and consented to the adoption and change of name, and the same is on file herein.

    Further, the Court finds that the said child has resided with the petitioners for more than six (6) months; and the Court, having examined Joseph S. Wright and Pauline O. Wright, each separate and apart from the other, is satisfied that each desires such adoption of his own free will and accord.

    THEREFORE, IT IS ORDERED, ADJUDGED AND DECREED that said adoption be and hereby is made, that the name of said child be and hereby is changed to Evan Samuel Wright, that said child shall hereafter be known by said name, and that from this day henceforth said child shall for all purposes in the adoption statutes of this state provided, be the child of Joseph S. Wright and Pauline O. Wright.

_____
                                  Probate Judge

Approved:

_____
        Attorney

Adoption: Figure 2. *Example of
final decree of adoption.*

to advancements made by him or her to the maker's donees (*see* DONEE) during his or her lifetime, and direct that such advancements be deducted from the donee's LEGACY. *See also* ADEMPTION.

Advance Sheets. *See* NATIONAL REPORTER SYSTEM.

Adversary (Adverse Party). The opponent in a legal controversy or litigation; party on the opposite side.

Adverse Possession. A method whereby one acquires title to land against all others through certain acts over an uninterrupted period. Adverse possession is actual, visible, open, notorious, hostile, under claim or right, definite, continuous, exclusive, and so on.

Advisory Opinion. A formal legal opinion, usually issued by a judge or law officer, upon a question of law, and requested by a government official or legislative body. It does not have the force of law, but is an advisory opinion only. For example, state attorneys are frequently asked to issue an opinion on the state of the law in regard to some issue.

Affiant. A person making an affidavit. The affiant may also be known as the *deponent*. *See* AFFIDAVIT.

Affidavit. A written statement of facts sworn to by the person making the statement in the presence of an officer authorized to administer the oath. The purpose of the affidavit is to help establish or prove a fact. (*See* figure 1.) For example, an affidavit may be used to prove a person's identity, age, marital status, and possession of property. It may also be used as an essential part of a court case or action.

An affidavit is always a complete instrument within itself, whereas an ACKNOWLEDGMENT is always part of, or rather an appendage to, another instrument. An affidavit is sworn to but an acknowledgment is not. Both the person making the affidavit and the officer administering the oath sign an affidavit; only the officer taking an acknowledgment signs it. An affidavit has a JURAT but an acknowledgment does not.

Essentials of an affidavit. Some affidavits are written in the first person and some in the third person, but they all have the following basic essentials:

1. *Venue.* When an affidavit is used in a court case, it is always preceded by the caption of the case. The affidavit itself begins with a recital of the venue.

2. *Name of affiant.* The name of the person making the affidavit is written in solid caps.

3. *Averment of oath.* The introduction to the affidavit avers that the affiant was sworn, or made the statement under oath.

4. *Statement of facts.* The body of the affidavit is a narrative of the facts that the affiant wishes to state.

5. *Signature of affiant.* The affiant always signs the affidavit, even those that are written in the third person.

6. *Jurat.* A jurat is a clause in an official certificate attesting that the affidavit or deposition was sworn to at a stated time before an authorized officer. It is often referred to as the "sworn to" clause.

STATE OF SOUTH CAROLINA   )

                              :   ss.

COUNTY OF DARLINGTON   )

        KENNETH V. KNOX, being duly sworn, deposes and says:

He is the Secretary of Knox Brothers Corporation, and that no stockholder of said Corporation has filed with the Secretary thereof a written request (other than such written request or requests as may have heretofore expired or been withdrawn) that notices intended for him shall be mailed to some address other than his address as it appears on the stock book of the said Corporation.

_____

                                   Secretary

Sworn to before me this

     day of   , 19—

_____

        Notary Public

Affidavit: Figure 1.

In a few states, the jurat recites the title of the officer and the state, or state and county, in which he is authorized to act. In a few other states, the name of the affiant is repeated in the jurat. The most common form of jurat is:

Subscribed and sworn to (or affirmed) before me this
. . . . day of . . . . ,
19 . . . .
                  Notary Public

7. *Signature of notary.* The notary signs immediately beneath the jurat. He also affixes his seal and the expiration date of his commission. In some states the expiration date precedes the signature.

Affidavit of Title. An AFFIDAVIT executed by the seller upon sale of REAL PROPERTY to assure the purchaser that there are no defects in the seller's TITLE to the property. The affidavit of title (figure 1) supplements a title examination; it covers matters that may not be revealed by a TITLE SEARCH. It furnishes additional protection to the purchaser, for a false affidavit of title may subject the seller to criminal prosecution. The affidavit of title also serves as a means of identifying the person executing the papers to be delivered on CLOSING TITLE to the satisfaction of the title company that insures the title. (See TITLE INSURANCE.)

FORM OF AFFIDAVIT OF TITLE

STATE OF NEW YORK ⎫
                    ⎬ ss.:
COUNTY OF   ⎭

Title No. ....
.... being duly sworn, says: I reside at No. ....Street, ... City, State of ....
I am the *.........
owner in fee simple of premises...... and......the grantee described in a certain deed of said premises recorded in the Register's Office of.............County in Liber..........of Conveyances, page ....

Said premises have been in my/its possession since 19......; that my/its possession thereof has been peaceable and undisturbed, and the title thereto has never been disputed, questioned or rejected, nor insurance thereof refused, as far as I know. I know of no facts by reason of which said possession or title might be called in question, or by reason of which any claim to any part of said premises of any interest therein adverse to me/it might be set up. There are no judgments against me/its unpaid or unsatisfied of record entered in any court of this state, or of the United States, and said premises are, as far as I know, free from all leases, mortgages, taxes, assessments, water charges and other liens and encumbrances, except.............

Said premises are now occupied by............
No proceedings in bankruptcy have ever been instituted by or against me/it in any court or before any officer of any state, or of the United States, nor have I/has it at any time made an assignment for the benefit of creditors, nor an assignment, now in effect, of the rents of said premises or any part thereof.

†I am a citizen of the United States, and am more than 21 years old. I am by occupation............ I am married to............who is over the age of 21 years and is competent to convey or mortgage real estate. I was married to her on the ....day of ......19.....I have never been married to any other person now living. I have not been known by any other name during the past ten years.

‡That the charter of said corporation is in full force and effect and no proceeding is pending for its dissolution or annulment. That all license and franchise taxes due and payable by said corporation have been paid in full.

There are no actions pending affecting said premises. That no repairs, alterations or improvements have been made to said premises which have not been completed more than four months prior to the date hereof. There are no facts known to me relating to the title to said premises which have not been set forth in this affidavit.

This affidavit is made to induce............to accept a ....of/on said premises, and to induce........Title Company to issue its policy of title insurance numbered above covering said premises knowing that they will rely on the statements herein made.

Sworn to before me this........
day of........., 19..........

_____

*If owner is a corporation, fill in office held by deponent and name of corporation.
†*This paragraph to be omitted if owner is a corporation.*
‡*This paragraph to be omitted if owner is not a corporation.*

Affidavit of Title: Figure 1.

Affirmance. See RATIFICATION.

Affreightment Contract. A contract by a carrier to transport goods. See BILL (of Lading); CHARTER-PARTY.

AFL-CIO. A united labor federation in the United States, formed by the merger of the AMERICAN FEDERATION OF LABOR and the CONGRESS OF INDUSTRIAL ORGANIZATIONS in December, 1955. George Meany was elected the first president of the AFL-CIO. See also LABOR UNION.

Agency. The relationship that exists when one person authorizes another to act for him or her. The one granting the authority is the *principal;* the one authorized to act is the *agent.* For an agent to act, a *third party,* with whom the agent contracts, is necessary. An agency relationship is created when a person gives a POWER OF ATTORNEY or a PROXY, and in other situations. An agency may be *general*—the agent has broad powers to represent the principal; or the agency may be special.

Aggrieved Party. A person who has been injured or suffered a loss; one whose personal or property rights have been violated by another person.

Agreement. See CONTRACT.

Aiding and Abetting. Words, acts, or presence by one person to assist another person, the principal, to do the physical acts in the commission of a crime. If one aids and abets, one is liable for the same punishment as the principal doing the act. The principal must actually commit the crime if the aider and abetter is to be liable. See ACCOMPLICE; ACCESSORY; CONSPIRACY.

Alias Summons. A SUMMONS that is issued when the original one is not effective because of defective form or improper manner of service. It is prepared like the original summons, except that *alias* precedes *summons.* If the alias summons is not served, and it is necessary to issue a following summons, the third one is designated as a *pluries summons.*

Alibi. An inference that one could not have committed a crime because one was elsewhere at the time of its commission.

Alien. A person born in a foreign country; one who is not a citizen of the country in which one resides.

Alienation (Real Property). The voluntary and absolute transfer or conveyance of title and possession from one person to another.

Alien Corporation. A CORPORATION organized outside the United States. See also FOREIGN CORPORATION; DOMESTIC CORPORATION; STATE OF INCORPORATION.

Alimony. Allowances that a court orders one spouse to pay the other for maintenance while they are separated or after they are divorced. The amount of alimony to be awarded is discretionary with the court. In determining the amount to be paid, the court considers each person's income and ability to provide for himself or herself and family.

Temporary alimony is an allowance made pending a suit for DIVORCE or SEPARATION. It includes a reasonable allowance for expenses in preparing the suit as well as for support. In determining the amount of temporary alimony, the court looks into the chances of the other person's success in the action.

For the purpose of federal income taxes, periodic alimony payments are included in the gross income of the recipient and are deductible by the payer in the year of payment. Generally, alimony payable in a lump sum or in a fixed number of installments is not deductible by the payer. *See* also PALIMONY.

Allegation. A statement made by a party who claims it can be proved as a fact. *See* also COMPLAINT.

Allocution. The requirement that a trial judge ask a defendant to show legal cause why the sentence should not be pronounced upon the verdict of conviction. In modern courts, the judge usually asks the defendant to offer evidence of mitigating circumstances before pronouncing sentence.

Allonge. (French) A piece of paper attached to a bill of exchange or PROMISSORY NOTE, on which to write endorsements when there is no room on the instrument itself.

Alternative Pleading. At common law, a pleading that alleges facts so different or mutually exclusive that it is difficult to determine which facts the plaintiff intends to rely on as a basis for recovery. Alternative pleading is generally permitted under modern procedure.

Amendment of the Constitution. A method of changing the Constitution, as provided by Article V in the Constitution itself. Amendments are proposed by two-thirds of each House of Congress. To become law, they must then be ratified by the legislatures or conventions in three-fourths of the states.

American Association of Law Libraries. An association of law libraries. They may be reached by writing:

American Association of Law Libraries
53 West Jackson Boulevard
Chicago, Illinois 60604

American Bar Association. A national association for lawyers, to which most lawyers belong. The American Bar Association has published a list of canons that govern the members' ethics. They are as follows:

1. A lawyer should assist in maintaining the integrity and competence of the legal profession.
2. A lawyer should assist the legal profession in fulfilling its duty to make legal counsel available.
3. A lawyer should assist in preventing the unauthorized practice of law.
4. A lawyer should preserve the confidences and secrets of a client.
5. A lawyer should exercise independent professional judgment on behalf of a client.
6. A lawyer should represent a client competently.
7. A lawyer should represent a client zealously within the bounds of the law.
8. A lawyer should assist in improving the legal system.
9. A lawyer should avoid even the appearance of professional impropriety.

The American Bar Association may be reached at:
1155 E. 60th Street
Chicago, Illinois 60637.

American Court System. The plan by which American courts are organized and conducted. The American court system consists of federal courts (table I) plus the various systems of all the states. The courts of the District of Columbia and Puerto Rico are part of the federal court system although both are organized similarly to state court systems.

The Supreme Court of the United States is the highest tribunal in our land—it is the apex in the hierarchy of courts, both federal and state. The power of this court demands respect from every member of the legal profession. There is no appeal from its decisions.

State Courts. Each state system consists of the state's highest APPELLATE COURT and of courts of original jurisdiction, that is, courts where suits are initiated (table I). States with a large volume of cases also have INTERMEDIARY APPELLATE COURTS to relieve the congestion of cases in the highest court. A case is brought and tried in a lower court and may be appealed to a higher court having appellate jurisdiction until it reaches the state's highest appellate court, or, in some cases, the United States Supreme Court.

Under most state systems, the state is divided into circuits or districts with a court for each. Usually court is held in each county seat and the judges travel the "circuit" to the county seats to hold court. Other states have only one superior, or trial court, which is composed of geographical divisions. The distinction is reflected in the wording of the captions on court papers. For example, Mississippi is divided into 17 judicial circuits, with a separate court for each. The captions on the court papers read:

IN THE CIRCUIT COURT OF THE FIRST JUDICIAL DISTRICT OF HINDS COUNTY, MISSISSIPPI

On the other hand, there is only one superior court of Massachusetts, which is composed of divisions according to counties. The captions on the court papers read as follows:

COMMONWEALTH OF MASSACHUSETTS

ESSEX, ss   SUPERIOR COURT

In many jurisdictions the courts are also divided into parts for the purpose of facilitating the court's work. There is no standard principle upon which the division is based. For example, the Chancery Court of Davidson County, Tennessee, is divided into Part One and Part Two, and members of the Nashville Bar can bring their suits in either part. The caption designates the part. In Kings County, New York, Part One of the Supreme Court is the part in which all cases are called when they appear on the ready day calendar. (See DOCKET CALL). The judge presiding in Part One sends cases to the different trial parts. After a case is assigned to a certain part, that part is designated in the caption.

The courts in one state have no control over, or relation to, the courts in another state—the hierarchy in each state is complete. Nor do the federal courts, with the exception of the Supreme Court of the United States, have any relation to the state courts.

Federal Courts. When our country first adopted its Constitution, a rivalry and jealousy existed among the states that made up the Union and between the federal government and the respective state governments. The citizens of one state were fearful that they would not receive a fair verdict from judge or jury in

Table I

STATE COURTS OF RECORD IN THE UNITED STATES
AND THEIR MEMBERS
*(Asterisks indicate intermediate appellate courts.
Municipal courts are not included.)*

State	Court	Members of Court
Alabama	Supreme Court	Chief Justice
		Associate Justices
	*Court of Appeals	Presiding Judge
		Associate Judges
	Circuit Courts	Judges
	Probate Courts	Judge
Alaska	Supreme Court	Chief Justice
		Associate Justices
	Superior Court	Judges
Arizona	Supreme Court	Chief Justice, Justices
	Court of Appeals	Judges
	Superior Court	Judges
Arkansas	Supreme Court	Chief Justice
		Associate Justices
	*Court of Appeals	Presiding Judge
		Associate Justices
	Circuit Courts	Judges
	Chancery Courts	Chancellors
	Probate Courts	Judges
California	Supreme Court	Chief Justice
		Associate Justices
	*Courts of Appeal	Presiding Justice
		Justices
	Superior Courts	Judges
Colorado	Supreme Court	Chief Justice, Justices
	Court of Appeals	Judges
	District Court	Judges
	Superior Courts	Judges
	County Courts	Judges
	Probate Courts (Denver only)	Judges
Connecticut	Supreme Court	Chief Justice
		Associate Justices
	Superior Court	Judges
	Courts of Common Pleas	Judges
	Probate Courts	Judges

(continued on following page)

(continued from preceding page)

State	Court	Members of Court
Delaware	Supreme Court	Chief Justice
		Associate Justices
	Court of Chancery	Chancellor
		Vice Chancellor
	Superior Court	President Judge
		Associate Judges
	Registers' Courts	Register of Wills
District of Columbia	U.S. District Court	Chief Judge
		Judges
	District of Columbia Superior Court	Chief Judge
		Associate Judges
Florida	Supreme Court	Chief Justice, Justices
	�֍District Courts of Appeal	Chief Judge, Judges
	Circuit Courts	Judges
	County Courts	Judges
	Probate Courts	Judges
Georgia	Supreme Court	Chief Justice
		Presiding Justice
		Associate Justices
	�֍Court of Appeals	Chief Judge
		Presiding Judge
		Judges
	Superior Courts	Judges
	Probate Courts	Probate Judges
Hawaii	Supreme Court	Chief Justice
		Justices
	�֍Circuit Courts	Judges
	District Courts	District Judges
Idaho	Supreme Court	Chief Justice
		Justices
	District Courts	Judges
Illinois	Supreme Court	Chief Justice
		Justices
	�֍Appellate Courts	Judges
	Circuit Courts	Judges
	Court of Claims	Chief Judge
		Judges
Indiana	Supreme Court	Chief Justice
		Associate Judges
	�֍Court of Appeals	Chief Judge
		Presiding Judge
		Associate Judges
	Superior Courts	Judges
	Circuit Court	Judges
	Probate Courts	Judges

(continued on following page)

(continued from preceding page)

State	Court	Members of Court
Iowa	Supreme Court	Chief Justice
		Justices
	✳Court of Appeals	Judges
	District Courts	Judges
Kansas	Supreme Court	Chief Justice
		Justices
	✳Court of Appeals	Judges
	District Court	Judges
Kentucky	Supreme Court	Chief Justice
		Associate Justices
	✳Court of Appeals	Commissioners of Appeals
		Special Commissioners
	Circuit Courts	Judges
	District Courts	Judges
Louisiana	Supreme Court	Chief Justice
		Associate Justices
	✳Court of Appeal	Judges
	(New Orleans only)	
	District Courts	Judges
Maine	Supreme Judicial Court	Chief Justice
		Associate Justices
	Superior Court	Justices
	State District Courts	Chief Judge, Judges
	Probate Courts	Judges
Maryland	Court of Appeals	Chief Judge
		Associate Judges
	Court of Special Appeals	Judges
	Circuit Courts	Chief Judges, Judges
	Orphans' Courts	Judges
Massachusetts	Supreme Judicial Court	Chief Justice
		Associate Justices
	✳Appeals Court	Justices
	Superior Court	Chief Justice
		Associate Justices
	Probate Courts	Judges
	Land Court	Judge, Associate Judges
Michigan	Supreme Court	Chief Justice
		Associate Justices
	Court of Appeals	Justices
	Circuit Courts	Circuit Judge
		Judges
	Court of Claims	Judge
	Probate Courts	Judges

(continued on following page)

(continued from preceding page)

State	Court	Members of Court
Minnesota	Supreme Court	Chief Justice Associate Justices
	District Court	Judges
	County Courts	Judges
	Probate Courts	Judges
Mississippi	Supreme Court	Chief Justice Associate Justices
	Circuit Courts	Judges
	Chancery Courts	Chancellors
	County Courts	Judges
Missouri	Supreme Court	Chief Justice Presiding Judge Associate Judges
	�֊Courts of Appeals	Presiding Judge Associate Judges
	Court of Common Pleas	Judges
	Circuit Courts	Judges
	Probate Courts	Judges
Montana	Supreme Court	Chief Justice Associate Justices
	District Court	Judges
Nebraska	Supreme Court	Chief Justice Judges
	District Court	Judges
	County Courts	Judges
Nevada	Supreme Court	Chief Justice Associate Justices
	District Court	Judges
New Hampshire	Supreme Court	Chief Justice Associate Justices
	Superior Court	Chief Justice Justices
	Probate Courts	Presiding Judges
New Jersey	Supreme Court	Chief Justice Justices
	✶Superior Court, Appellate Division	Senior Judge Judges
	Superior Court, Chancery Division	Judges
	Superior Court, Law Division	Judges
	County Courts	Judges
	Surrogate's Courts	Surrogates

(continued on following page)

(continued from preceding page)

State	Court	Members of Court
New Mexico	Supreme Court	Chief Justice Justices
	✳Court of Appeals	Chief Judge Judges
	District Court	Presiding Judge Judges
	Probate Courts	Judges
New York	Court of Appeals	Chief Judge Associate Judges
	✳Supreme Court, Appellate Division	Presiding Justice Justices
	Supreme Court	Justices
	County Courts	Judges
	Surrogates' Courts	Surrogates
	Court of Claims	Judges
	City and District Courts (in larger cities and counties)	Judges
North Carolina	Supreme Court	Chief Justice Associate Justices
	✳Court of Appeals	Judges
	Superior Courts	Judges
North Dakota	Supreme Court	Chief Justice Judges
	District Court	Judges
	County Courts	Judges
Ohio	Supreme Court	Chief Justice Justices
	✳Courts of Appeals	Judges
	Court of Claims	Judges
	Court of Common Pleas	Judges
Oklahoma	Supreme Court	Chief Justice Vice Chief Justice Justices
	✳Criminal Court of Appeals	Presiding Judge Judges
	✳Court of Appeals	Judges
	District Courts	Judges
Oregon	Supreme Court	Chief Justice Associate Justices
	✳Court of Appeals	Judges
	Tax Court	Judges
	Circuit Courts	Judges
	County Courts	County Judges

(continued on following page)

(continued from preceding page)

State	Court	Members of Court
Pennsylvania	Supreme Court	Chief Justice
		Justices
	Superior Court	Presiding Judge
		Judges
	Commonwealth Court	Judges
	Courts of Common Pleas	Judges
Rhode Island	Supreme Court	Chief Justice
		Associate Justices
	Superior Court	Presiding Justice
		Justices
	Family Court	Judges
	District Court	Judges
	Probate Courts	Judges
South Carolina	Supreme Court	Chief Justice
		Associate Justice
	Circuit Courts	Judges
	County Courts	Judges
	Probate Courts	Judges
South Dakota	Supreme Court	Presiding Judge
		Judges
	Circuit Courts	Judges
Tennessee	Supreme Court	Chief Justice
		Associate Justices
	※Court of Appeals	Presiding Judge
		Associate Judges
	※Court of Criminal Appeals	Judges
Tennessee (Continued)	Chancery Courts	Chancellors
	Circuit Courts	Judges
	County Courts	Judges
	Probate Courts, Shelby and Davidson Counties	Judge
Texas	Supreme Court	Chief Justice
		Associate Justices
	※Court of Civil Appeals	Chief Justice
		Associate Justices
	Court of Criminal Appeal	Presiding Judge, Judges
		Commissioners
	District Courts	Judges
	County Courts	Judges
Utah	Supreme Court	Chief Justice
		Justices
	District Court	Judges
	Circuit Courts	Judges

(continued on following page)

(continued from preceding page)

State	Court	Members of Court
Vermont	Supreme Court	Chief Justice
		Associate Justices
	Superior Courts	Judges
	Probate Courts	Judges
Virginia	Supreme Court	Chief Justice
		Justices
	Circuit Courts	Judges
Virgin Islands	District Court	Judge
	Territorial Courts	Judges
Washington	Supreme Court	Chief Justice
		Associate Judges
	Court of Appeals	Judges
	Superior Courts	Judges
West Virginia	Supreme Court of Appeals	President
		Judges
	Circuit Courts	Judges
	County Commissions	Commissioners
Wisconsin	Supreme Court	Chief Justice
		Associate Justices
	*Court of Appeals	Judges
	Circuit Courts	Judges
	County Courts	Judges
Wyoming	Supreme Court	Chief Justice
		Associate Justice
	District Courts	Judges

Table I

another state. The federal government feared that the state courts would not interpret and enforce the national laws to the best of their ability. To avoid any miscarriage of justice that might result from interstate antagonism, the Congress provided for a federal system of courts for the trial of cases involving federal laws and interstate commerce and, also, cases involving diversity of citizenship—cases brought by a citizen of one state against a citizen of another state.

The federal system of courts consists of the Supreme Court of the United States, 11 courts of appeal, 90 district courts, a court of claims, a customs court, an emergency court of appeals, and a tax court (See table II.) The United States is divided into 11 judicial circuits—10 are comprised of several states each, and there is in addition the District of Columbia Circuit. Table III gives a list of the states in each circuit; table IV lists the states alphabetically and shows the circuit each state is in.

Federal District Courts. Each state has at least one district court. Twenty-five of the states are divided into two, three, or four districts with a court for each district. The states that have only one federal dis-

Table II

FEDERAL COURTS OF RECORD IN THE UNITED STATES
AND THEIR MEMBERS

Court	Members
Supreme Court of the United States	Chief Justice
	Associate Justices
United States Court of Appeals for the District of Columbia	Circuit Justice
	Chief Judge
	Circuit Judges
United States Court of Appeals for the (First) Circuit	Circuit Justice
	Chief Judge
	Circuit Judges
United States District Court for the (Southern) District of (New York)	Chief Judge
Or where the state is all in one district	District Judges
United States District Court for the District of (Maryland)	
United States Court of Claims	Chief Judge
	Associate Judges
United States Court of Customs and Patent Appeals	Chief Judge
	Associate Judges
United States Customs Court	Chief Judge
	Judges
United States Court of Military Appeals	Chief Judge
	Associate Judges
The Tax Court of the United States	Chief Judge
	Judges
Temporary Emergency Court of Appeals of the United States	Chief Judge
	Associate Judges

Table III

JUDICIAL CIRCUITS AND THE STATES AND TERRITORIES IN EACH CIRCUIT

District of Columbia Circuit	District of Columbia
First Circuit	Maine, Massachusetts, New Hampshire, Puerto Rico, Rhode Island
Second Circuit	Connecticut, New York, Vermont, Virgin Islands
Third Circuit	Delaware, New Jersey, Pennsylvania, Virgin Islands
Fourth Circuit	Maryland, North Carolina, South Carolina, Virginia, West Virginia
Fifth Circuit	Alabama, Canal Zone, Florida, Georgia, Louisiana, Mississippi, Texas
Sixth Circuit	Kentucky, Michigan, Ohio, Tennessee
Seventh Circuit	Illinois, Indiana, Wisconsin
Eighth Circuit	Arkansas, Iowa, Minnesota, Missouri, Nebraska, North Dakota, South Dakota, Territory of Guam
Ninth Circuit	Alaska, Arizona, California, Hawaii, Idaho, Montana, Nevada, Oregon, Washington
Tenth Circuit	Colorado, Kansas, New Mexico, Oklahoma, Utah, Wyoming

Table IV

STATES AND TERRITORIES AND JUDICIAL CIRCUIT IN WHICH EACH IS LOCATED

State	Circuit	State	Circuit
Alabama	Fifth Circuit	Montana✳	Ninth Circuit
Alaska✳	Ninth Circuit	Nebraska✳	Eighth Circuit
Arizona✳	Ninth Circuit	Nevada✳	Ninth Circuit
Arkansas	Eighth Circuit	New Hampshire✳	First Circuit
California	Ninth Circuit	New Jersey✳	Third Circuit
Canal Zone✳	Fifth Circuit	New Mexico✳	Tenth Circuit
Colorado✳	Tenth Circuit	New York	Second Circuit
Connecticut✳	Second Circuit	North Carolina	Fourth Circuit
Delaware✳	Third Circuit	North Dakota✳	Eighth Circuit
Florida	Fifth Circuit	Ohio	Sixth Circuit
Georgia	Fifth Circuit	Oklahoma	Tenth Circuit
Guam	Eighth Circuit	Oregon✳	Ninth Circuit
Hawaii✳	Ninth Circuit	Pennsylvania	Third Circuit
Idaho✳	Ninth Circuit	Puerto Rico	First Circuit
Illinois	Seventh Circuit	Rhode Island✳	First Circuit
Indiana	Seventh Circuit	South Carolina	Fourth Circuit
Iowa	Eighth Circuit	South Dakota✳	Eighth Circuit
Kansas✳	Tenth Circuit	Tennessee	Sixth Circuit
Kentucky	Sixth Circuit	Texas	Fifth Circuit
Louisiana	Fifth Circuit	Utah✳	Tenth Circuit
Maine✳	First Circuit	Vermont✳	Second Circuit
Maryland✳	Fourth Circuit	Virginia	Fourth Circuit
Massachusetts✳	First Circuit	Virgin Islands	Second Circuit
Michigan	Sixth Circuit	Washington	Ninth Circuit
Minnesota✳	Eighth Circuit	West Virginia	Fourth Circuit
Mississippi	Fifth Circuit	Wisconsin	Seventh Circuit
Missouri	Eighth Circuit	Wyoming✳	Tenth Circuit

Only one district court.

Example 1

IN THE UNITED STATES
DISTRICT COURT FOR THE
DISTRICT OF <u>IDAHO</u>
(<u>SOUTHERN</u> DIVISION)

trict court are indicated by an asterisk in table IV.

Many of the district courts are divided into divisions. It is important to know whether or not a district court is divided into divisions because the division must appear in the caption on papers filed in that court. In the above examples, the underscored words change according to the state, district, and division.

Example 2

IN THE UNITED STATES
DISTRICT COURT FOR THE
<u>SOUTHERN</u> DISTRICT OF
<u>MISSISSIPPI</u>
(<u>JACKSON</u> DIVISION)

American Digest System. The most comprehensive DIGEST series, covering all printed cases in all American jurisdictions from the year 1658.

Organization. The American Digest system is tied in with the NATIONAL REPORTER SYSTEM. It is broken down as follows:

Century Digest	1658-1856	50 Vols.
First Decennial Digest	1897-1906	25 Vols.
Second Decennial Digest	1907-1916	24 Vols.
Third Decennial Digest	1916-1926	29 Vols.
Fourth Decennial Digest	1926-1936	34 Vols.
Fifth Decennial Digest	1936-1946	52 Vols.
Sixth Decennial Digest	1946-1956	36 Vols.
Seventh Decennial Digest	1956-1966	38 Vols.
Eighth Decennial Digest	1966-1976	50 Vols.
General Digest Fifth Series	1977-1979	17 Vols.

The bound volumes of the General Digest, cumulated about every four months, are followed by monthly pamphlets and by the weekly advance sheets of the reporters. The Decennials, as their names imply, are cumulated every 10 years and supersede the General Digest for that period.

The digest covers approximately 500 main topics, arranged alphabetically. The Century and Decennials are broken down alphabetically, each volume containing certain main topics. Thus, Volume 19 of the Fourth Decennial Digest, "Judgment to Kidnapping," contains a reference to each case published from 1926 to 1936 on the topics of Judgment, Judicial Sales, Jury, Justice of the Peace, and Kidnapping. Each volume of the General Digest Series contains a reference to all the cases on every topic published during the period covered by that particular volume. Thus, each volume of the General Digest, Third Series, contains the topic *Judgment.*

A detailed fact index constitutes part of the American Digest System. The index is contained in several volumes, with a binding differing from that on the digests, entitled DESCRIPTIVE WORD INDEX. The descriptive words are listed in black type in alphabetical order. Different situations involving the fact element are listed in lighter type and refer to the place in the digest where cases in point may be found. The reference is by means of topic and key number.

An analysis precedes each main topic. The digests of cases are grouped according to the point of law involved, and each point is given a key number. The key numbers in the First Decennial are preceded by the section symbol (§) instead of the key symbol, but the numbers correspond. The Century section numbers do not correspond to the key numbers but may be translated into key numbers (see below).

How to use the digest system. Suppose you are interested in the priority over other claims of an allowance by the executor to a widow.

1. The first step in finding the authorities through the digest system is to get the key number. There are three methods of getting the key number:

(a) If at least one case in point is already known, from the key numbers in the headnotes in the reporters, which correspond to the key numbers in the digests,

(b) From the Descriptive Word Index,

(c) From the analysis that precedes each topic.

2. The search may be started with any of the Decennials or with the General Digest and then worked forward and backward. All of the cases involving the suggested question will be found under

the topic Executors and Administrators, Key 182. The backbones of the volume will indicate in which volumes of the Decennials the topic Executors and Administrators can be found.

3. The topic is in every volume of the General Digest, First, Second, and Third Series, but there probably is not a case in point in all volumes. To avoid unnecessary research, use the cumulative tables of key numbers, which are paper pamphlets published in conjunction with the General Digest. These pamphlets list the topics in alphabetical order and list the key numbers under each topic. On a line with each key number are the numbers of the volumes of the General Digest in which reference is made to cases having that key number. Thus, in the table of key numbers to General Digest, Third Series, Volume 1-10, under the topic Executors and Administrators, is the notation:

Key
182—3, 5, 6, 7, 9

Thus, volumes 3, 5, 6, 7, and 9 refer to cases in point. There is no need to look in the other volumes of the General Digest, Third Series.

4. Continue the search for the key number through the monthly digests that are in pamphlet form and through the digests in the reporter advance sheets published subsequent to the latest monthly digest.

5. Then search in the Century for cases decided before 1897. The second Decennial refers to the volume, topic, and section number in the Century, if there is a case in point referred to in the Century. Thus, Key 182 under Executors and Administrators in the Second

Decennial shows this reference: Cent. Dig. & Ad. §§651, 686-693. If there is no reference, there are no cases in point digested in Century.

6. Possibly the search was begun with a reference in Century. It was found that cases in point were digested at §686 of the topic Executors and Administrators. To get subsequent authorities, translate the section number to the key number of the digest. In the front of Volume 21 of the First Decennial, there is a parallel table on pink sheets. The table gives under each topic, the section number in the Century and the corresponding key number in the Decennial.

Table of cases. If the name of a case is known, find where it is reported from the tables of cases. The last five volumes of the First Decennial (Volumes 21-25) cover the cases digested in the Century and in the First Decennial. The last volumes of the Second, of the Third, and of the Fourth Decennials are tables of cases. The back of each volume of the General Digest contains a table of cases. Since each unit of the American Digest System covers a particular period, the search is narrowed if the decade in which the case was decided is known.

American Federation of Labor (AFL). A voluntary association of national labor unions organized along craft lines. The AFL was formed in 1886 with Samuel Gompers its first president. In 1955 AFL merged with the CONGRESS OF INDUSTRIAL ORGANIZATIONS to form the AFL-CIO. See also LABOR UNION.

American Jurisprudence. A legal encyclopedia that gives comprehensive textual statements of American case law. *Am. Jur.,* as American Jurisprudence is commonly called, makes no attempt to cite *every* case in point in support of its text. It relies heavily on cases printed in the annotated case series (See AMERICAN LAW REPORTS), including *all* United States Supreme Court cases. *Am. Jur.* also cites and quotes pertinent RESTATEMENTS OF THE LAW.

American Law Reports (ALR). Annotated opinions of appellate courts (see APPELLATE COURT) in all jurisdictions. ALR contains a minimum of U.S. Supreme Court cases; they are taken care of by the annotations in the *Lawyer's Edition.* (*Law. Ed.*).

ALR cases are selected on the basis of probable usefulness to lawyers. They are illustrative of established principles and are not necessarily "leading cases." Parallel official and unofficial (see NATIONAL REPORTER SYSTEM) citations are supplied. The decision is summarized at some length and the subject of the annotation is noted. Headnotes are written by the editors and classified according to the *Permanent ALR Digest* classification. There are frequent cross-references to the legal encyclopedia, AMERICAN JURISPRUDENCE.

ALR puts out a *Blue Book* that brings each ALR case up to date by later cases in point.

ALR is indispensable to the lawyer who has official reports of cases decided in his or her own state, but is interested in cases on the same point decided in other jurisdictions.

Amortization Schedules. A printed-out breakdown of principal and inter-est after each monthly payment and showing balance due on a note and mortgage load. Two copies may be obtained for a nominal amount by writing to:

> The Financial Publishing Company
> 82 Brookline Avenue
> Boston, Massachusetts 02115

Send amount of loan, amount of monthly payment, rate and type of interest (monthly reduction, annual or semi-annual). It is not necessary to send the names of the mortgagor or mortgagee. The secretary should mark the name of the client on the letter ordering the schedules so she will be able to identify the schedules when they are returned, as there are no names on the schedules. After the initial order the company will send a convenient order card for the next order, or, if desired, prepaid order cards may be ordered. The order card is always sent back with the order, so the secretary may indicate the client's name on the order card to identify it when it is returned.

Ancillary. Auxiliary; subordinate. The term *ancillary letters* is used to apply to letters testamentary or letters of administration that are taken out in a state other than that of the decedent's domicile, but in which he or she had assets or debts. These letters are subordinate or supplementary to the letters issued in the decedent's domicile. The term *ancillary* also applies to court proceedings that are auxiliary to the main action—for example, a bill of discovery is ancillary to the principal action.

Annexed Paper. An additional piece of paper containing auxiliary material, which is attached to a NOTICE, such as a Notice of Appearance in Equity Case, Notice of Filing and Entry, Notice of Settlement and Notice of Motion. The addition is also referred to as an *attached paper*. Both the notice and the *annexed paper* are stapled together with the notice on top, unless the other paper is to be signed by the judge. Whenever a group of papers are given to the judge for signature, any paper that the judge is supposed to sign is placed on top, so he or she will not have to search for the appropriate paper.

In the endorsement on the back of the instrument, the name of the annexed paper is placed first because it is the more important paper. See LEGAL BACK.

Announcement Card. A printed or engraved notification sent to clients, colleagues, or other persons whom the lawyer wants to advise concerning the address at which he or she is practicing.

An attorney sends these announcement cards upon joining a new firm or moving offices. Figure 1 shows an announcement when the lawyer first enters practice; figure 2, when resuming practice; figure 3, when moving the offices.

The secretary can be very helpful in compiling and maintaining a permanent list of people to whom the announcements may be sent.

The cards may be mailed to the groups listed below.

1. Friends and acquaintances
2. Members of the local bar
3. County officials
4. Classmates
5. Other lawyers
6. Clients

Annuitant. One who receives the benefits of an ANNUITY.

Annuity. A fixed sum payable periodically and subject to certain limitations imposed by the grantor.

JOHN JEFFREYS
ANNOUNCES THE OPENING OF HIS OFFICE
FOR THE PRACTICE OF LAW
AT
101 MAXWELL AVENUE
ROCHELLE PARK, NJ 07662
201-221-4077

Announcement Cards: Figure 1.
Announcement when entering practice.

Twenty Pine Street
New York, NY 10017

Margaret F. Crosby, having completed her term as a Justice of the Supreme Court of the State of New York, announces her return to the practice of law with the firm of

Wynn, Kass & Crosby

January 15, 19 —   *212-222-4483*

Announcement Cards: Figure 2.

Announcement when resuming practice.

FLYNN, OLAN & DAVIS
ANNOUNCE THE REMOVAL OF THEIR OFFICES TO
711 TOWER STREET
BOSTON, MA 02210
WHERE THEY WILL CONTINUE THE GENERAL PRACTICE
OF LAW UNDER THE FIRM NAME OF
FLYNN, OLAN, DAVIS & DISHMON

AUGUST 1, 19—   617-223-5200

Announcement Card: Figure 3.

Announcement of removal of offices.

Annulment of Marriage. A judicial decision that makes a marriage void and of no effect from its beginning. A basis for annulment would be a misrepresentation that amounts to FRAUD. For example, before marriage a spouse promises to have a family and during the marriage refuses to have sexual intercourse or uses some artificial means of birth control.

Answer. The defendant's formal written statement of defense, signed by his or her attorney. It denies some, or all, of the allegations of the COMPLAINT and sets forth the grounds of the defendant's defense. It may also set up claims the defendant has against the plaintiff as counterclaims.

The answer consists of the following parts: (1) caption; (2) introduction; (3) denials of allegations of the complaint; (4) counterclaims, if any; (5) "wherefore" clause; prayer, if answer contains a counterclaim; (6) signature of attorney for defendant; (7) verification if the complaint is verified.

How to prepare the answer. The lawyer will dictate the answer, but it is the secretary's responsibility to set it up properly. Unless the lawyer indicates a preference, follow the style illustrated in figure 1.

1. Type on legal size or 81/2- by 11-inch paper depending on the practice of the firm or the court.

2. Make an original for the court, a copy to serve on each plaintiff's attorney, and a copy for the office file.

3. The caption is the same as that on the complaint, but if there are numerous parties the title of the case may be shortened on most subsequent documents by listing the first plaintiff or defendant only and adding et al., et ux, or et vir.

4. The index number must appear on the answer at the right of the box.

5. The title of the document is "Answer."

6. Number the paragraphs consecutively throughout, except the last paragraph, which is the "wherefore" clause. Do not start a new series of numbers for the paragraphs in each separate defense.

7. Type a line for signature of attorney.

8. The answer must be verified if the complaint is.

9. In some large cities, the attorney's name, address and telephone number must appear after the verification, but usually this is not necessary. The attorney's address is on the legal back if one is used.

10. Some large jurisdictions require attorneys to endorse a legal back for each copy except your office copy. See figure 2. The endorsement differs from the endorsement on the complaint in that it shows the court's index number and the name of the attorney for the plaintiff, on whom a copy of the answer is served. When the complaint was prepared, the secretary for the plaintiff did not know the index number or who would represent the defendant.

Some offices type a Certificate of Service at the end of the Answer instead of adding an endorsed back. An example is shown on the following page.

11. Collate and staple in backs if required in your jurisdiction.

12. After signature and verification, conform exactly.

Methods of service of answer on plaintiff's attorney. Although the practice

BMM:r 4/22/—1—2—1

IN THE CIRCUIT COURT OF THE ELEVENTH JUDICIAL CIRCUIT OF FLORIDA, IN AND FOR DADE COUNTY.

———————————————————— x
                      :

HENRY S. WRIGHT and JOANNA
M. WRIGHT,   :   Index No: 11660-19—

             Plaintiffs, :

     —against—   :   ANSWER

CENTRAL MANAGEMENT CORPORATION:
a corporation, and PATTERSON MILLS, INC.,
a corporation

                      :

            Defendants.

                      :
———————————————————— x

The defendant Central Management Corporation, answering the amended complaint herein by his attorneys, Troy & Campbell:

1. Admits _____

_____

_____ .

2. Denies that he has knowledge or information sufficient to form a belief as to the allegations contained in the paragraph of the complaint designated "SECOND."

FOR A FIRST SEPARATE AND COMPLETE DEFENSE, DEFENDANT ALLEGES:

3. On information and belief _____

_____

(Continued on following page)

(Continued from preceding page)

FOR A SECOND SEPARATE AND PARTIAL
DEFENSE, DEFENDANT ALLEGES:

4. _____

_____

FOR A DISTINCT SEPARATE AND AFFIRM-
ATIVE DEFENSE AND BY WAY OF A
COUNTERCLAIM, DEFENSE ALLEGES:

5. _____

_____

WHEREFORE, defendant demands that the complaint be dismissed

with costs and asks judgment in the amount _____

_____.

_____
Attorneys for Defendant
Central Management
Corporation

Answer: Figure 1.

may vary with the jurisdiction, the answer is generally served on the plaintiff's attorney by (1) handing him a copy, or leaving it at his office with his clerk or other person in charge of the office; or (2) by mailing it to the attorney. No regular process server is necessary in the majority of jurisdictions. The secretary, or a clerk in the attorney's office, may serve the papers.

Proof of service. The attorney on whom the answer is served, or the secretary if she is authorized, writes on the back of the original a receipt similar to the following.

Copy received.......... date
(firm name) ....
Attorneys for . (name of client)

Many offices have rubber stamps for this purpose.

Printed LEGAL BACKS have printed on them an admission of service, which

---

CERTIFICATE OF SERVICE

This will certify that a copy of the foregoing instrument was served on the Plaintiff/Defendant by mailing a copy thereof to his/her/its/their attorney of record, Mr. David L. Osmon, of Osmon, Wilber & Strother, 119 East 6th Street, Mountain Home, AR 72653, on this 6th day of June, 1982.

_____
(Attorney's signature)

Index No. 11660-19—,

IN THE CIRCUIT COURT OF
THE ELEVENTH JUDICIAL
CIRCUIT OF FLORIDA, IN
AND FOR DADE COUNTY, AT LAW

HENRY S. WRIGHT, et ux.,

Plaintiffs,

-against-

CENTRAL MANAGEMENT
CORPORATION, a corporation
et. al.,

Defendants.

ANSWER

Troy, Campbell & Hudson
352 E. Flagler St.
Miami, Florida 33130

Attorneys for Defendants
Central Management
Corporation

To Dodd & Hoyt, Esquires,
Attorneys for Plaintiffs.

Answer: Figure 2. *Endorsed back of answer.*

usually contains the words "due and proper" service, "timely" service, or the like. When a secretary accepts service, she should strike out these words. Although she might be authorized to accept service, it is not her responsibility to admit that it was due, proper, or timely.

In some jurisdictions, the attorney whose office is serving the answer endorses on the back of the original:

I do hereby certify that copy hereof has been furnished to
. . . . by mail
(or delivery), this . . . . . . day
of . . . . . ., 19. . .

Many jurisdictions require a formal affidavit when service is made by mail.

What to do about the answer.

1. Prepare the answer, and verification if required.

2. Have answer signed, and verified, after approval by the attorney.

3. Notarize verification.

4. See that the copy is served on the plaintiff's attorney.

5. Make certain that receipt of service is endorsed on back of original, or that affidavit of service is attached.

6. Conform office copy.

7. File original, with admission of service, in court, with fee if required.

8. Make entry in SUIT REGISTER of service and filing.

9. The secretary to the attorney on whom the answer is served makes a notation on the back of the answer of the date and hour it was served; also makes entry in suit register.

10. *Enter in diary* date by which next action must be taken. See also PLEADINGS.

Antenuptial Contract. A CONTRACT made before marriage. The property rights of the prospective husband or wife can be determined by contract. For example, there have been instances where a wife has given up all right to any portion of the estate of her husband by signing an antenuptial contract.

Antitrust Laws. Legislation that forbids monopolistic trade practices and prohibits conspiracies and trusts that restrain INTERSTATE COMMERCE. Antitrust statutes are the Sherman Act; the Clayton Act; the Federal Trade Commission Act; the Robinson-Patman Act; the Miller-Tydings Act; the Wheeler-Lea Act. Antitrust laws do not apply to labor unions.

Appeal. The legal procedure by which decision of a lower court is brought to a higher court for review.

The procedure for taking a case to a higher court is governed by the rules of the highest state tribunal. These rules are based upon the civil practice acts or codes of civil procedure and are usually found in an appendix to the act or code. They may also be obtained in pamphlet form from the clerk of the APPELLATE COURT or from the state judicial council. The United States Supreme Court makes the rules for appeals to it and, also, for appeals from the federal district courts to federal courts of appeal.

The secretary can easily find in these rules the information she should have to do her part of the appellate work in accordance with the court's requirements. The rules provide, among other things, for the following:

1. Methods for review,
2. Content of the RECORD ON APPEAL
3. Form of testimony (questions and answer, narrative, or abstract),
4. Preparation and format of record,
5. Preparation and format of BRIEF,
6. Time allowed for filing and service of papers,
7. Method of service on opposing counsel
8. Costs.

Methods for review by a higher court. The method for review by the higher tribunal is by appeal from the lower court to the higher court, in the majority of states. In a few states, the method is by a petition to the higher court for a WRIT of Error. At one time chancery cases were reviewed by means of an appeal and law cases by means of a writ of error. This distinction in appellate procedure no longer exists except in a few states. Regardless of the method for review, the procedure is loosely referred to as "taking an appeal" or "appealing a case." The use of the term *appeal* here embraces both appeals and writs of error.

A case may also be referred to a higher court, under special circumstances, by means of extraordinary writs, such as CERTIORARI, MANDAMUS, HABEAS CORPUS, PROHIBITION, QUO WARRANTO, and STAY writs. These writs eliminate the necessity of hearings and trials in the lower court.

In some states the appeal is to an intermediate appellate court and thence to the highest state court. In states that do not have intermediary appellate courts (and in certain cases even if they do), the appeal is direct from the trial court to the highest court. The procedure for taking an appeal to an intermediate appellate court is similar to, but not exactly the same as, taking an appeal to the highest state tribunal. The main variations are in the details, such as the time allowed for the various steps taken, disbursements to be paid, whether the papers are to be typewritten or printed, and the size and quality of paper that is to be used. The secretary should check the rules of the intermediate appellate court.

Parties to an appeal. The litigants in a legal action when the decision of a lower court is brought to a higher court for review. In almost all of the states the party appealing is referred to as the *appellant*, and the party opposing the appeal is referred to as the *appellee* or the *respondent.* When the defendant in a lower case is the appellant, the title of the case is reversed in the majority of the states. Thus, *John Smith*, v. *Alfred Jones* becomes *Alfred Jones v. John Smith.* But this is not the practice in all of the states. Eight methods of designating parties on appeal in the CAPTION are shown in figure 1. Table I lists the states and indicates the style followed in each state, assuming that the title of the case in the lower court was *John Jones v. Albert Smith* and the defendant brings the appeal to the highest state court. In cases where review is by petition for a writ, the party appealing is designated as the petitioner, and the other party as the *respondent.*

Although the designation of the parties changes in the title of the case, the briefs sometimes refer to the parties by their designation in the lower court. (Some rules require this designation.) Or the BRIEF might refer to a party by the

STYLES OF DESIGNATION OF PARTIES ON APPEAL BY DEFENDANT TO
HIGHEST STATE COURT WHEN TITLE OF CASE IN LOWER COURT WAS

John Jones, Plaintiff vs. Albert Smith, Defendant

Style 1 (Names reversed)
Albert Smith,
  Appellant,
 vs.
John Jones,
  Appellee.

Style 2 (Names not reversed)
John Jones,
  Plaintiff and Respondent,
 vs.
Albert Smith,
  Defendant and Appellant.

Style 3 (Names not reversed)
John Jones,
  Plaintiff and Appellee,

Albert Smith,
  Defendant and Appellant.

Style 4 (Names reversed)
Albert Smith,
  Plaintiff-in-Error,
 vs.
John Jones,
  Defendant-in-Error.

Style 5 (Names not reversed)
John Jones,
  Appellee,
 vs.
Albert Smith,
  Appellant.

Style 6 (Names not reversed)
John Jones,
  Respondent,
 vs.
Albert Smith
  Appellant.

Style 7 (Names reversed)
Albert Smith,
  Appellant and Defendant,
 vs.
John Jones,
  Respondent and Plaintiff.

Style 8 (Names reversed)
Albert Smith,
  Defendant Below, Appellant,
 vs.
John Jones,
  Plaintiff Below, Appellee.

Appeal: Figure 1.

lower court designation on one page and by the appellate court designation on the other. The change in designation is very confusing, and the lawyer might inadvertently refer to the defendant-appellant when meaning plaintiff-appellant, or to the plaintiff when meaning plaintiff-in-error. Before the lawyer dictates a brief to the secretary, the secretary should fix firmly in mind the designation of the parties in both the trial and appellate courts so she can observe any error in designation of parties.

Appellant. The party making an APPEAL to a higher court for review of a decision rendered by a lower court. See APPELLATE COURT.

Appellate Court. A tribunal empowered to hear arguments, pro and con, concerning the decision made by a lower court on a particular cause of ac-

---

TABLE I

DESIGNATION OF PARTIES ON APPEAL TO HIGHEST STATE COURT

State	Designation	State	Designation
Alabama	Style 1	Nevada	Style 7
Alaska	Style 1	New Hampshire[2]	
Arizona	Style 1	New Jersey	Style 2
Arkansas	Style 1	New Mexico	Style 3
California	Style 2	New York	Style 2
Colorado	Style 4	North Carolina[1]	
Connecticut	Style 3	North Dakota	Style 2
Delaware	Style 8	Ohio	Style 3
Florida	Style 1	Oklahoma	Style 4
Georgia	Style 4	Oregon	Style 6
Hawaii	Style 1	Pennsylvania	Style 5
Idaho	Style 2	Rhode Island[2]	
Illinois	Style 3	South Carolina	Style 2
Indiana	Style 1	South Dakota	Style 6
Iowa	Style 1	Tennessee	Style 1
Kansas	Style 5	Texas	Style 1[3]
Kentucky	Style 1	Utah	Style 2
Louisiana	Style 3	Vermont[2]	
Maine	Style 5	Virginia	Style 1
Maryland	Style 1	Washington	Style 6
Massachusetts[1]		West Virginia	Style 1 (Equity)
Michigan	Style 3		Style 4 (Law)
Minnesota	Style 2		
Mississippi	Style 1		
Missouri	Style 6	Wisconsin	Style 7
Montana	Style 2	Wyoming	Style 2
Nebraska	Style 3		

[1]*Not reversed. Designation the same as in the trial court.*
[2]*Title in both trial court and appellate court: John Jones vs. Albert Smith. There is no designation.*
[3]*Except that in the Supreme Court the person seeking relief is called the "Petitioner" and the other party is the "Respondent."*

tion or trial. The appellate court has the power to affirm, reverse, or remand the original decision for retrial.

For example, a case tried in a lower court may be brought on APPEAL to a higher court having appellate jurisdiction until it reaches the state's highest appellate court or, in some cases, the United States Supreme Court. (See SUPREME APPELLATE COURT.) States with a large volume of cases have INTERMEDIARY APPELLATE COURTS to relieve the congestion of cases in the highest court. The party who loses a lawsuit, or who is dissatisfied with a JUDGMENT or court order or DECREE, may ask a higher court to review the decision of the lower court with the hope that the higher court will reverse or modify the lower court's decision. *See also* BRIEF; RECORD ON APPEAL; TIMETABLE ON APPEAL; CAPTION (of Case on Appeal).

Appointment, Reminders of. *See* REMINDERS.

Arbitration. Submission of labor disputes to a third party for final and binding decision. Arbitration may be compulsory or voluntary. Compulsory arbitration takes place when a governmental agency compels the disputing parties to submit their differences to an outside body for settlement. Voluntary arbitration takes place by mutual and free consent of the parties. Most collective bargaining contracts provide for arbitration as the final step in grievance procedure. *See* MEDIATION; CONCILIATION.

Arms Length Sale. A transaction where the parties have equal bargaining power. One party does not exercise undue influence or superior knowledge over the other.

Arrest. *See* PROVISIONAL REMEDIES.

Arrest of Judgment. When the court withholds its judgment because of an error apparent from the face of the record. The court refuses to give the judgment because it would be erroneous.

Arson. The crime of maliciously burning the house of another. In several states arson is divided into three degrees. *First-degree arson* is the willful act of setting fire at night to a dwelling house with a human being in it; *second-degree arson* is the act of burning a dwelling house in the daytime with a human in it or the burning in the nighttime of an uninhabited building while endangering an adjoining building with human beings in it; *third-degree arson* is setting a fire under circumstances not amounting to first or second degree arson or the burning of property with the intent to defraud the insurers.

Articles of Incorporation. The instrument that creates a private corporation according to the corporation laws of the state.

Asportation. *See* LARCENY.

Assault and Battery. An *assault* is a threat made with the apparent intention of doing bodily harm to another. An essential element of assault is real or apparent ability on the part of the person making the threat to do bodily harm to another. Mere words do not constitute assault. A *battery* is the wrongful touching of another's person or clothing as a result of an assault. A battery always includes an assault, but an assault may be made without a battery. A person guilty of assault and battery is liable for damage to the injured party. Assault and battery may also be a crime punishable by the state.

Assessment. A tax levied upon property within a designated area to provide funds for local improvements, such as grading or widening streets, construction of sewers, and erection of bridges. Assessments are generally payable in yearly installments. See also TAX LIEN.

Assets. Anything of value that could be appropriated for the payment of debts; all money, property, and money-related rights owned by a person or organization.

Assignment. The transfer of one person's rights to another. Assignments are made (a) by the act of the parties, as in the case of a tenant assigning his or her lease to another; or (b) by operation of law, as in the case of death or bankruptcy. The party transferring a right is the *assignor;* the party to whom the rights are transferred is the *assignee.*

An assignment need not be in any particular form. It may be oral or written, unless it involves a contract required by the STATUTE OF FRAUDS to be in writing. It may be a formal document or an endorsement on the contract signed by the assignor. An assignment does not require any consideration, but it must effect an immediate transfer to a specific assignee.

Assignment of Errors. See RECORD ON APPEAL.

Assumption of the Risk. An affirmative defense that claims a plaintiff had knowledge of a condition or situation that is obviously dangerous but still exposed himself or herself to the hazard; the defendant is thereby relieved of legal responsibility.

Assured. Insured.

Attachment. The method by which a debtor's property, real or personal, is placed in the custody of the law and held as security pending the outcome of a creditor's suit. Until the case is decided, the debtor cannot dispose of the attached property or place it beyond the reach of the creditor. The most usual grounds of attachment are the following: (1) the debtor is a nonresident or a foreign corporation; (2) the debtor has left the state or is in hiding; (3) the debtor is about to remove, conceal, or dispose of his or her property.

In many states the attaching creditor must put up a BOND; a debtor may then release the property by putting up a counterbond. See also LIEN.

Attempt. An act done with the intent to commit a crime and tending but failing to effect its commission. Four elements necessary to constitute the crime of attempt are intention, an overt act, failure, and closeness of success. See MERGER.

Attestation. The act of signing a written instrument as witness to the signature of a party, at the party's request, for example, witnessing signatures to a CONTRACT or WILL. Because the witness signs the instrument he is called a *subscribing witness.* See also ATTESTATION CLAUSE.

Attestation Clause. The legend or clause that relates the circumstances surrounding the signing of an instrument. It usually precedes the signature of the attesting witnesses. For example, if Robert Niles were testator, the attestation clause in his will might read: "Signed, sealed, published and declared by Robert Niles, the above named testator, as and for his Last Will and Testament in our presence, and we, at his request, in his presence and in the presence of each other, have hereunto subscribed our names as witnesses this 5th day of September in the year of our Lord 19___." The wording of an attestation clause may be simply: "In the presence of." The clause is typed at the left of the signature. The legal secretary is often asked to attest documents that are signed in the attorney's office.

When the secretary of a corporation attests an instrument, he or she impresses the CORPORATE SEAL upon it. See also TESTIMONIUM CLAUSE.

Attorney at Law. A person licensed to practice law.

Attorney in Fact. One who is appointed by another, with the authority to act for the other in matters specified in the terms of the appointment. (See also AGENCY.) An ATTORNEY AT LAW may be an attorney in fact, but an attorney in fact is not necessarily an attorney at law. In a loose sense, the term is frequently used to mean all agents *except* attorneys at law.

Attractive Nuisance. A condition on private property that would be haz-ardous to children if they came in contact with it. The children, in states where the attractive nuisance doctrine applies, can be compensated for injury even though they are trespassers if it is foreseeable to the person who maintains the hazard that children might enter, be attracted to it, and become injured. New York, for example, has applied the doctrine in a case where children trespassed on personal property left on a public highway. The doctrine is an exception to the general rule that no duty of care is owed to a TRESPASSER.

Auditor. A public officer whose duty is to examine and approve the payment of public funds; more generally, any accountant who performs a similar function for private parties.

Authentication of Instruments. The process of certifying a document worthy of acceptance or a belief. The use of authentication is not usually limited to the recording of documents or instruments that will be filed in one state court and then, subsequently, in a second state court. Authentication is necessary for the second state court to give the document the authority it was given in the first state court.

Table I is a general outline of the states that require authentication of instruments that were notarized outside the state in which they are to be recorded.

Averment. A positive statement or allegation of facts in a pleading.

Table I

AUTHENTICATION OF INSTRUMENTS

State	When an instrument is notarized outside the state for recording within the state, must it be authenticated if notary affixes his seal?	Who authenticates acknowledgments taken by notary public in state for use in another state?
Alabama	No	Clerk of Circuit Court
Alaska	No	Lieutenant Governor
Arizona	No	Clerk of Superior Court
Arkansas	Yes[1]	Superior Court Clerk
California	Yes	Clerk of Court of Record
Colorado	No[1]	Secretary of State
Connecticut	Customary[1]	Clerk of Superior Court, Waterbury District Clerk
Delaware	No	Prothonotary
District of Columbia	No	Secretary of District Council
Florida	No	Secretary of State
Georgia	No	Clerk of Superior Court
Hawaii	No	Clerk of Circuit Court
Idaho	No	Clerk of District Court
Illinois	No	County Clerk or Secretary of State may grant certificates of magistracy to notaries
Indiana	No	Clerk of Circuit Court
Iowa	Yes	Secretary of State
Kansas	No[1]	Clerk of Court of Record
Kentucky	No[1]	Clerk of County (District) Court
Louisiana	No	Clerk of District Court
Maine	No[1]	Clerk of Court
Maryland	No	Clerk of Circuit Court (Clerk of Superior Court of Baltimore City)
Massachusetts ...	No	State Secretary; Clerk of Superior Court
Michigan	No	Clerk of County
Minnesota	No[1]	Clerk of District Court, Secretary of State
Mississippi	No	Chancery Clerk, Secretary of State
Missouri	No	Clerk of County Court (Clerk of Circuit Court for City of St. Louis)
Montana	No	Secretary of State or County Clerk
Nebraska	No[1]	County Clerk
Nevada	No[1]	County Clerk
New Hampshire ...	No[1]	Secretary of State or Clerk of Court of Record
New Jersey	Yes	County Clerk
New Mexico	Not required but customary	County Clerk
New York	Yes	County Clerk

(continued on following page)

From the book, *Legal Secretary's Complete Handbook*, 3rd ed., by Besse May Miller, revised by Mary A. DeVries. © 1980 by Prentice-Hall, Inc. Published by Prentice-Hall, Inc., Englewood Cliffs, N.J. 07632.

(continued from preceding page)

State	When an instrument is notarized outside the state for recording within the state, must it be authenticated if notary affixes his seal?	Who authenticates acknowledgments taken by notary public in state for use in another state?
North Carolina	No	Secretary of State or Register of Deeds
North Dakota	No[1]	Clerk of District Court
Ohio	No[1]	Clerk of Common Pleas Court
Oklahoma	No[1]	Secretary of State
Oregon	No	County Clerk or Secretary of State
Pennsylvania	No[1]	Prothonotary of Common Pleas Court
Rhode Island	No	Superior, Supreme, and District Court Clerks
South Carolina	No[1]	Clerk of Court
South Dakota	No	Clerk of Circuit Court
Tennessee	No	Clerk of County, Secretary of State for Notaries at Large
Texas	No	County Clerk
Utah	No	Secretary of State
Vermont	No	County Clerk
	(banks usually request authentication)	
Virginia	No[1]	Clerk of Court
Virgin Islands	No	Clerk of District Court
Washington	No	Secretary of State or County Clerk
West Virginia	No[1]	Clerk of County Court
Wisconsin	No[1]	Clerk of Circuit Court
Wyoming	No	County Clerk

[1]Uniform Recognition of Acknowledgments Act adopted.

B

Bail. The security given the COURT to obtain the release of a prisoner and insure his or her later appearance at trial. The security as well as the persons who give it is known as *bail*. A *bail bond* is the document evidencing the monetary obligation to the court, signed by the defendant and those who put up the money for the defendant's release. The obligation is extinguished when the defendant appears at trial.

Bailment. A delivery of personal property for some particular purpose, upon a contract, express or implied, that the property will be returned to the person delivering it after the accomplishment of the purpose for which it was delivered. An essential of the bailment is that return of the property is contemplated.

The person delivering the property is a *bailor;* the person receiving it is a *bailee.* If under the terms of the contract the bailee is obligated to pay a sum of money instead of returning the goods, the obligation is a debt and not a bailment. Thus, a conditional sale is distinguished from a bailment, even though

the contract calls the transaction a bailment. The parties to a consignment of goods expect that the goods will be sold for the account of or returned to the consignor; a consignment is therefore considered a bailment. A bailee is liable for breach of his or her contract to keep the property in a particular manner in a particular place for a particular purpose.

The following transactions are bailments: lease of a car for hire, deposit of goods for storage or safekeeping, and pledge of stocks as collateral. Title to the property remains in the bailor.

Bank Accounts. Law offices maintain two basic bank accounts: the *firm's* bank account and the *trust* bank account.

The *firm's bank account* reflects (1) deposits of all monies belonging to the firm, that is, money the lawyer or lawyers put into the bank when the law office was opened (the capital account); and all cash received from clients in payment for services rendered (accounts receivable); (2) cash withdrawals for operating expenses such as salaries, office supplies, and taxes.

65

The *trust bank account* reflects all bank transactions relating to monies belonging to the client, such as (1) deposits of advances made by clients for expenses, or deposits that represent any monies collected on behalf of clients; (2) all withdrawals—checks drawn on the trust bank account for purposes of remitting to the client those collections that have been made for the client or any other monies that may be due to the client. See ACCOUNTING RECORDS FOR THE LAWYER, Trust Accounts.

Bankruptcy. A state of INSOLVENCY in which the property of a debtor is taken over by a receiver or *trustee in bankruptcy* for the benefit of the creditors. This action is currently performed under the jurisdiction of the courts as prescribed by the National Bankruptcy Act of 1978.

Voluntary Bankruptcy. Voluntary bankruptcy is brought about by the filing of a petition in bankruptcy by the debtor. The form of the petition is prescribed by the act. By filing a voluntary petition, debtors seek, first, to have their assets equally distributed among all creditors, and, second, to free themselves of debt. They are thus able to begin business life anew, unencumbered.

Voluntary bankruptcy is open to all individuals, firms, and corporations, except banking, building and loan, insurance, railroad, and municipal corporations. No special amount of indebtedness is required; a person owing one dollar or several millions may file a petition in voluntary bankruptcy.

Involuntary Bankruptcy. Involuntary bankruptcy is brought about by the filing of a petition by the creditors against an insolvent debtor. If there are fewer than 12 creditors, 1 creditor may file the petition; if there are more than 12, 3 creditors must join in the filing. Before creditors can throw a debtor into bankruptcy, the following conditions must exist:

1. The debtor must owe the creditors filing the petition at least $5,000 more than the value of the liens the creditors hold on the debtor's property.

2. The debtor must have committed an act of bankruptcy within four months preceding the filing of the petition.

Involuntary bankruptcy proceedings cannot be brought against a wage earner, a farmer, or a banking, building and loan, insurance, railroad, or municipal corporation.

Steps in bankruptcy proceedings. After a petition is filed in the federal courts, in a form prescribed by the United States Supreme Court, the basic steps are: (1) application for receiver, (2) adjudication of the bankrupt, (3) referral to referee in bankruptcy, (4) filing of schedules by the bankrupt, (5) meetings of creditors, (6) election of trustee in bankruptcy, (7) proof and allowance of claims, and (8) discharge of the bankrupt.

Referee in bankruptcy. When the court signs a decree of adjudication it refers the case to a "referee" in bankruptcy. The referee, who is a lawyer, acts in place of the bankruptcy court, conducts all the usual proceedings, and grants the final discharge of the bankrupt from further liability for his or her debts. The referee presides over all creditors' meetings.

Filing of schedules by the bankrupt. Within five days after the debtor has been adjudged bankrupt he must file, in involuntary cases, a schedule of assets and liabilities on a form prescribed by the United States Supreme Court. If a voluntary petition is filed, the debtor must accompany the petition with similar schedules.

What to do. The secretary opens a file and processes a bankruptcy matter just as she does with any new matter. The secretary then makes diary entries and keeps a progress record sheet. The petition, application, schedules, and the like are prepared on forms prescribed by the United States Supreme Court. The secretary will have no difficulty filling them in. Most bankruptcies, however, are now handled by specialists. The attorney receives a percentage of the fee for the referral to a specialist.

Bar. 1. The collective group of lawyers permitted to practice law. 2. The court itself. 3. A defense that prohibits an action.

Bar Associations. Professional organizations for lawyers. May be national, state, or local. An attorney usually belongs to all three. *See* AMERICAN BAR ASSOCIATION.

Bastard. A child born of an illicit union and before the marriage of his or her parents. Nearly all of the states have statutory provisions relating to the liability of the father criminally, as well as to the care and support of the child. If the parents marry subsequent to the birth of the child, many states consider the child to be legitimatized with all the rights of a legitimate child. The question of whether a child is legitimate is important when a WILL is drawn up leaving money or property to the "children" of someone. The courts interpret "children" as meaning legitimate children.

Bequest. A gift of personal property passed by will. *See also* LEGACY.

Best Evidence Rule. A regulation that requires a person who testifies in court seeking to prove the contents of a writing to produce the original writing or satisfactorily to account for its absence. The rule prevents the fraudulent misrepresentation of the contents of a document. It also guards against errors arising from the inaccurate copying of the original writing, or from mistakes in reading it, or from faulty recollection of its contents. These dangers disappear when the writing itself is produced at trial.

Bigamy. A criminal offense whereby one marries when one has a living legal spouse. The law treats the second marriage as nonexistent and the innocent spouse is free to remarry.

Bill. 1. *of Attainder.* A law passed by Congress or a state legislature that inflicts punishment upon someone without the benefit of a judicial trial. The Constitution prohibits bills of attainder to prevent legislatures from usurping judicial functions.

2. *of Complaint. See* COMPLAINT.

3. *in Equity. See* COMPLAINT.

4. *of Lading.* Written evidence of a contract between a shipper and carrier for the carriage and delivery of goods. A bill of lading is signed by the carrier or the carrier's agent. It describes the goods to be carried, states the name of the con-

signor (the shipper), the terms of the contract of transportation, the place where the goods are to be delivered, and the person to whom, or to whose order, the goods are to be delivered. A bill of lading serves three purposes: it is a receipt for the goods; it is a CONTRACT that defines the terms under which the carrier agrees to transport the goods; it is a document of title.

When the bill of lading states that the goods are to be delivered to the order of a particular person, it is an *order* or negotiable bill of lading and can be transferred by the original shipper to a third party. Bills of lading are often transferred or "negotiated" in connection with the sale of the goods by shippers to others. The buyer can claim the goods from the carrier by presenting a bill of lading.

5. *of Particulars.* A written statement of information and details relating to a legal controversy furnished by one of the parties to the other. The information is produced either voluntarily in response to a DEMAND FOR BILL OF PARTICULARS, or in compliance with a judge's order for that purpose.

Usually the lawyer dictates the bill of particulars. The secretary should follow figure 1 for style unless otherwise instructed.

The bill of particulars is prepared like the demand for bill of particulars, except that in almost all jurisdictions it *must* have a VERIFICATION. The lawyer tells the secretary who is to verify the bill.

6. *of Rights.* The first ten amendments to the Constitution. They limit the federal government by guaranteeing to the individual certain fundamental personal rights. Among the guarantees are

FREEDOM OF SPEECH AND PRESS, and the RIGHT OF ASSEMBLAGE AND PETITION.

7. *of Sale.* A formal document issued by a seller to a buyer evidencing the transfer of title to the particular piece of personal property described in the instrument. Some transactions require a bill of sale for purposes of registration, for example, the sale of a motor vehicle.

Billing Client. Instead of billing clients once a month, the usual practice in a law office is to bill them when a case is completed, unless it is a long, drawn-out matter. Then the client is billed at intervals. The lawyer will probably dictate the bill.

Law firms generally have printed bill heads; otherwise, they use letterheads. The general practice is to make an original and two copies—the original for the client, a copy for the case file, and a copy for the invoice file. The bills are usually numbered and filed in the invoice file according to number. If they are not numbered they are filed according to date.

Charges made to clients. Fees for services and disbursements made in behalf of a client are charged to the client's account. The disbursements, which are itemized in the bill, include

Recording fees
Court costs
Fee paid process servers
Telephone charges
Office visits
Revenue or state documentary stamps
Postage, when for heavy priority or registered documents; also when a

JMH:p 8/23/— 1-2-1

DENNIS BOOKMAN and	*	IN THE
EMILY BOOKMAN,		
Plaintiffs	*	CIRCUIT COURT
	*	OF BALTIMORE COUNTY
vs.		
CUSTOM MANAGEMENT	*	
CORPORATION and		
BUSINESS SUPPLIES, INC.,	*	
Defendants		
	*	

* * * * * * *

BILL OF PARTICULARS

The following is a bill of the particulars of the plaintiffs' claim against the defendants, that is to say:

(a) The accident occurred on February 23, 19—, at approximately 9:30 o'clock A.M.

(b) The accident occurred in the aisle between the second and third counters from the entrance to defendants' store about midway between the ends of said counters and nearer to the third counter.

(c) The following amounts are claimed as special damages:

1.	Hospital bills	$1,758.03
2.	Physicians' services and medical supplies	1,023.50
3.	Nurses	1,160.00
4.	Household assistance	904.60
5.	Transportation to hospital and doctor's office	43.10

(d) Plaintiffs reside at 162 Westchester Avenue, Baltimore, Maryland.

JONES & MADISON

Attorneys for Plaintiffs

Bill of Particulars: Figure 1.

special job requires mailing a large number of letters

Stenographic services when an out-of-the-ordinary amount of clerical work is required

Long-distance telephone calls

Telegrams

All fees paid for investigations, accountings, abstracts, etc.

Photocopies

How the amount of the bill is calculated. When it is time to bill the client, the lawyer will want a report on the time costs. The secretary will provide a report of the total number of hours spent on the case by each lawyer from the time the case was opened, or from the date of the last bill. Each lawyer's time is listed separately, because the cost per hour varies with the lawyer. The lawyer knows the cost per hour of each member of the firm and of each associate lawyer (the secretary might not) and calculates the cost accordingly.

The lawyer will also want a record of the advances made for the client and the status of the account as a whole. This information will be taken from the client's account ledger sheet, or the secretary will supply a record of the disbursements. (See ACCOUNTING RECORDS FOR THE LAWYER (Business).) Whenever a client is billed, the secretary should examine the current petty cash record to see if any expenditures have been made in the client's behalf; she also examines records of toll telephone costs. After a client is billed, the lawyer cannot very well send a bill for 50 cents for a photocopy the secretary paid for out of petty cash, but numerous small advances add up to sizeable sums.

Binder. 1. *Real Estate.* An agreement to cover a down payment for the purchase of REAL PROPERTY as evidence of good faith on the part of the purchaser. The payment itself is also called a binder.

2. *Insurance.* A temporary agreement given by an insurance company to pay the loss if damage from the peril insured against should occur before the policy is written. A binder need not be in writing.

Blacklist. An index of persons to be held under suspicion or censure. Employers' associations have occasionally kept a file of the names of people discharged for labor agitation, union affiliation, participation in a STRIKE, or other behavior distasteful to the employer. If the employers' association covers a wide area, it becomes practically impossible for a person on the blacklist to obtain work.

Blackmail. The use of any letter or writing threatening to injure another's person, property, or reputation for purposes of EXTORTION. The crime of blackmail is established merely by showing the act and the intent; it is not necessary for the writing actually to produce fear on the part of the victim.

Blanket Mortgage. One MORTGAGE on a number of parcels of REAL PROPERTY. Provision may be made for release of each parcel as certain payments are made in reduction of the loan. In the absence of such a provision for *partial release,* the mortgagee (lender) cannot be required to release any one parcel from his or her blanket mortgage upon payment of a pro rata share of the debt; the mortgagee is entitled to hold all the properties as security until the debt is paid in full.

Blue Book. See AMERICAN LAW REPORTS.

Blue-Sky Laws. Statutes that have been enacted by most states to protect the public from FRAUD in the offering of securities. The term probably derives from the fact that promoters, practicing fraud, were accused of selling stock that had as much worth as a piece of blue sky. These laws supplement interstate regulation of securities offerings, securities exchanges, and speculative practices, through the Securities and Exchange Commission. Actually, protection is achieved through (1) specific legislation—blue-sky laws, and (2) through enforcement of antifraud statutes.

Board of Directors. A group of individuals elected by stockholders, who *as a body* manage a CORPORATION.

Who is qualified to act as director. Any person who is legally competent to contract can be a director, unless the statute, CERTIFICATE of Incorporation or BY-LAWS provide otherwise.

Ownership of stock is generally, but not always, a statutory, charter or bylaw requirement. Some statutes require residence in the STATE OF INCORPORATION by one or more directors; a few require United States citizenship.

Number of directors. A minimum, usually three, is generally fixed by statute; a maximum is also sometimes fixed by statute. Actually, a number within statutory limits is fixed by charter or bylaws of the corporation. This number may be increased or decreased by amendment to the charter when the charter fixes the number; or by amendment to the bylaws when bylaws fix the number.

Election. The certificate of incorporation usually names the first board of directors; statutes give stockholders the right to elect directors annually thereafter. Election must take place once a year when the statute or certificate requires an annual election; no corporate bylaw or regulation can modify a statute directing the method of election. In the absence of an election, incumbent directors are retained in office.

Terms of office. The term is usually fixed by the bylaws. Directors continue to hold office and must discharge their duties until their successors are elected.

Resignation. A director may resign at any time unless prevented by the certificate of incorporation or bylaws or by statute of the state of incorporation. A director who has made a contract with a corporation to serve a definite period is liable for damages caused by his or her resignation before the expiration of that period. Written resignation is preferable but an oral one is sufficient. Resignation should state when it is to become effective; otherwise, it is effective immediately.

Powers. The directors have power to conduct the ordinary business activities of the corporation. They are free to exercise their independent judgment upon all matters before them, without interference by the stockholders except in matters requiring stockholders' consent. In many states the laws provide that matters affecting all the property of the company must be referred to the stockholders; for example, a sale of the assets, lease of all the assets, consolidation or merger, amendment of the charter to increase or decrease capital stock.

Liabilities. Directors must act in good faith and with reasonable care, and must handle the affairs of the corporation with the prudence that an ordinary person would use. The law presumes that they know everything concerning the corporation that they might have learned from the use of reasonable care and diligence. They are not personally liable for losses resulting from accident or mistakes of judgment. Their relation to the corporation is FIDUCIARY and they are accountable to it for any secret profits. They are not to use their positions of trust and confidence to further their private interests. They need not volunteer information affecting the value of stock when trading with the individual stockholders. Directors also incur liabilities under certain federal and state statutes.

Meetings. Generally, directors can bind the corporation by their acts only when they are assembled in a meeting. Bylaws usually provide for the place of the meeting and the method of calling it. A majority of the members of the board is necessary to constitute a QUORUM. A director cannot vote by PROXY and is forbidden to vote on any matter in which the director is personally interested. It is advisable that the director leave the meeting when the board is considering a matter of personal interest, because some courts hold that favorable action will not be binding if the director's vote is

necessary to decide the question. (See DIRECTORS' MEETINGS.) Figure 1 shows a convenient form for recording the meeting minutes.

Compensation. Directors are not legally entitled to compensation for performing their duties as directors or for attending meetings in the absence of charter or bylaw provision. State corporation laws rarely regulate compensation of directors. Directors who perform duties beyond the scope of a director's duties are entitled to compensation for their services.

Bond. A written promissory agreement, under SEAL, by which one party, which may be a corporation, governmental unit, or other body, promises to pay a stated sum of money at some specified future time (known as the maturity date) and to pay interest at a stated rate at specified dates until the maturity date. The obligation or debt is evidenced by the written certificate for a stated amount and for a stated term. See also BOND AND MORTGAGE; BOND ISSUE: CORPORATE MORTGAGE BOND.

Bond and Mortgage. A legal instrument that is written evidence of an obligation under seal, the payment of which is secured by a MORTGAGE (the conditional conveyance) on the property of the issuer. In a *bond and mortgage* both the evidence of obligation and the terms and conditions of payment to be met are combined in the same document.

Bond Issue. A method of raising funds through issuance of a large number of similar bonds, all of which are covered by a trust indenture or DEED OF

	SECRETARY'S MEMORANDUM	
	MEETING OF BOARD OF DIRECTORS	

		Stated	Reg. Notice
		Annual	Personal
ORGANIZATION		Special	Waiver
DATE	19—	Hour	Standard
PRESENT	No. present	Necessary for quorum	
CHAIRMAN			
SECRETARY			
MINUTES			
STATEMENTS			
RESOLUTIONS			
#1	Proposed by	Seconded by	
		For	
	Votes	Against	
#2	Proposed by	Seconded by	
		For	
	Votes	Against	
#3	Proposed by	Seconded by	
		For	
	Votes	Against	
#4	Proposed by	Seconded by	
		For	
	Votes	Against	
#5	Proposed by	Seconded by	
		For	
	Votes	Against	
#6	Proposed by	Seconded by	
		For	
	Votes	Against	
#7	Proposed by	Seconded by	
		For	
	Votes	Against	
NOTES			
ADJOURNMENT			
DISBURSEMENT	Fees	Per member present	
	Expenses	" " present Sundries Total	

(Signed) ....
Secretary

Board of Directors: Figure 1. *Secretary's memorandum for entering notes of minutes of meeting*

TRUST that sets forth the obligations of the borrower, the rights of the bondholders, and the duties of a bank or trust company designated as trustee for the bondholders. The borrower may be an individual, but generally bonds are issued by a CORPORATION (see CORPORATE MORTGAGE BOND). Each BOND represents the corporation's written promise, under SEAL to pay a specified sum of money at a fixed time in the future, usually more than ten years after the promise is made, with interest at a fixed rate payable at specified interest dates.

Bottomry Loan. A loan made to the owner or master of a ship, usually in a foreign port in cases of emergency, for which the ship itself is pledged as security. The development of modern means of communication enabling masters to get assistance from the ship's owners in emergencies has rendered this device largely obsolete. The lender has a LIEN on the ship enforceable in ADMIRALTY upon its safe arrival at the port of destination. The lien becomes void, however, if the ship is lost before arrival. See also RESPONDENTIA; MARITIME LIEN.

Boycott. An effort of many persons to injure another by preventing anyone from doing business with the injured party. Boycotts have been used as a coercive weapon by workers against management. An effective boycott could hurt the workers as well as management because wages and employment may be reduced for some time through the partial destruction of the market once boycotted.

A *secondary boycott* is an effort to injure another by putting economic pressure on a neutral party. A secondary boycott may take the form of union members refusing to handle nonunion goods. Secondary boycotts are illegal because they tend to injure to a greater extent parties not involved in a labor dispute than those directly concerned.

Breach. 1. *of Contract.* The failure or refusal by one of the parties to a CONTRACT to perform some act the contract calls for. A contract may also be breached by making performance impossible, as when a person contracts to sell a car and wrecks it before delivery; or by "anticipatory" breach, as the unqualified announcement by a seller, before delivery date, that the seller will not deliver the goods.

Breach of a contract by one party may discharge the other from performance. Or the injured party may sue for damages representing the loss directly incurred from the breach. Damages cannot be obtained for speculative or possible losses that cannot be shown to have resulted directly from the breach.

2. *of the Covenant of Warranty.* A term used in the law of REAL PROPERTY. It refers to a failure of the seller's warranty of good title. The breach occurs when the buyer is evicted by a person claiming superior title to the property.

3. *of Duty.* The failure (or omission) to do something a person is bound to do by law or to do it in an unlawful manner. For example, one has a "duty" to keep one's car under control and a "duty" to watch for other traffic.

4. *of the Peace.* Conduct by acts or words that disturbs the public tranquility

and is likely to produce violence in others. An example of a breach of the peace is the conduct of a man who threatens another with violence, or who goes about in public with dangerous weapons in a threatening manner. One who commits a breach of the peace is also guilty of DISORDERLY CONDUCT.

5. *of Promise.* Failure to perform a promise, for example, "breach of promise to marry."

6. *of Warranty.* When a WARRANTY made by a vendor proves to be false, the warranty is said to be breached. For the breach, the buyer has a choice of four remedies: (1) Accept or keep the goods and set up the breach to reduce the purchase price. (2) Keep the goods and recover damages for the breach of warranty. (3) Refuse to accept the goods if title has not passed and bring an action for damages for breach of warranty. (4) Rescind the CONTRACT, or if the goods have been delivered, return them and recover any part of the purchase price that has been paid. The buyer can claim only *one* of these remedies.

Bribery. The act of offering, giving, receiving, or soliciting anything of value to influence a public officer's action in the discharge of legal or public duty. The crime is committed whether or not the official does the act requested. Modern statutes punish the giving, receiving, asking, and offering of bribes.

Brief (Litigation). A written document that an attorney prepares as the basis for his or her argument before an APPELLATE COURT.

The brief must contain a history of the case on APPEAL, a statement of the questions or points involved, and the argument. The history is a concise statement of the essential facts without argument. It states the purpose of the litigation, contains a chronological enumeration of the PLEADINGS, the issues, and the JUDGMENT of the trial court, giving references to applicable pages of the transcript. The questions or points should be stated as concisely as possible. Each one is numbered and set forth in a separate paragraph and is usually followed by a statement of whether it was answered in the negative or the affirmative by the trial court. The section of the brief entitled *Argument* contains a division for each of the questions involved, with discussion and citation of authorities.

Preliminaries to preparing the brief. Before dictating the brief, the lawyer *briefs* cases to be used in support of his or her position. This means the lawyer makes a summary, digest, or abstract of a case, quoting pertinent parts from the court's opinion. Although the lawyer will dictate notes of these abstracts to the secretary, the dictation will consist principally of instructions to TAKE-IN excerpts of the court's opinion. Each summary is typed on a separate sheet of paper. Put the name of the case and the CITATION at the top of the sheet, double-space the lawyer's language and indent and single-space the take-ins. No copy is necessary.

Check carefully the spelling of names and the volume and page number of citations. After typing the notes, have someone read back the take-ins, if possible. This is especially important if the book quoted from is a borrowed book that must be returned before the final brief is written.

Time element. The court rules provide that the appellant must file a brief within a specified number of days after the RECORD ON APPEAL is filed, and that the appellee in turn has a specified number of days thereafter to file a brief. The appellant then has an additional time in which to file a reply brief. The timing is close. If the brief is to be printed, there is a deadline by which the MANU-SCRIPT must reach the printer. Unfortunately, many lawyers are inclined to put off the preparation of a brief until the last minute, and there is nothing the secretary can do about it except remind the lawyer of the date the brief must be filed.

Preparation of the brief. A rough *draft* of the dictated brief is first typed. Occasionally the lawyer will dictate part of a brief and then, because of the press of other matters, be unable to complete the dictation for a day or two. In the meantime, the secretary should transcribe his or her notes and place a copy on the lawyer's desk for reference.

Number of copies. After the lawyer revises the draft, it is typed in final form unless the lawyer asks for a second draft. The number of copies depends upon the rules of the court where the brief is to be filed. If the brief is to be printed, an original and two copies are necessary—the original for the printer, a copy for the lawyer, and a copy for the secretary's file.

Format. Figure 1 shows a page of a typed brief. It is important to note that the *questions* or *points* are typed in solid caps or printed in bold face. Also, when several cases are cited in support of the same proposition, they are placed one under the other unless they are in a quotation.

Index and list of authorities cited. A brief of more than 12 pages (consult the rules) must be indexed and prefaced by an alphabetical list of the authorities cited. These pages are numbered with small roman numerals. The index is actually a table of contents. Figure 2 shows an index. In the alphabetical list of authorities cited, the titles of the cases are not necessarily underscored or in italics. Underscoring of a long list of authorities takes a lot of time.

It sometimes happens that a case is cited before the court's opinion is published in the reporter (see NATIONAL REPORTER SYSTEM) or even in the advanced sheets. The page and volume numbers are then left blank. Should the opinion be published before the brief is filed, the reference may be inserted.

Cover and binding. The cover of the brief contains the name of the court, the style of the case, identification of the brief (the party filing it), and the name and address of the attorneys representing the party filing the brief. When the brief is typed on legal size paper, a legal back, endorsed with these items, is used and stapled at the top. When the brief is typed on letter-size paper, double covers stapled at the side are used. Some rules specify different colors for the backs of the appellant's brief, the appellee's brief, and the appellant's reply brief. Figure 3 illustrates a brief cover.

Filing and service. The rules specify the number of copies of the brief that must be filed with the clerk of the appellate court and the number of copies that must be served on opposing counsel. Service on opposing counsel may be by

I

THE BROAD POWERS GIVEN UNDER THE WILL
CLEARLY INDICATE AN INTENTION TO PERMIT
THE EXECUTORS AND TRUSTEES TO MAKE THE
PROPOSED TEN-YEAR LEASE AND OTHER LONG-
TERM LEASES

By the terms of Article EIGHT of the Last Will and

Testament of _____

_____

Article EIGHT reads in part as follows:

"I hereby give to my Executors or
Executor and to my Trustees or Trustee, as the
case may be, and to such of them and their
successors or successor as shall qualify or may be
acting for the time being, full power, authority and
discretion to manage and operate any property
which I may leave; *** and in general to do and
perform all acts which seem to them wise and
necessary for the proper management, investment
and reinvestment of my estate, it being my
intention and direction that they should have the
widest possible powers, authority and discretion in
relation thereto." (Italics ours.)

Among the powers expressly conferred upon the Trustees

by the testator _____

_____

In Corse v. Corse, 144 N.Y. 569, 572, power to grant

leases for a term not limited _____

_____

See cases in point.

Goddard v. Brown, 12 R.I. 31, 46, 47 (1821);
Holland v. Bogardus-Hill Drug Co., 314 Mo. 214;
    284 S.W. 121, 1926;
Lord v. Roberts, 84 N.H. 517, 153 Atl. Rep. 1, 3 (1931);
Matter of Jones, 122 F. 2d 853 (1941).

Brief: Figure 1. *Page from typed
brief.*

Brief (Litigation)

INDEX

Brief: Figure 2. *Index to brief.*

===

IN THE SUPREME COURT OF FLORIDA

_____

WEST SHORE VILLAGE,
Appellant,

vs.

FOSTER PROPERTIES, INCORPORATED,
Appellee.

_____

BRIEF OF APPELLEE.

_____

Beame, Hitt, Jerome & Phillips
627 Towers Building,
Miami, Florida 33156
Attorneys for Appellee.

===

Brief: Figure 3. *Cover for brief on
letter-size, or smaller, paper.*

ARGUMENT. ⟩ 10 Baskerville Bold

PART I ⟩ 11 Baskerville

An Answer to the Spurious Questions Posed By ⟩ 10/14 Baskerville Bold
the Appellants.

Text: 11/13 Baskerville

The Court can dispose of this case either on narrow technical grounds that will result in its being tried over again and appealed again, or on broad equitable principles. We hope it will choose the latter and thus effectively put an end to this controversy that has already gone on too long and caused too much ill feeling in the Village.[1] The whole trend of modern judicial thought is away from decisions on pinpoints. This case was fully and fairly submitted to the Chancellor who gave the parties almost unlimited opportunity to present everything they had. The appellants failed miserably to establish any defense and are asking this Court to reverse the case on the sheerest technicalities.

The City's Brief. ⟩ 10 Baskerville

The first, second and fifth questions posed by the appellant, West Shore Village, can be treated together. They are:

"FIRST QUESTION." ⟩ 11 Baskerville

May a property owner resort to the courts for ⟩ 10/14 Baskerville Bold relief from alleged oppressive zoning without first having exhausted the administrative remedies?

3 em dash

---

[1]See Plaintiff's Exhibits Nos. 10 and 11 in Appendix. ⟩ 9 Baskerville

Brief: Figure 4. *Page of manuscript from brief, marked for printer.*

mail or in person. Proof of service must be made to the appellate court.

Procedure when having a brief printed. The secretary should follow all rules carefully when typing a brief and preparing it for the printer (see TYPING; MANUSCRIPT; PRINTING). Figure 4 is a page of typed manuscript from a brief, marked for the printer. Printers who specialize in court work are usually familiar with the requirements of the court rules.

Upon receipt of the galley proofs, the lawyer will read the brief again and make any desired changes. The secretary has the following responsibilities:

1. Proofread for typographical errors.

2. Check the makeup to see that material that should be in boldface type is in boldface, that quotations are indented, and so on.

3. Compare the quotations with the source from which taken or, if this is impractical, with the manuscript.

4. Check the citations, preferably by reference to the cited case in the reporter; otherwise, against the manuscript.

5. Check the record references against the record itself.

6. Return the corrected proof to the printer with instructions about the number of copies to be printed, stock and color of cover and the like.

Bulk Sales Law. Legislation designed to protect the creditors of a seller who liquidates all or most of his or her assets to a single buyer at a single time. Sometimes a merchant wanting to go out of business will find someone to buy all assets at once. To protect the creditors of such a merchant from being defrauded, most states have enacted bulk sales legislation. Although the laws vary in detail from state to state, in general they provide that the purchaser of all or a major portion of a merchant's stock, other than in the regular course of business, should obtain from the seller, under oath, a list of all the seller's creditors, their addresses, and the amount owed to each of them. The buyer is then obliged to give each creditor notice of the pending sale, usually ten days before possession is transferred and payment is made. This procedure allows the creditors a brief period in which to press or secure their claims before the assets are beyond their reach.

The bulk sales laws do not apply to court-conducted sales such as those resulting from proceedings in BANKRUPTCY or trusteeships. In some states the statutes apply only to retail merchants, in others to retailers and wholesalers, and in still other states to anyone disposing of most business assets to a single buyer.

A buyer failing to comply with the law may be liable to the seller's creditors on a pro rata basis up to the value of the goods received from the seller.

Burglary. A crime defined under the COMMON LAW as breaking and entering the house of another at night with the intent to commit a FELONY. Modern statutes have enlarged the scope of punishable burglary to include breaking and entering in the daytime into structures other than dwelling houses with the intent to commit a felony. Statutes have divided the crime into degrees, with burglary as defined under the common law bearing the severest punishment.

Business Law Articles, The. A loose-leaf periodical used as a "secondary" source; useful in the law library.

Business Trust. See MASSA-CHUSETTS TRUST.

Bylaws. The rules adopted by a CORPORATION for its own government and that of its stockholders, directors, and officers. Bylaws are permanent and continuing, except for the changes that may be made by amendment.

The general corporation law of each state usually empowers the corporation to govern its internal affairs by bylaws and prescribes a method for their adoption and amendment. When either the corporation law or the CERTIFICATE of Incorporation describes the manner in which bylaws should be adopted, they must be adopted in that prescribed way or they will not be valid.

Ordinarily the corporation may change its bylaws at will, provided the amended bylaw is (1) consistent with law, (2) consistent with the certificate of incorporation, (3) consistent with reason, (4) capable of being complied with, and (5) not violative of the rights of stockholders.

Preparation of bylaws. Like the certificate of incorporation, the bylaws usually follow a more or less routine pattern. The lawyer will dictate special clauses or paragraphs peculiar to the corporation being organized and will dictate a memorandum that includes the following information:

1. Place of stockholders' meeting,

2. Day and hour of annual meeting of stockholders,

3. Time when notice of annual meeting of stockholders must be given (usually ten days before meeting),

4. Who may call special meetings of stockholders (usually president, vice-president, or upon request of two directors or holders of 25 percent of the outstanding stock),

5. Time when notice of special meetings of stockholders must be given (usually ten days before meeting),

6. Percentage of stock that constitutes a QUORUM (usually a majority),

7. Place of directors' meetings,

8. When regular directors' meetings are to be held,

9. Time when notice of regular meetings of directors must be given (usually three or five days before the meeting),

10. Who may call special meetings of directors (usually president, vice-president, or upon request of two directors),

11. Time when notice of special meetings of directors must be given (usually three or five days before the meeting),

12. Number of directors to constitute a quorum (usually a majority),

13. Officers who are to sign and countersign checks,

14. Officers who are to sign and countersign stock certificates,

15. When the fiscal year of the company ends.

With the help of this memorandum and the certificate of incorporation the secretary will be able to follow a form and prepare the bylaws. Bylaws are too lengthy to be included here, but reference may be made to any book of

M.T. EDWARDS, INC.

BY LAWS

ARTICLE I.

Office.

The principal office of the Corporation shall be located in the Borough of Manhattan, City of New York,

_____

_____

ARTICLE II.

Meetings of Stockholders.

Section 1. Annual Meeting. The annual meeting of the stockholders of the Corporation after the year 19__

_____

_____

Section 2. Inspectors of Election. The annual election of Directors shall be conducted by two inspectors

_____

_____

ARTICLE III.

Directors.

Section 1. Management. The property, business and affairs of the Corporation shall be managed by a

_____

_____

Bylaws: Figure 1. *First page of bylaws.*

incorporating forms. A printed copy of the bylaws of corporations that are listed on a stock exchange may also be obtained. Figure 1 shows how the bylaws should be set up. Letter-size paper is preferable.

C

Cable. See TELEGRAPH.

Calendar Call. See DOCKET CALL.

Canvass. To scrutinize, discuss, solicit. Not to be confused with *canvas*.

Capital. In the *economic* sense, one of the three "factors of production." The other two are "land" and "labor."

In the *accounting* sense, the net worth of a business as shown in the capital account of a sole proprietor; the sum of the capital accounts of the partners in a PARTNERSHIP business; the sum of the capital stock (*see* no. 3, below) and surplus in a CORPORATION.

In the *legal* sense, that portion of the consideration received by the corporation upon the issuance of stock that has been set up on its books as capital in accordance with the laws of the state in which the corporation is organized. It cannot be impaired through the payment of dividends or the acquisition of the corporation's own stock.

In a *business* sense, actual wealth or assets of a business in money, tangible property such as plant and equipment, or intangible property such as GOOD-WILL, patents, and trademarks. Capital is used synonymously with total assets expressed in monetary forms.

1. *Capital Assets.* Under the capital gain and loss provisions of the federal income tax law, a capital asset is any property held by the taxpayer, except:

(a) Property held primarily for sale to customers or property that will physically become a part of merchandise intended for sale to customers,

(b) Accounts or notes receivable acquired in the ordinary course of your trade or business for services rendered or from the sale of any properties described in (a),

(c) Depreciable property used in your trade or business (even though fully depreciated),

(d) Real property used in your trade or business,

(e) A copyright, a literary, musical, or artistic composition, a letter or memorandum, or similar property created by your personal efforts; prepared or produced, in the case of a letter, memorandum, or similar property, for you; or acquired from a person who created the property or for whom the property was prepared, under circumstances entitling you to his or her basis (for example, by gift),

(f) U.S. government publications that

you received from the government free or for less than the public sales price or that you acquired under circumstances entitling you to the basis of someone who received the publications free or for less than public sales price, if you sell, exchange, or contribute the publication,

(g) Obligations of federal, state, and municipal governments issued on a discount basis and payable without interest at a fixed maturity date not more than one year from the date of issue.

The term *capital asset* includes intangibles such as shares of stocks and bonds unless they fall under one of the exceptions mentioned.

2. *Capital Gain and Loss.* The federal INCOME TAX law and some of the state income tax laws have special provisions for the treatment of gains and losses on the sale or exchange of capital assets by individuals and corporations. These are called the capital gain and loss provisions. The following explanation of the capital gain and loss provisions of the federal income tax laws, as applied to security transactions by an individual, shows the principal factors of the provisions.

Gain or loss on security transaction. The disposition of securities for money (a sale) or for other property (an exchange) or for a combination of both, almost always results in a gain or loss. This is so because there is usually a difference between what was paid for the security given up and what was received for it. Before the taxable gain or loss, if any, on a security transaction can be determined, the taxpayer must know these principal factors:

1. The cost or other basis of the securities disposed of,

2. The amount realized upon the disposal of the security,

3. The period the investment was held before it was disposed of.

Basis for gain or loss on security transactions. Basis is the term used in the tax law to indicate the amount to be compared with the sales proceeds to determine what the gain or loss is. The basis depends upon the manner in which the securities were acquired. It may be the actual cost, the fair market value, or a substituted basis.

The amount realized. The amount realized includes both money and fair market value of any property received on the sale or other disposition of the securities. Fair market value is a question of fact to be determined from evidence.

The period the investment was held. This factor is important because for a noncorporate taxpayer a deduction from gross income is allowed equal to 60 percent of the excess of the new long-term capital gain over the net short-term capital loss. Gains and losses from the sale or exchange of a security held for more than one year are long-term capital gains and losses, and gains and losses from the sale or exchange of a security held for not more than one year are short-term capital gains and losses.

It is essential that the exact length of time the investment was held be determined. An error of one day might convert a short-term capital gain or loss into a long-term capital gain or loss, or vice versa. This could make a substantial difference in the tax. That is why a careful record must be kept of the exact date the investment was acquired and the exact date it was disposed of. In computing the period held, the day on which the property was acquired is *excluded;* the day on which it was disposed of is *included.*

In certain security transactions, particular rules must be followed for determining when the security was acquired. These rules give the *date basis.*

Computation of income and deduction. A net capital gain is included in income. By reason of the so-called "alternative tax" (separate Schedule D, Form 1040) the tax on the gain will never be more than 28 percent of the actual gain.

Corporations may deduct capital losses only to the extent of capital gains. Any capital loss in the current year that exceeds capital gains is carried back to the three years preceding the year of loss and, if not completely absorbed, is then carried over for up to five years succeeding the loss year.

An individual may claim a capital loss deduction if capital losses exceed capital gains. The deduction is limited to the smallest of the following amounts: (a) taxable income for the year reduced (but not below zero) by the zero bracket amount, and computed without regard to either capital gains and losses or deductions for personal exemptions; (b) $3,000; or (c) net capital loss.

Net short-term capital losses are considered at 100 percent in arriving at a capital loss (subject to limitations (a) and (b) above). In other words, net short-term losses can be used to reduce your ordinary income dollar for dollar. Only

50 percent of the net long-term loss can be used to reduce your income. Therefore, $6,000 of net long-term capital losses are needed to produce a $3,000 deduction; $3,000 to produce $1,500; and so on.

3. *Capital Stock.* The aggregate proprietary interest of stockholders in a CORPORATION. This is not an interest in, or ownership of, any specific assets of the corporation; rather it is the collective ownership of the corporation itself. *See* also COMMON STOCK; PREFERRED STOCK; PAR VALUE STOCK; NO-PAR STOCK; CERTIFICATE (of Stock).

Capital, Capitol. *Capital* is a city that is the seat of a government; *Capitol* is the building in which Congress meets, or a building in which a state legislature meets. State capitols may be spelled with either upper or lower case C, but the United States Capitol is spelled with an upper case C. CAPITAL has several other meanings but they do not cause confusion.

Caption. 1. *of Legal Document or Court Paper.* The heading that is written on a legal document or court paper. The caption consists of the following parts:

(a) *Jurisdiction and venue.* Usually the jurisdiction, that is, the name of the court in which the case is brought, and the venue are recited together in phraseology similar to this:

IN THE DISTRICT COURT WITHIN
AND FOR OKLAHOMA COUNTY,
STATE OF OKLAHOMA

or

IN THE DISTRICT COURT OF
SEDGWICK COUNTY, KANSAS

In a few states the venue is recited separately from the jurisdiction, thus:

STATE OF ILLINOIS } ss.:
COUNTY OF COOK

IN THE CIRCUIT COURT THEREOF

(b) *Title of the case.* This gives the names and designations of the various parties to the action. The heading that appears on the summons and complaint is used throughout the action until it is appealed, unless (1) there should be a change of parties by amendment, or (2) there is more than one plaintiff or defendant. In the latter case, it is necessary to show only the first-named plaintiff and the first-named defendant, followed by appropriate words indicating that there are others, such as *et al., et ux., et vir.*

(c) *Index number.* The index, docket, or action number is assigned by the CLERK OF THE COURT. Although it is not known at the time the first paper is filed in court, it must be included on all future papers.

(d) *Title of the pleading.* Each litigation paper has a designation or title, such as a COMPLAINT, or NOTICE of Trial. The common practice is to include the title in the heading or just beneath it. All offices do not follow this practice.

How to type the caption. Court rules specify the information that goes into the caption, but only a few courts regulate the style in which the caption shall be typed. The secretary should ask the lawyer to designate the style he or she prefers.

2. *of Abstract.* An abstract of title, as it relates to real estate, will normally begin with the caption sheet. The caption sheet generally shows the exact description of the property covered by the abstract. As the lands covered by the abstract are increased or decreased, the caption of the abstract will be changed. It is common practice, when this is done, to change the caption sheet of the abstract. However, in some areas, a new caption sheet will be entered inside the body of the abstract, and the abstractor may or may not note on the original caption sheet that a new caption has been inserted. When an attorney is examining the abstract, the attorney will find the new caption sheet and will alert all parties dealing with the title to the land that the description of land is to be taken from the new caption sheet and will generally refer to the page number of the abstract where the new caption sheet is located. However, if a client asks for a deed and the secretary is preparing the deed from the caption sheet of the abstract, the secretary must be very careful to use the last caption sheet added to the abstract, whether it be on the front of or in the body of the abstract.

3. *of Case on Appeal.* The part of a motion (see MOTION) or BRIEF that gives the name of the parties (see PARTIES to an Appeal) and the name of the APPELLATE COURT where the APPEAL is being made. When the RECORD ON APPEAL is filed with the appellate court, the caption has changed from what is was in the lower court. The new caption indicates the name of the appellate court, and the designation of

the parties show their appellate status. The lower court's index number (see CLERK OF THE COURT) of the case is no longer indicated. For styles of designation of the parties on appeal and a table of the styles used in the 50 states, see APPEAL.

Carry-Back and Carry-Over. A tax law provision that allows an individual or CORPORATION to use an operating or capital loss (see CAPITAL Gain and Loss) in one year to reduce taxes for preceding (carry-back) or succeeding years (carry-over). See also INCOME TAX.

Case. Any action, suit or controversy, whether civil or criminal, at law or in equity.

Case Law. The essential substance of law created by judicial decisions, as opposed to law stemming from statutory or other sources. See also SUBSTANTIVE LAW.

Cause. 1. *Causa Mortis.* Latin term meaning "in anticipation of death." It is most often used in "gift causa mortis," meaning a gift given in anticipation of death. If the donor were to survive, the gift would be void.

2. *Causa Proxima.* Latin term meaning "proximate cause." Lawyers speak of proximate cause in relation to personal injury suits. It refers to the act or omission most closely related to the injury that justifies imposing liability on the actor.

3. *Causa Sine Qua Non.* Latin term meaning "the necessary cause." It is most often used in personal injury suits to refer to the cause but for which the injury would not have happened.

4. *Immediate Cause.* The nearest cause in reference to time. A cause may be immediate and yet not proximate. (See *Causa Proxima.*)

5. *Intervening Cause.* An independent cause that occurs between the original wrongful act or omission of the defendant and the injury. It is used in a time sense, as it refers to later events. An intervening cause may produce a result that could not reasonably have been anticipated.

6. *Superseding Cause.* An intervening cause so directly responsible for the resulting injury that it acts to cut off the liability of the preceding parties, regardless of their prior negligence.

7. *Supervening Cause.* See *intervening cause,* above.

Cause of Action. Facts sufficient to support the right to sue. A *right of action* is a legal right to sue; a *cause of action* is the composite of facts giving rise to a right of action. If a complaint fails to state enough facts, that is, fails to give rise to a cause of action, it will be dismissed.

Censorship. The denial of the right of FREEDOM OF SPEECH AND PRESS and of all those rights and privileges one expects under a free government. Totalitarian governments have generally censored on political grounds, but in democracies censorship has largely ceased, save on moral grounds or during wartime.

Certificate. 1. *of Good Faith.* A written statement by an attorney that he or she has filed a DEMURRER on behalf of a client in good faith and not for the purpose of delay.

2. *of Incorporation.* A written instrument that determines what the CORPORATION is authorized to do. It is sometimes referred to as *articles of incorporation, articles of association,* or *charter of the corporation.* The general corporation laws of each state provide what *must* and what *may* be included in the certificate. It is essential to valid incorporation that the provisions of the general corporation law prescribing the necessary contents of the articles be complied with.

Before the proposed certificate of incorporation is filed with the public official designated by law (usually the Secretary of State), it should be checked carefully to make certain that all provisions required by statutes are included. Failure to include a required provision may lead the designated public official to reject the proposed certificate, thus requiring redrafting and resubmission with attendant delay.

Generally, the certificate of incorporation must contain the following:

1. Name of corporation.

2. Purpose or objects of corporation or nature of its business.

3. Place of business.

4. Amount of CAPITAL stock and number of shares into which it is divided. If more than one class is created, a description of the different classes with terms on which respective classes are created.

5. Statement of maximum amount of indebtedness that may be incurred and prohibition against exceeding that amount.

6. Duration of corporate existence.

7. Name and residence of incorporators.

8. Statement indicating what officers are to conduct corporate affairs or statement that such information is contained in the bylaws.

9. Number of directors and names and addresses of directors selected for first year.

10. Statement showing compliance with requirements concerning subscription to, or payment for, capital stock, including amount required to be paid in before commencing business.

11. Designation and address of registered agent (person to receive SUMMONS in case of suit).

Preparation of certificate of incorporation. The law office will have, or the secretary will accumulate, a form file from certificates prepared for previous clients. These forms will serve as models in the preparation of the certificate for a corporation in the process of organization.

The secretary should observe these points:

1. Find out the number of copies the law requires. *Make three extra copies*—one to be kept at the principal office of the corporation, one for the file, and one for the minute book. (In some states an extra copy is required as an exhibit to the application for a permit to sell securities to the public. A copy of the charter must also be filed with the application to the Securities Exchange Commission.) Some states also require that a certified copy be filed in each county where the corporation owns real estate. The secretary will also have to make an extra copy for each state in which the proposed corporation expects to qualify. Two typings are necessary, the second being on minute paper.

2. Use either 8½- by 11-inch good quality bond paper, or legal cap. The trend is toward the use of the letter-size paper, except in those states where printed forms prepared by the state are used. When letter-size paper is used, the ribbon copy of the second typing is made on minute paper, thus saving the time required to copy the charter in the minute book.

3. If printed blank forms are used, be sure they are of the same date of printing; otherwise, they might not be exact copies.

4. When typing the charter, always use pica type and a very black ribbon, and double-space it. These requirements are mandatory in nearly every state. Otherwise, there is no specific form in which the certificate of incorporation must be typed. Figures 1, 2, and 3 illustrate the first, second, and last pages of a charter and will serve as a model for style. The following details are customary, although not mandatory:

(a) The title of the document and name of the corporation are written in solid caps.

(b) The following words are written with initial caps whenever they refer to the corporation that is being organized: Corporation, Certificate of Incorporation (or any other name by which the charter is known), Board of Directors, Bylaws.

(c) The left margin of indented material is indented five spaces from the principal left margin, and the first line of an indented paragraph is indented five additional spaces. The right margin is also indented.

(d) Subindentations are indented an additional five spaces.

(e) Numbered or lettered items are indented.

(f) Purpose clauses are indented.

(g) Pages are numbered.

(h) Numbers are written out, followed by figures in parentheses.

5. Type a signature line for each signer.

6. In almost all states the charter is a sealed instrument. If the state of incorporation requires the seals of the signers, type (L.S.) or (SEAL) after each signature line.

7. If an ACKNOWLEDGMENT is required, type the certificate of acknowledgment in the form required by the state of incorporation. The VENUE will recite the state and county where the incorporators sign, not the state of incorporation. The rules that govern the acknowledgment of any instrument govern the acknowledgment of a certificate. Some states require acknowledgments taken outside the state to be authenticated. Therefore, if the acknowledgment is to be taken in a state other than the state of incorporation, consult the statutes of the state of incorporation to see if AUTHENTICATION is necessary. If all incorporators sign at the same time, one certificate of acknowledgment is sufficient, but if they sign at different times, there must be a separate acknowledgment for each. Some states do not require that all incorporators who sign will acknowledge the instrument.

8. Prepare a cover for each copy except the one that is on minute paper. The only typing on the cover is, "Certificate of Incorporation (or articles, or charter, as the case may be) of (name of corporation)."

Execution of the certificate. In a few states all copies of the certificate of incorporation required to be filed with the designated public official must be ribbon copies, carbons not being acceptable. In others, an original and duplicate origi-

```
CERTIFICATE OF INCORPORATION
              OF
     GREENBRIAR MILLS, INC.
        _____

        We, the undersigned, for the purpose of associating to
establish a corporation for the transaction of the business and the
promotion and conduct of the objects and purposes hereinafter
stated, under the provisions and subject to the requirements of the
laws of the State of Georgia (particularly Chapter 1, Title 8 of the
Georgia Code and the acts amendatory thereof and supplemental
thereto, and known, identified and referred to as the "General
Corporation Law of the State of Georgia"), do make and file this
Certificate of Incorporation in writing and do hereby certify as
follows, to wit:
        FIRST, The name of the corporation (hereinafter called
the Corporation) is
        GREENBRIAR MILLS, INC.
        SECOND: The respective names of the County and of
the City within the County in which the principal office of the
Corporation is to be located in the State of Georgia are the County
of Dougherty and the City of Albany. The name of the resident
agent of the Corporation is The Prentice-Hall Corporation System,
Inc. The street and number of said principal office and the address
by street and number of said resident agent is 229 South State
Street, Atlanta, Georgia 30303.
```

Certificate of Incorporation:
Figure 1. *First page.*

nals or triplicate originals are acceptable. Some states will accept an original and conformed copies.

If the papers are to be executed in the office, notify the incorporators that the papers are ready for signature and arrange a time for them to come in to sign. (It is advisable to do this as soon as it is known when the papers will be ready,

in order to avoid delay.) If some or all of the incorporators are to sign outside the office, forward the document with a covering letter.

Each original, duplicate original, and triplicate original must be signed, but the copies that are to be conformed need not be signed. The signature must be the same on each copy, and must be written

THIRD: The nature of the business and of the purposes to be conducted and promoted by the corporation, which shall be in addition to the authority of the corporation to conduct any lawful business, to promote any lawful purpose, and to engage in any lawful act or activity for which corporations may be organized under the General Corporation Law of the State of Georgia, is as follows:

To _____

_____

_____

To _____

_____

_____

FOURTH: The name and place of each of the incorporators are as follows:

NAME	PLACE OF RESIDENCE
E.G. Barnes	Atlanta, Georgia
R.S. Patterson	Atlanta, Georgia
L.M. Wilson	Atlanta, Georgia

FIFTH: The Corporation is to have perpetual existence.

SIXTH: The total number of shares of stock which the corporation shall have authority to issue is _____ with par value of $_____ each [or with no par value]. All such shares are of one class and are Common Stock. [Add additional clauses if there are to be different classes of stock, and if shares are to have preemptive rights].

SEVENTH: _____
_____

EIGHTH: The effective date of the certificate of incorporation of the Corporation, and the date upon which the existence of the corporation shall commence, shall be _____ , 19____
[This clause is to be used if effective date of certificate of incorporation is to be a date after the date of filing and recording, but in no event later than 90 days after filing with the Secretary of State].

Certificate of Incorporation:
Figure 2. *Second page.*

exactly as in the document. Thus, if an incorporator signs his name *R.P. Edwards,* his name should not be written *Richard P. Edwards* in the document.

When acknowledgments are required, take the acknowledgment of the incorporators, and notarize all signed copies of the charter. Conform the unsigned copies.

Filing the certificate and payment of fees. After the certificate of incorporation has been executed, send the required number of copies to the proper state official, with a letter of transmittal and a

IN WITNESS WHEREOF, we, the undersigned, being all of the incorporators hereinabove named, do hereby further certify that the facts hereinabove stated are truly set forth and accordingly have hereunto set our respective hands and seals.

Dated at Atlanta, Georgia

October 31, 19--

_____ (L.S.)

_____ (L.S.)

_____ (L.S.)

STATE OF GEORGIA   )
) SS.:
COUNTY OF DOUGHERTY)

BE IT REMEMBERED that personally appeared before me, Robert R. Steele, a Notary Public in and for the County and State aforesaid, E.G. Barnes, R.S. Patterson, and L.M. Wilson, all the incorporators who signed the foregoing Certificate of Incorporation, known to me personally to be such, and I having made known to them and each of them the contents of said Certificate of Incorporation, they did severally acknowledge the same to be the act and deed of the signers, respectively, and that the facts therein stated are truly set forth.

Given under my hand and seal of office this 31st day of October, A.D. 19--.

_____
                           Notary Public

—10—

Certificate of Incorporation:
Figure 3. *Last page.*

check in payment of the organization tax and fees. The letter of transmittal might read as follows:

Secretary of State
State of Georgia
Atlanta, GA 30303

Dear Sir:

Re: Greenbriar Mills, Inc.

We are enclosing an original and two conformed copies of the Certificate of Incorporation of Greenbriar Mills, Inc. Please record the original of the Certificate in your offices and certify and return to us the conformed copies.

We are also enclosing our check for $70, covering (1) the organization tax, $10; (2) filing and indexing fee, $25; (3) recording fee, $15; (4) certification of copy for recording, $10; and (5) certification of one extra copy, $10.

Sincerely yours,
Holt & Rogers
Enclosures (4)

If the charter is acceptable, the public official will retain the original. He or she will mark the copy, or copies, to show that the charter has been filed and will endorse his or her approval upon it or attach a certificate of approval to it and return it, together with receipt for tax and fees, to your office.

(a) Conform the office copy, noting particularly the date of the official's filing marks. This date, rather than the date on which the charter was executed, is the date of incorporation.

(b) Draw a check for the local filing fee and file the certified copy of the charter in the appropriate local office if required.

(c) Note on the office copy the date the certificate was filed locally.

(d) Paste the tax receipt in the minute book.

3. *of Stock.* Written evidence of ownership of a certain number of shares in a CORPORATION. The certificate itself evidences the holder's right to a proportionate share in the declared dividends and in the assets of the corporation upon its dissolution. The certificate is an assignable CHOSE IN ACTION. See also CAPITAL (Stock).

4. *of Title.* An instrument, written and signed by a TITLE examiner, stating that in his or her opinion the seller has good title to property to be conveyed. A certificate of title may be issued by an attorney who examines the public records and gives an opinion about the validity of the title based on such examination. It offers no protection to the purchaser of property against any hidden defects in the title that an examination of the records could not reveal or against any unwarranted litigation attacking the title. The issuer of the certificate is liable only for DAMAGES due to negligence. A certificate of title is, in effect, TITLE INSURANCE. See also ABSTRACT OF TITLE.

Certified Check. A CHECK that has been guaranteed by the bank both as to signature and amount. Either the maker of a check or the holder can present the check for certification at the bank on which the check is drawn. The bank examines the drawer's account, charges the account immediately for the amount of the check, and marks the check "accepted" or "certified."

The check then ceases to be an order on the bank and becomes an obligation of the bank. Hence, certification of a check makes it equivalent to cash. Certified checks are used principally in real estate and securities transactions in which cash payment is required. When DRAWERS have checks certified, they accept the bank as their debtor. A drawer is not liable in case of insolvency of the bank before payment. Drawers of a certified check cannot stop payment on it. They should redeposit the check if it is still in their possession and not destroy it. If a bank certifies a check by mistake, it may withdraw the certification if it acts promptly, provided the holder has lost no right.

Certiorari. (Latin) To be informed of; to be made certain in regard to. A writ issued by a superior court to an inferior court directing it to send to the former court the record of a particular case. A WRIT of certiorari is an extraordinary remedy resorted to in cases obviously entitled to redress where no direct appellate proceedings are provided by law. A writ of certiorari cannot be used as a substitute for an appeal or a writ of error. It is distinguished from an APPEAL in that it brings up the case on the record, whereas on appeal a case is brought up on the merits. A litigant is entitled to a writ of error as a matter of right, but a writ of certiorari lies within the court's discretion.

The dissatisfied party in the lower court petitions the appellate court for a writ of certiorari. If, on the face of the record, the appellate court determines that the lower court has not proceeded in accordance with the law, it will consent to issue the writ and hear the case. If the record itself does not indicate that the petitioner has been wronged by the proceeding, the court will deny the petition for a writ of certiorari. The denial is, in effect, an affirmance of the lower court's decision on the point of law before the appellate court, but the issuance of the writ does not mean that the appellate court will decide in favor of the petitioner. The court may then order the certiorari dismissed; or return it to the lower court with instructions; or render a final judgment which must finally govern the case.

See also HABEAS CORPUS; STAY; PROHIBITION; QUO WARRANTO; MANDAMUS.

Chancery Court. A court or tribunal that has jurisdiction over EQUITY or chancery matters. Law actions usually have for their object the assessment of damages, but a court of equity or chancery goes further. It attempts to prevent the wrong itself or give the complainant what he or she bargained for.

A few states still have chancery courts (see Table I, AMERICAN COURT SYSTEM). Others do not separate cases in equity from cases at law, but apply equity principles when appropriate. In the majority of states, equity and law are organized under a single court, which has two dockets—one in equity and one in law.

Among the more common equity actions are injunction suits, partition suits, specific performance, rescission of contract, reformation of a contract, and all matters relating to trusts and trustees.

Charge to the Jury. Instructions given by the JUDGE to the jury on the principles of law that the jury is required to apply to the facts of the case to return a verdict. Many judges invite active participation by the lawyers in the preparation of a tentative charge. Each lawyer at a trial has an opportunity to object to the charge as finally given by the court.

How to prepare an instruction to the jury. Many offices keep printed forms of stock instructions, but the lawyer will dictate others.

1. Make an original for the judge, a copy for opposing counsel, and an office copy.

2. Type each instruction on a separate sheet of legal paper.

3. Number each instruction for identification purposes.

4. Identify the party submitting the instructions, thus, "Plaintiff's Instruction No. . . ." (This may be placed at the top or bottom of the charge; numbers are inserted later in the order in which the charge is given.)

5. There is no CAPTION.

6. Instructions are not stapled in a legal back and are not enclosed.

Charter-Party. A CONTRACT by which a ship or a portion of it is leased to another for a specified time or use. There are three main types of charter-parties.

Voyage Charter. A ship is engaged to carry cargo on a single voyage. The vessel is manned and navigated by the owner. The voyage charter is the form of charter-party most frequently encountered.

2. *Time Charter.* The ship is engaged by the charterer for a fixed period for the carriage of goods anywhere in the world on as many voyages as approximately fit into the charter period. As in the voyage charter, the owner's people continue to navigate and manage the vessel. The crew is under the charterer's orders as to the ports touched, cargo loaded, and other business matters.

3. *Demise Charter.* The charterer takes over the ship and mans it with his own people. In practice, virtually all demise charters are for a specified period. See also ADMIRALTY; MARITIME LIEN.

Chattel. An article of tangible personal property, as distinguished from real property (land and improvements) and intangibles (stocks, bonds, and the like). The term *chattel* derives from the word *cattle*, an early symbol of property.

Chattel Mortgage. A MORTGAGE on tangible PERSONAL PROPERTY (chattels). A chattel mortgage is distinguished from other instruments of conveyance by the condition contained in it that if the debt is paid by a day specified, the conveyance is void, and if payment is not made, the transfer is absolute. In some jurisdictions, a chattel mortgage, like a real estate mortgage, is not a conveyance transferring TITLE but merely a LIEN given as security for the debt. If the debt is not paid when due, or if some other condition of the mortgage has not been complied with, the mortgagee enforces his or her lien by a FORECLOSURE sale.

In some states, the foreclosure of a chattel mortgage, like the forecloseure of a real estate mortgage, can be effected only through court procedure. In many states the chattel mortgage must be recorded. The chattel mortgage does not in itself constitute notice of the mortgagee's rights in the chattel. Hence, the creditor who wants to protect his or her rights against third parties, must give public notice of his interest in the chattel. The creditor does this by filing the chattel mortgage or a true copy of it in a prescribed public place.

The duration of a chattel mortgage is limited in some states—sometimes to three or four years, after which time it becomes void automatically unless renewed. See also CONDITIONAL SALE; RECORDING (of Conditional Sale Contract).

Check. A written order drawn upon a bank by a depositor, requesting the bank to pay on demand a certain sum of money to the bearer, or to the order of some person or corporation named on the face of the check.

Postdated check. The holder may transfer a check before the date on which it is payable, but the drawer's bank will not honor it before that date. A postdated check is a promise to pay rather than an order to pay; therefore, the drawer generally cannot be prosecuted criminally if the check is refused for lack of sufficient funds.

Discrepancy in amounts. The Negotiable Instruments Law provides that the amount expressed in words is the sum payable where there is a discrepancy between that amount and the amount expressed in figures. Banks generally refuse to accept checks with discrepancies in amounts. The holder may endorse it, guaranteeing the correct amount, and deposit the check for collection.

Certification. (See CERTIFIED CHECK.)

Time within which check must be presented for payment. The Negotiable Instruments Law provides that a check must be presented for payment within a "reasonable time," determined by the circumstances of each particular case. Failure to present a check for payment within a reasonable time discharges the drawer from liability to the extent of loss caused by the delay. Thus, if the bank on which a check is drawn becomes insolvent so that the drawer loses the amount he or she had on deposit to meet the check, the loss must be borne by the one who was lax in presenting the check for payment.

Checks that "bounce." Occasionally, a check will be returned to the depositor by the bank for some stated reason. "Lack of endorsement" means the depositor failed to endorse the check. "No account" means the maker of the check has no account at that bank. Unless the depositor knows the appropriate steps to take when a check is returned, he or she should consult counsel within 24 hours.

Insufficient funds. One of the reasons why checks "bounce" is "insufficient funds." A person who, with fraudulent intent, issues a check knowing that he or she does not have sufficient funds for its payment is subject to criminal prosecution in many states.

Death of a drawer. This revokes the authority of the bank to pay. If a bank pays a check without knowledge that the drawer has died, it cannot be held liable for the amount.

Given in full settlement of claim. When the amount of a claim is *disputed*, a check reciting that it is in full settlement, accepted or collected by the creditor without objection, discharges the debt-or's obligation. A check should be re-turned at once if the amount is not acceptable.

Forged or raised check. A bank is lia-ble to a depositor for payment of a forged or raised check. The Negotiable Instruments Law provides, however, that the drawer must notify the bank within one year after return of the paid check that it was forged or raised.

Drawn on Sunday or holiday. Tech-nically, a check should not be drawn on Sunday or on a holiday, but few banks refuse payment for this reason.

Endorsement. The endorsement ap-pears on the reverse side of a check. When an endorsed check is received in payment of debts, there are two things to watch. (1) The spelling of the name in the endorsement should correspond ex-actly with the name of the payee on the face of the check. A check made payable to a business firm should be endorsed in the firm's name and signed by the au-thorized person of that firm. (2) Any ad-ditional words accompanying the signature. Any wording having unfamil-iar legal significance should be a warning to the recipient of the check to consult an attorney.

Check-Off. A system whereby the employer deducts the union dues and in-itiation fees from the paychecks of the employees and transfers these amounts directly to the union. The check-off saves the union time and money in collecting dues and also guarantees the union a fi-nancial security as a result of the continuing and steady payment.

Chinese Copy. See TYPING.

Chose in Action. A right to receive or recover a debt or DAMAGES in an ac-tion on a CONTRACT or in a TORT ac-tion. A chose in action is intangible personal property. Often the phrase in-cludes not only the right of action, but also the thing that forms the subject mat-ter of that right, for example, contracts, stocks, bonds, and bank accounts.

Circuit Court. A state court whose jurisdiction extends over several coun-ties. For example, in Arkansas there are 75 counties and 20 circuit courts. These courts have original jurisdiction and are courts of record (see AMERICAN COURT SYSTEM).

Circumstantial Evidence. See DI-RECT EVIDENCE.

Citation. 1. *in Admiralty Proceed-ing.* A written command by the United States Marshal served upon a vessel or party being sued in an ADMIRALTY ac-tion. The citation commands the party to admit or deny the assertions in the libel. (See LIBEL AND SLANDER in Admi-ralty Practice.) It is substantially the same as a SUMMONS in an action at COM-MON LAW except that an action in ad-miralty is "commenced" by the filing of the libel in the U.S. District Court, not by service alone. The citation, however, must be served reasonably soon after the libel is filed.

2. *in Probate Proceeding.* An official order notifying a person to appear be-fore a probate court. See PROBATE.

3. *to Legal Authorities.* Reference to an authority that supports a statement of law or from which a quotation is taken.

Citations most frequently occur in a BRIEF, MEMORANDUM OF LAW, and OPINION LETTERS. The lawyer speaks of *citing a case, a cited case, citing a report,* and the like. The references are principally to the following sources:

1. Constitutions, statutes, codes
2. Law reports
3. Texts and periodicals

SHEPARD'S CITATIONS is a service that indicates whether statutes and cases to be cited as authority are in fact valid for that purpose. In matters of style and form, the most widely used book of citations is *A Uniform System of Citation*, published by the Harvard Law Review Association in Cambridge, Massachusetts. It covers general rules of citation and style, citation forms for various kinds of authority, and specific citation forms and abbreviations. However, some state supreme courts require a different form of citation. Always check your own supreme court rules to see how the official state reporters should be cited in appellate briefs.

How to take citations in shorthand. It sometimes happens that citations, particularly volume, page, and section number, are incorrectly set down when dictation is rapid. The following procedure is recommended: Write down the volume number, allow a small space, and immediately write down the page or section numbers, going back to fill in the title of the volume. The memory more readily retains the title of the volume than it does the volume and page number. In the citation of a case, it is more important to obtain the correct numbers and title of the book than the correct names of the parties. The secretary can go to the law report and easily find the title of the case.

Accuracy of citations. The importance of accuracy of citations cannot be overemphasized. Check and double-check volume and page references and spelling of names. The secretary should check against the original reports, not against her notes. Check printed briefs against the original reports, not against manuscript. A judge is annoyed if he or she cannot find a case cited because of a typographical error in the citation. Misspelling of the name of a well-known case marks the lawyer as either careless or ignorant. Errors in citations are always avoidable, and it is the secretary's responsibility to see that no reflection is cast upon the lawyer through carelessness.

How to cite a constitution. Show the number of the article, or amendment, in Roman numerals; the section number in Arabic numerals. Give date if the constitution cited is not in force.

> U.S. Const. art. IV, §2
> U.S. Const. amend. VI, §2
> Ga. Const. art. XI, §3
> Ga. Const. art II, §1 (1875)

How to cite statutes and codes. Whenever full reference to a federal statute is necessary, cite date, chapter number, statute citation, and United States Code citation, thus: Section 1 of the Act of June 13, 1934, c. 482, 48 Stat. 948, 40 U.S.C. 276 b. Compilations of state statutes and codes are cited by chapter, title, or section number. See table I.

When citing statutes and codes, the secretary should observe these directions:

1. If a compilation in its preface gives the method of citing it, use that citation.
2. When the date is incorporated in the title of the compilation, show it.
3. When statutes or codes of one state

Table I

State	Title of compilation	How cited
Ala.	Code of Alabama, Recompiled 1958	Code of Ala. Tit. 10, § 101
Alas.	Alaska Statutes 1962	A.S. § 08.04.310
Ariz.	Arizona Revised Statutes Annotated	ARS § 10-101
Ark.	Arkansas Statutes Annotated 1947	Ark. Stats. (1947) Sec. 10-101
Calif.	Deering's California Codes (Code of Civil Procedure)	CCP § 101
Colo.	Colorado Revised Statutes, 1963	101-1-7, C.R.S. '63
Conn.	General Statutes, Revision of 1958	Conn. G.S. 1958 Sec. 101
Del.	Delaware Code Annotated, 1953	10 Del. C. § 110
D.C.	District of Columbia Code Annotated, 1961	D.C. Code 1961, Title 26, § 703
Fla.	Florida Statutes, 1967	Florida Statutes, 1967, § 101.011
Ga.	Code of Georgia, Annotated	Ga. Code Ann. § 10-1010
Hawaii	Revised Laws of Hawaii, 1955	R.L.H. 1955 § 172-1
Ida.	Idaho Code	Idaho Code, Sec. 26-1850
Ill.	Illinois Revised Statutes 1951	Ill. Rev. Stat. 1951 Ch. 10, § 101
	Smith-Hurd Illionis Annotated Statutes	S.H.A. Ch. 10, § 101
	Jones Illinois Statutes Annotated	Jones Ill. Stat. Ann. Ch. 10, § 101
Ind.	Burns Annotated Indiana Statutes	Burns Ann. St. Sec. 25-101
Iowa	Code of Iowa, 1966	Code of Iowa, 1966, § 110.10
Kans.	Kansas Statutes Annotated, 1963	K.S.A. 48-101
Ky.	Kentucky Revised Statutes, 1962	KRS 101.010 (1)
La.	Louisiana Revised Statutes of 1950	R.S. 10:101
Maine	Revised Statutes of Maine, 1964	R.S. of Maine 1964, T. 10 § 51
Md.	Annotated Code of Maryland, 1957	Md. Code (1957), Art. 10, Sec. 101
Mass.	Annotated Laws of Massachusetts, 1966	A.L., C. 8 § 10
Mich.	1948 Compiled Laws of Michigan	C.L. 1948, § 10.101
	Michigan Statutes Annotated	Stat. Ann. § 10.101
Minn.	Minnesota Statutes 1967	Minn. Stat. 1967, Sec. 101.51
Miss.	Mississippi Code, 1942, Annotated	Miss. Code, 1942, Ann., § 101

(continued on following page)

(continued from preceding page)

State	Title of compilation	How cited
Mo.	Missouri Revised Statutes, 1959	R.S. Mo. 1959, § 101.010
Mont.	Revised Codes of Montana, 1947, Annotated	RCM 1947, § 10-101
Nebr.	Nebraska Revised Statutes, 1943	Sec. 1-101, R.S. Nebr., 1943
	Reissue Revised Statutes of Nebraska, 1943	Sec. 1-101, R.R.S. Nebr., 1943
Nev.	Nevada Revised Statutes	NRS § 19.010
N.H.	1966 New Hampshire Revised Statutes Annotated	RSA 101:1
N.J.	Revised Statutes of New Jersey, 1937	N.J.R.S., 10:101-10
	New Jersey Statutes Annotated	N.J.S.A., 2A: 4-30.1
N.M.	New Mexico Statutes Annotated, 1953	NMSA Comp., 3-7-16
N.Y.	McKinney's Consolidated Laws of New York	Business Corporation Law, § 101
N.C.	General Statutes of North Carolina, 1965	G.S. § 10-101
N.D.	North Dakota Century Code Annotated, 1961	N.D.C.C.A. § 9-08-05
Ohio	Baldwin's Ohio Revised Code, Annotated	R.C. § 1110.10
Okla.	Oklahoma Statutes, 1961	10 O.S. 1961 § 101
Oreg.	Oregon Revised Statutes	ORS 11.010
Pa.	Purdon's Pennsylvania Statutes Annotated	10 P.S. § 101
R.I.	General Laws of Rhode Island of 1956	Gen. Laws 1956, 1-1-10
S.C.	Code of Laws of S.C. 1962	1962 Code, § 10-101
S.D.	South Dakota Code of 1939	SDC 10.1010 (10)
	South Dakota Code Supplement of 1960	SDC 1960 Supp. 11.0111
Tenn.	Tennessee Code Annotated	T.C.A., § 10-101
Tex.	Vernon's Texas Statutes, 1948	Vernon's Texas St. 1948, Art. 101
	Vernon's Texas Statutes, 1962 Supplement	Vernon's Texas C.C.P., 1962 Supp., Art. 5728
Utah	Utah Code Annotated, 1953	UCA 1953, 10-10-1
Va.	Code of Virginia, 1950	Code, § 10-101
Vt.	Vermont Statutes Annotated	VSA, Title I, § 51
Wash.	Revised Code of Washington 1968 Supplement	RCW 10.11.101
W. Va.	West Virginia Code Annotated (1966)	Michie's § 17-3-6
Wis.	Wisconsin Statutes 1967	Stats. § 84.12
Wyo.	Wyoming Statutes 1957	WS, § 10-10

are cited outside of that state, the name of the state is always indicated for identification purposes. For example, lawyers in Kansas cite the Kansas General Statutes as "G.S." but outside of Kansas the citation is Kan. G.S.

4. When citing an act or law that has been repealed and no longer appears in the latest compilation, give the date of the compilation cited.

Ill. Rev. Stat. C. 114, §88 (1889)

How to cite cases in official reports and reporters. Cases in OFFICIAL REPORTS (see table II) and reporters are cited alike. Directions for citing cases must be considered in the light of applicable court rules. Some courts lay considerable emphasis on how cases should be cited and where citation to the NATIONAL REPORTER SYSTEM (see table III) should be included. The following directions are the rules of thumb used in many law offices. (Also see *Illustrations of Citations,* below.)

Names of parties. 1. Cite the name of the case as it appears in the running head of the report, not as it appears at the beginning of the opinion. Do not abbreviate the first word.

2. When the United States is a party, do not abbreviate U.S. unless it is part of the name of a government vessel. (See example 1.)

3. Do not substitute the initials of a government agency or a labor union for its full name in briefs. It may be done in other legal writings. (See example 2.)

4. Use the first name of railways, but abbreviate the balance. (See example 3.)

5. When *Co.* and *Inc.* are both part of a name omit the *Inc.*

6. When the names of parties change completely on APPEAL, indicate that

fact by the use of *sub nom.* (See example 4.) This direction does not apply when the names of the parties are merely reversed.

Volume and page. Cite the volume and page number of the report or reporter in which the opinion is published. The reference is to the entire opinion and gives the page at which the opinion begins. A *spot page reference* follows when it is desired to call attention to a particular page, such as one from which a quotation is taken. (See example 5.)

The designation "2d" *must* be included in the citation of a volume in a second series. A reference to 58 N.E. is not the same as a reference to 58 N.E. 2d.

Date. Show in parentheses the year the decision is handed down by the court. It appears at the beginning of the court's opinion. Both *A Uniform System of Citation* and *Practical Manual of Standard Legal Citations* place the date at the end of the citation (example 1), but lawyers, when writing briefs, sometimes place it between the title of the case and the volume reference (example 5). Many lawyers do not show the date of the decision unless it is relevant to the argument.

Jurisdiction and court. When the name of the reporter does not indicate the JURISDICTION, show the jurisdiction in parentheses preceding the date. (See example 6.) Also show the name of the court deciding the case if it is not the highest court in the state. (See example 7.) This is always necessary when only the unofficial reporter is cited.

Parallel citations. Both the official and unofficial reports should be cited if available. Cite the official report first. (See example 8.) When the case has not been published in the official reports, but will be in the future, cite the name of the offi-

Table II

Official report	Cite as
Alabama Reports	Ala.
Alabama Appellate Reports	Ala. App.
Alaska Reports	P. 2d
Arizona Reports	Ariz.
Arkansas Reports	Ark.
California Appellate Reports	Cal. App.
California Appellate Reports, Second Series	Cal. App. 2d
California Reports	Cal.
California Reports, Second Series	Cal. 2d
Colorado Reports	Colo.
Connecticut	Conn.
Delaware Reports	By name of Rep., or by consecutive number, which is preferred
Delaware Chancery Reports	Del. Ch.
Florida Reports	Fla.
Georgia Reports	Ga.
Hawaii Reports	H.
Idaho Reports	Idaho
Illinois Reports	Ill.
Illinois Appellate Court Reports	Ill. App.
Indiana Reports	Ind.
Indiana Appellate Reports	Ind. App.
Iowa Reports	Iowa
Kansas Reports	Kan.
Kentucky Reports	Ky.
Louisiana Reports	La.
Maine Reports	Me.
Maryland Reports	Md.
Massachusetts Reports	Mass.
Michigan Reports	Mich.
Minnesota Reports	Minn.
Mississippi Reports	Miss.
Missouri Reports	Mo.
Missouri Appeal Reports	Mo. App.
Montana Reports	Mont.
Nebraska Reports	Neb.
Nevada Reports	Nev.
New Hampshire Reports	N.H.
New Jersey Equity Reports	N.J. Eq.
New Jersey Reports	N.J.
New Jersey Superior Court Reports	N.J. Super.
New Mexico Reports	N.M.
New York Appellate Division Reports	N.Y. App. Div.
New York Miscellaneous Reports	N.Y. Misc.
New York Reports	N.Y.
North Carolina Reports	N.C.

(continued on following page)

*From the book, *Legal Secretary's Complete Handbook*, 3rd ed., by Besse May Miller, revised by Mary A. DeVries. ©1980 by Prentice-Hall, Inc. Published by Prentice-Hall, Inc., Englewood Cliffs, N.J. 07632.

(continued from preceding page)

Official report	Cite as
North Dakota Reports	N.D.
Ohio Appellate Reports	Ohio App.
Ohio State Reports	Ohio St.
Oklahoma Reports	Okl.
Oklahoma Criminal Reports	Okl. Cr.
Oregon Reports	Or.
Pennsylvania Reports	Pa.
Pennsylvania Superior Court Reports	Pa. Sup.
Rhode Island Reports	R.I.
South Carolina Reports	S.C.
South Dakota Reports	S.D.
Tennessee Reports	Tenn.
Tennessee Appeals Reports	Tenn. App.
Texas Reports	Tex.
United States Reports	U.S.
United States Court of Appeals, District of Columbia	U.S. App. D.C.
Utah Reports	Utah
Vermont Reports	Vt.
Virginia Reports	Va.
Washington Reports	Wash.
Washington Reports, Second Series	Wash. 2d
West Virginia Reports	W. Va.
Wisconsin Reports	Wis.
Wyoming Reports	Wyo.

cial report, preceded and followed by blanks, thus, ___ Miss. ___, 55 So. 2d 477. (See example 9.)

Federal courts. When citing cases decided by the federal courts of appeals, show the circuit in parentheses. (See example 10.) The District of Columbia circuit is indicated by *D.C.* (See example 11.) When citing cases decided in the federal district court, show the district, but not the division, in parentheses. (See example 12.)

Selective case series. In some law report series, such as *American Law Reports* and *Law Reports Annotated*, only certain cases are published. These series are cited by the year of publication, the *letter* of the volume (A, B, C, or D), and page. (See example 13.) In parallel citations, they follow the National Reporter citation. It is customary to cite selective case series in briefs for state courts but not in those for federal courts.

Named reporters. Old court reports carry the name of the reporter. When citing cases in the U.S. reports before volume 91, always cite by the volume number and name of the reporter, not by the subsequently assigned consecutive U.S. number. To cite these volumes by the U.S. number is considered bad form. The following are the names of the old court reports and the number of volumes they reported.

4 of Dallas (cited as 1 Dall. 10)

9 of Cranch (cited as 1 Cranch 10)

12 of Wheaton (cited as 1 Wheat. 10)

16 of Peters (cited as 1 Pet. 10)

24 of Howard (cited as 1 How. 10)

2 of Black (cited as 1 Black 10)

23 of Wallace (cited as 1 Wall. 10)

When citing state cases, follow the local practice. For example, in Massachusetts the early reports are invariably cited by the name of the reporter, whereas in North Carolina a rule of court requires that they be cited by the consecutive number. When the named reporter is used, indicate the jurisdiction and date in parentheses. (See example 14).

String citations. When several cases are cited one after the other instead of on separate lines, the citation is referred to as a *string citation.* Separate the cases with a semicolon. (See example 15.)

How to cite an unpublished case. When citing a case that has not been reported, cite by name, court, the full date, and the docket number if known. (See example 16.)

How to cite slip decisions. Each opinion of the United States Supreme Court is published separately as soon as it is handed down. This form of publication is called a *slip decision.* Slip decisions are printed by the U.S. Government Printing Office and also by two unofficial publishers, Commerce Clearing House and U.S. Law Week. They are widely circulated and are frequently cited in briefs. Cite by number, court, date of decision, and source if unofficial. (See example 17.)

How to cite treatises. Cite by volume number (if more than one volume), author, title of the publication, page or section number, and the edition in parentheses. If the editor is well known, his name follows the edition. Underscore or italicize the title of the publication. (See example 18.)

In a few well-known works, the paging of the original edition is indicated by stars in differently paginated editions. (Cite by the star page. (See example 19.)

How to cite law reviews. Cite the volume and page number and the year. Underscore or italicize the title of the review. If an article is referred to, place it in quotation marks. Abbreviate *Law* (L.), *Review* (Rev.), and *Journal* (J.). (See example 20.)

How to cite legal newspapers. When citing a case that has not been published in either the official or unofficial reports but has been published in a legal newspaper, give the name of the newspaper, the volume and page number, the column, the court, and the exact date of the decision. (See example 21.)

Underscoring and italicizing. Underscoring and italicizing vary with the law office, but the following directions, some of which are arbitrary, are based upon the practices followed by many lawyers:

1. Underscore the names of the parties.

2. In a printed brief, the underscoring of *v.* or *vs.* is optional. Continuous underscoring gives a more even appearance on the typed page and requires less care than breaking the underscoring at the desired points. Printers usually set the *v.* or *vs.* in roman type.

3. When a previously cited case is referred to in the text of the brief by part of the title used as an adjective, italicize it.

Under the authority of the *Daoud* case the Court held . . .

When the reference is repeated under the same point of the brief, do not italicize it.

4. Italicize *case* or *cases* only when it is part of the usual name of the case.

5. It is preferable not to underscore

Table III

REPORTERS OF NATIONAL REPORTER SYSTEM

Name of reporter	Cite as	Courts covered
Supreme Court Reporter	S. Ct.	United States Supreme Court
Federal Reporter	F.	United States Circuit Courts of Appeals and the District Courts
Federal Reporter, Second Series	F. 2d	United States Courts of Appeals, United States Court of Customs and Patent Appeals, United States Emergency Court of Appeals
Federal Supplement	F. Supp.	United States District Courts, United States Court of Claims
Atlantic Reporter Atlantic Reporter, Second Series	A. A. 2d	Connecticut Delaware Maine Maryland New Hampshire New Jersey Pennsylvania Rhode Island Vermont District of Columbia
New York Supplement New York Supplement, Second Series	N.Y. Supp. N.Y.S. 2d	New York Court of Appeals Appellate Division of the Supreme Court Miscellaneous Courts
Northeastern Reporter Northeastern Reporter, Second Series	N.E. N.E. 2d	Illinois Indiana New York Massachusetts Ohio
Northwestern Reporter Northwestern Reporter, Second Series	N.W. N.W. 2d	Iowa Michigan Minnesota Nebraska North Dakota South Dakota Wisconsin

(continued on following page)

Reporters of National Reporter System—*continued*

Name of reporter	Cite as	Courts covered
Pacific Reporter P. Pacific Reporter, Second Series P. 2d	}	Alaska Arizona California Colorado Hawaii Idaho Kansas Montana Nevada New Mexico Oklahoma Oregon Utah Washington Wyoming
Southeastern Reporter S.E. Southeastern Reporter, Second Series S.E. 2d	}	Georgia North Carolina South Carolina Virginia West Virginia
Southern Reporter So. Southern Reporter, Second Series So. 2d	}	Alabama Florida Louisiana Mississippi
Southwestern Reporter S.W. Southwestern Reporter, Second Series S.W. 2d	}	Arkansas Kentucky Missouri Tennessee Texas

words and expressions between citations of the same case that relate to its history, such as *affirmed, certiorari denied,* and the like. (*See* example 22.)

Spacing of abbreviations. In briefs the parts of an abbreviation are separated by a space, thus *N.E. 2d.* In other legal writings, the general practice is to close up the citation, thus *N.E.2d.*

Placement of citations. Unless a citation is part of a quotation, it is indented and placed on the line following the quo-

tation. If it runs over one line, the carry-over line is indented.

". . . should be denied, as proposed allegations would add nothing to the equity of the bill."

Volunteer Security Co. v. Dowl, 159 Fla.
  767, 33 So. 2d 150, 152 (1947)

When several citations are given in support of a point, list them one under the other.

Illustrations of citations. The following examples of citations illustrate the fore-

going directions. Parts appearing in italics would be underscored on the
typewriter. Apparent inconsistencies in
the italics and in the placement of the
dates in the examples demonstrate the
variations in accepted practices. However, the secretary should be consistent
throughout a brief.

Example   Citation
1. *United States* v. *Texas & Pacific
   Motor Transport Co.,* 340 U.S. 450,
   71 S. Ct. 422 (1951)
2. *United States* v. *Congress of Industrial Organizations,* 335 U.S. 106,
   68 S. Ct. 1349, 48 A.L.C. 1164,
   aff'g 77 F. Supp. 355, 48 A.L.C.
   559 (D.C. Cir. 1948)
3. *Nashville, C. &. St. L. Ry.* v. *Wal-
   ters,* 294 U.S. 405, 55 S. Ct. 486
   (1934)
4. *Blaustein* v. *United States,* 44F. 2nd
   0106163 (C.C.A. 3), certiorari
   denied *sub. nom. Sokol* v. *United
   States,* 283 U.S. 838, 51 S. Ct. 486
5. *Green Point Savings Bank* v. *Board
   of Zoning Appeals* (1939) 281 N.Y.
   534, 24 N.E. 2d 319, 321
6. *Harrington* v. *Board of Adjustment,
   City of Alamo Heights* (Tex. 1939)
   124 S.W. 2d 401, 404
7. *Rayl* v. *General Motors Corp.* (Ind.
   App. 1951) 101 N.E. 2d 433;
   Janice v. *State,* 107 N.Y.S. 2d 674
   (Ct. Cl. 1951)
8. *People* v. *Davis,* 303 N.Y. 235, 101
   N.E. 2d 479
9. *Hughes* v. Wilson (1961) . . . .
   Ohio St. . . . ., 174 N.E. 2d
   789
10. *American Fruit Machinery Co.* v.
    Robinson Match Co., 191 Fed. 723
    (3rd Cir. 1911)

11. *Barbee* v. *Capital Airlines, Inc.*
    (D.C. Cir. 1951) 191 F. 2d 507
12. *Standard Oil Co.* v. *Atlantic Coast
    Line R. Co.* (W.D. Ky. 1926) 13 F.
    2d 633
13. *Hanover Star Milling Co.* v. *Allen &
    Wheeler Co.,* 208 Fed. 513, 1916D
    L. R. A. 136 (7th Cir. 1913)
14. *Forward* v. *Adams,* 7 Wend. 204
    (N.Y. 1831)
15. *Rubin* v. *Board of Directors of City
    of Pasadena* (2940) 16 Cal. 2d 119,
    104 P. 2d 1041; *Harrington* v.
    *Board of Adjustment, City of Alamo
    Heights* (Tex. 1939) 124 S.W. 2d
    401; *Green Point Savings Bank* v.
    Board of Zoning Appeals (1939)
    281 N.Y. 534, 24 N.E. 2d 319
16. *Roe* v. *Doe,* No. 152 U.S. Sup. Ct.,
    Jan. 10, 1961
17. *Torcaso* v. *Watkins,* No. 40, U.S.
    Sup. Ct., No. 373, 1961 (29 U.S.
    Law Week)
18. 2 Pomery, *Equity Jurisprudence*
    §428 (5th Ed., Symonds, 1941)
19. 2 Bl.Comm. *358
20. 42 *Yale L.J.* 419 (1933)
21. *Marine Midland Trust Co. of N.Y.* v.
    Dow, 146 N.Y. L.J. 9, Col. 2 (Sup.
    Ct. Spec. Term Sept. 8, 1961)
22. *In re Morse* (1928) 220 App. Div.
    830, 220 N.Y. Supp. 858, Rev'd on
    the other grounds, 247 N.Y. 290,
    160 N.E. 374

Citators. See SHEPARD'S CITA-
TIONS; FEDERAL TAX CITATOR.

Citizenship. Membership in a political community. Citizenship may pertain
either to a state or to the United States or
to both. Each status carries with it certain
obligations of the citizen and also gives

the citizen the enjoyment of full CIVIL RIGHTS that are protected against encroachment by governmental power.

Civil Court. A body in the government delegated to administer justice in connection with *civil wrongs*, that is, wrongs arising from the relationship between individuals as such, as distinguished from wrongs against the public (See CRIMINAL LAW.) Civil wrongs infringe on private rights and duties; remedy against them is sought by private action. TORT and BREACH of Contract are among common civil wrongs. See also CIVIL LAW.

Civil Law. A term generally used to designate Roman jurisprudence. The law of the Romans under Emperor Justinian was condensed and digested into a code known as Corpus Juris Civilis. The laws of Justinian were lost in the Western Empire during the early Dark Ages, but a complete copy was found about 1137. The laws were then revised and became the basis of jurisprudence for most of continental Europe. The present law on the Continent is therefore referred to as the Roman or civil law. The term may also be used to designate that part of the law concerned with noncriminal matters, or it may refer to the body of laws prescribed by the supreme power of the state, as opposed to natural law. See COMMON LAW; CRIMINAL LAW; CIVIL COURT; CRIMINAL COURT.

Civil Rights. Rights belonging to a person by virtue of his CITIZENSHIP in a state or community. The failure of the Constitution to guarantee many of the personal rights the people regarded as fundamental led to the almost immediate adoption of a BILL of Rights in the form of the first ten amendments.

Civil Wrongs. See CIVIL COURT.

Claimant. In ADMIRALTY law, the term *claimant* has two meanings, each almost opposite to the other. (1) When a vessel is sued *in rem*—that is, no individual or corporation is sued—the owner of the ship appears, files a *claim of owner*, and defends the action on behalf of the ship. In such a case, the owner is called a claimant. (2) When a steamship owner whose vessel has been in a disaster petitions to limit his liability, the parties who have claims against the limitation fund (who are really plaintiffs) file their claims against the fund and are called *claimants*.

Clean Hands. Equitable relief may be denied on ground of deceit or impurity of motive. A party with "unclean hands" cannot ask a court of conscience (the equity court) to come to his or her aid.

Clear and Present Danger. A classic test applied by Justice Holmes in determining what limitations may constitutionally be put upon FREEDOM OF SPEECH AND PRESS. The test would be applied to determine if a person should be stopped from making a speech where there appears to be a "clear and present danger" that an uncontrollable riot would occur because of it. The law cases stress that by "clear and present danger" is meant something more than public inconvenience, annoyance, or unrest. One of the functions of free speech is to invite dispute, and it may not be abridged merely because it stirs people to anger and creates a condition of unrest.

Clerk of the Court. The official recorder of all court business. He or she receives all court papers such as complaints, answers, amendments, motions, and appearances, assigning them numbers according to what is known as the *clerk's index system.*

The secretary's contact with the court is chiefly through the Clerk of the Court. Almost all correspondence is addressed to the clerk. For the proper form of address in writing to the Clerk of the Court, see CORRESPONDENCE (Addressing Officials). The Clerk of the Court answers inquiries, written or telephonic, about pending court cases, court rules, the calendar, and any other matters pertaining to the office. The clerk and personnel in the clerk's office can be of considerable help to the lawyer's secretary. It is frequently necessary for the secretary to look up something in the records of the clerk's office or to telephone for information regarding a case. It is necessary for the secretary to maintain cordial relations with the personnel in the clerk's office at all times. Although the systems of keeping records in clerk's offices vary in detail because of statutory requirements and custom, they are fundamentally the same.

1. *Index System.* The method by which the Clerk of the Court receives and records all court papers such as complaints, answers, amendments, motions, and appearances. (See *Permanent Record Book.* below.) As soon as the summons and complaint, or other first pleading is filed, the clerk assigns an index number, also called a *docket number,* and an *action number,* to the case. The numbers are consecutive. In some courts, an initial is used to indicate the court in which the case is filed. For example, *S* for Superior, *C* for Circuit, *P* for Probate. In courts that have separate law and EQUITY divisions, the letter *L* or the letter *E* will be a part of the index number. In some courts, the successive numbering of cases starts over at the beginning of each year, and the number includes the year. Thus the index number might read 80S-1328, or 1328/80, or 1328-1980, indicating that the case was filed in 1980. When a clerk uses this system of numbering, the year is as important as any part of the number. The clerk keeps a cross-index of the cases, arranged alphabetically according to the name of the plaintiff, and also, in some courts, a cross-index according to the name of the defendant.

How to use the index number. (a) If the secretary files the first pleadings, she must get the index number from the Clerk of the Court or from the clerk's records so the secretary may enter it in the office file. If an attorney in the office files the paper, that attorney should get the number and give it to the secretary or she may ask for it. The index number should be procured as soon as possible after it is assigned to a case.

(b) After an index number is assigned

to a case, the secretary *must* type that number on all papers thereafter prepared in the case in that court. Before filing a paper or giving it to an attorney to file the secretary should check to see that the proper index number is endorsed on it, both on the paper itself and on the backing.

(c) The secretary must have the index number to get information about the status of a case.

2. *Minute Books.* The books in which the Clerk of the Court enters abstracts of all court orders. The clerk does this numerically according to index number. There might be separate books for law, chancery, divorce, and the like.

How to use the minute book. If the secretary wants any information about the court's orders in a case, she can get it by consulting the minute book. She must have the index number. Usually the clerk's office will give the secretary the information over the telephone.

3. *Permanent Record Book.* The standing register, kept by the Clerk of the Court, of all records of legal papers filed in a particular case. The cases are entered consecutively according to index number, a case to a page. The permanent record book may be called also the *docket* or *register.* The clerk enters on the docket sheet the index number, the title of the case, the names and addresses of the attorneys, and the date the SUMMONS was served. The clerk also enters on the docket sheet all subsequent proceedings.

How to use the register. Although the lawyer keeps his or her own record of the information in the clerk's register (See SUIT REGISTER), it is sometimes necessary to consult the court register for the purpose of checking on dates that papers were filed by opposing counsel. Besides, an attorney is frequently interested, for one reason or another, in the developments in a case in which he or she is not representing a litigant. The attorney is usually interested in knowing the status of cases immediately preceding on the court calendar, to judge when his or her case will be reached.

If the secretary wants information on any case in court, she looks in the alphabetical index unless, of course, she already has the number. Then she turns to that page number in the docket and reads the entries made there. When the secretary wants to read the original papers on file, she gives the clerk the index number and asks for the papers. Sometimes the clerk will let the secretary get them herself; if so, she must be sure to put the papers back exactly where she found them.

Clients, Charges to. See BILLING CLIENT.

Close (or Closed) Corporation. A corporate enterprise whose capital stock is held by a limited group; its shares are ordinarily not sold in the securities markets. A close relationship between ownership and management is an identifying characteristic as well as a main objective. Usually a close corporation is small. (The Ford Motor Company was an exception.)

Theoretically, there is no difference between meetings of stockholders or boards of directors of great enterprises and those of close corporations (See DIRECTORS' MEETINGS). Statutes and judicial decisions spell out the meticulous care that must be taken in fulfilling technical requirements. In practice, however, it is a recognized fact that a CORPORA-TION having relatively few stockholders holds meetings without extensive advance preparation.

Closed Shop. An agreement whereby all employees must be members of a union before they can be hired by the employer. The closed shop is the strongest form of union security. See OPEN SHOP.

Closing. See CLOSING TITLE.

Closing Statement (Real Estate). The provision in a CONTRACT OF SALE that contains an adjusted and prorated summation of certain charges against REAL PROPERTY and the income from it. For example, a seller who has paid the insurance for a year in advance is entitled to receive an adjustment from the buyer. If the seller has collected the rents for an entire month in advance, the buyer is entitled to an adjustment. This prorating or adjustment results in credits in favor of each party. A statement of the charges and credits is known as the *closing statement,* sometimes called a *settlement sheet.*

Forms of closing statements vary. Printed forms are available and are widely used. When the printed forms do not provide for all the items that must be entered on the closing statement, the statement is typed. This situation frequently arises in large, complicated deals. The statement cannot be prepared in final form until the closing is held, because all of the necessary information is not available. It is prepared on

the basis of the figures agreed upon by all parties at the closing (See CLOSING TITLE). However, the lawyer for each party usually calculates the adjustments and prepares a memorandum of them before the closing. The secretary will probably have the responsibility of calculating the adjustments. See ADJUST-MENT OF CHARGES AND INCOME.

Closing Title. A transaction in which the formalities of a sale of REAL PROPERTY are executed. When the purchaser agrees to buy, he or she generally pays a deposit and enters into a contract with the seller. The contract designates a certain day, and sometimes hour, when the deed and mortgages, if any, shall be delivered and the balance of the purchase price paid.

Preparations for closing. As soon as a CONTRACT OF SALE is received in the lawyer's office, the secretary should enter the date of the closing in her diary (see REMINDERS). The following checklists show some of the preparations that the secretary has to make before the closing.

Checklist of preparation by secretary to seller's attorney. (The asterisks indicate items that are to be delivered to the buyer at the closing.)

*1. Prepare the DEED.

2. Prepare the purchase money mortgage and bond or note, if any. (See MORTGAGE, *purchase money mortgage.*)

*3. Prepare, or obtain from the seller, a list of the tenants, rents paid and unpaid, and due dates.

*4. Obtain a certificate, properly acknowledged, from the holder of any mortgage that the purchaser assumes, showing payment on account or the amount actually due at the closing date.

5. Prepare memorandum of closing figures (*see* CLOSING STATEMENT). (A copy of the memorandum might be mailed to the attorney for the purchaser, thus saving time in adjusting figures at the closing.)

6. Prepare letter to tenants advising them to pay future rent to the purchaser.

*7. Prepare assignment of any service contracts, such as exterminator's contracts, that are to be assigned to the purchaser.

8. Notify seller of the exact time, date, and place of the closing. Tell him to bring to the closing the following papers:

(a) Receipts for last interest payment on mortgages

*(b) Insurance policies and assignment of them

*(c) Last receipts for taxes, special assessments, gas, electricity, and water

*(d) Leases and assignments

*(e) Securities or cash deposited by tenants as security for rent

9. If seller is an individual, tell the seller that his or her spouse must also be present at the closing to sign the deed.

10. If seller is a corporation, indicate the two officers who are to sign the deed and who, therefore, should be present at the closing. Also, advise the officers to bring the corporation's seal.

11. Notify others who might be present in behalf of seller of closing date—broker, accountant, title closer.

Checklist of preparations by secretary to purchaser's attorney.

1. Order ABSTRACT OF TITLE.

2. Type opinion of title after lawyer dictates it.

3. Prepare a memorandum of closing figures (*see* CLOSING STATEMENT). (This might be mailed to the seller's attorney, thus saving time in adjusting figures at the closing.)

4. Notify purchaser of the exact time, date, and place of the closing. Tell him or her to bring to the closing the following:

(a) Certified check for approximate amount that will be due to the seller. (The figure is in the memorandum of closing figures.)

(b) Cash (e.g., bring a blank check) for any additional amount owed the seller.

5. If purchaser is a corporation indicate the two officers who are to sign the purchase money mortgage and who, therefore, should be present at the closing. Also advise the officers to bring the corporate seal with them.

6. Notify others who might be interested in behalf of the buyer of the closing date—accountants, insurance broker, title closer.

7. Prepare for the attorney a checklist of papers that are to be delivered to the buyer at the closing. This list will include the items marked with an asterisk in the foregoing checklist of preparations by the seller's secretary.

Code Address. See TELEGRAPH.

Codes and Statutes. Compilations of the laws that have been enacted by the Congress of the United States and the various state legislatures. They are systematically sorted and arranged in chapters and subheads to facilitate their use. These compilations, known as *codes* and *statutes* usually contain also, the Constitution of the United States and of the particular state.

Every lawyer has the compilation of her or his own state; law firms that practice in several states have the compilations for those states; nearly all lawyers have the United States Code; law association libraries and law college libraries usually have the compilations of every state.

The majority of the compilations are kept up to date by pocket parts and supplements, but in some states the session laws for all years after the date of the compilation must be used in conjunction with the compilation. Florida and Wisconsin publish a new compilation after every session of legislature.

How to find a law. The secretary should familiarize herself with the plan of arrangement of the compilation for her state. She will find that the preface contains explanatory and useful material. All of the compilations contain a general index, and some of them also have an index in each volume. The indexes vary in their completeness and usefulness, but with a little perseverance she will be able to find the desired section of the law. After the secretary searches the compilation, she should search the supplements and pocket parts, if any, and all session laws since the date of the compilation or since the date of the latest supplement. The section of the law in which she is interested might have been amended or repealed since the compilation, or a new law on the subject might have been enacted.

When a lawsuit involves a statute, the court's judicial interpretation and construction of that statute becomes as much a part of the law as the statute itself.

Table I, CITATIONS, describes the approved method of citing compilations of statutes and codes.

Codicil. A supplement to a WILL that changes its provisions. The same procedures and formalities that are necessary to execute a will properly must be observed when making a codicil.

Coercion. Compulsion; constraint; compelling by force of arms.

COGSA (Carriage of Goods by Sea Act). A federal statute (46 U.S. Code Sec. 1300) passed in 1936 that is this country's adoption of the Hague Rules, which were drafted by representatives of the major maritime nations at an international convention. The statute defines the rights, liabilities, and obligations of shippers and carriers of goods brought to or from the United States. Most of the leading maritime nations have adopted similar legislation See also ADMIRALTY; GENERAL AVERAGE LOSS; MARITIME LIEN.

Cohabitation. The act of living together, which may or may not be as husband and wife. When a man and woman live together in a manner that makes people believe they are married, the law will presume that they are legally and validly married. In a case that seeks to disprove the existence of a valid marriage, such as one involving the legitimacy of a child, it would take very strong evidence to overcome this presumption of validity where there has been cohabitation. *See also* COMMON-LAW MARRIAGE.

Collateral. Something of value, easily converted into cash, deposited as a pledge with a lender to secure the repayment of a loan; its value is usually substantially more than the amount of the loan. If the borrower is unable to meet the loan when due, the lender is free to sell the collateral and collect the debt from the proceeds of the sale.

Collating. *See* TYPING.

Collection Agency. A firm specializing in collecting overdue accounts receivable. It has no means of collection not available to the creditor, but is frequently successful in obtaining payment of past due accounts after the creditor's collection system has failed. The agency is often successful because it has no interest in keeping the good will of the customer and can press its demands more vigorously. The customer also knows that his or her credit rating will suffer if he fails to respond to the agency's demand.

Claims, or accounts, are taken on a contingent basis—if there is no collection, there is no charge. Rates depend on the amount of money collected and whether the collection is made by letter or personal call.

Collections. Past due accounts that the lawyer undertakes to collect for others. Collections may be turned over to the lawyer by local clients, or they may be forwarded from another town by a COLLECTION AGENCY or by another

lawyer. Unless suit is filed, collections are handled on a contingent fee basis, usually at standard Commercial Law League rates. Although some commercial items involve large amounts, the majority of them are for small sums, with a correspondingly small fee. It is, therefore, desirable in the case of small items to curtail the usual office procedure as much as is consistent with efficiency. Collections are usually segregated from the other cases and are handled in a special manner. The procedure is routine and, after it has been established, the secretary can assume responsibility for the entire operation of the collection department.

Office procedures affecting collections. The office procedures affecting collections involve the following:

1. Files
2. Follow-up system
3. Acknowledgment of claim
4. Letters to debtor
5. Reports to forwarder
6. Records of collections
7. Remittance to forwarder
8. Forwarding collection items
9. Suit

How to file collection matters. As soon as a collection item is received, a file folder should be made for it. The folders are filed alphabetically under the debtor's name. In conformance with the policy of keeping office procedure at a minimum, file index cards are not made. If the lawyer prefers that index cards should be made, the secretary uses plain 3- by 5-inch cards and keeps them separate from her other index cards. Show on the card the name of the creditor, the name of the debtor, and the name of the forwarder.

DEBTOR'S NAME *Jackson, L. E.*			ADDRESS *405 South Adams, City*				A
CREDITOR *A. B. Corporation*			ADDRESS *307 South Main St., Chicago*				B
FORWARDER			ADDRESS				C
SENT TO			ADDRESS				D
AMOUNT OF CLAIM $	INTEREST	DATE OF CLAIM	DATE DUE	DATE RECEIVED		LIST	E
NATURE OF CLAIM (Check proper space)	ACCOUNT	AFFIDAVIT	NOTE	ACCEPTANCE	DRAFT	JUDGMENT	F
COLLECTION RATE	COST ADVANCED	REGISTERED	PROOF FILED				G

CORRESPONDENCE WITH

Forwarder	Debtor	General	CALLS MADE	SUIT MEMORANDA			
				COURT			H
				SUIT FILED		RETURNABLE	
				CONTINUANCE			I
				TRIAL	JUDG. COSTS	$ $	J
				EXECUTION ISSUED	"	$	K
				SUPPLEMENTARY			
				CITATION	COSTS	$	L
				GARNISHMENT	COSTS	$	
				FINAL DISPOSITION			M
				TOTAL	JUDG. & COSTS	$	N

CASH ACCOUNT

FOLLOW UP DATES

DATE	MEMO	REC'D	DISB.

REMARKS:

O P Q R S T U V W X Y Z

STICK GUMMED TAB ON BACK LEAF OF FOLDER OPPOSITE INDEX LETTER IN POSITION INDICATED BELOW.

Jackson, L. E.
Debtor's Name and Address

1 2 3 4 5 6 7 8 9 10 11 12 13 14 15 16 17 18 19 20 21 22 23 24 25 26 27 28 29 30 31

Forwarder's Number

Office Number

Jackson, L. E.

MADE IN USA—COMMERCIAL LAW LEAGUE OF AMERICA—STANDARD VERTICAL COLLECTION FOLDER, NO. 8—LETTER CASE

Collections: Figure 1.
Collections folder with name tab.

The secretary will notice that the printed file folder in figure 1 has space for a file number. When the numbering system of filing is used for collections, cross-reference index cards are essential.

When suit is brought on a collection, the case is transferred to a legal folder and handled like any other litigated case. Since default judgment is obtained in the majority of collection cases, considerable clerical work can be saved by not transferring the file unless the suit is contested.

Follow-up system. A desirable method of following collections is to use a file folder that has the days of the month printed on the top edge of the folder (See figure 1.) The alphabet on the folder is ignored. Folders without any printed matter except the days of the month are also obtainable. A metal tab is placed on the date that the file should come up for action, and the folder is filed alphabetically under the name of the debtor. Thus, regardless of the follow-up date, the folder is always in its proper alphabetical position in the filing cabinet. Each morning the secretary pulls all folders that have the metal tab placed on the current date. After the necessary action is taken, the metal tab is moved to the date on which the file again should come up for action.

Another popular method of follow-up for collections is a follow-up file with the folders tabbed so that they can be located alphabetically. The folder illustrated in figure 1 is also appropriate for this system; the dates on the top edge are ignored. Each file drawer, if more than one is necessary, is arranged as a follow-up file, with guides for the months and dates. Each drawer is operated as a separate follow-up file.

How can a folder be located if it is needed before the follow-up date? The letters of the alphabet printed near the top edge of the front leaf of the folder make this possible. A small gummed tab marked with the debtor's name is pasted on the back leaf of the folder, opposite the index letter printed near the top of the front leaf. Thus, the name *Jones* is on the folder opposite *J*; the name *Smith* is opposite *S*, and so on. It makes no difference under what date the folder is filed: the *J*'s are always in one line in one position in the file, and so is each letter of the alphabet. By looking at the proper line, the secretary can easily find the proper folder at any time. The folder can be returned to the correct follow-up date, because the last date in the space for follow-up dates, on the front of the folder, shows where it is to be filed. This system simplifies the task of pulling the folders each morning, because all folders to be brought up on a certain date are together. It also eliminates moving the metal tabs, which are sometimes difficult to move without tearing the folder.

Acknowledgment of claim. Simultaneously with the preparation of the folder, the claim should be acknowledged. Promptness in acknowledging the collection is very important, because the forwarder is naturally interested in knowing that the matter is receiving immediate attention. The acknowledgment might read:

Dear Sir:

Re: Thrifty Stores, Inc. v.
J.C. Adams, Amount
$345

We acknowledge receipt of the above claim and accept the claim for collection on the basis of the terms and regulations of the Commercial Law League of America.

Since you are recognized as the client's agent, we will report developments and make remittances directly to you.

Sincerely yours,
McHenry & Stone

Reports to the forwarder. The forwarder is interested in developments. As soon as contact is made with the debtor, write the forwarder telling what the prospects for collection are. It is helpful to the forwarder to send reports in duplicate, especially those in which the lawyer recommends suit or some special arrangement. The forwarder can then send a copy to the client, thus saving the time and trouble in copying the report.

See also COMMERCIAL LAW LISTS; INSTALLMENT COLLECTIONS.

Collection Letters. Correspondence sent to a debtor with the purpose of collecting the debt. The secretary will probably be called upon to draft collection letters. If so, she should keep these premises in mind:

1. The purpose of the letter is to collect money; therefore, do not hesitate to ask for a check.

2. Do not take the attitude that the account "probably has been overlooked," because numerous demands for payment are made before the account is given to the attorney.

3. Use *dated action.* That is, tell the debtor that a certain action is expected by a given date, or within a given number of days, not in the "near future."

4. The *divided urge* is a serious fault in a collection letter. Suggest only one course of action—do not mention an alternative. For example, do not tell the debtor that you expect a check by a certain date and then suggest that he or she should telephone if payment is impossible.

5. The period between letters should be short—from 5 to 10 days.

A first letter to the debtor from the attorney on May 3 might read:

Dear Mr. Adams:

Thrifty Stores, Inc. has retained us to collect your past due account in the amount of $345.

Since this account has been delinquent for six months, it is imperative that you give it your immediate attention. Please let us have your check in full by May 13.

Sincerely yours,

After this letter is written, mark the file for follow-up for May 15. If the debtor does not reply by that date, another letter might be sent that reads:

Dear Mr. Adams:

We have received no reply to our letter of May 3 concerning your past due account with Thrifty Stores, Inc. in the amount of $345. We will be compelled, therefore, to bring suit against you for the above amount, together with costs, disbursement, and interest, unless your check in full payment is received at this office by May 20.

Sincerely yours,

Collective Bargaining. The negotiation, administration, and enforcement of written agreements between employers and unions. The agreements set forth joint understandings about policies and procedures governing wages, hours, and other conditions of employment. Collective bargaining is the principal method of determining wages and other conditions of employment for those who earn their living by working for others. By substituting group action for individual action in making and enforcing agreements, the worker has protected himself or herself and improved his or her economic status. See LABOR UNION.

Collusion. A conspiracy between two or more persons for a fraudulent or deceitful purpose. In DIVORCE law, collusion is a conspiracy of the husband and wife to obtain a decree of divorce by false testimony, such as testimony of ADULTERY when none, in fact, occurred.

Color of Title. The semblance of title. Facts that appear to support a claim of present title to land, but that fall short of establishing it. One who possesses a forged deed has mere color of title.

Combing-Back. The process of moving forward from week to week reminders of matters that require attention at an indefinite date until a definite date is established or until the matter is completed. See also REMINDERS (Diary); TICKLER CARD FILE.

Comity. The practice by which the courts of one state or country follow a statute or JUDGMENT of another on a like question, though not legally bound to do so. A state will not give the judgment of a foreign country comity if it contravenes its own public policy. Under full faith and credit, as contrasted to comity, the judgment of a sister state must be recognized no matter how erroneous and unjust it may seem to be.

Commercial Law Lists. Names of lawyers who handle COLLECTIONS of commercial items. It is from these lists that out-of-town lawyers select an attorney in the debtor's locality to handle the claim. It is from these lists that the lawyers in the secretary's office will select attorneys to whom to forward accounts against debtors in another jurisdiction.

Usually the forwarder of an item will mention the law list from which the lawyer's name was obtained. Some lists produce better results than others. The secretary, therefore, should keep a record of the items the lawyer received through each list and the fees earned by reason of the lawyer's representation on that list. The lawyer can then determine whether continued representation on a special list is warranted. A simple record is sufficient. Keep a separate sheet for each law list and show on it the forwarder, the item (creditor, debtor, amount), and when the matter is closed, the amount of the fee. The secretary might keep these sheets in a folder in the front of the file drawer in which the collection cases are filed. See also COLLECTION, Letters.

Commercial Lease. A binding CONTRACT, for the possession of lands and improvements to be used in the conduct of business (such as retail stores, office buildings, theaters, shopping centers, parking facilities, hotels and motels) in return for a specified rent. See also LEASE; RESIDENTIAL LEASE; COMMERCIAL PROPERTY.

Commercial Property. REAL PROPERTY used in connection with all activities of business, industry, and trade, for the purpose of producing income. These may include: (1) residential property such as an apartment house or hotel; (2) industrial property, such as a factory building or loft; (3) business property, such as a retail store, office building, gasoline station, garage, warehouse, market, motel or resort property; and (4) amusement and recreation properties, such as theaters, taverns, bowling alleys, dance halls, and skating rinks.

Common Carrier. One whose business it is to transport goods or passengers.

Common carriers of goods are responsible for all loss or damage of merchandise during transportation from any cause except the act of God or the public enemy. They may, however, qualify this liability by CONTRACT. The responsibility of the carrier terminates after the goods have arrived at their destination and a reasonable time has elapsed for the owner to receive them. After that, the carrier may put them in a warehouse and is only responsible for ordinary care. Carriers, both by land and water, when they undertake the general business of carrying every kind of goods, are bound to carry for all who offer; if they refuse, without just excuse, they are liable to an action at law.

Common carriers of passengers, un-

like common carriers of goods, are not responsible as insurers of their cargo. Passenger-carriers, however, do have the duty to exercise a high degree of care and watchfulness to their passengers. There is no responsibility when injury results directly from the passenger's NEGLIGENCE.

Common Law. A system of law, or body of legal rules, derived from decisions of judges based upon accepted customs and traditions. It was developed in England. It is known as the *common law* because it is believed that these rules were generally recognized and were in full force throughout England. Common law is now the basis of the laws of every state of the Union, except Louisiana, which bases its laws upon the early laws of France. Statutes have been enacted to supplement and supersede the common law in many fields; the common law, however, still governs where there is no statute dealing with a specific subject. Although the common law is written, it is called the *unwritten law* in contradistinction to STATUTORY LAW enacted by the legislatures.

Common-Law Marriage. A marriage not solemnized in the ordinary way, but created by an agreement to marry, followed by COHABITATION. Most states declare a marriage to be valid only if there is a formal procedure prescribed by statute. Common-law marriages legally contracted in a state that does consider them valid, however, must be given full faith and credit by all the other states. See also COHABITATION.

Common-Law Trust. *See* MASSA-CHUSETTS TRUST.

Common Stock. Corporate stock characterized first by the fact that it entitles its holder to a DIVIDEND only after the rights of the holders of PREFERRED STOCK have been satisfied, and second by the fact that it usually has voting rights attached.

Common stock represents the basic ownership of the CORPORATION. With only nominal exception, all corporations have common stock. Some corporations have common stock only; others have common and preferred and/or a variety of hybrids.

Upon the dissolution of a corporation, common stock entitles its owners to all that is left after allowance for claims having priority. During periods of prosperity common stockholders are in the enviable position of having an unlimited interest in the profits and assets of the corporation while the holders of preferred stock have only the right to receive dividends at a fixed or stated rate. However, during periods of business decline the position of common stockholders is less desirable because by the time prior claimants have received their due, there may be nothing left for the holders of common stock.

Common stock generally carries with it voting rights that enable the holders to participate in the management of the corporation and thereby to exercise a certain amount of control of the corporate assets, which, basically, they own. Sometimes common stock does not have the voting privilege.

Community Property. In some states a system exists whereby all earnings of either husband or wife constitute a common fund of the husband and wife. The property is known as *community property.* The central idea of the system is the same in all states where community property exists, but statutes and judicial decisions have directed the development of the system along different lines in the various states. For example, in some states only property that is acquired by the exertion or labor of either party is *common,* whereas in other states income from separate property is also considered community property. Generally, either husband or wife may have "separate" property, such as that belonging to either of them at the time of marriage, real estate acquired in a state that does not recognize community property, or property given to or inherited by either at any time. Property acquired in exchange for separate property is *separate property;* that acquired for community property is *community property.* In some states the husband may dispose of, or encumber, the community property, but the wife may not; nor may the community property be attached for the wife's debts, except for those contracted for necessities for herself and her children.

In states having community property laws, a SEPARATION AGREEMENT should provide for the disposition of community property with sufficient exactness to avoid the implication that the question of division remains unsettled.

In community property states, the prevailing rule at the death of a spouse is that the half belonging to that spouse descends to his or her heirs, except when it has been disposed of by WILL.

To correct the inequalities in tax treatment between residents of community property states and residents of noncommunity property states, the federal government passed statutes allowing joint INCOME TAX returns, and a MARITAL DEDUCTION for the federal ESTATE TAX and GIFT TAX.

Company Union. An organization of employees that is dominated by the employer. This type of union has been generally opposed by the labor movement because the workers have to be represented by bargaining specialists who are dependent upon the company for their livelihood. Company unions have been initiated by management when it seemed necessary to forestall outside organizing threats. See LABOR UNION.

Competent Parties. Parties who have the legal right to make a CONTRACT.

Complaint. In the practice of law, the name given to the statement of the case of the PLAINTIFF or complaining party. (See PARTIES TO AN ACTION.) It is a formal and methodical specification of the facts and circumstances surrounding the cause of action. Known also as the plaintiff's *first pleading* (see PLEADINGS), the *complaint* sets forth in detail the grounds upon which the plaintiff is suing the DEFENDANT, and asks the court for damages or other relief. The first pleading is called the *com-*

plaint in the majority of states; the *petition* or the *declaration* in a few states; still other states distinguish between actions at law and in EQUITY and call the first pleading the *bill of complaint* in an action at law, or *bill in equity* in an equity case.

Regardless of the variance in terminology in the various states, a *complaint* follows a standard pattern, which consists of the following parts:

1. *Caption.* The CAPTION to the complaint designates the court in which the action is brought and lists the full names of all plaintiffs and defendants. It does not show the clerk's index number because that is not available at the time the complaint is prepared. (See CLERK OF THE COURT, Index System.)

2. *Introduction.* The opening paragraph of the complaint simply states, "The plaintiff, by his attorney, John Jones, complaining of the defendant, alleges as follows:" or words to that effect.

3. *Body.* The body of the complaint states the facts and circumstances that are the basis for the action. The complaint may contain one or more causes of action, each of which is a separate and complete division within itself. These divisions are referred to as *counts* in some jurisdictions. A cause of action, or count, is composed of one or more *allegations*. These are statements that the plaintiff expects to prove. Complaints in certain actions must contain standard allegations, which the lawyer dictates from memory or from a practice manual. (See FORMS.) For example, when a domestic corporation is the plaintiff, the allegation will allege the corporate status in a form similar to the following: *That at all*

times hereinafter mentioned, the plaintiff was and still is a domestic corporation, organized and existing under and by virtue of the laws of the State of . . . . When a corporation is the defendant, the allegation is introduced by the words: *Upon information and belief . . . .*

4. *Prayer.* The prayer, also called the WHEREFORE CLAUSE, is the final paragraph of the complaint and "demands" judgment against the defendant for a specified sum, or, in equity actions, "prays" for or seeks other relief to which the plaintiff believes he is entitled. The complaint will also demand interest if the action is for a definite amount of money owed by the defendant, as when the action is on a stated account or a promissory note.

5. *Signature.* Either the plaintiff or the plaintiff's attorney must sign the complaint. The original must be signed manually in every state except New York, where a typed signature is sufficient. In federal courts, pleadings must be signed by an attorney in his or her individual name, not in the firm name.

6. *Verification.* The law in the various states specifies which complaints must be verified, but many lawyers follow the practice of having all complaints verified. The VERIFICATION is signed before a notary public.

Figure 1 illustrates a *complaint* as the secretary might type it.

Conciliation. The act of a third party helping two contending parties settle their differences. A conciliator transmits information between the parties as requested and otherwise tries to keep negotiators at their appointed tasks. The conciliator is not supposed to evaluate or to express a judgment on the merits of opposing contentions. See ARBITRATION; MEDIATION.

Conclusion of Fact. An inference drawn from the presentation of the facts, without resort to rules of law.

Conclusion of Law. Conclusion reached through application of rules of law.

Concurrent Powers. Political powers exercised independently in the same field of legislation by both federal and state governments. The concurrent power of the states is potentially subordinate to that of the federal government; it cannot be exercised unless Congress consents. Congressional consent may be given expressly or it may be implied. An example of concurrent power to regulate commerce is a case that held that where, in the absence of congressional legislation on the matter, a state was permitted to dam a navigable river. The theory used was that the commerce clause did not affect the power of the states where the federal power was not exercised. See EXCLUSIVE POWERS.

Conditional Sale. An installment sale. The buyer usually gives the seller a promissory note secured by a conditional sale contract or a chattel mortgage. A *conditional sale contract* is a contract for the sale of goods under which the goods are delivered to the buyer but the title remains in the seller until the goods are paid for in full, or until the conditions

IN THE CIRCUIT COURT OF THE ELEVENTH
JUDICIAL CIRCUIT OF FLORIDA, IN AND
FOR DADE COUNTY.   AT LAW.

```
————————————————————— x
                                :
WILLIAM O. MADISON and EVELYN   :
T. MADISON                      :
                                :
                                :
              Plaintiffs,       :
                                :
                                :
      -against-                 :      COMPLAINT
                                :
                                :
                                :
BARKLEY MANAGEMENT CORPORA-     :
TION, a corporation, and CLASSICS, :
INC., a corporation.            :
                                :
                                :
              Defendants.       :
                                :
————————————————————— x
```

Plaintiffs by their attorneys, Ewing & Snow,
complaining of the defendants above named, allege:

FOR A FIRST CAUSE OF ACTION:

FIRST: That the plaintiffs _____

_____

_____

SECOND: Upon information and belief, that _____

_____

FOR A SECOND CAUSE OF ACTION:

THIRD: Plaintiffs repeat, reiterate _____

(continued on following page)

(Continued from preceding page)

WHEREFORE, plaintiffs demand judgment against defendants for the sum of Five thousand three hundred twenty-five and 36/100 dollars ($5,325.36), with interest thereon from the 20th day of December, 19—, together with the costs and disbursements of this action.

Ewing & Snow
Attorneys for Plaintiffs

Complaint: Figure 1.

of the contract are fulfilled. When a chattel mortgage is used, the seller transfers the goods to the buyer who, in turn, executes a chattel mortgage in favor of the seller. This instrument gives the seller a lien on the goods.

The seller's choice of security instrument depends upon the laws in the seller's state. The seller studies the laws and selects the type of instrument that provides the most protection with the least inconvenience. The instrument usually includes a provision that if an installment is not paid for when due, the entire debt becomes payable at once. This clause, called the ACCELERATION CLAUSE, is essential in any installment contract. Otherwise the seller would have to sue for the amount of each installment as it became due, or would have to wait until the debt matured. See also CONTRACT; RECORDING (of Real Estate Instruments).

Condominium. System of separate ownership of individual units, with undivided interest in the common facilities and common areas of the building(s) and grounds used by all residents. Management of the building(s) and grounds is usually undertaken by an association composed of the condominium owners.

Condonation. The conditional forgiveness by a husband or wife of a marital indiscretion committed by the other. Condonation is a valid defense in a DIVORCE action based on ADULTERY. COHABITATION with the guilty party, with knowledge that he or she committed adultery, amounts to conclusive evidence of condonation. The cohabitation after knowledge of the adultery must be voluntary and free from duress in order to constitute the defense of condonation.

Confession. An acknowledgment of guilt by a person charged with having committed a crime. A judicial confession is made before a judge during a trial or preliminary examination; an extrajudicial confession is an acknowledgment of guilt elsewhere than in court or before a magistrate. See CORROBORATING EVIDENCE.

Conforming Documents. The writing or typing on copies of documents, the signatures, dates, recording data, and notarial data inked or stamped on the original.

In typing the signature, there is no need to type *Signed* in front of the typed copy. In a conformed copy of an executed document bearing an official or corporate seal, CORPORATE SEAL, OFFICIAL SEAL, or NOTARY'S SEAL, as the case may be, is written in brackets at the left of the official or corporate signature. Seals of individuals are indicated by SEAL unless written otherwise on the original.

When a county clerk's certificate is attached to an original document, it is sometimes sufficient to make a notation such as:

County Clerk's Certificate for .... County, State of .... attached to original.

on the conformed copies. But it is sometimes important to attach a copy of the entire certificate to the conformed copies, especially where a certified copy of an original instrument is required. The lawyer instructs the secretary on this point.

Congressional Directory. See OFFICIAL CONGRESSIONAL DIRECTORY.

Congressional Record. A daily record of the proceedings of Congress, including a complete history of all legislation. Texts of bills are not included. Indexes give names and subjects of bills and a history of them under their respective numbers. The final index to a volume, covering one session, thus provides references to the complete history of all legislation introduced during that session.

Congress of Industrial Organizations (CIO). A LABOR UNION formed in 1938 to encourage and promote organization of workers in the mass production industries. The founders of the CIO broke away from the AMERICAN FEDERATION OF LABOR because of its emphasis on craft union organization. In 1955 the CIO merged with the AFL to form the AFL-CIO.

Consequential Damages. DAMAGES resulting not from taking any part of physical property, but as a consequence of some act in connection with the property. For example, a city may raise the grade of a street without taking any additional land but in such a way that adjoining property is left an objectionable distance below the new street grade. The property owner may be entitled to consequential damages. This is different from SEVERANCE DAMAGE, where a part of an original lot may be taken with damage to the remaining portion.

Conservator. See GUARDIAN and GUARDIANSHIP.

Consideration. The price, motive, or matter inducing a party to make a contract. See CONTRACT, Consideration. See also MORTGAGE, Statement and Clauses, Mortgage Consideration.

Consolidation of Corporations. The unification of two or more corporations into a single new CORPORATION, which acquires the property and assets and assumes the debts and liabilities of those passing out of existence.

In a MERGER, an existing corporation absorbs one or more other corporations and remains in existence, the absorbed corporations being dissolved. The distinction between a consolidation and a merger may be of great importance in such matters as tax liabilities, JURISDICTION of the courts, and special statutory privileges and exemptions. It may be also important to creditors who seek satisfaction of unpaid claims against the constituent companies.

Conspiracy. An agreement between two or more persons to commit a crime. All the conspirators must share the intention to accomplish, by concerted action, the act that they plan. The act the conspirators agree to do need never be done; the conspiracy itself is a crime. See AIDING AND ABETTING.

Constitution, United States. The written instrument agreed upon by the people of the Union as the absolute rule of action and decision for all departments and officers of the government in respect to all the points covered by it. The Constitution has become adapted to modern times through amendment, cus-

tom, statute, and judicial interpretation. See AMENDMENT OF THE CONSTITUTION; BILL (of Rights).

Constructive. In a legal sense, the term *constructive* generally applies to that which amounts in the eyes of the law to an act, although the act itself is not necessarily performed. The law presumes the act to have been performed, and applies the term to many situations to prevent a miscarriage of justice. For example, the holder of a warehouse receipt has *constructive possession* of the goods represented by the receipt, although the holder does not have actual personal occupancy or possession of the property.

Some of the circumstances under which the law will presume an act are indicated by the following: constructive abandonment, constructive delivery, constructive desertion, constructive eviction, constructive fraud, constructive gift, constructive notice, constructive possession, constructive process, constructive receipt of income, constructive service, and constructive trusts.

1. *Constructive Delivery.* Arises when actual, or manual, delivery is impossible or undesirable. Constructive delivery includes those acts that are equivalent to actual delivery although they do not confer real possession. Acts that bar a lien or a right to stoppage in transit, such as marking and setting apart goods as belonging to the buyer, constitute constructive delivery.

2. *Constructive Notice.* Notice that arises from a strictly legal presumption that cannot be controverted. The presumption is one of law and not of fact, as

distinguished from implied notice that arises from an inference of facts. The presumption of constructive notice is conclusive against the actual facts. Thus, a mortgage recorded with the proper public authorities is constructive notice of the mortgagee's interest in the property.

3. *Constructive Receipt.* Constructive receipt of income usually constitutes taxable income under the various tax laws. For example, any time during the year commissions may be credited on a firm's books to a salesperson who may draw upon the firm to the amount of the credit. The commission is said to be constructively received. Whatever amount is credited to the salesperson would have to be reported by the salesperson as income in the year the amount was credited on the books, even if the money was not drawn until the following year.

Contempt of Court. Any act meant to embarrass the court or lessen its authority and dignity. Contempt of court committed in the presence of the court, and which interrupts its proceedings, may be punished immediately by order of the presiding JUDGE. Constructive contempts are those that arise from a refusal to comply with an order of the court. The punishment for contempt of court is a fine or imprisonment.

Contingent Fee. A charge for services to a client based on an agreement that the fee will be dependent on the lawyer's successful handling of the case. Contingent fees are customary in personal injury cases, especially if the client

is unable to pay for the lawyer's time except out of the damages he might recover. The lawyer usually agrees to take a case for a client for a percentage of the amount recovered.

Contract. An agreement between two or more parties whereby each promises to do or refrain from doing some act. A contract may be oral or in writing, sealed or unsealed, except that state statutes, designated as the STATUTE OF FRAUDS, require certain agreements to be in writing. A contract may be express or implied. An *express contract* is one in which the terms are set forth by the parties involved, either orally or in writing. An *implied contract* is a contract implied by law. For example, when a person sits down in a restaurant and orders a meal, it is implied that he or she will pay for it, although there is no express promise to that effect.

If a contract has been fully performed by all the parties to it, it is referred to as an *executed contract*. Sometimes a contract is *executed* on the part of one party and *executory* on the part of the other. For example, when a merchant delivers a television set to a customer who has purchased it on credit, the merchant's contract is executed. He or she has completed his or her part of the agreement. On the other hand, the customer's contract is executory, until such time as the final payment on the television set is made.

To be enforceable at law, a contract must have the following elements:
Offer and acceptance. Before a contract can be formed, there must be an offer by one party, called the *offeror*, to do

or to refrain from doing a certain thing, and an acceptance of the proposal by another party, called the *offeree*.

An offer is considered open until it is revoked, rejected, or accepted, or until after the lapse of a reasonable time. The only case in which an offeror cannot withdraw an offer before acceptance is the case in which he or she has entered an OPTION contract, which is an agreement supported by the payment of a sum of money, or for some other consideration, to hold an offer open for a definite period.

An *acceptance* is an indication by the offeree of his willingness to be bound by the terms of the offer. The acceptance may take the form of an act, the signing and delivery of a written instrument or of a promise communicated to the offeror. Silence on the part of the offeree is not an acceptance unless the previous dealings between the parties create a duty upon the part of the offeree to accept or reject the offer. The acceptance must be unequivocal and must show an intention to accept all the terms of the offer. In the language frequently used by the courts, there must be a "meeting of the minds" of the offeror and the offeree.

Competent parties. All persons are presumed to have unlimited power to contract—except infants, insane persons, intoxicated persons, and corporations.

Legally, a person is in his infancy until he reaches the age of majority, which is set by the state legislatures (usually between the ages of 18 and 21). Some states provide that marriage removes the infancy status. Contracts by infants are not void, but generally they may be disaffirmed by the infant. An infant is not bound by an executory contract unless he or she affirms the contract after coming of age; failure to affirm implies disaffirmance. An infant may disaffirm an executed contract during infancy or within a reasonable time after attaining majority; failure to disaffirm within a reasonable time implies affirmance. Contracts for necessities, such as food, clothing, shelter, medical care, education, and the like, may be binding upon an infant.

Like infants, insane persons are not absolutely incapable of making contracts; their contracts are voidable, not void, and they may be held liable for necessities. A person who is so drunk that he or she is deprived of reason and does not understand the nature of his or her acts is in the same position as a mental incompetent; such a person may disaffirm his or her contracts if the disaffirmance does not injure third persons, and provided this person disaffirms immediately upon restoration of his or her faculties.

Under the COMMON LAW a married woman has few contractual powers, but the statutes in most states have modified the common law. In general, a married woman may now contract as freely as a single woman, but in some states she cannot contract with her husband, enter into partnership with him, or act as surety for him.

A corporation's ability to contract is limited by its charter and by various statutes.

Legality of subject matter. A contract is illegal if it calls for the performance of an act forbidden by law or against public policy. Gambling and wagering contracts and usurious contracts (see USURY), for example, are generally held to be illegal. In some states any contract entered into on Sunday is illegal.

Federal and state laws make illegal those contracts that restrain trade, fix prices, or result in unfair practices.

Consideration. Something of benefit to the person making a promise must be given, or some detriment must be suffered by the person to whom a promise is made to make a contract binding. *Consideration* is the price, motive, or matter inducing the contract; it may consist of (a) doing some act that one is not obligated to perform; (b) refraining from doing something that one would otherwise be free to do; (c) giving some money or property; (d) giving a promise. The value of the consideration is generally immaterial.

Contracts under seal. The placing of a SEAL on a contract has lost the significance formerly attached to it, but it is still customary, and required in some states, to place a seal on contracts of major importance. Deeds, mortgages, and other conveyances of real estate are among the contracts requiring a seal.

Figure 1 illustrates an agreement between two corporations. See also DEFAULT.

The above contracts are usually bilateral contracts.

Rescission of contract. To *rescind* a contract means to abrogate, annul, void, or cancel a contract; particularly, nullifying a contract by the act of a party to it.

1. *Bilateral Contract.* One in which there are rights and duties on each side, each party being both a promisor and a promisee. In a CONTRACT OF SALE, one party becomes bound to deliver the thing sold, and the other to pay the price of it.

2. *Cost-Plus Contract.* A contract where the contractor charges his or her cost plus a stated percentage of the cost

that represents the contractor's profit. Often used in government contracts.

3. *Oral Contract.* One that is not in writing or that is not signed by the parties.

4. *Output Contract.* Where one promises to deliver the entire production to another and the other promises to purchase the entire production supplied.

5. *Unilateral Contracts.* Where one party makes an express engagement or undertakes a performance, without receiving in return any express engagement or promise or performance from the other. For example, an offer of a reward would be a unilateral contract. There is an offer but no specific acceptance.

Contract of Sale (Real Estate). A formal CONTRACT entered into between a seller (known as VENDOR) and a buyer (known as VENDEE) of REAL PROPERTY, setting forth in full all the terms of the agreement between them for the conveyance of title within a specified time. The contract of sale, often called Purchase and Sale Agreement, sets in motion the various investigations of title and encumbrances, arrangements for financing, and preparation of instruments to be signed upon CLOSING TITLE. It is important that the contract of sale be prepared carefully to include all the terms of the agreement between buyer and seller and to state them clearly, for if any dispute should arise, the courts will not admit any oral testimony in variance of the written contract.

How to prepare a contract of sale. Each locality has a contract form approved by the local real estate board.

THIS AGREEMENT, entered into on the ___ day of
_____, 19—, by and between _____ CORPORATION, a
corporation organized and existing under and by virtue of the laws of the
State of _____, and having its office at _____, _____,
hereinafter referred to as "_____," and THE _____ COMPANY,
a corporation organized and existing under and by virtue of the laws of the
State of _____, and having its office at _____,
_____, hereinafter referred to as "_____,"

WITNESSETH:

WHEREAS _____
_____; and

WHEREAS _____
_____
_____

NOW, THEREFORE, in consideration of the premises
_____
_____,

IT IS AGREED:

1. _____
_____

2. _____
_____.

IN WITNESS WHEREOF the parties hereto have on the day
and year first above written caused these presents to be executed in their
behalf and in their corporate names respectively by their proper officers
hereunto duly authorized and their respective corporate seals to be hereto
attached by like authority.

(Corporate Seal)   _____ CORPORATION

(continued on following page)

(continued from preceding page)

ATTEST: By _____
                                                        President

_____
                    Secretary

                                         THE _____ COMPANY

(Corporate Seal)   By _____
                                                      Vice President

ATTEST:

_____
                    Secretary

Contract: Figure 1. *Agreement between two corporations with seals attested.*

Printed forms of the contracts are available from stationery stores and, also, from abstract and title companies. (See ABSTRACT COMPANY.) The forms are easy to complete and require little explanation. The lawyer will provide a memorandum of the information necessary to complete the form.

Four copies should be made—original and duplicate original for the seller and buyer, a copy for the broker, and a copy for the lawyer's file. Both the seller and the buyer sign the contract and, usually, the seller's spouse signs also. Generally an ACKNOWLEDGMENT is not necessary, because ordinarily the contract is not recorded. If the form has an acknowledgment printed on it, it should be completed. The form will also indicate whether it should be witnessed.

Checklist of information necessary to fill in form.

1. Date of contract
2. Name and residence of seller
3. Name of seller's spouse if spouse must join in deed that is to be delivered
4. Name and residence of the buyer
5. Description of property to be conveyed (See LAND DESCRIPTION)
6. Purchase price, the exact amount being named
7. Amount to be paid when contract is signed (EARNEST MONEY)
8. Amount to be paid at closing, when DEED is delivered
9. Whether existing mortgage, if any, is to be assumed or property purchased subject to it
10. How balance is paid, and when
11. Name of trustee in those states where a deed of trust is the security instrument
12. Unpaid taxes and assessments
13. Fire insurance data
14. Name of broker
15. Closing date
16. How long offer is open

17. Evidence of title; whether abstract of title, title insurance, or certificate of title
18. Possession date
19. Expiration date of offer

Contributory Negligence. Lack of care by the person suing in a NEGLIGENCE action, which, concurring with the defendant's negligence, was a PROXIMATE CAUSE of his or her injury. Most courts hold that if the complaining party in any way negligently contributes to his or her own injury, DAMAGES may not be collected. See also LAST CLEAR CHANCE.

Conventional Mortgage. See MORTGAGE.

Conversion. The unlawful taking or possession of the CHATTEL of another. When, for example, title to the goods has passed on a sale, but the seller has refused to deliver the goods to the buyer, the buyer may sue for conversion. Conversion may also take the form of an unauthorized destruction or alteration of another's property.

Copyright. A protection granted by national governments through statutory enactment covering the production, publication, and sale of the content and form of literary and artistic work, and advertisements.

When a person creates a book, song, or picture, he or she has a COMMON LAW right to the exclusive ownership of this creation. One need not publish one's work and may prevent others from doing so. Once a person does publish, however, the common law right is lost. Upon publication one must obtain a *statutory copyright* in place of the common law right or lose one's right in the published work forever.

To obtain a statutory copyright, a sufficient inscription or notice of claim must be on the published work. Promptly after publication, two copies of the published work must be filed in the Copyright Office, at the Library of Congress in Washington, D.C., accompanied by application for copyright and statutory fee.

Under the new law passed in 1976, copyrights are now granted for a period of 50 years after the author's death. This will permit heirs to collect royalties for a period of 50 years after the author's death. A copyright may be assigned, given away, or mortgaged by an instrument in writing signed by the owner of the copyright, or may be bequeathed by WILL. The ASSIGNMENT should be recorded by the assignee in the Copyright Office within three months after its execution to protect the assignee's rights if there is any subsequent assignment or mortgage by the original owner.

Corporal Punishment. Generally used to distinguish physical punishment such as imprisonment from pecuniary punishment such as a fine.

Corporate Mortgage Bond. A written promise, under seal, to pay a specific sum of money at a fixed time in the future, usually more than ten years after the promise is made. It is generally one of a series of similar bonds, all of which usually carry interest at a fixed rate, covered by a TRUST DEED or MORTGAGE in which the corporation's property is mortgaged to the trustee for the benefit of the bondholders. These bonds are evidence of indebtedness on the part of the borrower to the lender; the lenders, however, may not enforce the mortgage covenants directly as in the case of individually owned mortgages, but must have the trustee act in their behalf to enforce mortgage convenants or to carry out FORECLOSURE. See also BOND ISSUE; DEED OF TRUST.

Corporate Seal. An engraved symbol used by a corporation to make an impression upon its business papers. The seal usually recites the name of the corporation and the year and state of incorporation. The BYLAWS of a corporation usually provide that any instrument signed on behalf of the corporation shall be impressed with the corporate seal. An officer of the corporation impresses the seal on the instrument at the time it is signed. In many cases the corporate secretary must bear witness or *attest* to the fact that the imprint on the paper is the seal of the corporation. (See ATTESTATION.) When the document recites that the seal is to be attested, the following is typed on the left-hand side of the page, opposite the signature lines:

ATTEST

. . . .
Secretary

Corporation. A collection of persons who act together to accomplish some monetary, ideal, or governmental purpose. A corporation is a legal entity separate and apart from the persons who

are interested in and control it. The state authorizes its existence and gives it certain powers. It also has certain powers that it gives itself, within the limits prescribed by the state, when it goes through the formalities of organization. A corporation has fundamental characteristics that make it the most popular form of business organization. Probably the most favorable aspect of the corporate form is the assurance of limited liability to the persons who put capital into the business.

Corporations may be classified as public corporations, corporations not for profit, and corporations for profit, each class being organized under different statutes.

1. *Public Corporations.* All the subdivisions of the state, such as cities, tax districts, and irrigation districts. They also include government-owned corporations, such as the Commodity Credit Corporation.

2. *Corporations Not for Profit.* Those organized for purposes other than the pecuniary gain of their members. Nonprofit corporations do not have CAPITAL stock or pay a DIVIDEND. Those who are interested in and control the corporation are referred to as its members, rather than its stockholders or shareholders as in a corporation for profit. These corporations include religious, civil, social, educational, fraternal, charitable, and cemetery associations.

3. *Corporations for Profit, or Business Corporations.* Those with capital stock that carry on an enterprise for profit. Business corporations fall into three groups: (1) banks and insurance companies, which are known as *moneyed corporations;* (2) corporations that

135

furnish public utility services to the public, such as transportation and electricity, which are known as *public service corporations;* and (3) corporations engaged in ordinary business pursuits, such as manufacturing, which are known as *private corporations.* The first two classes are subject to stricter governmental control than the private corporation.

The organization procedure herein described relates to a private business corporation, but it is adaptable to other corporations.

Incorporating procedure. To organize a corporation means to bring it into existence. Each state designates a specific department and official through which the lawyer must work. Certain steps are necessary. These involve routine procedure that the secretary can follow at the lawyer's direction without detailed instruction.

The usual steps in the organization of a corporation are:

1. RESERVATION OF CORPORATE NAME
2. Preparation of incorporating papers
3. Execution of papers
4. Filing of papers
5. First meeting of INCORPORATORS
6. First meeting of directors (see BOARD OF DIRECTORS).

See also CERTIFICATE (of Incorporation); STATE OF INCORPORATION; DE JURE CORPORATION; DE FACTO CORPORATION; SUBSIDIARY CORPORATION; CLOSE (OR CLOSED) CORPORATION.

Corpus Juris Secundum System. A complete statement of the body of American law in encyclopedic form. The Corpus Juris Secundum and Corpus Juris are broken down into approximately 430 titles. The text of Corpus Juris Secundum supersedes the corresponding text of Corpus Juris. Each title of the Secundum brings down to date the same title in Corpus Juris. The authorities cited in the notes in the Secundum are the cases decided since that title in Corpus Juris was written. If there are earlier cases on the point, footnote references in Corpus Juris Secundum direct the searcher to the precise page and note in Corpus Juris where they will be found. The absence of a footnote reference to Corpus Juris is conclusive evidence that there are no earlier cases. Thus, although the text of Corpus Juris is superseded by Corpus Juris Secundum, Corpus Juris remains a vital part of the law library because of the footnotes.

The titles embraced by the system are alphabetically arranged. Judicially defined words, phrases, and maxims are alphabetically interspersed through the titles. The backbone of each volume shows the first and last words in that volume and also the volume number. Volume 72 of Corpus Juris is a complete DESCRIPTIVE WORD INDEX to all volumes of Corpus Juris. Each volume of the Secundum has an index to the titles contained in that volume.

How to use Corpus Juris Secundum System. There are three methods of finding the discussion and supporting authorities in the Corpus Juris Secundum System.

1. *The fact, or descriptive, word index.* Find the descriptive word in the index to the title in the back of the volume. For example, if looking for the extent of an implied agency, the title would be *Agency.* In the index "Implied agency"

shows the section and page number where implied agency is discussed. At the head of the section is an analysis of points covered in the section, which enables the search to be narrowed.

Each volume of Corpus Juris does not contain an index. If the pertinent title has not been published in the Secundum, look for the descriptive word in Volume 72, "Descriptive-word Index and Concordance," of Corpus Juris.

2. *The general analysis preceding each title.* At the beginning of each title is an analysis, or breakdown, of the contents of the title. The topics are in bold-face capitals and are numbered with roman numerals. Each of the topics has a subanalysis. Judge which topic should cover the point and then look at the subanalysis for the specific point. "III Creation and Extent of Relation" should cover implied agency. In the subanalysis of that topic will be found, "§24. Implied Agency—p. 1045."

If it cannot be determined which topic should cover the problem, look at each of the subtopics, but this, of course, is a slower method of research.

3. *Words and phrases alphabetically arranged throughout the set.* If an important word or words in the problem can be picked out, refer to those words in CJS and find cross-references to related topics in which the words have meaning or importance.

How to cite. Cite by volume number, title, and page and section number.

57 C.J., Set-Off and Counterclaim, p. 476, §22
24 C.J.S., Criminal Law, p. 147, *§* 1606

Correspondence. *Styles of letters.* Letters in a law office are usually prepared in one of three styles: full-block,

block, or semiblock. Informal letters are sometimes set up in the official style.

1. *Full-block style.* The full-block style uses no indentations; all structural parts begin flush left, so very few typewriter adjustments are needed. The complimentary close and dateline, for example, are aligned with the paragraphs at the extreme left. Open punctuation is often used.

2. *Block style.* In the block style the inside address and paragraphs are blocked flush with the left margin. The salutation and attention line, if any, are also positioned flush left. However, the dateline and reference line are flush right and the complimentary close is placed slightly to the right of center page. Both lines of the signature are aligned with the complimentary close. Open punctuation is often used.

3. *Semiblock style.* In the semiblock style all structural parts of the letter begin flush with the left margin, but the first line of each paragraph is indented five to ten spaces. Carry-over lines in the address are indented three spaces. All lines of the typed signature are aligned with the complimentary close. The dateline is typed flush with the right margin. Open punctuation is often used.

4. *Official style.* In the official style the inside address is placed below the signature, flush with the left-hand margin, instead of before the salutation. The address is blocked. The identification line and enclosure notations, if any, are typed two spaces below the last line of the address.

Punctuation. 1. *Mixed punctuation.* No end-of-line punctuation in the inside address. However, you do use a colon after the salutation and a comma after the complimentary close.

2. Open punctuation. The omission of punctuation marks after the inside address, salutation, and complimentary close, unless a line ends in an abbreviation.

Address forms. 1. *Names.* Some law firms omit the comma between names of the members of the firm; others insert the ampersand between each name. Some companies include *Company, Co., The, Inc.* or *&* as part of the official name. Always write a name the way the owner writes it. If a letter is addressed to a particular department in a company, place the name of the company on the first line and the name of the department on the second line. In addressing an individual in a firm, corporation, or group, place the individual's name on the first line and the company's name on the second line.

2. *Titles.* Always precede the name by a title (Mr. John Snow, President), unless initials indicating degrees or *Esquire* follow the name. The use of a business title or position or of *Sr.* or *Jr.* after a name does not take the place of a title. Some law offices always address a lawyer as *Esquire* (Donald O. Toll, Esquire; Joan F. King, Esq.). Although *Esquire* is traditionally a title for men, it is now being used for women in the legal profession too. Use *Esquires* after a firm name composed of two or more surnames. *Messrs.* is also used for addressing a firm of attorneys (Messrs. Allen, Seale & Hill.) It may be used in addressing a business firm of men or men and women when the names denote individuals but not in addressing corporations or other business organizations that bear impersonal names. After the name of a person, use only initials of the highest degree (Ellen E. Lewis, Ph.D. *not* Ellen E. Lewis, A.B., A.M., Ph.D.). Use more than one degree

only when the degrees pertain to different fields and then place the one pertaining to the person's full-time occupation first (John Morris, D.D., LL.D.). Do not use a scholastic title with a degree (Professor Max Stone *not* Professor Max Stone, Ph.D.). *Mr., Mrs., Miss,* or *Ms.* precedes a person's name, and the business title follows it (Ms. Edna McReynolds, Treasurer). In the inside address, omit a person's business title if it would cause the address to run over four lines.

Addressing women. 1. *Firm composed of women.* Use *Mesdames* or *Mmes.*, whether the women are married or unmarried.

2. *Unmarried woman.* Use *Miss* or *Ms.* When you do not know if a woman is married, use *Ms.*

3. *Married women.* Socially a married woman is addressed by her husband's full name preceded by *Mrs.* In business, she may be addressed either by her husband's name or by her given name and her married name, preceded by *Mrs.* Use the form the woman prefers if you know it.

4. *Widow.* Socially a widow is addressed by her husband's full name preceded by *Mrs.* In business either her husband's full name or her given name and her married name, preceded by *Mrs.* is correct. Use the form that she prefers if you know it.

5. *Divorcee.* If a divorcee retains her married name, the title *Mrs.* is preferable to *Miss.* If she uses her maiden name, she may use either *Miss* or *Mrs.* In business she may be addressed by her given name combined with her married name or by both her maiden and married names. Follow the form she prefers if you know it. Socially she is addressed by

her maiden name combined with her married name.

6. *Wife of a titled man.* Do not address a married woman by her husband's title. Address her as *Mrs. John A. Watts*, for example. If she is addressed jointly with her husband, the correct form is Dr. and Mrs. John A. Watts. (If a married woman is titled and her husband is not, the correct form would be Mr. John A. and Dr. Mary B. Watts.)

7. *Professional women.* Address a woman with a professional title by her title, followed by her given and last names. A married woman sometimes uses her maiden name and, if so, should be addressed by it. In social correspondence her title is sometimes dropped in addressing her and her husband. When you do not know whether an addressee is a man or woman, use the form of address appropriate for a man.

Addressing officials. Table I presents the correct form of address for persons in honorary or official positions. Women in official positions are addressed just as men in similar positions, except that *Madam, Mrs., Miss,* or *Ms.* replace *Sir* or *Mr.*

Street address. The inside address and the address on the envelope are the same. The following instructions for writing it are standard, although various authorities give different rules for writing the address.

1. Do not precede the street number with a word or a sign (20 Third Avenue *not* #20 Third Avenue).

2. Spell out the numerical names of streets and avenues if they are numbers of 12 or under (2 Seventh Avenue). Do not follow figures with *d, st.,* or *th.* (*not* 23rd). Use figures for all house numbers except *One* (One Sixth Avenue). Separate a house number from a numerical name with a space, hyphen and a space (117 - 71 Street).

3. If a room, suite, or apartment number is part of the address, it should follow the street address. If the address is an office building the suite number may precede the name of the building (500 Ocean Drive, Room 214; 2020 Tower Building).

4. Never abbreviate the name of a city. States, territories, and possessions should be abbreviated by their official two-letter designations (IL, OH, CA, etc.). A list is available from your local post office.

5. The zip code should appear on the last line of the address following the city and state. Leave one or two spaces between the last letter of the state and the first digit of the code.

6. Even if there is no street address, keep the city and state on the same line.

7. Use a post office box number if you have it instead of the street address.

Salutations. Capitalize the first word, the title, and the name. Capitalize *Dear* when it is used as the first word of the salutation. Use a colon following the salutation. A comma is used only in social letters, particularly in those written in longhand. *Mr., Mrs.,* and *Dr.* are the only titles that are abbreviated.

1. *Correct forms of salutation.* The form of salutation varies with the tone of the letter and the degree of acquaintanceship between the lawyer and the client. The trend today is toward the less formal salutation. (See also table I.) If the letter is addressed to an individual, make the salutation singular (Dear Sir). If the letter is addressed to a company or group, make it plural (Gentlemen or Dear Sirs). *Dear Sirs* is preferable when

Table I

FORMS OF ADDRESS: HONORARY AND OFFICIAL POSITIONS

UNITED STATES GOVERNMENT OFFICIALS

Personage	Envelope and Inside Address (Add City, State, Zip)	Formal Salutation	Informal Salutation	Formal Close	Informal Close	1. Spoken Address 2. Informal Introduction or Reference
The President	The President The White House	Mr. President:	Dear Mr. President:	Respectfully yours,	Very respectfully yours, Very truly yours, or Sincerely yours,	1. Mr. President 2. Not introduced (The President)
The Vice-President of the United States	The Vice-President of the United States United States Senate	Mr. Vice-President:	Dear Mr. Vice-President:	Very truly yours,	Sincerely yours,	1. Mr. Vice-President or 2. Mr. Blank The Vice-President
The Chief Justice of the United States Supreme Court	The Chief Justice The Supreme Court of the United States	Sir:	Dear Mr. Chief Justice:	Very truly yours,	Sincerely yours,	1. Mr. Chief Justice or Sir 2. The Chief Justice
Associate Justice of the United States Supreme Court	Justice Blank The Supreme Court of the United States	Sir:	Dear Mr. Justice: or Dear Madam Justice or Dear Justice Blank	Very truly yours,	Sincerely yours,	1. Mr. Justice Blank or Madam Justice Blank or Justice Blank 2. Mr. Justice Blank or Madam Justice Blank
Retired Justice of the United States Supreme Court	Justice William R. Blank (local address)	Sir:	Dear Justice Blank:	Very truly yours,	Sincerely yours,	1. Mr. Justice Blank or Justice Blank 2. Mr. Justice Blank
The Speaker of the House of Representatives	The Honorable William R. Blank Speaker of the House of Representatives	Sir:	Dear Mr. Speaker: or Dear Mr. Blank:	Very truly yours,	Sincerely yours,	1. Mr. Speaker or Mr. Blank 2. The Speaker, Mr. Blank (The Speaker or Mr. Blank)

UNITED STATES GOVERNMENT OFFICIALS *continued*

Personage	Envelope and Inside Address (Add City, State, Zip)	Formal Salutation	Informal Salutation	Formal Close	Informal Close	Spoken Address 1. / Informal Introduction or Reference 2.
Cabinet Officers addressed as "Secretary"[1]	The Honorable William R. Blank / Secretary of State / The Honorable William R. Blank / Secretary of State of the United States of America (if written from abroad)	Sir:	Dear Mr. Secretary:	Very truly yours,	Sincerely yours,	1. Mr. Secretary or Secretary Blank or Mr. Blank 2. The Secretary of State, Mr. Blank (Mr. Blank or The Secretary)
The Attorney General	The Honorable William R. Blank / The Attorney General	Sir:	Dear Mr. Attorney General:	Very truly yours,	Sincerely yours,	1. Mr. Attorney General or Attorney General Blank 2. The Attorney General, Mr. Blank (Mr. Blank or The Attorney General)
Under Secretary of a Department	The Honorable William R. Blank / Under Secretary of Labor	Dear Mr. Blank:	Dear Mr. Blank:	Very truly yours,	Sincerely yours,	1. Mr. Blank 2. Mr. Blank
United States Senator	The Honorable William R. Blank / United States Senate	Sir:	Dear Senator Blank:	Very truly yours,	Sincerely yours,	1. Senator Blank or Senator 2. Senator Blank
United States Representative or Congressman[2]	The Honorable William R. Blank / House of Representatives / The Honorable William R. Blank / Representative in Congress (local address) (when away from Washington, DC)	Sir:	Dear Mr. Blank:	Very truly yours,	Sincerely yours,	1. Mr. Blank 2. Mr. Blank, Representative (Congressman) from New York or Mr. Blank

[1]Titles for cabinet secretaries are Secretary of State; Secretary of the Treasury; Secretary of Defense; Secretary of the Interior; Secretary of Agriculture; Secretary of Commerce; Secretary of Labor; Secretary of Health and Human Services; Secretary of Housing and Urban Development; Secretary of Transportation; Secretary of Energy; Secretary of Education.

[2]The official title of a "congressman" is *Representative*. Strictly speaking, senators are also congressmen.

UNITED STATES GOVERNMENT OFFICIALS *continued*

Personage	Envelope and Inside Address (Add City, State, Zip)	Formal Salutation	Informal Salutation	Formal Close	Informal Close	1. Spoken Address 2. Informal Introduction or Reference
Territorial Delegate	The Honorable William R. Blank Delegate of Puerto Rico House of Representatives	Dear Sir: or Dear Mr. Blank:	Dear Mr. Blank:	Very truly yours,	Sincerely yours,	1. Mr. Blank 2. Mr. Blank
Resident Commissioner	The Honorable William R. Blank Resident Commissioner of (Territory) House of Representatives	Dear Sir: or Dear Mr. Blank:	Dear Mr. Blank:	Very truly yours,	Sincerely yours,	1. Mr. Blank 2. Mr. Blank
Directors or Heads of Independent Federal Offices, Agencies, Commissions, Organizations, etc.	The Honorable William R. Blank Director, Mutual Security Agency	Dear Mr. Director (Commissioner, etc.):	Dear Mr. Blank:	Very truly yours,	Sincerely yours,	1. Mr. Blank 2. Mr. Blank
Other High Officials of the United States, in general: Public Printer, Comptroller General	The Honorable William R. Blank Public Printer The Honorable William R. Blank Comptroller General of the United States	Dear Sir: or Dear Mr. Blank:	Dear Mr. Blank:	Very truly yours,	Sincerely yours,	1. Mr. Blank 2. Mr. Blank
Secretary to the President	The Honorable William R. Blank Secretary to the President The White House	Dear Sir: or Dear Mr. Blank:	Dear Mr. Blank:	Very truly yours,	Sincerely yours,	1. Mr. Blank 2. Mr. Blank
Assistant Secretary to the President	The Honorable William R. Blank Assistant Secretary to the President The White House	Dear Sir: or Dear Mr. Blank:	Dear Mr. Blank:	Very truly yours,	Sincerely yours,	1. Mr. Blank 2. Mr. Blank

UNITED STATES GOVERNMENT OFFICIALS *continued*

Personage	Envelope and Inside Address (Add City, State, Zip)	Formal Salutation	Informal Salutation	Formal Close	Informal Close	Spoken Address / Informal Introduction or Reference
Press Secretary to the President	Mr. William R. Blank Press Secretary to the President The White House	Dear Sir: or Dear Mr. Blank:	Dear Mr. Blank:	Very truly yours,	Sincerely yours,	1. Mr. Blank 2. Mr. Blank

STATE AND LOCAL GOVERNMENT OFFICIALS

Personage	Envelope and Inside Address (Add City, State, Zip)	Formal Salutation	Informal Salutation	Formal Close	Informal Close	Spoken Address / Informal Introduction or Reference
Governor of a State or Territory[1]	The Honorable William R. Blank Governor of New York	Sir:	Dear Governor Blank:	Respectfully yours,	Very sincerely yours,	1. Governor Blank or Governor 2. a) Governor Blank b) The Governor c) The Governor of New York (used only outside his or her own state)
Lieutenant Governor	The Honorable William R. Blank Lieutenant Governor of Iowa	Sir:	Dear Mr. Blank:	Respectfully yours, or Very truly yours,	Sincerely yours,	1. Mr. Blank 2. The Lieutenant Governor of Iowa, Mr. Blank or The Lieutenant Governor
Secretary of State	The Honorable William R. Blank Secretary of State of New York	Sir:	Dear Mr. Secretary:	Very truly yours,	Sincerely yours,	1. Mr. Blank 2. Mr. Blank
Attorney General	The Honorable William R. Blank Attorney General of Massachusetts	Sir:	Dear Mr. Attorney General:	Very truly yours,	Sincerely yours,	1. Mr. Blank 2. Mr. Blank

[1]The form of addressing governors varies in the different states. The form given here is the one used in most states. In Massachusetts by law and in some other states by courtesy, the form *His (Her) Excellency, the Governor of Massachusetts*.

143

STATE AND LOCAL GOVERNMENT OFFICIALS *continued*

Personage	Envelope and Inside Address (Add City, State, Zip)	Formal Salutation	Informal Salutation	Formal Close	Informal Close	1. Spoken Address 2. Informal Introduction or Reference
State Representative, Assemblyman, or Delegate	The Honorable William R. Blank House of Delegates	Dear Sir:	Dear Mr. Blank:	Very truly yours,	Sincerely yours,	1. Mr. Blank 2. Mr. Blank or Delegate Blank
District Attorney	The Honorable William R. Blank District Attorney, Albany County County Courthouse	Dear Sir:	Dear Mr. Blank:	Very truly yours,	Sincerely yours,	1. Mr. Blank 2. Mr. Blank.
Mayor of a city	The Honorable William R. Blank Mayor of Detroit	Dear Sir:	Dear Mayor Blank:	Very truly yours,	Sincerely yours,	1. Mayor Blank or Mr. Mayor 2. Mayor Blank
President of a Board of Commissioners	The Honorable William R. Blank, President Board of Commissioners of the City of Buffalo	Dear Sir:	Dear Mr. Blank:	Very truly yours,	Sincerely yours,	1. Mr. Blank 2. Mr. Blank
City Attorney, City Counsel, Corporation Counsel	The Honorable William R. Blank, City Attorney (City Counsel, Corporation Counsel)	Dear Sir:	Dear Mr. Blank:	Very truly yours,	Sincerely yours,	1. Mr. Blank 2. Mr. Blank
Alderman	Alderman William R. Blank City Hall	Dear Sir:	Dear Mr. Blank:	Very truly yours,	Sincerely yours,	1. Mr. Blank 2. Mr. Blank

COURT OFFICIALS

Personage	Envelope and Inside Address (Add City, State, Zip)	Formal Salutation	Informal Salutation	Formal Close	Informal Close	1. Spoken Address 2. Informal Introduction or Reference
Chief Justice of a State Supreme Court[1]	The Honorable William R. Blank Chief Justice of the Supreme Court of Minnesota[2]	Sir:	Dear Mr. Chief Justice:	Very truly yours,	Sincerely yours,	1. Mr. Chief Justice or Judge Blank 2. Mr. Chief Justice Blank or Judge Blank

[1] If his or her official title is *Chief Justice* substitute *Chief Judge* for *Chief Justice*, but never use *Mr., Mrs., Miss* or *Ms.* with *Chief Justice* or *Judge.* For example, the highest court in New York State is called the Court of Appeals.
[2] Substitute here the appropriate name of the court.

144

COURT OFFICIALS *continued*

Personage	Envelope and Inside Address (Add City, State, Zip)	Formal Salutation	Informal Salutation	Formal Close	Informal Close	Spoken Address, Informal Introduction or Reference
Associate Justice of a Supreme Court of a State	The Honorable William R. Blank Associate Justice of the Supreme Court of Minnesota	Sir:	Dear Justice Blank:	Very truly yours,	Sincerely yours,	1. Mr. Justice Blank 2. Mr. Justice Blank
Presiding Justice	The Honorable William R. Blank Presiding Justice, Appellate Division Supreme Court of New York	Sir:	Dear Justice Blank:	Very truly yours,	Sincerely yours,	1. Mr. Justice (or Judge) Blank 2. Mr. Justice (or Judge Blank)
Judge of a Court[1]	The Honorable William R. Blank Judge of the United States District Court for the Southern District of California	Sir:	Dear Judge Blank:	Very truly yours,	Sincerely yours,	1. Judge Blank 2. Judge Blank
Clerk of a Court	William R. Blank, Esquire Clerk of the Superior Court of Massachusetts	Dear Sir:	Dear Mr. Blank:	Very truly yours,	Sincerely yours,	1. Mr. Blank 2. Mr. Blank

[1]Not applicable to judges of the United States Supreme Court.

addressing a firm of lawyers. Never use a designation after a salutation (*not* Dear Mr. Jones, C.P.A.). The salutation in a letter addressed to an organization composed of men and women is *Ladies and Gentlemen*; to a man and woman, *Dear Sir and Madam*; to a married couple, *Dear Mr. and Mrs. Jones*; *Dr. and Mrs. Jones*; or *Mr. and Dr. Jones*. Never use a business title or designation of position in a salutation (*not* Dear Secretary Anderson). However, some lawyers address others in their profession as *Dear Brother Jones* or *Dear Sister Jones*. If a letter addressed to a firm of lawyers is to the attention of an individual lawyer, the salutation is to the firm, not to the individual. Follow a title with the surname (Dear Dr. Altman).

2. *Forms of salutation for women.* Do not use *Miss, Mrs.,* or *Ms.* as a salutation unless it is followed by a name (*not* Dear Miss:). If the letter is addressed to a firm of women, the salutation is *Ladies* or *Mesdames*. Do not use "Dear" or "My dear" with either of these salutations. The salutation to two women with the same name is *Dear Mesdames Hart* (married) or *Dear Misses Hart* (unmarried). When in doubt whether the addressee is a man or woman, use the salutation appropriate for a man.

Complimentary Close. The form of complimentary close varies with the tone of the letter and the degree of acquaintanceship between the lawyer and the client. In the interchange of letters between lawyer and client, observe how the client closes the letter and be guided by his or her taste. (See also table I). Among colleagues and most clients the trend is toward a more informal close (*Sincerely*; *Sincerely yours*) rather than the more

formal close (*Yours very truly*; Respectfully).

Signature. Firms of attorneys frequently sign letters manually with the firm name, particularly if the letter expresses a professional opinion or gives professional advice. In some offices the firm name is typed on the letter and the lawyer who dictated it signs his or her name:

WEST, HALL & MICHAELS

By *Joseph West*

A letter signed in the firm name, whether manually or typed, is written in the first person plural, not the singular. Many letters are signed by the dictating attorney or by a partner without having the firm name appear in the signature. The purpose of typing a signature is to enable the recipient of the letter to decipher a difficult signature. There is no need, therefore, for the lawyer's name to be typed in the signature if it appears on the letterhead. If a firm has alternate forms of signatures, the dictator will indicate his or her preference. Type the firm name in capitals exactly as it appears on the letterhead. If the signature of the dictator is typed, type it exactly as the dictator signs his or her name. The typed signature should never extend beyond the right margin of the letter and no title except *Miss* or *Mrs.* precedes either the written or typed signature.

Envelopes. The items in the address on the envelope are the same as those on the inside address. Even if there is no street address, keep the name of the state on the same line as the name of the city. Use the proper two-letter postal abbreviation for the state. Write the name of a foreign country in capitals on the envelope; use initial capitals in the inside address.

Attention line. Strictly business letters addressed to a firm are often directed to the attention of an individual by the use of an attention line, in preference to addressing the letter to the individual. This practice ensures that the letter will be opened in the absence of the individual to whom it is directed. Type the attention line two spaces below the address. The word *of* is not necessary. The attention line has no punctuation and is not underscored (*Attention Mr. John R. Snow*). When a letter addressed to a firm has an attention line, the salutation is *Gentlemen* because the salutation is to the firm, not the individual. It is permissible to direct the letter to the attention of an individual without including his or her given name or initials, if they are unknown.

Identification line. This shows who dictated the letter and who typed it. The only purpose of the identification is for reference by the firm writing the letter. It does not belong on the original of a letter, but many firms have the line typed on the original because it saves time. The usual position of identification marks is two spaces below or on a line with the last line of the signature, flush with the left margin. If the dictator's name is typed on the letter, there is no need for his or her initials to appear in the identification marks.

Personal notation. "Personal" or "Confidential" should be used only when no one but the addressee is supposed to see the letter. Type the word four spaces above the address. In the official style of letter place the personal notation at the top of the letter. The notation is also typed, in solid caps underlined, on the envelope two spaces above the address.

Reference line. If a file reference is given in an incoming letter, include a reference line in your reply. Place your own reference beneath the incoming reference. When letterheads have a printed notation such as *In reply please refer to*, type the reference line after it. Otherwise, type it about four spaces beneath the date.

Mailing notation. When a letter is sent by any method other than regular mail, type a notation of the exact method on the envelope, in the space below the stamps and above the address. Make a similar notation on the carbon copy of the letter.

Enclosure mark. When a letter contains enclosures, type the word *Enclosure* or the abbreviation *Enc.* flush with the left-hand margin one or two spaces beneath the identification line. If there is more than one enclosure, indicate the number. If the enclosures are of special importance, identify them. If an enclosure is to be returned, make a notation to that effect.

Copy distribution notation. When a copy is to be sent to another person, type the distribution notation flush with the left-hand margin, below all other notations. If space permits, separate it from the other notations by two spaces. The abbreviation *c.c.* or *cc* is often used for *carbon* copies, and the words *Copy to* are often used with photocopies. Type a blind-copy notation in the upper left-hand portion of the letter on the carbons only. This indicates that the addressee of the letter does not know that a copy was sent to anyone.

Postscript. When it is necessary to add

a postscript to a letter, type it two spaces below the identification line or the last notation that is on the letter. The left margin of the postscript should be indented five spaces from the left margin of the letter itself. You may include or omit the abbreviations "P.S." Type the dictator's initials after the postscript.

Heading on succeeding pages. Law firms generally have continuation sheets, loosely called second sheets, with the firm name, but no address, engraved or printed on them for use when a letter runs more than one page. If your office does not have printed continuation sheets, use a plain sheet of the same size and quality as the letterhead. Type enough descriptive matter at the top of the succeeding pages to make them recognizable if they should become separated from the first page. The name of the addressee, the number of the page, and the date should be sufficient.

Enclosures. When it is necessary to fasten enclosures together or to a letter, use staples. The U.S. Postal Service objects to pins or metal clips because they injure the hands of employees and the clips damage post office canceling machines.

1. *Enclosures the size of the letter.* These are easily folded and inserted, with their accompanying letters, into commercial envelopes of ordinary size. If the enclosure consists of two or more sheets, staple them together but do not fasten the enclosed material to the letter. Fold the enclosure, then fold the letter, and slip the enclosure inside the last fold of the letter.

2. *Enclosures larger than the letter.* These include briefs, abstracts, and other legal documents too large to fit into a commercial envelope of ordinary size.

They are generally mailed in large manila envelopes. Enclosures of this kind may be handled in one of three ways: (a) The letter is inserted with the enclosure in the large envelope, which is sealed. First-class postage is charged for both letter and enclosure. (b) A combination envelope is used. This is a large envelope with a flap that is fastened by a patent fastener of some kind, but not sealed. A smaller envelope of commercial size is affixed on the front of this envelope in the process of manufacture. The letter is inserted into the small envelope and the flap is sealed. Postage is affixed to the large envelope at the third-class rate and to the smaller envelope at the first-class rate. (c) The enclosure may be sent, unsealed, in one envelope and the letter, sealed, in another. In this case, the letter should not refer to an enclosure but should state that the material is being sent separately.

3. *Enclosures smaller than the letter.* These should be stapled to the letter in the upper left-hand corner, on top of the letter. If two or more such enclosures are sent, put the smaller one on top.

Corroborating Evidence. Evidence supplementary to that already given and tending to strengthen and confirm it. Under certain circumstances the testimony of a witness, even though uncontradicted, is not sufficient to establish the truth of a certain fact unless the testimony of the witness is corroborated. Examples of this are the provision in the federal Constitution (see CONSTITUTION, UNITED STATES) that the crime of treason can be proved only by the testimony of two witnesses to the same overt act, and the statute found in about half the states that an accused cannot be convicted by the uncorroborated testimony of an ACCOMPLICE.

Counterclaim. A CAUSE OF ACTION is set up by a DEFENDANT, to be tried at the same time as an original cause of action alleged by a plaintiff. The defendant takes advantage of the suit against him to ask the court for relief against the plaintiff, when otherwise he or she would be compelled to institute an action of his own. For example, the maker of a note might claim that the payee is indebted to him or her for certain sums in connection with a matter not related to the note.

Counterfeiting. See FORGERY AND COUNTERFEITING.

County Court. See COURTS OF SPECIAL JURISDICTION.

Court. In the legal sense *court* relates to the law in these commonly used senses:

1. *Court* refers to the *persons* assembled under authority of law, at a designated place, for the administration of justice. These persons are the JUDGE or judges, clerk, marshal, bailiff, reporter, jurors, and attorneys, and they constitute a body of the government. Thus, the lawyer's secretary says that her employer "is in court this morning," meaning that he or she is appearing before this duly assembled body in the interest of a client. It is not necessary that all of these persons be present to constitute a court—court is frequently held without a jury.

2. The word refers to the authorized *assembly* of the persons who make up the court. Thus, we say, "Court will be held . . ." meaning that the judge, clerk, attorneys, and so on will gather together to administer justice. Or we say, "Judge Smith's court . . .," meaning the clerk, attorneys, jurors, and so on over which Judge Smith presides.

3. *Court* refers to the judge or judges themselves, as distinguished from the counsel or jury. Thus, we have the expression, "In the opinion of the Court . . .," "May it please the Court . . .," "The Court stated . . ." In this sense, the word is written with a capital, because it is personified when it stands for the judge.

4. The word *court* is used occasionally to refer to the chamber, hall, or place where court is being held. Thus, a spectator is present "at court," in the courtroom, but the defendant is "in court" because he or she is part of the assembly.

5. The name of a specific court always includes the word *court*, which is capitalized; for example, Probate Court, Essex County. Neither probate nor court is capitalized if reference is made to probate courts generally; for example, "Petitions for letters of administration are filed in probate courts."

Court procedure. The method by which the court operates. All court proceedings are conducted for and on behalf of the litigants (see PARTIES TO AN ACTION) by attorneys at law. It is permissible for a party to a lawsuit to represent himself in court, but a layman seldom has the required technical knowledge. Court actions consist of a series of written statements of the claims and defenses of the parties to a court action. These written statements are known professionally as PLEADINGS.

Court proceedings vary from a simple hearing in the judge's office to a full-dress jury trial. In an informal hearing in the judge's chambers, only the judge (or on occasion the special master assigned), the litigants, and their attorneys are present. In a more formal courtroom hearing, the litigants, their attorneys, and the presiding judge are joined by the CLERK OF COURT, the court reporter, and one or more bailiffs.

At a jury trial, before the judge arrives, the plaintiffs and their attorneys and the defendants and their attorneys are present in the courtroom along with the court reporter, a bailiff, and any members of the public who want to attend. All present stand while the jury is brought into the courtroom and seated in the jury box. Everyone then rises at the order of the bailiff and remains standing until the judge has entered the courtroom and is seated behind the bench.

The clerk declares the court in session and announces the first case. The plaintiff, if it is a civil case, or the prosecution, if it is a criminal case, begins by making an OPENING STATEMENT. Sometimes the defense attorney will make an opening statement immediately after that. The prosecution or the plaintiff then presents his or her evidence. Witnesses are called and questioned in turn by the plaintiff's attorney or the prosecution, as the case may be.

The defendant's attorney has a turn to cross-examine the same witness. Afterward, the prosecution or plaintiff may ask further questions of the witness on what is called *redirect examination.* Re-

direct is limited to questioning on matters brought up on CROSS-EXAMINATION. Occasionally redirect examination is followed by a *recross-examination* by the defendant's attorney. Upon completion of the evidence for his or her side, the plaintiff or prosecution rests. The same routine is followed by the defendant's *case in brief.* When both sides have completed presenting all of their evidence, the attorneys present their *closing arguments* to the jury.

Finally, before the jury retires to deliberate on the evidence, the judge gives a CHARGE TO THE JURY. The jury may ask the judge for further instructions. Otherwise, the case is complete when they return with their verdict. In a criminal case, the judge may sentence the defendant immediately upon the return of a guilty verdict, or he or she may defer sentencing.

Court Bond. Litigants at law are required many times to file a bond or other security guaranteeing that, if unsuccessful in litigation, they will pay to the other party the monetary DAMAGES awarded by the court. These bonds are known as *court* or *judiciary bonds.* Another class of court bonds is known as *probate bonds.* They are issued to executors, administrators, and other fiduciaries to guarantee the faithful performance of their legal duties.

Court of Appeal. See APPELLATE COURT.

Court of Last Resort. The final tribunal in the APPELLATE COURT structure to which a case may be taken for

APPEAL. Each state has its highest court; the court of last resort in the federal judiciary system is the SUPREME COURT OF THE UNITED STATES.

Court Register. See CLERK OF THE COURT, Permanent Record Book.

Courts of Intermediate Review. Courts that are established to relieve congestion in a state's highest APPELLATE COURT. (See table I, AMERICAN COURT SYSTEM.) These courts exercise appellate jurisdiction only, except that in some states they have original jurisdiction to issue writs of MANDAMUS, CERTIORARI, HABEAS CORPUS, and the like. They have jurisdiction of matters of appeal from the final judgments, orders, or decrees of superior courts (see DECREE), usually in both law and chancery matters. (See CHANCERY COURT.) The appellate jurisdiction of intermediate courts is frequently restricted. For example, the Georgia Court of Appeals, which is a court of intermediate review, does not have jurisdiction over appeals involving the Constitution of Georgia or of the United States. The appellate courts of Illinois do not have jurisdiction over criminal appeals other than misdemeanors. In New Jersey and New York, divisions of the superior court (New York's equivalent of superior courts is called Supreme Court) exercise intermediate jurisdiction. See also the AMERICAN COURT SYSTEM; APPELLATE COURT; SUPERIOR COURTS; INFERIOR COURTS; COURTS OF SPECIAL JURISDICTION.

Courts of Record. Judicial organized tribunals where acts and proceedings are permanently enrolled. Courts of record may be federal or state. For a listing of federal and state courts of records in the United States, see AMERICAN COURT SYSTEM.

Courts of Special Jurisdiction. Tribunals of ORIGINAL JURISDICTION to administer justice in certain restricted matters. Some states have courts of special jurisdiction in some fields; other states, in other fields. The most common courts of special jurisdiction are probate courts, criminal courts, chancery courts, juvenile courts, county courts, and municipal courts in large cities.

1. *Probate Courts.* Sometimes called Surrogate Courts. They have jurisdiction over the probate of wills, administration of a decedent's estate, and guardianship of minors and insane people.

2. *Criminal Courts.* Have jurisdiction over criminal cases. Criminal trial courts may be called *oyer & terminer* (hear and determine).

3. *Chancery Courts.* Have original jurisdiction over criminal cases. See CHANCERY COURT.

4. *Juvenile Courts.* Usually have exclusive original jurisdiction over all neglected, dependent, or delinquent children under eighteen.

5. *County Courts.* Have widely diverse jurisdictions in the different states. For example, in Alabama they are courts of criminal jurisdiction; in Colorado, they have jurisdiction over probate matters, over delinquent children in some counties, and in civil actions if the amount involved is not over $1,000; in Mississippi, they have concurrent jurisdiction with

circuit and chancery courts if the amount involved does not exceed $10,000.

6. *Municipal Courts.* In large cities they are frequently courts of record and have concurrent jurisdiction with superior courts, if the amount involved does not exceed a stated sum, usually $3,000. See also INFERIOR COURTS; SUPERIOR COURTS; the SUPREME APPELLATE COURTS; the APPELLATE COURT; AMERICAN COURT SYSTEM.

Covenants. Agreements of legal validity between two or more persons to do or to refrain from doing some act, or that a given state of facts exists or does not exist. Covenants may arise by implication of law or from the conduct of the parties and may be divided into two classes: (1) personal covenants, and (2) covenants running with the land, known as restrictive convenants. See Covenant of Title, below.

1. *Covenants in Deeds.* Promises made by the GRANTOR and GRANTEE in the sale of REAL PROPERTY. The usual covenants by the grantor, which are printed in the deed, relate to the TITLE to the property and to its quiet and peaceful enjoyment by the grantee. The grantor might make special promises not included in the usual printed form, such as agreeing to construct and maintain roadways. Covenants by the grantee are less common than covenants by the grantor. The most frequent use of covenants by the grantee is in connection with the sale of lots in subdivisions; they usually relate to the type of structure that may be erected on the premises. These covenants are not included in the usual printed form of deed, but special deeds that contain them are usually printed for the sale of lots in a specific subdivision.

Example of covenant by grantee:

And the said grantee does hereby for himself, his heirs and assigns, covenant with the said grantor, his heirs, executors, and administrators, that he will not, at any time hereafter, erect, or cause, or suffer, or permit, to be erected upon the hereby granted premises, or any part thereof, any building other than a brick or stone private dwelling house, not less than three stories in height.

2. *Covenants of Title.* Guarantees or assurances by the GRANTOR contained in a WARRANTY DEED that the DEED conveys a good and unencumbered TITLE. These guarantees differ in scope in various localities, but generally the covenants guarantee the following:

Covenant of seizin. That the grantor is seized of the property in FEE SIMPLE and has good right to convey. If the grantor owns only part of the title conveyed, or has only a LIFE ESTATE, he or she has violated the covenant of SEIZIN and is liable to the GRANTEE for DAMAGES caused by such violation.

Covenant of quiet enjoyment. That the grantee shall quietly enjoy the premises. The purpose of this warranty is to make certain that the possession of the grantee after he or she takes title will not be disturbed by anyone having a better title or LIEN.

Covenant against encumbrances. That the premises are free from encumbrances, other than those mentioned in the deed. Such encumbrances may include a MORTGAGE, tax lien, judgment lien, restriction on the use of the land. Even if the grantee knew of the ENCUMBRANCE, the grantor is liable if any encumbrance not indicated in the deed exists.

Covenant of further assurance. That the grantor will execute or procure any further necessary assurance of title. Additional instruments needed to confirm title to the premises are usually executed at the purchaser's expense. Requests for further assurance must, of course, be reasonable.

Covenant of warranty. That the grantor will forever warrant the title to the premises conveyed. This imposes a personal obligation upon the seller to defend the title of the purchaser and, in effect, includes the covenant of quiet enjoyment and the covenant of further assurance.

Craft Union. See LABOR UNION.

Credibility. That quality in a witness which makes his or her evidence worthy of belief. Whether a witness' testimony is to be accepted as true is normally a question for the jury to decide.

Credible, Credulous, Creditable. *Credible* means believable; *credulous* mean easily imposed upon, believing too easily; *creditable* means praiseworthy.

He is not a *credible* witness.

The readers are indeed *credulous* if they believe the editorial completely.

Her summation of the case was *creditable.*

Crime. An act that a government regards as injurious to the public. One charged in court with the commission of a crime is prosecuted by the state or federal government, depending on whether the act violates a state or federal criminal statute. In the United States the law of crimes is covered solely by statute. A TORT, on the other hand, is an infringement on the rights of an individual rather than the community as a whole and is prosecuted by the injured party. See also FELONY; MISDEMEANOR.

Criminal Court. A government tribunal empowered to administer justice in connection with public wrongs, that is, crimes of *treason, felony,* or *misdemeanor.* Criminal trial courts may be called *oyer & terminer* (hear and determine). See CRIMINAL LAW; CIVIL COURT.

Criminal Law. The statutes and general dicta that forbid certain actions or conduct as detrimental to the welfare of the state and that provide punishment therefor. Criminal acts are prosecuted by the state, whereas civil wrongs (see CIVIL LAW), are prosecuted by a private individual. A wrong may be both a criminal wrong and a civil wrong; for example, ASSAULT AND BATTERY. A crime may be a treason, a felony, or a misdemeanor. The Constitution of the United States states that *treason* "shall consist only in levying war against them or in adhering to their enemies, giving them aid and comfort." *Felonies* are crimes punishable by death or by imprisonment in a federal or state prison. They include murder, GRAND LARCENY, ARSON, and RAPE. *Misdemeanors* are crimes of lesser importance than felonies and are punishable by a fine or imprisonment in the local jail. They include petty larceny, drunkenness, disorderly conduct, and vagrancy. Violation of traffic ordinances, building codes, and similar city ordinances are not crimes but are termed "petty offenses," "public torts," or *mala prohibita.* See TORT; CRIMINAL COURT; CIVIL LAW.

Cross-Examination. The interrogation of an adverse witness after the witness has testified on DIRECT EXAMINATION for the party who called him or her. Cross-examination of unfriendly witnesses is a matter of right in every trial of a disputed issue of fact and is recognized as the best means of discovering truth.

Cruelty. A ground for DIVORCE and SEPARATION in many states. If one is claiming physical cruelty, it is wise to produce medical testimony and, if possible, photographs of bruises and lacerations.

Mental cruelty is more difficult to prove because the insults made by husband and wife are often in private and rarely result in sufficient proof. The classic example of successfully proving mental cruelty is evidence of the subjection of the innocent spouse to ridicule, humiliation, and scorn in the presence of friends, relatives, or members of the community.

Cul de Sac. (French for the bottom of a sack): a blind alley; a street that is open at one end only.

Cumulative Preferred Stock. A class of PREFERRED STOCK, which, if

dividends are not paid in any given year or DIVIDEND period, entitles the owner to the arrearage in subsequent years. Ordinarily, if the CERTIFICATE of Incorporation does not specify whether the stock is to be cumulative, the law will hold the preferred stock to be cumulative. See NONCUMULATIVE PREFERRED STOCK.

Cumulative Voting. A system of voting for directors of a CORPORATION under which each stockholder is entitled to a number of votes equal to the number of shares he or she owns multiplied by the number of directors to be elected. The stockholder may cast all the votes for one candidate—cumulate them—or distribute the votes among the candidates any way desired. This system enables the minority stockholders to elect one or more of the directors. The right to cumulative voting cannot be claimed unless provided for (1) by statute, (2) by the corporation's charter or bylaws, or (3) by contract among all the stockholders, provided the agreement is not otherwise illegal.

Curtesy. The right of the husband to enjoy during his life and after his wife's death any land that his wife might own during marriage, provided she had legitimate children born to her during the marriage. This is a COMMON LAW right that has largely been abolished by statute. See DOWER.

Custody of Children. The care and control of infants as determined by a court. The court's basic consideration when it gives orders and directions concerning the custody of children is the welfare of the particular child. Courts will often consult a child to find out with which parent the child prefers to live. A child may be taken away from a parent or legal guardian, a charitable agency or welfare commissioner, or even from one to whom the court itself had granted custody.

Customs. The government agency concerned with collecting duties and enforcing the rules and regulations that govern the export and import of merchandise. The United States Customs Service is under the jurisdiction of the Treasury Department; it maintains staffs in all American ports of entry and has representatives in many important foreign ports.

Imported goods must be "entered" upon arrival with customs officials either by the importer or his authorized agent, the broker, regardless of whether the goods are dutiable or duty free. *See also* CUSTOMS COURT.

Customs Court. A tribunal delegated to hear appeals in connection with the tolls and levies upon merchandise, exported or imported, that have been imposed by the customs appraisers and are payable by law.

Cy Pres Doctrine. (French for "as near as.") An ancient doctrine applicable to the construction of instruments in EQUITY, whereby the intention of the party making the instrument is carried out as nearly as possible when it is impossible to carry out the precise intention. The doctrine, although ancient, is especially useful in modern times as a device to render charitable trusts useful. For example, if funds left to a charitable trust are insufficient to carry out the provisions of the testamentary trust, the fund does not necessarily revert to the estate, but may be used for a charitable purpose similar to that provided for in the trust. The doctrine is not accepted in all states.

D

Daily Time Sheet. A record of the time the lawyer spends on particular tasks, kept for the purpose of arriving at an estimated cost of each job. Figure 1 illustrates a daily time sheet.

Many offices prefer to combine the daily time sheet with the diary. See figure 2.

Still another method of posting the time the lawyer spends for each job is the system used in keeping the *lawyer's diary*. Figure 3 shows a page from the lawyer's diary.

Damages. A monetary compensation that may be recovered in the courts by any person who has suffered loss or injury because of the unlawful act or NEGLIGENCE of another.

1. *General Damages.* Presumed by the law to have stemmed from the wrong because they necessarily result from the injury; they do not refer to the special character, condition, or circumstances of the plaintiff. General damages include compensation for physical injury, physical pain, and mental anguish.

2. *Special Damages.* The natural, but not the necessary, result of the injury. Unlike general damages, special damages can generally be computed exactly. In a negligence action they usually consist of reasonable amounts spent for hospital, medical, and related services.

Dead Freight. See FREIGHT.

Debentures. Bonds issued without security and therefore not protected by any specific LIEN upon property. They are simply the promise of the borrower to pay a certain sum of money at a stipulated time and place, with interest at a fixed rate. The bonds are issued under a trust indenture, which distinguishes them from ordinary notes. Debentures are issued by corporations that (1) have a relatively small percentage of tangible assets, which prevents them from issuing secured bonds, (2) have unquestionable credit ratings and can readily market unsecured bonds, or (3) have mortgaged all of their tangible assets and therefore must resort to debentures to raise funds.

Trust indentures under which debentures are issued usually contain provisions or restrictions designed to protect the investment of the unsecured bondholders. The most common types of provisions are (1) covenants regarding future mortgages or pledges of property, (2) restrictions against additional indebtedness, and (3) dividend restrictions while debentures are outstanding. See also DEED OF TRUST; CORPORATE MORTGAGE BONDS.

HALL and DOBB

DAILY SERVICE REPORT OF

Date

CLIENT	CASE	CHARACTER OF SERVICES	TIME	
			HOURS	TENTHS

Key CHARACTER OF SERVICES

TT, telephone to
TF, telephone from
LT, letter to
LF, letter from

SL, study of law
PF, preparation of facts
MT, memorandum to
MF, memorandum from

Ct. T, court trial
Ct. M, court motion
Ct. A, court argument
CW, conference with

Ex, examination of title
PP, passing papers
RP, recording papers
RT, reviewing title

Daily Time Sheet: Figure 1.

HOUR	PLACE	SUBJECT
9:00	Office	C. L. Schum - Drafting lease
10:00	Probate Court	Williams Estate - Hearing
11:30	Office	Conference re income tax
12:00	Office	Hugh Bailey - Auto accident
12:45	Biltmore Hotel	Luncheon with Clemens
2:30	Mathews' office	Community Chest Committee meeting
3:30	Office	Henry Fowler - Escrow agreement

HOUR	CASE NUMBER	✓	CLIENT	NATURE AND CLASSIFICATION	NEW	ESTIMATED FEE	TIME	CHARGE EXPENSE	FEE
8:00									
8:30									
9:00 9:30	3		C. L. Schum	Drafting lease			1		
10:00 10:30			Williams Estate	Hearing					
11:00									
11:30	4		Rogers	Conference re income tax			50		
12:00			Hugh Bailey	Auto accident	X	50	.75		
12:30									
12:45 1:00			Luncheon	Clemens - Biltmore					
1:30									
2:00									
2:30									
3:00				Community Chest					
3:30	3		Henry Fowler	Conference	2	200	1.25		
4:00									
4:30									
5:00									
5:30									
EVENING 9:00				Churchill Dinner - Waldorf					

Daily Time Sheet: Figure 2.

Daily time sheet combined with diary.

Saturday, APRIL 21   112th Day

9:45 Dept. 2 - King V. Smith - Trial

11:00 - Mr. S. A. Murray (Tr 7491)

(ax. - 7230 - chg Smith V. City)

4:30 - Harbor Committee Meeting

Last day to file Op. Br. - Allen V. City
Pay jury fee Deposit - Linn V. Fall

Client's Name and Address	Work Done	Time
King (Arthur L.) 207 Sunset Ave.	Briefing Trial	2 hrs 4 hrs

Daily Time Sheet: Figure 3.

Page from the lawyer's diary.

Decedent's Estate. The property left by a deceased person. See WILL; PROBATE; LETTERS OF ADMINIS- TRATION; LEGACY.

Declaratory Judgment. An edict of the COURT that simply states the rights of the parties or expresses an opinion on a question of law. For example, a party would want a *declaratory judgment* to determine who has TITLE in a piece of property when there is another claimant.

Decree. The judicial decision of a litigated cause by a court of EQUITY. See also JUDGMENT; INTERLOCUTORY DECREE.

Deed. A formal written instrument by which TITLE to REAL PROPERTY is conveyed from one person to another. (See also DEED OF TRUST.) The legal effect of the deed is to transfer ownership from the seller to the purchaser, taking away from the seller the use and enjoyment of the property and relieving the seller of its burdens. The deed is usually prepared by the seller's attorney, and is signed and delivered upon CLOSING TITLE.

The parties to a deed are the *grantor*, who conveys his or interest in the property, and the *grantee*, to whom the conveyance is made. The grantor is the seller, and the grantee is usually the purchaser, but not necessarily. The purchaser may buy the land for the grantee. Only the grantor signs the deed, unless the grantee makes special covenants.

1. *Bargain and Sale Deed.* A deed in general use for the transfer of title where there are no warranties made by the grantor. The deed transfers whatever interest the grantor has in the property at the time of its execution.

2. *Warranty Deed.* A deed under which the GRANTOR (seller) agrees that he or she will forever guarantee title to the premises conveyed. It assures that the grantor is the true owner and has the right to pass title; guarantees that there are no encumbrances on the property, such as a MORTGAGE or tax lien, except those that have been specifically mentioned; and guarantees that the GRANTEE will have quiet possession, that neither the grantee nor the grantee's heirs will be dispossessed because of defect of title. The grantor further agrees to

obtain and to give to the grantee and his or her successors any legal documents that may be necessary (such as a quitclaim from the heir of a deceased previous owner) to perfect the title. Most important, the grantor guarantees the title. If a flaw in the title should develop later, the grantee or the grantee's successor is entitled to recover up to the full value of the property at the time of the sale.

Figure 1 is a printed form for a Warranty Deed and figure 2 is an endorsed back.

3. *Quitclaim Deed.* A deed that merely releases the grantor's interest in the property and nothing further.

4. *Deed of Gift.* A deed of gift is given in consideration of the "love and affection that the grantor has for the grantee. A deed of gift passes TITLE as completely as a deed for which there is a monetary consideration.

5. *Statutory Deed.* A short form of deed approved by some states to save the space required for recording deeds. By statute, certain covenants and warranties are made part of the deed and, although not set forth in the deed, are binding on the grantor and his or her heirs. Since the statute is actually part of the deed and a state statute is not effective outside of the state enacting it, a statutory form of deed can be used only in the specific state that makes statutory provision for it.

See also RECORDING (of Deed).

6. *Fiduciary Deed.* A fiduciary deed may have a grantor as an executor, administrator, trustee, guardian, receiver, or commissioner. Some states permit a statutory form to be used, wherein the main difference between the fiduciary deed and a general warrant deed is that

the fiduciary must state his source of authority.

7. *Sheriff's Deed.* A deed usually prepared by the sheriff for real estate sold at public sale.

Tenancy by the entirety. See TENANCY BY THE ENTIRETY.

Contents of deed. Regardless of the type or form of deed, the secretary should be sure the instrument contains the following:

1. Date of execution.

2. Whether grantor is an individual, a partnership, or a corporation.

3. Full name of grantor who has FEE SIMPLE as determined by abstract, title insurance or deed, residence of grantor. Full description of grantor's office and authority if he or she is conveying in a representative capacity.

4. Marital status of grantor.

5. Full name of spouse if spouse must join in the conveyance.

6. Full name and residence of grantee.

7. Description of property. See LAND DESCRIPTION.

8. Whether deed is to be a warranty, bargain and sale, quitclaim, or gift deed. If printed form is used, the type of deed will be printed on the form. Printed forms come for corporation to individual, corporation to corporation and individual to corporation.

9. Consideration to be expressed in deed. Consideration is the price given for the property or the motive for giving it.

10. A recital of any MORTGAGE or other ENCUMBRANCE on the property. The statement of encumbrances, if any, follows the description of the property.

11. HABENDUM CLAUSE. States that the grantee is to have the property transferred to him or her.

12. COVENANTS. Promises made by the grantor and grantee. The most usual ones, such as the grantee's right to quiet enjoyment of the property, and the assurance that the grantor has the right to pass title, are printed in the forms for deeds. The lawyer will dictate any unusual covenants.

13. TESTIMONIUM CLAUSE. Closing clause immediately preceding the signature. The introductory words to the testimonium clause, *in witness whereof, in testimony whereof,* and the like, are usually typed in solid caps. The word following begins with the lower case unless it is a proper name. A comma usually follows the introductory words.

14. Names and official positions of officers signing and acknowledging deed, if grantor is a corporation.

Preparation of deed.

1. Make three copies—the original for the grantee, a copy for the grantor, and a copy for the office files.

2. Use LEGAL CAP, if a printed form is not used.

3. Remember the responsibility and distribution line (see TYPING Court Papers) at the top of the first page. (This goes on the office copy only of a printed form.)

4. Double-space.

5. Type the LAND DESCRIPTION.

6. Number all pages of typed deed.

7. If a printed form is used, be sure the "Z" appears after the land description. See "Z" Ruling, FORMS.

8. Make sure there are at least two lines of typing on the signature page.

WARRANTY DEED   Form 1001   Published by Tennessee Title Company

For and in consideration of the sum of $1.00 ....
- - - - - - - - - - - ONE AND NO/100 - - - - - - - - - - - - DOLLARS

cash in hand paid by the grantees herein, and other good and valuable considerations, the receipt
of which is hereby acknowledged,
We, John Albert Green and wife, Ellen Blake Green,

_____ have bargained and sold, and by these presents do transfer and convey
unto the said   ROBERT COLE BROWN and wife, MARY HOWARD BROWN

_____ heirs and assigns, a certain tract or parcel of land in Davidson County, State of
Tennessee, described as follows to wit:

Land in Davidson County, Tennessee, being Lot No. 26 on the Plan of the Resubdivision of
Part of Royal Oaks Subdivision, as of record in Book 1424, page 31, Register's Office for said
County.
Said Lot No. 26 fronts 165 feet on the northerly side of Sunnybrook Drive and runs back
271.3 feet on the easterly line and 262.8 feet on the westerly line, to a dead line in the rear,
measuring 182.8 feet thereon.

Being the same property conveyed to John Albert Green and wife, Ellen Blake Green, by deed
from Royal Highland Land Company, of record on book 2063, page 25, said Register's Office.

To have and to hold the said tract or parcel of land, with the appurtenances, estate, title and
interest thereto belonging to the said Robert Cole Brown and wife, Mary Howard Brown,   .
_____their_____heirs and assigns, forever.
And we do covenant with the said Robert Cole Brown and wife, Mary Howard Brown, that we are
lawfully seized and possessed of said land in fee simple; have a good right to convey it, and the same
is unencumbered.
And we, John Albert Green and wife, Ellen Blake Green

do further covenant and bind ourselves, our heirs and representatives, to warrant and forever
defend the title to the said land to the said Robert Cole Brown and wife, Mary Howard Brown,
their_____ heirs and assigns against the lawful claims of all persons, whomsoever.
    Witness our hands this 15th day of   December   , 19 ___

_____   *John Albert Green*

_____   *Ellen Blake Green*

STATE OF TENNESSEE
Davidson County

    Personally appeared before me_____ James D. White _____ , a Notary Public in and
for said County and State, the within named _____John Albert Green and wife,_____
Ellen Blake Green

the bargainor_s, with whom I am personally acquainted, and who acknowledged that they
executed the within instrument for the purposes therein contained. Witness my hand and official
seal at_____Nashville_____ , Tennessee, this 15th day of _____December_____ , 19 ___
Commission expires_____May 1, 19_____   *James D. White*
                                                        Notary Public

Deed: Figure 1. *Warranty deed*
from husband and wife.

```
┌─────────────────────────────────┐
│  ═══════════════════════════    │
│       WARRANTY DEED             │
│  ═══════════════════════════    │
│           FROM                  │
│   JOHN ALBERT GREEN and         │
│  wife, ELLEN BLAKE GREEN        │
│                                 │
│                                 │
│            TO                   │
│                                 │
│   ROBERT COLE BROWN and         │
│  wife, MARY HOWARD BROWN        │
│                                 │
│                                 │
│                                 │
│  ═══════════════════════════    │
│                                 │
│                                 │
│                                 │
│                                 │
│                                 │
│                                 │
│                                 │
│  ═══════════════════════════    │
│         Published by            │
│             ᛏᛖ                  │
│   TENNESSEE TITLE COMPANY       │
│     NASHVILLE, TENNESSEE        │
│         Zone Office             │
│  LAWYERS TITLE INSURANCE        │
│        CORPORATION              │
│     of Richmond, Virginia       │
│  ═══════════════════════════    │
│  HESSEY 10M 11-49               │
└─────────────────────────────────┘
```

Deed: Figure 2. *Back of warranty deed endorsed by husband and wife.*

9. Prepare signature line for the grantor. The grantee does not sign a deed except in special circumstances.

10. In the case of an individual grantor, type *L.S.* in caps at the end of the signature lines. In the case of a corporate grantor, be sure that the authorized officer, usually the corporate secretary, affixes the seal.

11. Type witness lines and ATTESTATION clause when required.

12. Prepare certificate of ACKNOWLEDGMENT.

13. Collate (see TYPING).

14. Check and double-check spelling of names.

15. Have someone compare the land description with you.

16. Endorse back of printed form. If deed is typed, prepare LEGAL BACK.

17. Arrange for the grantor to come in and sign the deed and acknowledge it.

18. Get the lawyer's approval of the instrument *before* it is signed. Have the grantor sign the original only. Make sure that the grantor's signature agrees with name typed in the deed.

19. Have the deed notarized. If the secretary is the notary, she should take the acknowledgment.

20. Affix documentary stamps if they are required by the state.

21. Conform copies to original upon completion of signature and acknowledgment.

22. Get the lawyer's approval and then have the deed recorded. The secretary makes a notation that the deed is to be returned to the lawyer's office. (The secretary to the lawyer for the grantee attends to the recording.)

23. When the deed is returned by the recorder, send it to the grantee with a covering letter, or have the grantee call for it.

Deed of Trust. An instrument in use in some of the states and the District of Columbia by which legal title to real estate is conveyed to a *third party* to be held in trust for a lender until the debt secured by the instrument is paid. It is, in effect, a MORTGAGE with three parties: the borrower, the lender, and the trustee. This security instrument is also known as TRUST DEED, but the term *trust deed* is more generally applied to the security for a corporate bond issue.

De Facto Corporation. An organization started in good faith by people who attempted to organize a CORPORATION under a valid statute and have failed in some minor particular, but have thereafter exercised corporate powers. Failure to have incorporators' signatures on applications for CERTIFICATE of Incorporation notarized is an illustration of noncompliance with statutory requirements. The decided weight of authority is that a de facto corporation can do everything that a properly organized corporation can do. See also DE JURE CORPORATION.

Defamation. See LIBEL AND SLANDER.

Default. The failure to perform what is required by duty or law.

1. In litigation, a plaintiff or defendant is in default when he does not appear at court within the time prescribed by law to prosecute his claim or prosecute his defense. The JUDGMENT entered when the defendant does not appear is called a *judgment by default.* When a plaintiff defaults he or she may be nonsuited.

2. A *borrower* is in default when he fails to meet his obligation to pay. If security has been given for the debt and the borrower defaults, the lender has a right to look to that security for the satisfaction of the debt. See BOND AND MORTGAGE; PLEDGE.

Defeasance Clause. A provision in a MORTGAGE that if the indebtedness is paid in accordance with the terms of the mortgage agreement, the mortgage will be null and void.

165

Defendant. In a lawsuit, the party against whom action is brought. The defendant is the person required to make answer in the action or suit. See also PARTIES TO AN ACTION.

Deferred Payments. Payments extended over a specified period; put off to a future date. (*Installment payments* are a series of equal deferred payments.) See also INSTALLMENT CONTRACT.

De Jure Corporation. A CORPORATION that has complied with the letter of the law governing incorporating procedure. A de jure corporation is distinguished from a DE FACTO CORPORATION in that a de facto corporation has done something that less than fully complies with the state's incorporating procedure. A de jure corporation exists in law as well as in fact.

Demand. A formal requisition or request that the party under obligation do a particular thing specified under a claim of right on the part of the person making the request. For example, when property is sold to be paid for on delivery, a *demand* would have to be made before an action for failure to deliver the goods might be instigated.

Demand for Bill of Particulars. Under the federal rules the demand for bill of particulars was abolished, leaving the liberal discovery rules to accomplish this purpose. In jurisdictions that retain the motion, it is a demand by one of the PARTIES TO AN ACTION for more definite information from the other party. A BILL of Particulars is usually desired when PLEADINGS have been served that do not give *details* about time, place, or circumstance of what is to be proved. For example, some of the particulars that may be required in a personal injury action are date and time of day of the occurrence, its approximate location, a general statement of the acts constituting the NEGLIGENCE claimed, a statement of injuries, and medical expenses. A party demands this statement of details within a specified time. He or she may request from the court an order for the bill of particulars, in which case the procedure is like that in any other MOTION. The demand for the bill of particulars is addressed to opposing counsel. No VERIFICATION of a demand is necessary.

Parts of demand for bill of particulars. The demand for bill of particulars consists of the following parts: (1) caption; (2) salutation; (3) introduction; (4) details demanded; (5) date line; (6) signature of attorney demanding the bill; (7) name and address of attorney on whom demand is made.

How to prepare the demand for bill of particulars. Usually the lawyer dictates the demand for bill of particulars. Unless otherwise instructed, follow figure 1 for style.

1. Make an original for the court (some courts require an extra copy), a copy to serve on each opposing counsel, and a copy for the file.

2. The caption is the same as that on the complaint; the title of the case may be shortened.

3. The salutation is to opposing counsel. It is typed in solid caps, and reads:

SUPREME COURT OF THE STATE OF NEW YORK

COUNTY OF RICHMOND

ROY M. LONDON and JANET
R. LONDON,

       Plaintiffs,   :   DEMAND FOR BILL
              :   OF PARTICULARS

  -against-

THE WILSHIRE CORPORATION,
and TOYLAND, INC.

       Defendants. :

SIRS:

   PLEASE TAKE NOTICE that the above named defendants hereby demand that the plaintiffs serve upon the attorneys for the defendants within ten days a Bill of Particulars showing in detail the following:

   (1) The date and the time of day of the occurrence as closely as the plaintiffs can fix it.

   (2) Its location, identifying as closely as possible the display counters and the place on the floor between them as described in paragraph FIFTH of the complaint.

(continued on following page)

(continued from preceding page)

(3) A statement of the injuries and a description of those claimed to be permanent.

Dated, New York, August 23, 19—,

Respectfully yours,

SCHUBERT & LEE
Attorneys for Defendants,
99 Broad Street
New York, NY 10004

TO:

BRUCE & MURRAY
Attorneys for Plaintiffs,
117 Madison Avenue
New York, NY 10016

Demand for Bill of Particulars:
Figure 1

SIRS: (if to an all-male law firm)
SIR: (if to one male lawyer)
or TO . . . . ,
ATTORNEY FOR . . . . :

In some jurisdictions the demand for bill of particulars is addressed to the party *and* his or her attorney.

4. Number consecutively and indent the details demanded.

5. Type the dateline at the left margin, three spaces beneath the last numbered paragraph.

6. Type a line for signature of attorney demanding the bill. Beneath the signature line, indicate the party he or she represents.

7. Type name and address of counsel to whom the demand is addressed at the left margin, several spaces beneath the signature. If the attorney's name is given in the salutation, this is not necessary.

8. There is no verification to a demand for bill of particulars.

9. Endorse legal back, if one is used, for original and all copies except the office copy.

10. Collate and staple in backs.

What to do about the demand for bill of particulars.

1. Prepare the demand for bill of particulars.

2. Ask attorney to sign.

3. See that copy is served on opposing counsel.

4. Be sure that receipt or certificate of service is endorsed on back of original.

5. Conform the office copy.

6. *Make diary entry* of date bill of particulars must be served.

7. File original in court.

8. Make entry in suit register of service and filing.

9. The secretary to the attorney on whom the demand is served makes a notation on back of the copy of date and hour of service. *Enter in diary date by which bill of particulars must be served.* Also make entry in suit register.

Demise. Used most often as a synonym for "let" in a lease; a conveyance of an estate in REAL PROPERTY, usually for a term of years.

Demise Charter. *See* CHARTER-PARTY.

Demurrage. In ADMIRALTY law, the money allowed to a shipowner whose vessel has been held by a charterer or shipper beyond the number of days allowed by the CHARTER-PARTY or BILL of Lading for loading and unloading or for sailing. The term is sometimes used to refer to the period during which demurrage accrues.

Demurrer. A pleading that raises an issue of law, not of fact. It objects to defects that are apparent from the pleading itself. Insteady of denying facts alleged in the COMPLAINT, as an ANSWER does, a demurrer to a complaint takes exception to the complaint because it is *insufficient on some legal ground*. In effect, the demurrer declares that even if everything stated in the complaint were true, it does not state facts sufficient to constitute a CAUSE OF ACTION. For example, a defendant may demur to a

complaint on the ground that the plaintiff does not have legal capacity to sue. The defendant may also demur to the plaintiff's reply. But a demurrer is not a pleading to be used by the defendant only. A plaintiff may demur to the defendant's answer, or to a cross-complaint. Each cause of action (count), or each defense, is demurred to separately. Many states have abolished demurrers, but they are still permitted as a pleading in some states. Under the Federal Rules of Civil Procedure, the demurrer is replaced by a motion to dismiss. If the motion to dismiss is denied, the case simply goes to trial on the merits.

A demurrer consists of the following parts:

1. Caption
2. Introduction
3. Grounds of demurrer, each stated separately
4. Signature of attorney
5. Attorney's certificate of good faith when required
6. Points and authorities

The statutes name the grounds for demurrer. These grounds usually include, among others, the following: (1) that the court has no jurisdiction; (2) that the plaintiff has no legal capacity to sue; (3) that the complaint (or answer) is ambiguous, unintelligible, uncertain. A demurrer is supported by legal points and authorities sustaining the grounds of demurrer.

How to prepare the demurrer. The statement of a specific ground for demurrer usually follows a standard form, with which the secretary quickly becomes familiar. Although the lawyer ordinarily will dictate the demurrer, he or she might ask the secretary to follow a form. Unless otherwise instructed, type the demurrer in a style similar to that illustrated by figures 1 and 2. Figure 3 illustrates the points and authorities supporting a demurrer.

1. Type on the size paper specified by the court.

2. Make an original for the court, a copy for the opposing party's counsel, and a copy for your file.

3. The caption is the same as that on the complaint, but the title of the case may be shortened.

4. The index number must appear on the demurrer, at the right of the box.

5. The title of the document is "Demurrer to Complaint," or "Demurrer to Answer," as the case may be.

6. Number the grounds of demurrer to each cause of action or count (or each defense) consecutively, beginning with "I."

7. Type a line for the attorney's signature.

8. There is no verification because a demurrer does not allege or aver facts.

9. Type the attorney's certificate of good faith in jurisdictions where it is required by the court rules.

10. Begin the points and authorities on a separate page.

11. Endorse a legal back for each copy except your file copy. The endorsement is similar to the endorsement on the back of the answer in that it shows the index number and the name of opposing counsel on whom a copy of the demurrer is served.

What to do about a demurrer.

1. Prepare the demurrer and points and authorities.

2. Staple original and copies in endorsed legal backs, if used.

3. Get attorney to sign original and copies, and also certificate of good faith if required.

4. Serve copy on attorney for opposing party.

5. See that admission of service is endorsed on back of original.

6. Conform the office copy.

7. File original in court, with fee if required.

8. Make entry in SUIT REGISTER of service and filing.

9. The secretary to the counsel *on whom the demurrer is served* makes a notation on the back of that copy of the date and hour the demurrer was served and an entry in the SUIT REGISTER. See also PLEADINGS.

Depletion. An exhaustion or gradual reduction of an asset. Depletion in the federal income tax law applies to the exhaustion of assets such as oil, gas, timber, mineral deposits, and other natural resources. To compensate for the wasting away of the taxpayer's assets, an annual depletion deduction is allowed when computing INCOME for the federal INCOME TAX. See also DEPRECIATION.

Deponent. A person making an AFFIDAVIT.

Depositary, Depository. *Depositary* applies to the person or authority entrusted with something for safekeeping. It may also be used to apply to the place where something is deposited or stored. *Depository* applies only to the place where something is deposited or stored.

Deposition. Testimony of a witness under oath taken in writing to be introduced at a trial, hearing, investigation, or at arbitration proceedings.

Many occasions arise when the secretary in a law office is required to take the testimony of a person under oath. The

8   IN THE SUPERIOR COURT OF THE STATE OF CALIFORNIA

9   IN AND FOR THE COUNTY OF LOS ANGELES

10

11   DIANE CARTER,   )
)   No. 14788
12   Plaintiff,   )
)
13   vs.   )   DEMURRER
)   TO
14   WILLIAM FROST,   )   COMPLAINT
)
15   Defendant.   )
)
16   _____)

17   Comes now the above named defendant, WILLIAM

18   FROST, and demurs to Count One of the Complaint on file herein

19   upon the following grounds and each of them:

20   I

21   That Count One of said complaint fails to state

22   facts sufficient to constitute a cause of action against

23   this defendant.

24   II

25   That Count One of said complaint fails to state

26   facts sufficient to constitute a cause of action against

27   this defendant in this, that it affirmatively appears there-

28   from that the purported cause or causes of action therein

29   set forth are barred by the provisions of §§ 339(1), 343

Demurrer: Figure 1. *First page.*

1
2
3
4
5
6
7
8
9
10
11
12
13
14
15
16
17
18
19
20
21

IV

That Count One of said complaint is ambiguous for each of the reasons heretofore set forth for its uncertainty.

That Count One of said complaint is unintelligible for each of the reasons heretofore set forth for its uncertainty.

DEMURRER TO COUNT TWO

Defendant demurs to Count Two of said complaint upon the following grounds and each of them:

I

(Continue as in the demurrer to Count One.)

WHEREFORE, this demurring defendant prays that this demurrer be sustained without leave to amend and that he be dismissed with his costs.

_____
W.H. SAMUELS
Attorney for Defendant

I hereby certify that this demurrer is filed in good faith; that it is not filed for the purpose of delay, and in my opinion the grounds are well taken.

_____
W.H. SAMUELS
Attorney for Defendant

Demurrer: Figure 2. *Last page.*

POINTS AND AUTHORITIES

POINT ONE

A PARENT IS NOT BOUND TO COMPENSATE THE OTHER

PARENT FOR THE VOLUNTARY SUPPORT OF HIS CHILD WITHOUT AN

AGREEMENT FOR COMPENSATION.

Civil Code § 208

POINT TWO

AS BETWEEN THE PARENTS OF MINOR CHILDREN, THEIR

RESPECTIVE OBLIGATIONS OF SUPPORT OF EACH OTHER AND TO THE

MINOR CHILDREN MUST BE DETERMINED IN THE PROCEEDING FOR

DIVORCE, AND IN THE ABSENCE OF SOME SPECIFIC PROVISION TO

THAT EFFECT, THE FATHER WHO HAS BEEN DEPRIVED OF THE

CUSTODY OF THE MINOR CHILDREN IS NOT OBLIGATED FOR THEIR

SUPPORT.

Calegaris v. Calegaris, 4 Cal. App. 264, 87 Pac. 561;

Ex Parte Miller, 109 Cal. 643, 42 Pac. 428;

Lewis v. Lewis, 174 Cal. 336, 163 Pac. 42.

Respectfully submitted,

_____

W.H. SAMUELS
Attorney for Defendant

Demurrer: Figure 3. *Points and authorities supporting demurrer.*

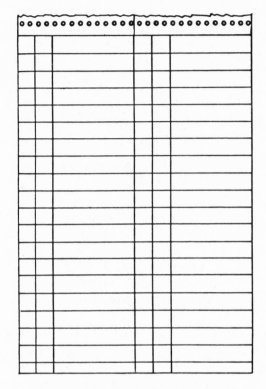

Deposition: Figure 1. *Notebook
ruled for question and answer
testimony.*

testimony is usually in question and answer form and is referred to as a *deposition*. Counsel for both sides are present at the examination.

The secretary takes the testimony verbatim and transcribes it verbatim, without editing even glaring grammatical errors. If the exchange of questions and answers is too rapid and the secretary falls behind in her notes, she should raise her left hand as a signal to the attorney conducting the examination to slow down. It is essential that every word of the testimony be reported accurately.

Depositions are often tape-recorded, but it is desirable to have a stenographer record the proceedings at the same time. Occasionally, depositions are video-taped for use in court, but a written record is also usually made.

To take testimony, use a notebook that has a vertical line down the center of the page. Divide each half of the page into three columns by lightly penciled vertical lines in the positions shown in figure 1. (It is assumed you customarily write only to the dividing line, treating each column as a separate page.)

Notes of the questions by the examining attorney are placed on the page in the same position as notes are ordinarily placed. Each question begins at the extreme left of the page, extends to the center line, and, if it takes more than one line, continues at the extreme left of the next horizontal line.

Notes of the witness' answers begin at the right of the first vertical line and extend to the center line. If more than one line is necessary, the answer continues on the next horizontal line at the right of the first vertical line. The witness' answers never extend to the left of that line.

Notes of the interpolations by opposing counsel begin at the right of the second vertical line and extend to the center line. If more than one line is necessary, the interpolation continues on the next horizontal line at the right of the second vertical line and extend to the center line. if more than one line is necessary, the interpolation continues on the next horizontal line at the right of the second vertical line. Remarks by opposing counsel never extend to the left of that line.

Notes of actions that must be indicated, such as marking exhibits for identification, are enclosed in brackets, thus distinguishing them from notes of the testimony. They are written in the same positions as notes of the questions by the examining attorney.

Notes are written on the right half of the page in the same manner as on the left half, the center vertical line representing the left edge.

The preceding method of arranging the shorthand notes on the page of the notebook increases your speed by eliminating the writing of "Q" and "A," punctuation after the questions and answers, and the name of the opposing counsel when he makes an objection. It also facilitates reading back.

Figure 2 illustrates a transcription of testimony.

Court stenographers. Some attorneys use court stenographers for depositions and do not call on their secretaries for this purpose. Many of the court stenog-

raphers use shorthand machines (Stenotype), which are much speedier. They will furnish a transcribed copy of the deposition with as many additional copies as desired.

Depreciation. The decline in value of an asset caused by wear, tear, and obsolescence. A corporation may deduct depreciation as an expense on its federal income tax return. An individual may take a deduction for depreciation of income-producing property from his or her adjusted gross income. (See INCOME.) The depreciation allowance that is taken during the useful life of the property should be part of a reasonably consistent plan (not necessarily the same rate each year) authorized under federal income tax law. The total depreciation deductions may not exceed the difference between the cost (or other basis) and the salvage value of the property.

Derivative Action. A suit brought by a shareholder on behalf of the CORPORATION to compel management to act properly for the protection of the corporation's rights. The relief, if granted, is in favor of the corporation. The suit may involve restitution from the directors who have misappropriated assets, or who, by their NEGLIGENCE have brought a loss upon the corporation. Before a stockholder may maintain a derivative suit, he or she must make a demand to the BOARD OF DIRECTORS that they act properly and redress any wrongs, and the directors must refuse to do so. See also REPRESENTATIVE ACTION.

Descriptive Word Index. An alphabetical list of topics with references to the place these topics are found in

WALTER V. KING

DIRECT EXAMINATION BY MR. JONES:

Q. Mr. King, what is your full name?

A. Walter V. King.

Q. What is your address? A. 226 Haskell Avenue, Van Nuys, California 91406.

Q. Where are you employed, sir? A. The Swanson Company, 25 Central Street, Van Nuys, California 91406.

Q. How long have you been employed there? A. Since 1970.

Q. What is your position at Swanson's? A. Salesman.

Q. Do you know Mrs. Lola Miller, the plaintiff in this action? A. Not too well, I know her as a customer.

Q. In April 1981, did you see her when she brought in the necklace to Swanson's? A. No.

Q. What officer or employee did see her? A. Another salesman.

Q. What is his name? A. Fred Rochefort.

Q. You don't know what he said to her concerning the work to be done?

MR. WOOD: I object to the form of that question.

A. No, only from our records.

Q. What records do you have with you that show the delivery of the necklace to Swanson's?

(continued on following page)

(continued from preceding page)

[Mr. King produces record and Mr. Jones studies it.]

MR. JONES: I offer that in evidence.

MR. WOOD: Can I see that?

MR. JONES: Certainly, I thought you had already seen it.

MR. WOOD: It should not be admitted in evidence but should be marked for identification.

[Marked Plaintiff's Exhibit 1 for Identification.]

Q. Mr. King, with reference to plaintiff's exhibit marked Exhibit 1 for identification on your examination, do you recognize the handwriting in pencil on the notations on that exhibit? A. Yes, sir, that's Mr. Rochefort's.

MR. JONES: I have no further questions at this time. Mr. Julio, would you like to cross-examine?

Deposition: Figure 2.
Transcription of question and answer testimony.

multivolume reference works such as AMERICAN DIGEST SYSTEM and CORPUS JURIS SECUNDUM SYSTEM.

Desertion. A voluntary separation from a spouse without justification and with the intention of not returning. In some states, desertion is a ground for DIVORCE; in others, for SEPARATION. The courts hold that a justified absence does not constitute desertion. As an example, a wife is justified in leaving her husband's home if she fears bodily injury from him. This is not an act of desertion even though she does not intend to return to him. Desertion is sometimes also known as ABANDONMENT.

Devise. A gift of real property by WILL. One who receives a devise is a *devisee.* See also LEGACY.

Diary. See REMINDERS.

Dictum. An opinion expressed by a court is not necessary in deciding the question before the court. When, in addition, such opinion does not relate to the question before the court, it is called *obiter dictum* (Latin for "remark by the way"). Dicta carry legal weight in courts deciding subsequent questions but not to the extent that court decisions do. Court decisions are binding precedents; the dicta expressed in the opinion are not.

Digest (Law). An index arranged by subject matter to the rules of law raised or discussed in reported cases. A digest is the most important and necessary single tool of the lawyer for getting at the law as stated in judicial opinions.

The digest is a collection of separate paragraphs, each of which is related to the others only because they belong in the same subject grouping. There is no editorial comment on the case, no statement as to jurisdictional rules, historical developments, majority and minority views. Each rule is there on its own. The lawyer must be constantly on the alert, therefore, to the law's changes, both by decision and statute.

Digests vary in scope. The AMERICAN DIGEST SYSTEM, covering all printed opinions in all American jurisdictions, from 1658 to date, is the most comprehensive.

Dilatory Plea (Plea in Abatement). A plea constituting a defense that simply delays or defeats the present action, leaving the cause unsettled, for example, a challenge to jurisdiction. A plea in abatement does not go to the merits and has largely disappeared in modern practice.

Direct Evidence. Sworn testimony by a person that he or she saw the acts done, or heard the words spoken, that

are in question and have to be proven.

On the other hand, *circumstantial evidence* consists of facts introduced that tend to prove indirectly a point in dispute. For example, a person's reputation for honesty or dishonesty may be shown when he or she is on trial for LARCENY.

Direct Examination. The first interrogation or examination of a witness by the attorney for the party on whose behalf the witness is called. Direct examination is followed by CROSS-EXAMINATION, which is conducted by the adverse party, or ADVERSARY.

Directed Verdict. A verdict returned by the jury at the discretion of the trial judge. In civil actions, either party may receive a directed verdict. In criminal actions, there can be a directed verdict of acquittal, but not a directed verdict of guilty.

Director. See BOARD OF DIRECTORS.

Directors' Meetings. Formal meetings or assemblies of the individual directors of a CORPORATION for the purpose of taking joint action on business of the corporation. The BOARD OF DIRECTORS, acting as a body, has sole authority to manage the corporation in those matters not reserved for action by stockholders. The stockholders cannot take this authority from the board and give it to an individual.

Notice of directors' meetings. Follow the provisions of the BYLAWS in sending notices of meetings to directors.

Even if notice of a regular meeting is not required by the bylaws, it is advisable to notify the directors of the meeting. If a special meeting is to be called, telephone or telegraph the directors to determine whether the time is convenient for all of them. Send a written notice after the time of the meeting is definitely fixed. The list of the directors that is kept in the current meeting folder should be tabulated, with columns showing the date each was notified, the date a follow-up notice was sent, and the replies.

Notices of directors' meetings are usually typewritten on the corporation's letterhead. Printing, mimeographing, or photocopying the notice on cards or paper slips, with blanks for the date, time, and place of the meeting, is a timesaving expedient. A light stock for card notices is preferable, since heavy stock is not suitable for insertion in the typewriter to fill in necessary information.

The notice is sent in the name of the corporate secretary. It should specify the date, the place, and the hour at which the meeting is to be held. It is advisable, although not obligatory unless required by statute or bylaw, for the notice of a special meeting to state the purpose for which it is to be held.

Quorum at directors' meeting. A directors' meeting cannot be held unless a QUORUM is present. Consult the bylaws for the number of directors necessary to constitute a quorum. A quorum at a directors' meeting differs from a quorum at a stockholders' meeting in that the representation is based upon the number of directors and not upon the amount of stock owned by them.

If you learn that a quorum will not be present, telephone those directors who expect to attend and arrange, with approval of the person calling the meeting,

to have the meeting postponed. This is particularly important if the directors are coming from a distance.

A director cannot give a PROXY for a directors' meeting. But corporate action may be taken without a formal directors' meeting when written consent is obtained from all or a majority of the directors.

Preservation of notice. Keep a copy of every notice of meeting, with the date of mailing noted on it. If the notice has been published in the newspapers, keep a clipping of the published notice and the name of the publication and dates of publication.

The agenda. The *agenda* consists of an itemized list of matters to be brought up at a meeting. The secretary lists them from the accumulated material in the current meeting folder. The agenda should follow the order of business as set forth in the bylaws.

Here is a typical agenda prepared for a director's meeting:

1. *Read minutes of last meeting.* (Attach a typewritten copy of the minutes of the previous meeting to the corporate secretary's copy of the agenda.)

2. *Submit the following statements:* (Here enumerate the reports of officers and committees to be presented to the meeting. Copies of the reports may be attached to the agenda.)

3. *Adopt resolution approving minutes of executive committee meetings.* (If minutes are long, copies may be made and attached to the agenda.)

4. *Business of the meeting.* (Here enumerate business to be acted upon indicating each item by a summary of the resolution that is required.)

Begin preparation of the agenda several days before the meeting. Have it completely in order the evening before the meeting. Prepare a copy for each director. Attach to the agenda the exhibits, supporting papers, reports, and the like that contain the information necessary to supply the groundwork for discussion.

Reservation and preparation of the meeting room. If a meeting is to be held in a room that is used for other purposes, notify the person who is responsible for the room to have it available at the time of the meeting. When entering the date of the meeting in the corporation's calendar, also enter at an earlier date a reminder to reserve the room. This should be done in ample time to avoid conflict, the time of the advance notice depending upon the demand for the room.

In preparing the room for the meeting, have it dusted, properly heated, and ventilated. See that sufficient costumers and coat hangers are available. Provide stationery, memorandum pads, pen and ink, and pencils for each person who is expected to attend the meeting. Have a supply of clips, pins, rubber bands on the table, and put an ashtray and matches at each place.

Directors' fees. The fee payable to directors for attendance at a meeting is usually fixed by resolution adopted by the board of directors. When preparation for the meeting is the lawyer's responsibilty, payment of the fees might be his or her responsibility also. In this case, arrange with the treasurer of the corporation to have the money at the meeting. If any money is left over because of nonattendance, return it to the treasurer. Give the money to the directors after the meeting, preferably enclosed in an envelope.

Material to take to meetings. Take the following materials to directors' and stockholders' meetings:

1. Pamphlet copy of the corporation laws of the state in which the corpo-

ration is organized;

2. Copy of the CERTIFICATE of Incorporation, with marginal notations of amendments and copies of them;

3. Copy of the bylaws, with marginal notations of amendments and copies of them;

4. Separate sheet for order of business;

5. Rules and regulations of the corporation, if any, governing the conduct of meetings;

6. Proof of the mailing of notices of the meeting and, where necessary, of publication;

7. The original call for the meeting, and if there has been a demand for a call, the original of the demand;

8. The minute book;

9. The corporate seal;

10. Current papers pertaining to the meeting;

11. Blank affidavits, oaths, and the like.

Directory of Post Offices. A manual that lists the post office and zip code number of every city or town in the United States that has a post office. However, the most valuable feature of this manual is that it gives the county in which each post office is located. This may be used in typing acknowledgments on deeds which will be acknowledged out of the community in which the law office is located. The manual is sold by the United States Government Printing Office, Washington, D.C. 20402. Zip code directories are also published by commercial organizations and sold through bookstores and by mail.

Disbarment. Expulsion of a lawyer from the legal profession or from the bar of a particular court. Although the disbarment of an attorney is not a conviction for crime, disbarment may result from such a conviction.

Discharge of Contract. The release of the parties to a contract from the obligations under it. Contracts may be discharged by the following methods: (1) *Performance,* or the carrying out of the terms of the contract. (2) *Agreement.* The parties may agree to discharge one another from further liability under the contract. There must be sufficient consideration for the agreement. (3) *Impossibility of performance.* When a contract is based on an implied condition that certain factors shall continue to exist and performance is impossible, the contract is discharged. (4) *Operation of law.* A change in the law in effect at the time the contract was made may bring about a discharge of the contract, or a law itself may operate as a discharge. Thus, a contract to build a garage on a certain site would be discharged by a zoning ordinance forbidding the erection of a garage within that zone. (5) *Breach.* If one party breaches a contract the other may be discharged. (See BREACH of Contract.)

Disclosure. See PATENT.

Discovery. A procedure designed to obtain facts known by the defendant, or referred to in papers in his possession. In general, either party may obtain discovery about any matter that is not privileged and that is relevant to the subject matter involved in the pending action. Even information that may be inadmissible at trial may be discoverable if it appears that the information will lead to admissible evidence. Parties may obtain discovery by DEPOSITIONS, written INTERROGATORIES, production of documents, physical and mental examinations and requests for admissions.

Discovery and inspection. A procedure whereby an attorney may obtain information contained in books, papers, documents, photographs, or other articles of property that are under control of the adverse party. This procedure is extremely helpful in preparing a case for pleading or for trial.

Dishonor. Refusal to pay a NEGOTIABLE INSTRUMENT when due. Notice of dishonor is usually given to endorsers and drawers, who, in addition to the maker, are liable on the instrument. Notice of dishonor may be given orally or in writing. If it is not given, endorsers and drawers are discharged from liability. See also PROTEST.

Dismissal. 1. An order or judgment finally disposing of an action, suit, motion, and so on by sending it out of court, although without a trial of issues involved. Dismissal of MOTION is a denial of the motion; dismissal of an APPEAL is a confirmation of the JUDGMENT of the lower court.

2. A release or discharge from employment.

Disorderly Conduct. A term of indefinite meaning (except when occasionally defined in statutes), but signifying generally any behavior that is contrary to law and tends to cause a BREACH of the Peace or to shock the public morality. One who commits a breach of the peace is guilty of disorderly conduct, but not all disorderly conduct is necessarily a breach of the peace. Soliciting by a prostitute is an example of disorderly conduct that is not a breach of the peace.

District Courts. See AMERICAN COURT SYSTEM.

Divided Damages Rule. A doctrine developed by ADMIRALTY that divides DAMAGES equally when two vessels collide and both are at fault. Most of the leading maritime nations have adhered to an international convention, the Brussels Collision Convention of 1910, under which damages are proportioned in accordance with the party's degree of fault, that is, a party 20 percent at fault bears 20 percent of the resulting loss and the party 80 percent at fault would be taxed for 80 percent of the loss. Under the COMMON LAW rule, recovery would be barred to both parties because of each one's CONTRIBUTORY NEGLIGENCE.

Dividend. That portion of the profits and surplus funds of a CORPORATION that has actually been set aside by a valid act of the corporation for distribution among the stockholders of record on a fixed day, in proportion to their holdings. The declaration of a dividend and the fixing of the amount, time, and terms of payment rest generally in the discretion of the BOARD OF DIRECTORS.

Divorce. The legal separation of husband and wife, founded on matrimonial wrong, by the JUDGMENT of a court dissolving the marriage. A divorce may be granted by the state where the parties have their legal DOMICILE. A decree of divorce must be given full faith and credit in every other state. There has been much abuse in divorce practice because of the different standards in each state about what constitutes grounds for divorce. Fraudulent claims of domicile

are often made to obtain a divorce in a state with less strict standards.

No-fault divorce. Since 1969 some 32 legislatures have passed statutes that provide for the dissolution of a marriage without regard to the fault of the parties. *The court must find* that the underlying relationship of the spouses to each other has broken down to the extent that a marriage exists in name only and that there appears to be no hope of reconciliation. The statutes vary widely in their terminology, but they basically provide for a legal dissolution of the marriage upon a finding by the court that the marriage is no longer viable. The statutes shift the inquiry of the court from a determination of the relative "fault" of the parties to an examination of the status of the marriage itself, thus the popular term *no-fault divorce.* The idea is to replace the concept of "fault" and substitute marriage failure or "irretrievable breakdown" as a basis for a decree dissolving a marriage. (*Am.Jur. 2d Desk Book,* item 121, gives the statutory grounds for divorce in the various states.)

Docket (Court). A formal record of all the important acts done in court in the conduct of each case from its beginning to its end. *Trial docket* is the name sometimes given to the list of causes set to be tried at a specified term and prepared by the clerks for use of the court and bar. See also CLERK OF THE COURT, Permanent Record Book.

Docket Call. The time when the judge reviews all cases filed and sets a time for hearing each case, if it is ready for trial.

Docket Number. *See* CLERK OF THE COURT, Index System.

Domestic Corporation. A CORPORATION doing business in a state in which it was incorporated. *See also* FOREIGN CORPORATION; ALIEN CORPORATION; STATE OF INCORPORATION.

Domicile. That place where a person has his or her true and permanent home and to which, whenever the person is absent, he or she has the intention of returning. People who go away temporarily on business or vacation do not change their domiciles. A person can have only one domicile at any one time. Domicile is important for purposes of taxation and JURISDICTION. *See also* RESIDENCE; VENUE.

Dominant Estate (Tenement). Where the owners of one estate are entitled to the beneficial use of another's property. Often the beneficial use is in the nature of an EASEMENT, so the dominant estate has a right of easement in the servient estate.

Donee. The recipient of a GIFT or LEGACY. Also one who is given a POWER OF APPOINTMENT.

Donor. One who gives or makes a GIFT or LEGACY or confers a POWER of appointment.

Double Jeopardy. The situation where a person is twice put in danger of punishment for committing the same offense. The Fifth Amendment bars a second prosecution where a party has already been put in jeopardy. For a plea of double jeopardy to be valid, the offense charged in the second indictment (see GRAND JURY INDICTMENT) must be the same as that charged in the first, and both prosecutions must take place within the same JURISDICTION. *See also* BILL (of Rights).

Dower. An allowance the law gives a widow from the real estate of her deceased husband and for her support and the care of the children. Whether or not a widow is entitled to dower depends on the law of the state where the real estate is situated. *See* CURTESY.

Dower by Common Law. The ordinary kind of dower in English and American law, consisting of a life interest in one-third of the lands the husband or wife was seized in fee at any time during the coverture. The dower interest must be released by the spouse signing the Warranty Deed if the real estate is conveyed to a new party or the title is defective to the new party.

Drawee. One to whom a check directs a request to pay. Usually the bank is the drawee, the person writing the check is the DRAWER, and the person to whom the sum of money is to be paid is the payee.

Drawer. One who executes a check directing a request to pay. (See DRAWEE.)

Due Care. In tort law, a term used to indicate the standard of care (legal duty) one owes to others. NEGLIGENCE is the failure to use due care.

Due Process of Law. Provisions in the Fifth and Fourteenth Amendments to the Constitution that prohibit the federal government and states from depriving any person of life, liberty, or property without *due process of law.* The clauses have been interpreted by the courts as protecting the individual from arbitrary government activity and the unreasonable use of POLICE POWER.

Dun & Bradstreet, Inc. An agency that gathers and distributes credit information about persons and firms engaged in all lines of trade, in contradistinction to special agencies that limit their fields of operation to special trades.

Dun & Bradstreet "rates" a business on the basis of information gathered by reporters and correspondents about the owners and managers, giving consideration to character and ability to make good on obligations. The ratings cover capital and credit. They are condensed conclusions that show, by means of symbols, (1) the range of a concern's estimated financial strength, and (2) its grade of credit, reflecting past record, ability, and business prospects. Letters, from *Aa* to *L*, denote the estimated financial strength; numbers, from *A1* to *E*, denote the composite credit appraisal.

Duplicate Original. See TYPING.

Duress. Coercion causing action or inaction against a person's will through fear. Duress may take the form of physical force, imprisonment, bodily harm, improper moral persuasion, or the threat of any of these. Threat of criminal prosecution constitutes duress, but threat of civil prosecution does not. A contract made under duress is avoidable at the option of the party subjected to duress.

Duty. Conduct obligated to be performed by one person to another. In tort law, duty is legally sanctioned. A BREACH of duty results in the liability of the actor. In tax law, a duty is a tax levied on imports and exports.

Dying Declaration. A statement by a dying person, who has been injured by another and is aware of his or her impending death, about the person who inflicted the fatal injuries. This statement is admissible at the trial for HOMICIDE where the killing of the declarant is the crime charged to the defendant. This is an exception to the rule that would ordinarily exclude such a statement as HEARSAY. The reasons for this exception are the declarant's death and the probability of the trustworthiness of a declaration made by someone who feels death is imminent.

Earnest Money (Real Estate). The payment of part of the purchase price to bind a sale. The cash deposit made by the buyer is an element of all contracts of sale, and is the indication that the buyer intends to go through with the purchase if the seller furnishes good title to the property. The deposit is also referred to as the *binder*, although this term is more frequently applied to a deposit made under informal agreements than to deposits made in connection with formal contracts drawn up by the lawyer. If the buyer fails to consummate the deal, the earnest money is retained by the seller; if the buyer does perform his or her part of the contract, the earnest money is applied as part payment of the purchase price. If the seller cannot convey good title to the property, the deposit is returned to the buyer. The amount of earnest money depends upon the agreement between the parties. It is ordinarily sufficient to cover the broker's commission, expenses of the title search, and compensation to the seller for the loss he or she might sustain should the buyer fail to go through with the deal.

Easement. A right or privilege by one owner of land to use the land of another for a specific purpose. For example, *A* owns adjoining lots. He constructs a driveway on the common boundary line between the lots and sells one lot to *B*. *B* has an implied easement to use the driveway. An easement may be created by express grant, reservation, or agreement, or as a right acquired by lapse of time.

1. *Easement Appurtenant.* An easement that requires a dominant estate to which the benefit of the easement attaches. An easement appurtenant passes with the dominant estate to all subsequent grantees and is inheritable.

2. *Easement in Gross.* A personal interest in or the right to use another's land. It is not appurtenant to a dominant estate and is therefore not inheritable, but "dies" with the person who acquired it.

3. *Easement of Necessity.* An easement necessary for the continued use of the land when a larger tract of land has been subdivided. Every owner has the right to be able to get to his or her land. If without the easement either the GRANTEE or GRANTOR cannot make use of his or her property, the existence of an easement of necessity is implied by law.

Ejectment. A form of action brought to regain possession of real property and to obtain DAMAGES for its unlawful retention. The action of ejectment is used to test or establish TITLE to REAL PROPERTY.

Emancipation. The act whereby one is set free from the control of others. When a child is emancipated from his or her parents the duty of care is renounced along with the right to the custody and earnings of such child.

Embezzlement. The fraudulent appropriation of property or money by a person to whom it has been entrusted lawfully. In embezzlement the original taking of the property was lawful or with the consent of the owner; in LARCENY the felonious intent must have existed at the time of the taking.

Eminent Domain. The power of federal, state, and local governments to appropriate property for public use or the public welfare. When such property is taken, the owner is reimbursed according to a fair appraisal and has the right to sue for a greater amount. PUBLIC UTILITY corporations are also given the power of eminent domain.

Encumbrance. A burden or charge on property, either REAL PROPERTY or PERSONAL PROPERTY, consisting of a legal right or interest in favor of a person other than the owner. Frequently there is an indebtedness against real property that is being sold, or taxes or assessments are owed on it. These are *encumbrances* against the property, and the DEED recites the agreement between the parties regarding them. The person who holds the encumbrance is

the *encumbrancer*. The statement of encumbrances, if any, either follows the property description (see LAND DESCRIPTIONS) or is made a part of the HABENDUM CLAUSE. It is usually dictated by the lawyer.

The said premises are conveyed subject to a mortgage in the sum of Forty Thousand Dollars ($40,000), with interest, made by Roger L. Thompson to Edgar N. Wilson, dated the fifteenth day of January, 19 . . , and recorded in Book 27 or Conveyances, page 359, in the office of the Clerk of said county.

Subject to a purchase money mortgage made by the Grantee to the Grantor delivered and intended to be recorded simultaneously herewith.

Endorsed Legal Back. The manuscript cover of a legal instrument or court paper, on which has been written certain data referred to as the *endorsement*. See LEGAL BACK.

Endorsement. Writing one's name, either with or without additional words, on a NEGOTIABLE INSTRUMENT or on a paper (called an ALLONGE) attached to it. By an endorsement, the endorser becomes liable to all subsequent holders in due course for payment of the instrument if it is not paid by the maker when properly presented, and if he or she is given notice of dishonor. (See DISHONOR.)

1. *Blank Endorsement.* The writing of one's name on an instrument, or an allonge, without any additional words, is a *blank endorsement.* Its effect is to make the paper payable to the bearer. Thus, a finder or thief might transfer the note to a third party for a consideration, and the third party may then enforce payment against the maker or the endorser.

2. *Special Endorsement.* The designation of a certain person to whom the instrument is payable is a *special endorsement.* Thus, if an instrument is endorsed "Pay to John Jones," or "Pay to the order of John Jones," followed by the endorser's signature, no one but John Jones can receive payment for the instrument or transfer it.

3. *Restrictive Endorsement.* An endorsement that transfers possession of the instrument for a particular purpose is a *restrictive endorsement.* Examples: "Pay to John Jones only. Mary Brown." "Pay to National City Bank for collection. Mary Brown." A restrictive endorsement terminates the negotiability of the instrument.

See also HOLDER IN DUE COURSE.

Entrapment. In criminal law, an affirmative defense that excuses a defendant from criminal liability for crimes induced by police persuasion or trickery. The majority "subjective" view of entrapment requires that the defendant prove that but for the objectionable police conduct, he or she would not have committed the crime.

Equal Protection of the Laws. A guarantee made by the Fifth and Four-teenth Amendments that neither Congress nor the states may impair equal protection and security to all in their enjoyment of their personal and CIVIL RIGHTS. The clause refers to rights already in existence; it does not create any new rights.

Equitable Title. A person's right to obtain absolute ownership of property to which another has TITLE at law.

Equity. 1. *Courts.* A branch of remedial justice by and through which relief is afforded to suitors in CHANCERY COURT, or a court of equity. The word *equity* in the legal sense means "fair dealing," and that is the purpose of the system of legal rules and procedures known as equity.

Remedies at the COMMON LAW in England were frequently inadequate to give the wronged party a fair deal. He or she would then take his or her case to the King's Chancellor, who tempered the strict letter of the law with fairness. As a result of this practice, *chancery courts,* in which equity is practiced, were established, presided over by a chancellor instead of a judge. A few states still have chancery courts. See table I, AMERICAN COURT SYSTEM.

In the course of its development, equity has established certain fundamental principles or maxims, which the lawyer frequently uses in dictating a BRIEF. Among these are the following:

He or she who seeks equity must do equity. If I seek the return of property that I was induced to sell through FRAUD, I must offer to return the purchase price.

He or she who comes into equity must come with clean hands. If I induce you to BREACH a contract and to make one with me instead, and then you breach the contract with me, a court of equity will not compel specific performance of your contract with me.

Equity will presume that to be done which should have been done. If I unlawfully take possession of your cow, a calf from the cow will belong to you, because a court of equity will presume that I was holding the cow for you.

Equity aids the vigilant, not those who slumber on their rights. Where the STATUTE OF LIMITATIONS has not run, but a claimant has delayed unreasonably in bringing suit, a court of equity may bar the claim by reason of such delay.

Equity follows the law. Except where the common law is clearly inadequate, equity follows the precedents of the common law and the provisions of the statutes. Thus, if a deed is void by common law or statute, the mere fact that a holder has given valuable consideration for it will not make the deed valid in equity.

Equity regards substance rather than form. Common law is normally governed by legal forms. Corporations, for example, are regarded in law as artificial beings, separate from their stockholders, directors, and officers. To accomplish justice, equity may disregard the corporate fiction and examine the substance of the dispute. For example, several men sold out a fish business and agreed not to go into the fish business in the same locality. They immediately formed a corporation to carry on a fish business in competition with the purchaser. The court ignored the corporate entity and granted an injunction against this violation of the agreement not to compete.

2. *in Accounting and Finance.* The value of the owner's interest in property in excess of all claims against it. Examples: (a) An owner's equity in his or her home is its present value less the amount of the mortgage. (b) The equity of the stockholders of a business is its net worth; hence, the interest of the stockholders as measured by capital and surplus, or the value of the assets of the business in excess of its liabilities. Sometimes, however, equity refers to the unlimited interest of common stockholders. (The equity of a person who has bought securities on margin is the present market value of the securities less the sum borrowed from the broker to make the purchase.) 3. *of Redemption.* The right of a mortgagor to redeem his or her property after defaulting in the payment of the mortgage by paying the mortgage debt plus all costs and interest. It is a right available to mortgagors before actual foreclosure.

Escheat. The return of land to the state if the owner dies without legal heirs. Unclaimed personal property may also go to the state. Escheated personal property is called *bona vacantia*.

Escrow. A conditional delivery of something to a third person to be held until the happening of some event or the performance of some act. To place an instrument or fund in escrow is to deliver the instrument or fund to a person charged with its custody and disposition under the terms of a specific agreement, known as the *escrow agreement*. For example, a GRANTOR may deliver a DEED in escrow to a trust company until the grantee makes certain payments on the purchase price, at which time the trust company delivers the deed to the grantee.

Necessary components of escrows for the sale of REAL PROPERTY are:

1. A valid and enforceable contract for the sale of land,

2. An escrow agreement,

3. A disinterested third party, usually a bank, to act as escrow holder (*escrowee*). Neither buyer nor seller nor their agents or attorneys can act as escrowee.

Many banks, trust companies, building and loan associations, and title companies maintain special departments for escrow transaction.

Escrow upon exchange of property. Placing the transaction "in escrow" is particularly helpful in a deal involving the exchange of real estate in one city for property in another city. When TITLE on both properties has been cleared and all the details attended to, arrangements can be made by telephone between the escrow agent in one city and the correspondent in the other city for simultaneous recording of the deeds.

Estate by the Entirety. See TENANCY BY THE ENTIRETY.

Estate Tax. A federal or state excise tax, usually levied on a graduated basis, on the right to transfer property from the dead to the living. It includes transfers taking effect at death and certain other transfers that are defined by the law as having been made in "contemplation of death."

Estate taxes should not be confused with INHERITANCE TAXES, which are EXCISE TAXES levied by all of the states, except Nevada, on the right of the living to receive property from the dead. Inheritance taxes are payable by the heirs and not by the estate of the deceased, or must be paid by the estate if so directed in the decedent's Last Will and Testament. See also MARITAL DEDUCTION.

Estoppel. A barrier raised by law preventing a person from taking a position, denying a fact, or asserting a fact, in court, inconsistent with his or her previous conduct or statements. Example: *A* sells *B* a house that *A* does not own, giving *B* a covenant and warranty deed in which *A* warrants that he has title to the house. Later, *A* obtains title from the actual owner and attempts to eject *B* on the ground that *A* is now the true owner and *B* is not. *A* would be estopped from disputing what he formerly warranted, namely, that he was the true owner when he sold the house.

In real estate an *estoppel certificate* is the legal instrument commonly used when a mortgage is assigned. It shows the unpaid principal and interest due on a MORTGAGE. It is executed by a mortgagee or holder of a LIEN and bars the signer from making a claim inconsistent with the instrument.

Estoppel Certificate. See ESTOPPEL.

Ethics of the Legal Secretary.
The law secretary is bound by the same code of ethics as her employer. She cannot solicit business; she must regard everything about a client or a case as confidential. She never divulges the contents of a written document in the office without permission from the lawyer. She must never talk outside of the office about a case, even if the talk is merely an anecdote. If tempted to entertain friends with interesting tidbits about socially prominent clients, she always resists the temptation. Irreparable harm can result from mentioning anything about what is transpiring in a case. Facts and information received from clients by a secretary in the course of her work are PRIVILEGED COMMUNICATIONS. A copy of the American Bar Association (ABA) code of professional responsibility is available from ABA, 1155 East 60th Street, Chicago, IL 60637.

Euthanasia. Practice of causing death painlessly to end suffering. This practice is very controversial. The controversy is over what is called brain death. The Harvard Medical School has drawn up guidelines to define brain death. Several states have incorporated these guidelines into their laws.

Eviction. The dispossession of tenant from the use and possession of REAL PROPERTY.

There are two forms of eviction: (a) *actual eviction,* by which the landlord forces the tenant to quit the property in advance of the termination of the lease; and (b) *constructive eviction,* where the tenant is forced to leave the property because it has become uninhabitable or not useful for the purpose for which leased (destruction by fire, for example).

Both types of eviction are subject to widely varied laws and to specific agreements written into the contract. See also FORCIBLE ENTRY AND DETAINER; EJECTMENT.

Evidence of Title. See TITLE.

Examination Before Trial. See DEPOSITION.

Excise Taxes. Federal, state, and local taxes imposed on acts rather than on property. For example, excise taxes are levied on the sale of gasoline and tobacco rather than on the items themselves.

Excise taxes may be levied either against the seller or the purchaser. Manufacturers' excise taxes are levied against persons who sell various articles, but admissions taxes and communications taxes are borne by the consumer. However, excise taxes paid by the consumer are usually collected by the seller and remitted by him to the taxing authority.

Federal excise taxes are deductible for federal INCOME TAX purposes only when paid or incurred as an ordinary and necessary expense of carrying on a trade or business, or incurred as "nonbusiness" expense. *Nonbusiness expenses* are ordinary and necessary expenses paid or incurred by an individual in connection with (1) the production and collection of income, or (2) the management, conservation, or maintenance of property held for the production of income, or (3) the determination, collection or refund of any tax.

State excise taxes are deductible as such for federal income tax purposes. Since these taxes are deductible as such and not as expenses, the deductibility does not depend on whether the tax is connected with the taxpayer's business or "nonbusiness" activities. State excise taxes are deductible by the person on whom they are imposed. However, a state tax separately stated may be deducted by the buyer even if it is imposed on the seller. The person on whom the tax is imposed depends on state or local law.

Whether federal and state excise taxes are deductible for state income tax purposes depends on the tax law of the particular state.

Exclusions. *See* INCOME.

Exclusive Powers. Those powers delegated by the Constitution solely to Congress. Powers are exclusive with Congress and denied to the states either by express provision in the Constitution or where exercise of a similar power by the states would be inconsistent with congressional action. Congress is given exclusive powers to do things such as coin money, declare war, provide and maintain a navy, and to establish post offices and post roads.

The Tenth Amendment provides that the powers neither delegated nor prohibited by the Constitution to the states are "reserved to the states respectively or to the people." *See* STATES' RIGHTS; CONCURRENT POWERS.

Execution. 1. *of Judgment.* A legal writ directing an officer of the law to carry out a judgment is an *execution of judgment.*

2. *of an Instrument.* The signature and delivery of a written instrument constitutes *execution of the instrument.* In law office parlance, *execution* more frequently refers merely to the signing of an

instrument by the party or parties described in it. *See* ATTESTATION CLAUSE; TESTIMONIUM CLAUSE.

Execution of Lease. *See* LEASE.

Executor. The person or corporation named by a testator in his or her will to administer the estate. The testator may name as many executors as desired. Often a person names a spouse and a bank as co-executors; the bank can advise the spouse and relieve him or her of a lot of work involved in the administration. (A woman is called an *executrix.*) *See also* ADMINISTRATOR.

Exhibit. 1. *in Trial.* A document or any other tangible item that has been received in evidence at a trial. The general rule is that a jury is permitted to take exhibits into the jury room at the court's discretion. In criminal cases, permission may be granted for the jury to have exhibits in the jury room only upon the consent of the defendant and the counsel for the prosecution.

2. *of an Instrument.* Attachment to a legal instrument that is too lengthy to be typed in the body of the document itself or provides further explanation of the document. Usually marked "Exhibit A," "B," and so on.

Expense Account. A statement of an individual's costs incurred for a specific period and purpose, usually for a particular assignment on behalf of the person's company. Sometimes a lawyer's firm will advance money, and the lawyer returns the unused portion. Or the lawyer may use his or her own funds, and the company will reimburse the lawyer.

If the lawyer accounts to the firm for expenses incurred on its behalf, the lawyer need not report on his or her income tax return those expenses for which the lawyer was reimbursed. The expenses and reimbursements balance, thus having no effect on the lawyer's income. However, the lawyer must state on the return that reimbursements did not exceed expenses, or if they did that the excess was included in income.

If the lawyer does *not* account to the firm for expenses, he or she must report them on the return. The lawyer must also attach a statement showing the total of all amounts received from the firm including the amounts charged to it.

The lawyer's secretary should keep a record of expenses incurred on behalf of the firm. The record shows the company the amount spent for each item and also serves as a record for income tax purposes. Any form of record that shows the date, description and amount of the expenditures is satisfactory. If the lawyer takes many trips, a columnar sheet similar to that illustrated in figure 1 is appropriate.

Expert Witness. A person selected because of knowledge or skill to examine, estimate, and ascertain things and to make a report of his or her opinion at trial. An expert can draw from facts inferences that a layman could not make, and in this way the expert aids the jury. The facts upon which the expert's opinion is based may have been personally observed by the expert or incorporated in a hypothetical question put to him or her. Whether a witness is qualified to speak as an expert is a preliminary question of fact to be determined by the trial court. A few examples of specialized fields where an expert's testimony would be necessary are medicine, ballistics, chemical analysis, psychiatry, and engineering.

Ex Post Facto Law. Any retroactive legislation that has the effect of substantially prejudicing the rights of the accused or convicted party in a criminal proceeding. An example of an ex post facto law is one that designates an act as criminal after it has been committed. Another example is the passage of a law that would increase the penalty for a crime already committed. The Constitution denies to both Congress and the states the right to pass ex post facto laws.

Extortion. The wrongful act of compelling payments by means of threats of injury to a person or to a person's property or reputation. Extortion is distinguished from ROBBERY in that the intimidation can be done at one place and the money taken at another. See also BLACKMAIL.

Extradition. The surrender by one state to another state of a party who has fled to escape prosecution. The state desiring extradition must be competent to try the party and must demand the surrender.

Mo. Day	Description	Fares	Meals	Lodging	Tips	Automobile Expenses	Misc.

Expense Account: Figure 1.
Record of expenses of business trip.

False Arrest. Unlawful arrest; any unlawful restraint of someone's personal liberty or freedom of movement. False arrest may be a criminal offense and/or the basis of a civil action for damages.

False Imprisonment. The substantial restraint of a person's freedom of movement, without authority of law and against that person's will. Arresting the wrong person under a WARRANT is an example of false imprisonment. An action for DAMAGES may be brought against the offender.

Featherbedding. Payment by an employer for services not performed or not to be performed. Legislation bans featherbedding, but the problem exists in particular cases as to whether an employee is needed or merely on the payroll for doing nothing. An example of what management considers featherbedding is the employment of stand-by musicians.

Federal Court. See AMERICAN COURT SYSTEM.

Federal Reporter. See NATIONAL REPORTER SYSTEM.

Federal Rules Decisions. See NATIONAL REPORTER SYSTEM.

Federal Supplement. See NATIONAL REPORTER SYSTEM.

Federal Tax Citator. A loose-leaf publication that gives a complete judicial history of every federal tax case and ruling. It shows where to find everything that has been said about any federal tax case or ruling in all succeeding cases or rulings. The Federal Tax Citator covers all standard court reporting systems, and other official sources, such as tax court, appeal and review memoranda, revenue rules, treasury decisions, income tax unit rulings, mimeograph rulings, and internal revenue bulletins.

The cases are arranged in alphabetical order. Cross references insure that the title under which each CITATION is listed may be readily found. In those cases in which the government, the commissioner, or the collector is a party, the citations are listed under the name of the taxpayer. The names of companies are listed as court decisions without reference to initials or first names of parties.

The Federal Tax Citator is the only CITATOR system on federal taxes that indicates the *exact page* in the *exact volume* of whatever reporter system is being used. It is standard equipment in the offices of leading tax practitioners. Supplements are mailed approximately once a month to subscribers.

The Federal Tax Citator is published by Prentice-Hall, Inc., Englewood Cliffs, New Jersey 07632.

Fees (Lawyer's). Compensation for the legal services rendered to clients. The fees that a lawyer charges usually depend on a number of factors. When fixing fees, the lawyer considers the amount of money involved in the controversy, the time spent, the difficulty and importance of the questions of law and fact involved, the ability of the client to pay, and the results accomplished. See FORWARDING FEE; CONTINGENT FEE.

Fee Simple. The absolute ownership of REAL PROPERTY. It gives the owner and his or her heirs the unconditional power of disposition and other rights.

Felony. A crime punishable by death or imprisonment in a state prison. See MISDEMEANOR.

Felony-Murder. The act of killing in the perpetration or attempted perpetration of a FELONY. Felony-murder is a crime that may be punishable by death. The offender's intent in felony-murder is the intent to commit the underlying felony and not the intent to kill. Killing someone while in the act of burglarizing a house is an example of felony-murder.

Fictitious Names. Names (either imaginary or only partly accurate) that are used temporarily in preparing legal papers in an action, with the express intention that the true names be substituted as soon as they are learned.

Since someone frequently has an interest that the plaintiff (see PARTIES TO AN ACTION) does not know about, or someone whose name is unknown has an interest in the suit, several fictitious names are added as defendants can be brought into the action without the necessity of serving an amended complaint on all defendants. Perhaps an interested party's last name is known but not his first; a fictitious first name is given to that defendant thus:

"Richard" Neilson, first name "Richard" being fictitious, defendant's first name being unknown to the plaintiff.

The complaint usually alleges that the names are fictitious. The true names are substituted as soon as they are learned. In all subsequent papers filed in the case, the caption reflects the substitution.

Fiduciary. A person or organization such as a CORPORATION holding a position and acting in the capacity of trust and special confidence so that he, she, or it is obliged to act with the highest degree of good faith, and to place ahead of his, her, or its own interests the interest of those represented; as an adjective—having the nature of a trust. Attorneys, guardians, directors of corporations, and public officers are fiduciaries.

Fiduciary Account. An accounting of receipts and disbursements made to the Probate Court by a guardian for his or her ward or an executor or an administrator for a decedent. Accounts are usually numbered "First Account," "Second Account," and "Third, Final and Distributive Account," when an estate is closed or the guardianship is terminated.

Filing. The following classification of files is appropriate for the typical law office.

1. *Clients' business.* All matters relating to clients, with the exception of commercial collections when handled in volume. Some offices separate the material into litigation and nonlitigation matters. Other offices segregate files relating to a particular field of law if a large part of the practice is in a specific field. Still other offices segregate matters relating to a retainer client with a large volume of business. The least confusing method, however, is to keep all of the files of each client together.

2. *Commercial collections.* Where a fair volume of commercial collections is handled, the files are segregated from other clients' business because of the close follow-up on these cases. (See COLLECTIONS, How to file collection matters.)

3. *Personal files.* Contain material relating to the lawyer's personal business matters, correspondence, and outside activities, such as bar association committees.

4. *General correspondence files.* The miscellaneous or "catch-all" file. It contains all material not relating to clients' business or to the lawyer's personal matters. Office administation material, such as personnel applications and records, correspondence about office equipment, correspondence with law book publishers, and the like would be placed in this file. Correspondence about a case that the lawyer does not accept would be filed here.

5. *Periodicals, bulletins, etc.* Every office accumulates pamphlets, booklets, periodicals, and the like that contain information likely to be needed in the future.

6. *Subsidiary files.* Files for material such as sample legal blanks. Some secretaries keep sample forms in a loose-leaf notebook; others prefer to keep such material in file folders.

Centralized filing. A system of keeping records whereby all correspondence and materials are entrusted to one main filing center for safekeeping. Law offices generally maintain a *centralized* filing system. In a small office the secretary might be responsible for the centralized file. In addition, she would maintain her lawyer's confidential or personal file apart from the regular centralized file.

Numerical filing system. Each file is given a number, and the folders are arranged in numerical sequence. This is an *indirect* filing system since it must be used in connection with a cross-index. The subject and number of each file are put on an index card, and the cards are arranged alphabetically. Advantages are the rapidity and accuracy of refiling and the maintenance of the auxiliary card index and the necessity of making two searches, one of the index and one of the files, whenever papers or folders are withdrawn.

1. *How to use the numerical system in a law office.* Give a key number to a

client instead of to a case. Each case for that client is given the client's key number plus an identifying number or letter.

(a) Assign a key number to the client in numerical sequence. His or her general file has this number. Then assign an identifying *number* to each matter that is litigation and an identifying *letter* to each matter that is not litigation. For example, client Brown & Rogers, Inc. has a file of general correspondence, a profit-sharing plan for employees, and a suit against Ellis & Lewis Co. You give the general file the number 85, the profit-sharing file number 85-A, and the suit number 85-1. The next suit will be 85-2.

(b) Make index cards under each name that appears in connection with the matter. In some instances, for example estate matters, the client's name does not appear in the subject of the file; nevertheless a card should be made in the client's name.

Type on the card the title of the case, the number assigned to it, and the client's name if it does not appear in the title. In a matter of litigation the card under the defendant's name will read *defendant ads. plaintiff*, instead of plaintiff vs. defendant. If the matter is not a suit or claim, type on the card, in addition to the client's name, an identifying description of the subject matter.

For example:

Brown & Rogers, Inc.
Profit-sharing Plan

It is not necessary but the secretary might also make a card under the subject which would read:

Profit-sharing Plan
Brown & Rogers, Inc.

Make index cards and cross-index cards freely, and be liberal in the information you type on them. (See figure 1.)

(c) File the index cards alphabetically. When there is more than one card under a client's name, place them in this order: general card, nonlitigation cards arranged alphabetically according to subject, litigation cards arranged alphabetically according to opposing party. Suppose a client has a general file and five other files. The cards will be arranged as follows:

Brown & Rogers, Inc.	52
Brown & Rogers, Inc.—Arbitration	52-B
Brown & Rogers, Inc.—Legislation	52-C
Brown & Rogers, Inc.—Profit sharing Plan	52-A
Brown & Rogers, Inc. vs. Jones	52-2
Brown & Rogers, Inc. ads. Matthew	52-1

If the client's cases are numerous, the secretary might put a guide card between the litigation and nonlitigation cards to facilitate locating the desired card.

(d) File the folders in numerical sequence according to key number. If there is more than one file for a client, arrange those bearing identifying letters in alphabetical sequence; follow with those bearing identifying numbers in numerical sequence. Thus, in the cabinet, all files pertaining to one client are together; all of his nonlitigation matters are together and all suits and claims are together.

(e) Keep a card showing the key number to be assigned to the next client in front of the index box.

(f) When a client brings a case to the office, give the client a key number and assign the case an identifying letter or

Jones, John v. Smith, Allen				81-5
Correspondence	DOCUMENTS	PRINTED PAPERS	GENERAL SAFE	
81-5	81-5	*Cabinet 2*		
Cabinet #2 - Extra copies of Briefs, case on appeal, etc.				

Filing: Figure 1. *File index card.*

number. Reserve the key number, without identifying letters or numbers, for the client's general correspondence should it become desirable to have a file of that nature for him.

(g) Reserve a key number for miscellaneous clients, who might want a letter written for them or have some smaller matter involving only one or two papers. These matters can be filed under the same key number, but all necessary index cards should be made.

2. *Assigning numbers according to type of case.* A group of numbers is set aside for each category. For example, cases involving litigation will be numbered 1 through 199; probate cases, 200 through 399, and so on. The client does not have a key number. A list of available numbers is kept for each category, and the number of a closed file is placed on the appropriate list and used again.

Another method of numbering when files are separated according to type of case is for each category to have a separate sequence of numbers. There might be, for example, a Claim 485 and a Probate 485. Different colored labels or folders should be used for each category.

3. *Transferring numerical files.* The procedure followed by many firms is to retain in the office as many closed files as space permits and from time to time to send the oldest closed files to outside storage, replacing them in the office with more recently closed files. When there are retired files in the office, the active files might be kept in the top drawers of the filing cabinets and the retired files in the lower drawers. We use the word *closed* and *retired* interchangeably here.

Law files are not retired periodically but are closed when the matter is presumably completed. As soon as a secretary is informed that a matter has been completed, she should stamp the file jacket "Closed." Then when time permits, she can go through the filing cabinets and withdraw all closed cases and process them for retirement. Use old jackets for storage files.

(a) Withdraw from the active index all cards relating to the closed case. Stamp the cards "Closed" with a small rubber stamp. If the secretary wishes she might also stamp the date on the card. Figure 1 has a column that can be designated *storage*.

(b) Withdraw from the active files all jackets or folders holding papers that relate to the completed case. The index card will indicate whether there are extra copies or printed papers that have been removed from the regular filing cabinet. (See figure 1.) The documents in the safe will not be sent to storage. They will be returned to the client, or other appropriate disposition will be made of them.

(c) Keep the index of closed files separate from the index of active files. (Some offices, however, prefer to keep cards for inactive files in the master file so the secretary need look only in one place to see if something is active or inactive.)

(d) If your policy is to segregate active and inactive cards, file the index cards in the closed card index, alphabetically, just as they were filed in the current index.

(e) File the closed files in the transfer cabinets numerically just as they were filed in the active files.

4. *Terminal digit filing.* The numerical sequence follows the terminal digits. This system is used often by insurance companies for filing dailies.

Alphabetical filing. Clients' folders are filed alphabetically according to name or subject. A cross-index is not necessary with this system of filing but is sometimes

desirable. The principal advantage of this system is that it is not necessary to look up a file number in a cross-index. The disadvantages are that the system does not lend itself to expansion as readily as the numerical system, and it requires more shifting of folders.

1. *How to use the alphabetical system.* Each client has a general folder and each of his or her matters has a separate folder. All matters of a specific client are filed under that client's name. The order of arrangement of the various folders is similar to that of the index cards in a numerical system: the general folder comes first and is followed by the nonsuit files arranged alphabetically according to subject. These are followed by the litigation files arranged alphabetically according to opposing party. The various matters of Client Desmond & Lake, Inc. might be labeled and filed as follows:

Desmond & Lake, Inc.—General
Desmond & Lake, Inc.—Arbitration—
  R.E. Brown
Desmond & Lake, Inc.—Arbitration—
  L.F. Jones
Desmond & Lake, Inc.—Profit-sharing
  Plan
Desmond & Lake, Inc. ads. Bates & Co.
Desmond & Lake, Inc. vs. Cordell
  Lighting Effects Co.

If the active files of a client are very numerous, they might be numbered and a card index made of that client's files.

Another method of using the alphabetical system in a law office is to file under the name of the plaintiff, whether or not the plaintiff is the client. Lawyers have a tendency to think of suits and claims in terms of plaintiff vs. defendant. Nonlitigation matters are filed under the name of the client. When this method of filing is followed, cross-index cards are desirable. The secretary makes the index cards in the name of the client and others connected with the case, and shows on the card under which name the folder is filed.

2. *How to transfer alphabetical files.* Assign the file a transfer number and make cross-index cards for each party connected with the matter. Then place the files in the storage files in numerical order. This avoids shifting of files.

Some offices transfer alphabetically. The file drawers are then numbered and the drawer number in which the file is placed is indicated on the cross-index cards. Each year's transferred files may be filed together alphabetically. However, this entails shifting of files from drawer to drawer unless ample space under each letter is kept open for files to be stored under that letter in the future.

Personal file. A combination name and subject file. The alphabetical system of filing is used for it. The file relates to matters of direct personal concern to the lawyer and is separate from those matters that relate to the lawyer's clients and legal work of the office. A 25-division alphabetical guide is probably sufficient; no cross-index is needed.

1. Make a folder for each letter of the alphabet. File the correspondence under the first letter of the correspondent's last name, according to date. Thus, correspondence with Mr. Moss and with Mr. Matthews will be in the same folder. If the lawyer has prolific correspondence with a certain person, make a separate folder for that correspondent. Also make a separate folder for each separate business matter and outside activity. Thus, if the lawyer is on the Grievance Committee of

the American Bar Association, there will be a folder labeled, "American Bar Association—Grievance Committee," and the folder will be filed under the letter A. Should the material for any particular subject become voluminous withdraw it from the alphabetical file and file it under a guide of its own.

2. Close these files periodically by moving them to another drawer in the office where they will be available for reference if necessary. The correspondence folders can probably be transferred intact, or several letters of the alphabet combined in one folder to save space. However, it will probably be necessary to go through the subject folders, such as the "American Bar Association—Grievance Committee" folder, and extract material that is pertinent to the forthcoming year. Transfer the closed files from the office to storage when they are several years old, to make room in the office for the more recent personal files.

General correspondence file. Records of all routine office letters, general in nature, separate from the clients' files and the lawyer's personal file. The file is operated in the same manner as the personal file. The secretary always keeps it alphabetically according to the name of the correspondent. The division of the alphabetical guide needed will depend upon the volume of miscellaneous material. No card index is necessary.

The secretary closes and transfers these files periodically by the same method used to transfer the lawyer's personal file.

Filing periodicals, bulletins, etc. Magazines, bulletins, law journals, are generally filed alphabetically according to subject. The filing cabinet used for them need not be fireproof, and a 25-division alphabetical guide is usually sufficient. This material often consists of government bulletins, advertisements, catalogues, announcements of changes in law firms, announcements from law schools, any other material of this nature that the lawyer wishes to keep. Periodically the secretary should go through the file and discard material that is out of date.

Preparation of Material for filing.

1. Segregate papers belonging in different files: clients' matters; personal; general correspondence.

2. Check to see if the lawyer has initialed the paper for filing. (In offices with more than one attorney, there should be a hard and fast rule that no paper is to be filed until the responsible attorney has initialed it.)

3. Check through all papers that are clipped or stapled together to see whether they should be filed together.

4. Remove all paper clips.

5. Mend torn papers with cellophane tape.

6. See that all legal documents have been conformed.

7. Mark on all court papers the date they were filed with the CLERK OF THE COURT or served upon opposing counsel. (This information is stamped by the clerk of the court on the back of the paper and is not evident when the paper is fastened to the folder unless noted on the face of the paper.)

8. Note on the paper where it is to be filed. For numerical files, write the key and identification numbers in the upper right-hand corner; for a name file, underline the name in colored pencil; for a subject file, write the subject in colored pencil in the upper right-hand corner, or underline it in colored pencil if it appears on the paper.

9. Punch a hole or holes in the *exact* place where the paper should be fastened to the folder. An electric gadget that punches holes in the paper is a valuable time saver when thick documents must be stapled into folders.

10. When fastening the paper in the folder, check the number and name on the paper being filed with the number and name on the folder.

11. Sort unfiled material into categories and keep it nearby in one or more folders to save time in searching for unfiled items.

12. Fold oversized papers so the written material is on the outside, easily read without having to open a paper or remove it.

13. Use follow-up files (see below) to avoid needless searching for items needing follow-up.

14. File the latest material at the front of loose-leaf books to avoid paging through everything when searching for current items.

Typing index tabs and labels. Use the briefest possible designations. Abbreviate, omitting punctuation whenever possible. Index tabs need to be legible only a normal reading distance. Guide labels should be legible at two or three feet. File drawer labels should be legible at six feet.

Use initial caps whenever needed. Full caps, especially in elite and pica type, do not increase the legibility of label designations; they decrease the amount of light background around the letters and make reading more difficult. Do not underline.

1. *Folder labels.* The most important part of a folder label is the eighth of an inch immediately below the scoring (the place at which the label is folded when it is pasted on the folder tab). Frequently this space is the only part visible in the file. Therefore, start at the first typing space below the scoring. Typing should begin in the first or second typing space from the left edge of the label, except for one or two character designations. If this is done, all folder labels in the file drawer will present an even left margin.

Use initial caps and indent the second and third lines so the first word of the first line will stand out.

In typing labels for a numbered subject or name file, leave space between the number and first work; type the subject in block form. Avoid exceptionally long file numbers if possible.

2. *Guide labels.* For file guide labels, use the largest type available. Begin the typing as high on the label as the guide tabs will permit. Center one- and two-character designations. Start all other designations in the second typing space from the left edge. Use abbreviations or shortened forms and omit punctuation, except for large numbers such as 10,000.

3. *File drawer labels.* In preparing labels for file drawers, use the largest type available. Center the typing on the label and leave a double space above and below detailed reference information. It is better to print file drawer labels because typing is not legible at a distance.

Arrangements of papers in file folders. A file in a law matter consists of at least two parts: correspondence and formal documents, whether they be court papers or legal instruments such as agreements, leases, and the like. Each file must have a correspondence folder and a document folder, both of which are kept together in the file jacket. it does not matter what kind of "folder" is used, as long as it has enough firmness to serve as a backing sheet to which the papers may be fastened with a brad or other fastener that permits removal when desired. Correspondence and papers are both filed in their respective folders according to date, usually with the latest on top, although some lawyers prefer the reverse order. Always keep the correspondence folder on top of the document folder in the jacket.

A file might consist of more than two parts. Separate folders are required for briefs and law memoranda; drafts; extra copies; miscellaneous memoranda, such as interoffice memos, notes made by the lawyer, and so on. If a file contains both legal instruments (agreements, contracts, and the like) and court papers, a separate folder is made for each. If a case has papers filed in more than one court, a separate folder is made for each court. A law file might also contain a folder for "hold papers," that is, papers belonging to the client other than those kept in the safe. The "hold papers" should not be fastened in the folder. Always indicate on the index card the folders that are made up in each case.

As a file grows, it is broken down into volumes, with all letters together in one or two folders, all court papers together, and so on. Law files frequently become so voluminous that two or more jackets are required. All of the jackets in a particular case have the same number. On each jacket, write the classification of the contents of that jacket—that is, the folders that are in the jacket—so you will not have to open more than one jacket to

Filing: Figure 2. *File jacket
properly labeled.*

find the desired papers. Some offices make a separate index card for each jacket.

For a matter that will not become sufficiently voluminous to warrant separate folders and a jacket, use a legal-size folder and fasten the documents to the right side and the correspondence to the left. Some offices do not put the file folders in a jacket but simply file them together. This eliminates having to open a jacket to get out the folder that is needed.

Write the title of the case, the client's name, and the numer of the file on each folder and on the jacket. (See figure 2.)

Filing loose-leaf publications. Most business and professional advisers subscribe to one or more loose-leaf services. These publications usually contain an explanatory text (compilation) and report on new laws, regulations, administrative interpretations, judicial decisions, and other developments affecting the subjects covered. Lawyers, tax consultants, accountants, and other businessmen use these services.

The original compilation is furnished in a large loose-leaf binder. Periodically, loose-leaf report bulletins are sent to the subscribers to highlight recent developments and furnish new pages that bring the compilation up to date. This material is numbered by page and paragraph and is filed in the loose-leaf binders. With loose-leaf binders it is easy to remove pages as they become obsolete, and replace those pages with new ones giving up-to-date information.

The loose-leaf services the lawyer finds most helpful are Prentice-Hall's *Wills, Estates, and Trusts* and *Corporation* services and federal and state tax services. Each week, the secretary receives in the mail report bulletins and

---

```
CONTENTS[1]

Report No. 5
```

Pages not required[2]	Pages in this report[3]	Reason for change[4]
9293-9294[5]	9293-9294	Reference added in ¶9217
12,201-12,208[6]	None	Obsolete Regulations removed
None[7]	28,801-28,806	New Regulations added
30,101-30,107[8]	30,101-30,104	Editorial Revision to conform with new law provisions
36,201-36,208[9]	36,201-36,218	Annotations added

Explanations:

[1]*Contents* means these are the items in the report that must be replaced, added to, or removed from the volume.

[2]*Pages not required* means that the pages in this column are to be replaced or removed.

[3]*Pages in this report* means that the pages in this column contain the latest information and are to be inserted.

[4]*Reason for change*

[5]*9293-9294 9293-9294*	In this case pages 9293-9294 are being replaced by the same number of new pages, which have new information.
[6]*12,201-12,208 None*	The secretary removes these pages and nothing is to take their place.
[7]*None $28,802-28,806*	There are no comparable pages in the volume to be removed. The addition is inserted in the numerical sequence of pages already in the volume.
[8]*30,101-30,107 30,101-30,104*	The obsolete material removed is larger than the new material to be inserted.
[9]*36,201-36,208 36,201-36,218*	The material to be removed is replaced with a larger amount of material.

Filing: Figure 3. *Weekly instruction sheet.*

new pages for the services. She follows the enclosed directions *carefully and promptly.* Figure 3 explains the use of an instruction sheet.

Preparation for closing a file. Go through the file carefully and remove all paperclips, pins, and the like. This procedure eliminates the possibility of storing papers that do not belong in that particular file. Quite often a misplaced paper is found, and removal of the clips reduces the size of the file. If a file has several jackets, the secretary might be able to combine the contents into one jacket.

Papers and folders in a closed file may be packed more tightly than those in an active file.

Out file control. To control folders removed from the files, the secretary uses guides that are the same height as the file folders but of different-colored stock, with the word *out* printed on the tab. The *out* guide provides space on which to make an entry of the date, the material taken, who has it, and date it should be returned. The secretary should place the guide in the files where the removed material was located.

A secretary in a private office does not put an *out* guide in her file every time she withdraws material for the lawyer. She uses the guide under these circumstances: (1) Someone outside her immediate office wants the material. (2) The lawyer expects to take the material out of the office, say, while on a trip. (3) She expects her employer to keep the material a week or so, say, to prepare a BRIEF.

When a paper is removed from a folder, the secretary makes a note of the removal and inserts it in the folder. Many law offices have a rule that no one may remove a paper from a folder except the person responsible for the filing.

Follow-up filing system. The follow-up file is a check on whether correspondence has been answered or any other desired action has been taken. A notation or reminder, usually a carbon copy, is placed in the follow-up file while the material itself remains in its proper place in the regular files. If the material itself is placed in the follow-up file instead of in the regular file, it cannot be located if it is needed before the follow-up date.

1. *Checklist of material to be placed in follow-up files.* Court cases are preferably followed through the diary or SUIT REGISTER, but the following matters are generally followed through follow-up files rather than through the diary (see also REMINDERS).

(a) Matters that are referred to other lawyers or law clerks in the office for information, comment, or action,

(b) Correspondence or memoranda awaiting answer,

(c) Collection letters,

(d) Covering letters enclosing documents sent by registered mail, until receipt is received,

(e) Requests for acknowledgments of documents, etc.,

(f) Receipts for documents left with court clerks or other officials for recording,

(g) Letters of Register of Deeds, or other officials, enclosing papers for recording, to be kept until papers are returned and delivered to client,

(h) Letter to ABSTRACT COMPANY.

2. *Equipment for follow-up system.* The only equipment necessary is a file drawer and file folders. Make a set of file folders consisting of (a) 12 folders labeled from January through December, (b) 31 folders labeled from 1 through 31, and (c) 1 folder marked "Future Years." If you have a heavy volume of follow-up material, it is advisable to have two sets of folders labeled by days—one for the current month and one for the succeeding month.

Tabbed guides marked 1 through 31 and removable separators tabbed with the months will make it easier to locate a particular folder, but these are not necessary to the efficient functioning of the system.

3. *Arrangement of folders for follow-up.* Arrange the folders labeled by days in numerical order in the front of the file. Place in these the follow-up material for the current month. The folder labeled for the current month is at the back of the other monthly folders ready to receive any material to be followed up in the same month next year. Immediately following the numerical daily folders is the folder for the coming month, followed by the folder for the succeeding month, and so on.

4. *Operation of the follow-up system.*

(a) Make an extra copy of correspondence or memoranda that require a follow-up, preferably on paper of a different color. Mark on the extra carbon the date on which it is to be followed up. When there is no carbon copy of material for follow-up write a brief memo. The memo should indicate where the material is filed. File any pertinent papers in the regular files.

(b) Place material that is to be followed up in the current month in the proper date folders. Each day transfer the empty daily folder in back of the folder for the coming month. Thus there are always 31 daily folders for follow-ups, part of them for the remaining days in the current month and part of them for the first part of the coming month. Place material that is to be followed up more than 30 or 31 days in the future in the proper month folder, regardless of the day of follow-up.

(c) On the first of each month, transfer the material from the folder for that month into the folders labeled by days. To avoid filing material for follow-up on Saturdays (if the office closes), Sundays, or holidays, reverse the folders for those days so that the blank side of the label faces the front of the file.

5. *How to handle material in the daily follow-up file.* Each day when examining the follow-up file the secretary will find that a large part of the material has been answered without a follow-up. She should destroy these carbons or memoranda. If a heavy schedule keeps her from giving attention to all the material in the daily folder, she marks the less important items for follow-up at a later date.

Move indefinite follow-ups forward from week to week until a definite date is established or until the matter is completed. This procedure is often referred to as *combing-back*.

6. *Follow-ups on a small scale.* When the secretary has only a small amount of correspondence or other matters to follow up, a set of follow-up file folders is not necessary. She marks the carbons with the follow-up date and files them chronologically in one folder, with those marked for the earliest follow-up on top.

Tickler card file. A small card file that acts as a reminder system. The tickler card file has a tabbed guide for each month of the year and 31 tabbed guides, one for each day of the month. The daily guides are placed behind the current month guide. Memoranda are made on cards or slips, which are filed behind the daily guide according to the date on which the matter is brought up.

Use of tickler file with diary. Generally secretaries in law offices do not like to depend upon tickler cards as reminders for deadlines, hearings, trial dates, and other legal work. It is too easy to lose or misplace a small 3- by 5-inch card or slip, and the resulting damage might be irreparable. Furthermore, tickler cards do not constitute a permanent record of the day's activities, as a diary does.

Tickler cards can be used in conjunction with a diary very satisfactorily. They reduce the work necessary in making diary entries. Recurring items can be put on one card, and the card can be moved from week to week, month to month, or year to year. Thus if a certain check is made out each Friday, the secretary can make one card and move it each week, instead of making 52 entries in her diary. Also, she can put all necessary information on the card so that she or anyone else can attend to the task without referring to any other material. Tickler cards are also particularly useful for indefinite date follow-ups. Suppose a lawyer has told the secretary he or she wants to do a certain job sometime within the next few months. She makes a card and moves it from time to time if the lawyer does not do the task immediately.

The secretary should refer to the diary every afternoon for the following day and to the tickler each morning.

Information storage and retrieval systems. Information storage and retrieval devices provide high-density storage and rapid retrieval for active index cards used as a cross-reference to cases or account data. The card carriers are arranged in ferris-wheel fashion. As the operator presses a button, the carrier with the card tray is moved to operator's position in about three seconds. Reference is easier; vital records are protected against tearing, bending, and soiling; and records are always within immediate reach.

In one unit, the operator touches the keyboard and within seconds the desired slide or frame is delivered to the desk area ready for reference, revision, updating, insertion, or withdrawal. The visible margin of each card combined with colored signals ensure positive interpretation and evaluation. This combination assures faster retrieval and saves valuable executive and secretarial time.

Automated records retrieval systems for case files and client records are geared to the law office that has an active filing operation consisting of six or more file cabinets. From a seated or standing position the operator touches a button and carriers for letter, legal, or larger

sized folders rotate in either direction and stop in front of the operator for rapid media withdrawal or addition. Not only does this save time, it can also save the law office up to 50 percent of its floor space and ensure better client service and relations.

Some systems, such as microfilming, reduce data for storage on film. Rapid retrieval brings the film to a machine where it is magnified for reading. Certain models will produce a photocopy of the document being read.

Findings of Fact and Conclusions of Law. A statement of the facts and the applicable rules of law in a particular jurisdiction, prepared by the attorney at the direction of the court. At the trial of a case, certain facts are determined from the pleadings and evidence. Certain rules of law are applicable to those facts. After the trial of a case by the court without the jury, the court directs the attorneys to prepare a statement of the facts and applicable rules of law. This statement is designated *findings of fact and conclusions (or rulings) of law*. In other jurisdictions, the court directs counsel for both sides to prepare findings of fact and conclusions of law. In some jurisdictions, the court directs counsel for only one party to prepare the statement; opposing counsel then has a specified time within which to file objections and submit his or her proposed findings.

How to prepare findings of fact and conclusions of law. The lawyer dictates the findings of fact and conclusions of law.

1. Make an original for the court, a copy for each counsel, and a copy for the file.

2. The caption is the same as on the complaint.

3. The document is entitled "Findings of Fact and Conclusions of Law."

4. The findings of fact are enumerate   beginning with FIRST, or I.

5. The conclusions of law are enumerated, beginning with FIRST, or I.

6. The dateline is typed below the last conclusion of law, at the left margin.

7. Type a line for the judge's signature.

8. Endorse legal backs and all copies except office copy.

What to do about findings of fact and conclusions of law.

1. As soon as the court directs counsel to prepare findings of fact and conclusions of law, *enter in diary* the date by which the statement must be prepared.

2. See that copy is served on opposing counsel.

3. See that receipt of copy is acknowledged, or make an affidavit of service by mail.

4. *Enter in diary* date by which opposing counsel must file objections and submit his or her proposed findings.

5. The original, with proof of service on opposing counsel, is submitted to the judge who tried the case.

6. Make entry in suit register of service, submission to judge, signing, and filing.

First Pleading. See PLEADINGS.

Fixture. Something that has become physically attached to REAL PROPERTY such that its removal would damage the property; thus it is considered part of the realty. Examples of fix- ture are wall-to-wall carpeting and built-in bookcases.

Flotsam. See JETTISON.

Force Majeure (French). Superior or irresistible force. Corresponds in a general way to "Act of God," for example an earthquake or the sudden death of a person. If a party to a contract is prevented from executing it by a *force majeure,* that party may not be held liable for damages. If the vendor of a contract for the sale of real estate dies before the contract is completed and the contract states that it includes the vendor's executors, administrators, heirs and assigns, the decedent's executor or administrator may bring an action for the completion of the contract.

Forcible Entry and Detainer. A remedy provided by statute in some states to enable the lessor (landlord or owner) to recover possession of his or her property, upon one or more of the following violations by the lessee (tenant):

(1) holding over after termination of the LEASE, (2) failure to pay rent a fixed number of days after it is due, after specified notice has been given by the lessor, (3) violating other terms of the lease, (4) committing waste.

Foreclosure. A proceeding against property securing a debt, brought upon DEFAULT, to cut off the mortgagor's equitable right to redeem the property (see REDEMPTION). The most common method is by *foreclosure* suit in a court of EQUITY. In a few states foreclosure may also be effected by exercise of a power of sale given in the mortgage (Colorado, for example), by entry and possession (New Hampshire, for example), or by writ of entry (Maine, for example). The mortgage may provide that the holder of the mortgage is entitled to the appointment of a receiver in any action to foreclose it.

Foreclosure procedure. The legal action taken by a lawyer on behalf of a creditor against a debtor who has defaulted in payment on a secured debt or MORTGAGE.

The first steps in the foreclosure proceeding are (1) the preparation of the notice of LIS PENDENS; (2) the preparation of the SUMMONS and COMPLAINT, which are prepared like the summons and complaint in any civil action. Because the foreclosure action generally has numerous defendants, the secretary usually types the summons instead of using a printed form.

Parties to a foreclosure action.

1. *Parties plaintiff.* The owner of the mortgage—the mortgagee or his or her beneficiary or assignee— is the plaintiff in a foreclosure action. The suit must be brought in the name of the actual owner of the mortgage. For example, if the mortgage is held by Richard Barth as trustee for Thomas Jones, the action is brought by *Richard Barth, Trustee for Thomas Jones,* not by Richard Barth. If the mortgage is owned jointly, say by husband and wife, the action is brought in the name of both owners.

2. *Parties defendant.* Every person who has any interest in the property covered by a mortgage is made a party defendant to the foreclosure action. These might include the mortgagor; the mortgagor's heirs, devisees, or legatees; wife of the mortgagor; *cestui que trustent* (*see* LATIN TERMS, *cestui que trust*); persons in possession as tenants or occupants; the people of the state; and others.

See also FICTITIOUS NAMES.

Filing and service of lis pendens, summons, and complaint. After the lis pendens, summons, and complaint are prepared, the procedure is the same as in any civil action. The notice of *lis pendens* must be filed with the proper county official (the official varies with the jurisdiction); the summons is issued for service and the complaint is filed with the CLERK OF THE COURT. The summons and complaint must be served on the defendants within a specified time after the *lis pendens* is filed.

The secretary must not forget to make diary and SUIT REGISTER *entries accordingly.*

Follow-up of process service. Follow-up of process service is necessary in all civil actions, but is particularly important in foreclosure actions because of the number of defendants. Numerous foreclosure actions are delayed because service of process is lax. It is the secretary's responsibility to see that the process server makes every effort to effect service expeditiously on all defendants. (See also NOTICE of Appeal, Service on Opposing Counsel.)

Other steps in foreclosure proceedings. After the summons, complaint, and *lis pendens* have been filed and served, the procedure in foreclosure litigation varies. The following steps are among those that will have to be taken, depending upon the jurisdiction and the circumstances of the case.

1. Application for receivership. If the

property involved is income producing, the plaintiff will ask for the appointment of a receiver to collect the income and make the necessary disbursements.

2. Application for appointment of guardian *ad litem.* If the parent of an infant defendant will not ask for the appointment of a guardian *ad litem,* the plaintiff does.

3. *Ex parte* motion to obtain leave to sue "arm of court," such as a trustee in BANKRUPTCY.

4. Entry of DEFAULT judgment.

5. Reference to compute or reference to master in chancery.

6. Hearing before referee or master. The lawyer will want the following papers to take to the hearing:

   (a) Referee's oath,

   (b) Referee's report ready for signature,

   (c) Bond or note,

   (d) MORTGAGE or DEED OF TRUST,

   (e) Assignments,

   (f) True copies or photocopies of (c), (d), and (e), so the originals may be withdrawn when the hearing is over,

   (g) Receipted bills for taxes, assessments, water rates, penalties or interest, if any, paid by mortgagee,

   (h) Receipt for payment of insurance if paid by mortgagee,

   (i) Summons with affidavit of service,

   (j) Check to order of referee.

7. Judgment or DECREE of foreclosure and sale.

8. Publication of notice of sale.

9. Sale.

Checklist of what to do in foreclosure action.

1. Make file and process as any other new matter.

2. *Keep diary entries* and progress record.

3. Order ABSTRACT OF TITLE continuation.

4. Prepare all papers, as directed by the attorney.

5. See that summons, complaint, and *lis pendens* are filed and served.

6. Follow process server closely.

7. Have copies (typed or photocopy) made of mortgage or deed, trust, bond or note, and assignments.

8. Prepare party sheet and keep it up to date.

9. If a receiver is appointed, keep after him for regular reports.

10. Gather together papers for the lawyer to take to the hearing (see preceding paragraph).

11. Make bookkeeping entries of all disbursements and receipts, just as in any case.

Foreign Corporation. A CORPORATION transacting business in a state other than the one in which it is incorporated is known as a foreign corporation in that state. A foreign corporation is obliged to observe all the requirements of the state in which it seeks to do business with respect to right of admission, service of process, taxation, etc. See also ALIEN CORPORATION; DOMESTIC CORPORATION; STATE OF INCORPORATION.

Forfeiture of Lease. The right of a landlord to terminate the LEASE if the tenant fails to pay rent or commits any other violation of the terms of the leases. Practically all leases provide that the lease may be forfeited and the tenant evicted for nonpayment of rent or for any other violation of the terms of the lease. Some leases require the landlord to give the tenant both notice of intention to forfeit and a period of grace. Upon forfeiture, the landlord has the right to enter and take possession of the property, unless he or she has waived the violation. *Waiver* may be implied if the landlord accepts rent with knowledge of the violation.

When the landlord evicts a tenant because of the latter's DEFAULT, the tenant's liability for future rent is ended unless the lease contains a *survival clause,* providing for continuance of such liability after EVICTION. Landlord's remedies, under a survival clause, are much the same as in the case of abandonment of the premises by the tenant. See ABANDONMENT.

Forgery and Counterfeiting. The act of copying or altering a writing with the intent to defraud. Although a forgery and a counterfeit are frequently regarded as the same, there is a distinction. A *forgery* is a false object of which there is no genuine original; a *counterfeit* is a false object of which there is a genuine original.

Forms. A term that refers to practice manuals, books of legal forms, and forms files. Forms are also called "printed lawblanks."

1. *Practice Manuals.* Books that contain forms of pleadings, which the lawyer

usually follows when dictating. Since the wording of pleadings differs with the state, a practice manual is used only in the state for which it is prepared. With the aid of a practice manual a secretary can draft many pleadings without dictation. The forms always indicate by italics, by parentheses, or in some other manner, the wording that must be changed with each case, such as names, dates, and various clauses applicable to a particular situation. In addition to the complete forms, the manuals contain many clauses applicable to various circumstances, which may be substitued for the clauses contained in the complete form.

2. *Books of Legal Forms.* Books that contain forms of instruments and documents as distinguished from litigation papers. Although the statutes prescribe the wording of many instruments, books of legal forms are generally useful for all states. They call attention to statutory requirements and often give forms for each state. For example, *Jones Legal Forms Annotated,* published by Bobbs-Merrill, Indianapolis, one of the best known books of legal forms, gives forms of acknowledgments, deeds, mortgages, and wills that meet the requirements of each state. Some forms books cover only forms in one particular field. Numerous clauses, as well as complete forms, enable the user to pick out the appropriate clause to suit his or her pupose. In giving instructions for the preparation of a legal instrument, the lawyer frequently tells the secretary to copy certain forms or clauses from a forms book.

3. *Forms Files.* Files that contain frequently used forms set up alphabetically in folders for ease of access. A well-organized forms file saves time for the

lawyer and the secretary. For example, a lawyer with an extensive practice in probate law would have in his or her forms file the recommended forms for probate of an estate. These forms vary from state to state; in Arkansas for instance, some 23 forms might be used in the probate of an estate. Which forms are applicable depends on the circumstances in each case. A lawyer with an extensive practice in real estate law should have copies of the many different forms of deeds used in his or her practice.

In addition to forms files, most legal secretaries keep handy a ring binder or file folder with a topical arrangement of sample instruments for easy reference. For example, under the topic "Chancery Court" could be found things such as confirmation of title, foreclosure actions, and divorce actions.

4. *Printed Law Blanks.* Commercially prepared legal instruments set up in printed form, with blank spaces to be filled in with specific information. For example, a printed law blank of a MORTGAGE or DEED will need only to be filled in with the necessary information to complete the document, such as the names of the parties and the description of the property being mortgaged or sold.

Printed law blanks are widely used in drawing up legal instruments. Law blank printers publish a catalog showing the numbers and titles of the blanks that they print. Each law blank has its title and, usually, the printer's catalog number, printed in small letters on it. The blanks are obtainable at almost any stationery store. Frequently the secretary can fill in these blanks without any dictated instruction. When it is necessary to dictate the material to be inserted in the blanks,

the usual manner of giving instructions is as follows:

The dictator numbers in pencil the spaces to be filled in—1, 2, 3, and so on. He or she then dictates the material that should be typed in each numbered blank, thus eliminating any confusion about where each dictated insertion should be typed.

(a) *Typing on ruled lines.* Make certain that the typing is adjusted so the bases of letters with tails that extend below the line of type (g, p, and y) just touch the ruled line.

(b) *Date of printing.* Printed forms bear a printer's mark showing the number of copies printed and the date of the printing. When filling in more than one copy use forms that were printed at the same time, because a change might have been made in the form.

(c) *Registration of printing.* Before attempting to fill in more than one blank form at a time by using carbon paper, make sure that the printing on all copies registers exactly. To do this, place the edges of the forms together and hold to the light. The printed matter in one copy should be exactly over corresponding material in the other copy. After the forms and carbon are inserted in the typewriter, if the forms are not perfectly aligned, loosen the typewriter platen and adjust the edges of the forms. They must be exactly even or the typing will not be properly spaced on the copies.

(d) *Fill-ins on both sides of sheet.* When making carbon copies of a form that has fill-ins on both sides of the sheet, take particular care to avoid having one side the ribbon copy and the other side the carbon copy, thus rendering the form unfit for execution. Double sheet forms are particularly apt to cause trouble in this respect.

(e) *Small blanks*. When the blanks on the form are small, fill in each form individually; do not use carbons. Be careful not to overlook any of the small blanks. In many forms they are not indicated by underlining, but only by a small space. Many of them call only for letters identifying the person or persons signing the document. For example, a printed mortgage form might include the following: "Said mortgagee___, ___h___ heirs or assigns." If there is more than one mortgagee, *s* is added to *mortgage* and ___ h___ becomes *their*. If there is only one mortgagee, the first blank is not filled in, and ___h___ becomes her or his.

(f) *"Z" ruling*. Frequently the material typed on a printed form does not fill the space provided. To protect the instrument from alteration draw a "Z" ruling, as illustrated here, with pen and ink in the unused space.

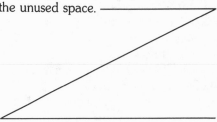

Forwarding Fee. Payment to a lawyer for referring a client to another attorney. Frequently a case is referred to a lawyer by an out-of-town firm. Often, although not always, a percentage of the fee earned is sent to the forwarding attorney.

Franchise. Special privilege conferred by the government upon individuals. For example, a city may grant a franchise to a local bus company that will give it sole authority to operate buses for a certain number of years. Franchise also refers to the right given to a person or corporation to market another's product within a certain area. Thus, the owner of a McDonald's franchise will have the exclusive right to open a McDonald's restaurant in a given area. A franchise tax is imposed on corporations by most states and must be paid before a corporation can do business in the state.

Fraud. A false representation of a fact, whether by words or by conduct, that deceives and is intended to deceive another so the other person will act upon it to his or her legal injury. For example, if a jewelry salesperson tells a customer that a piece of glass is a diamond, the salesperson is committing fraud.

The elements of fraud are (1) a false and material misrepresentation made by someone who either knows it is false or is ignorant of the truth; (2) the maker's intent that the representation be relied on by the person and in a manner reasonably contemplated; (3) a person's ignorance of the falsity of the representation; (4) a person's rightful or justified reliance; and (5) proximate injury to the person.

1. *Constructive Fraud (Legal Fraud).* All acts or omissions, contrary to equitable or legal duty, trust, or confidence and resulting in damage to another. There need be no evil intent.

2. *Extrinsic Fraud.* Fraud that is grounds for equitable relief from a judgment. Some intentional act or conduct by which the winning party has pre-

vented the losing party from having a fair trial of all issues involved in a controversy.

3. *Fraud in Fact (Positive Fraud)*. Actual fraud. Concealing something or making a false representation with an evil intent that causes injury to another. It is used in contrast to constructive fraud, which does not require evil intent.

4. *Fraud in Law*. Fraud inferred by law from the circumstances, where the one who commits it need not have any evil intent. Fraud in law is a constructive fraud.

5. *Fraud in the Factum*. Generally arises from a lack of identity between the instrument executed and the one intended to be executed, for example, when a blind or illiterate person executes a deed that has been read falsely to him after he asked to have it read. It renders the deed voidable through proper court action.

6. *Fraud in the Inducement*. Fraud that intended to and that does persuade one to execute an instrument or make an agreement. The person signing is induced to sign the instrument through fraudulent misrepresentation about what will be the results of his or her signing.

7. *Intrinsic Fraud*. Fraudulent representation that is presented and considered in rendering a judgment. Generally, it is not sufficient grounds for granting equitable relief from a judgment. For example perjury is intrinsic fraud, because it does not prevent a completely adversary proceeding. It only influences the judgment, so it will not be a ground for equitable relief from any judgment that results from it.

Freedom of Speech and Press. A guarantee, provided by the First and Fourteenth Amendments, against governmental restrictions upon public speeches and publications. The Constitution, however, has not been interpreted as granting an absolute right to speak without responsibility whatever one chooses. As Mr. Justice Holmes stated in one of his opinions, "The most stringent protection of free speech would not protect a man in falsely shouting fire in a theater and causing a panic." When deciding free speech and press cases, the courts are faced with difficult questions of degree, questions involving the balancing of the public protection and an individual's CIVIL RIGHTS. See also CLEAR AND PRESENT DANGER; BILL (of Rights).

Freight. In ADMIRALTY law, the money paid to a shipowner for transporting goods; the term is sometimes used by laymen to refer to the goods themselves.

Dead freight is the amount paid by a shipper or charterer for that part of the vessel's capacity he or she has reserved but fails to occupy.

Fresh Pursuit. Generally refers to the power of a police officer to make an arrest without a warrant when in immediate pursuit of a suspect. A police officer also has a right under the COMMON LAW to cross jurisdictions to make an arrest.

Frisk. A quick search of the outer clothing to detect, by the sense of touch, if a concealed weapon is being carried.

Fruit of the Poisonous Tree Doctrine. A rule fashioned by the courts that refuses to allow evidence that is the direct result or product of illegal conduct on the part of the police. It is based on the due process clause of the Fourteenth Amendment. The name of the rule comes from the idea that once the tree is poisoned (primary evidence is obtained illegally), the fruit of the tree (secondary evidence) is also tainted by the police misconduct and may not be used.

G

Garnishment. A legal proceeding by a JUDGMENT CREDITOR to compel a third party owing money to, or holding money for, a judgment debtor to pay the money to the creditor instead of to the debtor. The third party against whom the proceedings are brought is called the *garnishee*. Not only wages and salaries, but trust funds, insurance disability payments, and the like may be garnished. The laws that govern the right of garnishment and the procedures in effecting garnishment differ greatly in the various states.

Collecting a judgment by garnishment is particularly useful to a retail creditor whose customers are composed largely of salaried people or wage earners.

General Average Loss. A loss arising out of voluntary sacrifice made, or extraordinary expense incurred, for the joint benefit of a ship and its cargo when both are imperiled by a common danger. When the property of one is sacrificed to save the property of all, it would be unfair to make the owner of the sacrificed property bear the entire loss with no right of contribution from the owners of the property saved. Consequently, from the earliest times, ADMIRALTY has required that a loss occasioned for the benefit of all must be made good by the contribution of all. See also JETTISON; PARTICULAR AVERAGE LOSS; YORK-ANTWERP RULES.

General Damages. See DAMAGES.

General Strike. See STRIKE.

Gift. A voluntary transfer of property made gratuitously, and not for any CONSIDERATION.

A *gift inter vivos* is perfected when there is an intent of the DONOR to make a gift, a delivery of the gift, and an acceptance by the DONEE. Control over the subject of the gift is lost by the donor upon delivery, and the gift takes effect immediately. There can be no revocation of such a gift by the donor.

A *gift causa mortis* is made by the donor in contemplation of his or her death from some existing ailment or some other impending peril. If the donor does not recover, the gift takes effect upon death; the gift is void if the donor does recover. It has been held that real estate cannot be the subject of a *gift causa mortis*. The gift may be revoked by the donor any time until death.

Gift Causa Mortis. See GIFT.

Gift Inter Vivos. See GIFT.

Gift Tax. A tax that applies to gratuitous transfers of property during the taxpayer's life. The purpose of the gift tax law is to impose a tax on the donor that measurably approaches the ESTATE TAX that would have been payble on the donor's death if the GIFT had not been made and if the property given as a gift was part of the donor's estate at death. The value of property for gift tax purposes is determined as of the date the gift was made. See also MARITAL DEDUCTIONS.

Goodwill. An intangible asset arising from the reputation of a business and its relations with its customers. When an established business is offered for sale, goodwill has a marketable value.

Government Survey. See LAND DESCRIPTION, Section and township.

Graduated (progressive) Taxes. Taxes for which the rate increases as the income, or some other taxable base, increases. Graduated tax rates are found in taxes on individual incomes, corporation incomes, estates and inheritances. See INCOME TAX; ESTATE TAX; INHERITANCE TAXES.

Grand Jury Indictment. An accusation in writing found and presented by a jury charging that a person therein named has done some act which is a public offense.

The Fifth Amendment requires that criminal cases in federal courts be instituted with a grand jury indictment. The Constitution imposes no such restriction on the states.

Grand Larceny. The unlawful appropriation of property whose value is above a certain statutory amount. If the value of the stolen property is below the amount, the crime is classified as *petit larceny*. Many states have abolished the distinction between grand and petit larceny in their statutes. The states that do maintain the distinction provide for a harsher penalty when the amount stolen classifies the crime as grand larceny. See LARCENY.

Grantee (Real Estate). The person to whom REAL PROPERTY is conveyed by DEED. A deed must have a grantee to be valid. The grantee may be a minor or an insane person. A misspelling of the grantee's name does not render the deed invalid if his or her identity is apparent. A grantee may even take TITLE in an assumed name, but a deed to an entirely fictitious person is void. The name of the grantee should appear in the body of the deed correctly and in full. The deed should state the address of the grantee, otherwise it may not be accepted for recording.

The grantee is often designated in the deed as the "party of the second part," but the grantee does not sign the deed.

Grantor (Real Estate). The person who conveys REAL PROPERTY to another by DEED. The grantor is often designated in the deed as the "party of the first part." The grantor must be of legal age and of sound mind. If the grantor is a corporation, EXECUTION of the deed must be duly authorized by the directors or stockholders as required by state law. If the grantor is a trustee or executor, the trust instrument or WILL must be examined to determine whether the grantor has power to convey real estate. The marital status of the grantor is usually stated in the deed—for example, bachelor, widow, spinster (or unmarried), married, or divorced and not remarried. Whether the grantor's spouse must join in the deed depends upon the law of the state where the land is situated. *See also* GRANTEE.

Gross Income. *See* INCOME.

Guaranty. (The term is used interchangeably with *suretyship* by courts and lawyers as well as laypersons.) A contract of guaranty or of suretyship is a contract whereby one person agrees to be responsible to another for the payment of a debt or the performance of a duty by a third person. It must be in writing and is not enforceable if made orally.

The term *guaranty* (or *guarantee*) is often loosely used in the sense of WARRANTY. In a strict legal and commercial sense, it is the essence of a contract of guaranty that there should be a principal, liable directly to perform some act or duty. An agreement by a third party guaranteeing the honest and faithful performance of a contract of sale is a contract of guaranty; an agreement in a sales contract "guaranteeing" the efficient performance of a product for a certain number of years is a contract of warranty.

The words *guarantee* and *guaranty* are frequently used incorrectly. For the verb, always use *guarantee*. Business convention has established a specialized use of *guaranty* as a noun, as illustrated above. However, *guarantee* is never wrong, even in these expressions. A safe rule to follow is: When in doubt, use *guarantee*.

Guardian. The person appointed by a Probate Court to act for and guard the property of a minor, or an incompetent person, known as the "ward."

Guardian Ad Litem. *See Ad litem* in the list of LATIN TERMS.

Guardianship. Guardianships may be created for minor children or mentally or physically incompetent persons. A suitable guardian is appointed by the Probate Court after serving notice upon the "ward" and the ward's mother and father or next of kin, and letters of guardianship are issued to the guardian. The guardian then gathers together all of the assets of his or her ward and files an inventory with the Court that lists all of the ward's property, real or personal. The property might consist of real estate or monthly income from the Veterans Administration, Social Security or Railroad Retirement or other retirement benefits such as annuities. The guardian opens a checking account at the bank to handle the funds of his or her ward. The account is in the name of the guardian and the guardian signs the checks. The guardian must make regular accountings to the Probate Court (usually once a year or sometimes once every two years, depending on the state) of receipts and disbursements that come into the guardian's hands and show the balance left in the estate. The guardian must make an itemized statement in the account of all funds, that is, checking account balance, savings account balance, certificates of deposit, and so on. The guardian pays all of the debts of his or her ward and banks all the income.

What to Do. If the guardian is the attorney, the secretary may receive and deposit all income and type out checks for bills as they come in, keeping an accounting sheet of all receipts and disbursements and balance as she goes. The secretary may note in her diary when an accounting is due and prepare the account for the guardian's signature. If V.A. funds are coming into the guardianship, an extra copy of the account should be filed with the court for the V.A. Office. A file copy should be made and fastened down in the file when the account is filed in court with the date of filing shown on the file copy.

H

Habeas Corpus (Latin for "You have the body"). A writ commanding the person having custody of another to produce the person detained at a certain place and time so the court may determine if the detention is lawful.

A provision in the U.S. Constitution puts it beyond the power of the government to abolish this procedure and the powers of the courts in relation to it, except in case of war when the "public safety shall require it." The provision does not bind the states, but there is commonly a similar provision in state constitutions.

Habendum Clause. The clause in a DEED or MORTGAGE that states that the GRANTEE is to have the property transferred to him or her. The habendum clause derives its name from the Latin phrase *habendum et tenendum* and, accordingly, begins with the words *to have and to hold.* Its purpose is to define the extent of the interest conveyed. When special circumstances surround the transfer of the property, the lawyer dictates a substitute habendum.

Examples:
TO HAVE AND TO HOLD the premises herein granted unto the Party of the Second Part, his heirs and assigns, forever,

TO HAVE AND TO HOLD the granted premises, with all the rights, easements, and appurtenances thereto belonging, to the said John L. Thompson, his heirs and assigns, to his/their own use forever,

SUBJECT, HOWEVER, to all rights of the lessees, tenants and occupants of, or in said granted premises, or in any part, or parts, thereof.

Habitual Criminal. A description given in many states to a person who is convicted of a FELONY, having been previously convicted of any crime. It has been held that an offender is not put in DOUBLE JEOPARDY for one crime when, upon conviction for a second crime committed later, his or her punishment is increased because a statute categorizes the offender as an habitual criminal.

Heading. The designation of the jurisdiction, the VENUE, the title of the case, index number, and title of the pleading that appears on a legal document or court paper. See CAPTION.

Hearsay. Written or oral evidence that seeks to establish the existence of a fact based not on the witness' own personal knowledge or observation, but on what someone else said. Hearsay evidence is generally excluded at a trial because there is no opportunity for CROSS-EXAMINATION of the declarant to lay bare whatever weakness there may be in the witness' story. See DYING DECLARATION.

Heir. One who inherits or is entitled to inherit. See WILL; LEGACY.

Hereditaments. Things capable of being inherited, whether corporeal or incorporeal, real or personal, or mixed, and including not only lands and everything thereon, but also heirlooms and certain furniture, which, by custom, may descend to the heir together with the land.

Holder in Due Course. The transferee of a NEGOTIABLE INSTRUMENT who acquires the instrument under the following conditions: (1) The paper must be complete and regular on its face. (2) It must be purchased before maturity. (3) The purchase must be in good faith for a valuable consideration. (4) The purchase must be made without notice of defects in the title or of defenses against payment to the transferor. A holder in due course may enforce collection of the instrument against prior parties regardless of their claims, defenses, and offsets against one another. A transferee may acquire the rights of a holder in due course without being one himself. For example: *A*, the holder in due course of a note procured by the payee through fraud, endorses the note to *B*, who knew of the fraud and hence was not a holder in due course. *B*, however, acquires *A's* right as a holder in due course to collect the note regardless of the fraud, provided *B* has no part in the fraud. See NEGOTIABLE INSTRUMENT.

Holding Company. A CORPORATION organized for the purpose of owning and holding the stock of one or more other corporations. The term is generally applied to a corporation that owns enough of the voting stock of another corporation to have working control over it. Companies that conduct a business of their own in addition to owning the controlling stock of another company are called *holding-operating companies*. Companies that do not operate a business but merely direct the activities of their subsidiaries are called *pure holding companies*. The holding company is the *parent* and the companies whose controlling stock it owns are *subsidiaries*. See SUBSIDIARY CORPORATION. The assets of the holding company consist mainly of stocks of the subsidiaries and from these stocks the holding company derives its income. Holding companies may be vulnerable to prosecution under ANTITRUST LAWS when used as a device to suppress competition or to create a monopoly.

Holographic Will. See WILL.

Homicide. The act of one human being killing another. Homicide is a necessary ingredient of the crimes of MURDER and MANSLAUGHTER. It is possible, however, to kill someone without criminal intent and without subsequent criminal prosecution. For example, killing in self-defense or as the only means of arresting an escaping felon.

House Agency. A fictional collection establishment created by a creditor to convey the impression that it is an independent and bona fide COLLECTION AGENCY. It is but a name and address used by the creditor for its final collection effort. The advantage is that by use of the "agency's" stationery the creditor can press with all the vigor of a regular collection agency. See also COLLECTIONS.

Hung Jury. A jury wherein the members cannot reach a verdict because of differences of opinion.

Illegitimate Child. See BASTARD.

Impleader. The process of bringing into an action a third party who may be liable to the defendant. See also PARTIES TO AN ACTION. The purpose of impleader is to avoid a multiplicity of actions and to encourage a determination of all the controversies existing between the parties in one suit. For example, if a person gets sick from tainted meat he or she bought, that person can sue the butcher. The butcher can then, in the same action, implead the meat packer, and the rights of all the parties will be determined in the single action.

Inchmaree Clause. The portion of an ocean marine insurance contract that covers against perils such as bursting of boilers, breakage of shafts, damage through any latent defects in the machinery, hull, or appurtenances, or from faults or errors in navigation and/or management of the vessel by the master, mariners, mates, engineers, or pilots.

Inchoate. Begun but not completed, as a contract not executed by all parties. An instrument that the law requires to be recorded is an *inchoate instrument* until it is recorded, in that it is good only between the parties and privies (see PRIVITY). A wife's interest in her husband's lands that becomes a right of dower upon his death, is an inchoate right of dower during his lifetime. An interest in real estate that may become a vested interest unless barred is an *inchoate interest*. Other phrases are *inchoate equity, inchoate lien, inchoate title*.

Income (Federal tax law). The return in money, property, or services from one's business, labor, or invested capital.

1. *Gross Income.* To determine gross income, subtract from income the income that is exempt from taxes. Items of income that are exempt from federal INCOME TAX are called *exclusions*. Some examples of exclusions are gifts, inheritances, and interest on state bonds.

2. *Adjusted Gross Income.* Gross income less business expenses of the taxpayer. Adjusted gross income is computed by individuals only, not by corporations.

3. *Taxable Income.* Gross income less deductions allowed by law. For individuals, adjusted gross income less additional deductions for personal expenses and personal exemptions is the taxable income. Individuals may take a standard deduction in lieu of itemizing deductions for personal expenses. The standard de-

duction is *in addition to* deductions for adjusted gross income, but *instead of* deductions for personal expenses. In every case, the amount of the standard deduction depends on the amount of the taxpayer's adjusted gross income.

For corporations, taxable income is gross income less deductions. Many expenses incurred by corporations are deductions.

4. *Prepaid Income.* Income that is received before it is earned. See also WITHHOLDING; CAPITAL (Gain and Loss).

Income Tax. A federal, state, or local tax that is levied on the INCOME of individuals and corporations, estates, and some trusts. The federal income tax is expressly authorized by the Sixteenth Amendment to the Constitution.

Under the federal pay-as-you-go income tax collection system, most individuals pay all or a substantial part of their income tax during the year in which they receive their income. The tax is withheld from their wages (see WITH-HOLDING) or is paid in quarterly installments based on a declaration of estimated tax, or both.

Most income taxes are GRADUATED TAXES. The rates increase as the amount of income reported increases. See also INTERNAL REVENUE SERVICE.

Incompatibility. Incapability of existing together. Incompatibility is not ordinarily grounds for DIVORCE, although in some states it is.

Incorporating Procedure. See CORPORATION.

224

Incorporators. Those who unite for the purpose of forming a CORPORATION. They tell the lawyer the kind of business the corporation will engage in and other details that are necessary for the lawyer to know before he or she commences the legal organization procedure. They also put up the capital for the corporation. Only natural persons may incorporate, although they may actually be representing a corporation or a PARTNERSHIP.

A large majority of the states require three or more incorporators. Many states also require that one or more of the incorporators be a resident of that state, or that the organization meeting of the corporation be held in that state. For these reasons, and for convenience, the incorporators are frequently *dummies*. They are not the principals who are actually interested in the organization of the corporation, but merely act for them until the organization meeting. Secretaries frequently act as dummy incorporators. See also CERTIFICATE (of Incorporation).

Indemnity. An undertaking, either express or implied, to compensate another for loss or damage, or for expenses or trouble incurred, either in the past or in the future. Under a contract of indemnity, the indemnity is the obligation or duty resting upon a particular person or company to make good any loss or damage another has suffered, or may suffer, upon the happening of a specific event. The person giving the indemnity (agreeing to indemnify) is the *indemnitor,* corresponding to the insured. The term *indemnity* also applies to the sum paid as compensation or remuneration in the event of loss or damage to the indemnitee. The indemnity may be payable to the indemnitee or to someone else in behalf of the indemnitee. For example, the payments that are made to an injured workman under workmen's compensation insurance are indemnities. They are payable to the worker in behalf of his or her employer, who is the indemnitee.

Indenture. A formal written instrument between two or more parties, involving reciprocal rights and duties —for example, a lease. In ancient times, the practice was to write two or more copies of the instrument on the same piece of parchment. The copies were then separated by tearing the parchment in irregular fashion so the indentations of each torn part would fit the other. Hence, the term *indenture*.

Independent Contractor. A person who is hired to perform services and is responsible for the end results of his or her labor. The hirer has no control over the method of performance or details of the independent contractor's work. The general rule is that a hirer is not liable for a TORT committed by an independent contractor. To avoid any later controversy over the status of an independent contractor (e.g., that he or she is not an employee), some organizations request that such persons sign an agreement clarifying their status and the nature of their services. See figure 1.

Index Number. See CLERK OF THE COURT, Index System.

Index to Foreign Legal Periodicals. An index to legal periodicals used as a "secondary" source by the lawyer. It was started in 1960 as a quarterly with annual cumulations.

Index to Legal Periodicals. An index to legal periodical publications by law schools and professional associations used as a "secondary source" by the lawyer.

Indictment. An accusation in writing found and presented by a grand jury, legally convoked and sworn, to the court in which it is impaneled, charging that a person therein named has done some act, or been guilty of some omission, that, by law, is a public offense, punishable on indictment.

Indirect Taxes. See DIRECT TAXES.

Industrial Union. See LABOR UNION.

Inferior Courts. Judicial tribunals that have limited jurisdiction and powers. The most common inferior courts are justice of the peace courts, small claims courts, and a class of courts whose jurisdiction is confined to violations of city ordinances. Courts of this class are variously called police, magistrate's, municipal, or recorder's courts. All inferior courts have a narrow jurisdiction. In criminal matters, they are restricted to preliminary hearings or inquiries except in minor matters. In civil actions, they have jurisdiction over actions involving

AGREEMENT FOR INDEPENDENT CONTRACTOR

AGREEMENT dated _____, 19 ___, between _____, hereinafter called (Company) (Corporation) (last Name) and _____, hereinafter called (Contractor) (Last Name).

WHEREAS, THE (Corporation) desires to enter into this agreement with (Contractor) to the extent and upon the terms and conditions hereinafter set forth, and

WHEREAS, (Contractor) is willing to enter into this agreement with respect to his time, services, and workmanship upon the terms and conditions hereinafter set forth

NOW, THEREFORE, in consideration of the premises and the mutual agreements hereinafter set forth, the parties hereto agree as follows:

1. *Relationship Between Parties.* The (Contractor) shall perform and contract as an independent contractor and nothing herein contained shall be construed to be inconsistent with this relationship or status.

2. *Duties/Services.* (as required)

3. *Time Requirements.* (as required)

4. *Compensation.* (as required)

5. *Workmanship.* (as required)

6. *Working Supervision by (Contractor).* The (Contractor agrees to be responsible for and will supervise the execution of all works covered by this ·agreement.

7. *(Contractor) to Furnish Labor and Materials.* The (Contractor) shall furnish at his own expense all labor, materials, equipment, and other items necessary to carry out the terms of this contract.

IN WITNESS WHEREOF, (Corporation) has caused this agreement to be executed in its corporate name by its corporate officers, and (Contractor) has set his hand and seal, as of the date and year first above written.

(CORPORATION):   (CONTRACTOR):

By _____   _____

Attest _____
       Secretary

CORPORATE SEAL

Independent Contractor: Figure 1.
Contractor agreement form.

small amounts only, the amount varying with the state. For example, in Arkansas, justice of the peace courts have jurisdiction over claims of $300 or less. Inferior courts are usually courts not of record, but their proceedings may be recorded. Sometimes, the judge of an inferior court is not a lawyer. The decisions of these courts are subject to review or correction by higher courts. Actually, circuit and district courts are "inferior" to appellate or supreme courts, but the term is usually applied to the courts not of record described here. See also SUPERIOR COURTS; COURTS OF SPECIAL JURISDICTION; COURTS OF INTERMEDIATE REVIEW; AMERICAN COURT SYSTEM.

Ingress, Egress, and Regress. These words express the rights of a lessee to enter, go upon, and return from the lands in question.

Inheritance Taxes. Levies by some of the states on the right of the living to receive property from the estate of the deceased. Inheritance taxes are EXCISE TAXES payable by the heirs and not by the estate of the deceased unless decedent specifies in his or her Last Will and Testament that the estate pay the inheritance taxes, in which case it is mandatory that the estate pay the taxes. See ESTATE TAXES.

Injunction. A writ restraining a person or corporation from doing or continuing to do something that threatens or causes injury, or requiring the defendant to do a particular act. The writ may be granted by the court to which the case is brought or by a judge of the court. Injunctions may be classified as prohibitory and mandatory. A *prohibitory injunction* restrains the commission or continuance of an act. Thus, a prohibitory injunction may restrain a board of elections from placing a certain candidate's name on the ballot. A *mandatory injunction* commands acts to be done or undone. For example, a mandatory injunction may compel a property owner to open a road the owner had closed by constructing a fence across it, thus depriving another property owner of the use of the road.

Injunctions may also be classified as (1) restraining orders, (2) temporary injunctions, and (3) permanent injunctions. A *restraining order* may be granted without notice to the opposite party, for the purpose of restraining the defendant until the court has heard an application for a temporary injunction.

A *temporary injunction* is granted on the basis of the application, before the court has heard the case on its merits. It restrains the defendant during the litigation of a case and may be either dissolved or made permanent when the rights of the parties are determined. Temporary injunctions are also called preliminary, interlocutory, or injunction *pendente lite* (see LATIN TERMS). *Permanent injunctions* are granted on the merits of the case. They are often called "final injunction." See PROVISIONAL REMEDIES.

In Perpetuity. Existing forever.

Insanity. A lack of reason, intelligence, and a memory that prevents a person from understanding the nature of his acts or from distinguishing between right and wrong conduct. This legal definition is to be distinguished from the medical idea of insanity, which has to do with a prolonged departure of the individual from his natural mental state. Insanity in law covers nothing more than the relation of the person and the particular act that is the subject of judicial investigation.

A few examples of legal proceedings where insanity may be shown are a criminal proceeding where insanity is alleged as a defense, a proceeding to defeat a WILL on the ground of the insanity of the maker, and a suit to avoid a CONTRACT.

Insolvency. The inability to pay debts as they mature. The word is used in two senses: (1) A debtor whose assets exceed his liabilities but who is temporarily unable to meet his obligations as they mature because his assets are not readily convertible to cash, is insolvent in the *equitable* sense. (2) A debtor whose total assets are less than his liabilities is insolvent in the *bankruptcy* sense.

Installment Collections. Receipt of partial payments of debts. Litigation as a means of collecting a small sum should be a last resort; it is expensive, and the JUDGMENT may be as difficult to collect as the debt. For this reason, attorneys will "play long" with the debtor and accept partial payments. Usually the arrangement is that the debtor will pay a certain amount at regular intervals. An arrangement of this type is often made

after judgment is obtained against the debtor. It is the secretary's responsibility to bring up the file for attention on the dates that payments are due. If a payment is not made as promised, upon instruction from the lawyer, she should communicate with the debtor, either by telephone or mail. See COLLECTIONS.

Installment Contract. An agreement in which credit is extended upon the promise to pay a certain part of a particular debt at certain regular times. The credit may be granted as a loan of money. For example, a person may borrow money from a bank or a personal finance company on his or her personal credit with an agreement to repay a certain portion of it each month, or each week. Or the credit may be extended upon the sale of goods. For example, a person buys furniture and agrees to pay a certain part of the price at regular intervals instead of paying the entire price immediately. See Also CONDITIONAL SALE.

Installment Credit. That form of credit that involves the repayment or amortization of an obligation by payments of fixed portions at regular intervals. Installment credit is granted as a loan of money or extended upon the sale of goods. When extended for consumer goods, the credit is known as *consumer* or *retail installment credit;* when extended for commercial or business use, the credit is known as *productive* or *mercantile installment credit.*

Instructions to Jury. See CHARGE TO THE JURY.

Insurable Interest. A person has an insurable interest if he or she might be financially injured by the occurrence of the event insured against. Under American law, if an insurable interest is not present, the contract is a mere wager and is not enforceable.

1. *in Property.* Insurable interest must exist at the time the loss occurs. Title to the property insured is not necessary; an owner, lessee, mortgagee, or purchaser has an insurable interest. Thus, the interest (a) may be contingent, as the interest of a purchaser under contract of sale; (b) may be conditional, as the interest of a purchaser under a contract of CONDITIONAL SALE until the conditions of the sale have been met; (c) may arise from possession as in the case of a bailee (see BAILMENT).

2. *in Life.* Insurable interest must exist at the time the policy is written but need not exist at the time death occurs. Every person has insurable interest in his or her own life and may name anyone desired as beneficiary. Other examples of relations giving rise to an insurable interest are those of (a) employer and valued employee; (b) several partners of a partnership; (c) creditor and debtor; (d) corporation and its officers; (e) wife and husband; (f) dependent children.

Insurance. A social device designed to eliminate pure risk. Almost everything is insurable, if a person wants to pay the premium. General classifications of insurance are fire and extended coverage, casualty, accident and health, life, and marine. Also available to the homeowner is the homeowner's policy, which covers a number of perils. Available to the businessperson and attorney are special multiperil policies that cover fire, extended coverage, burglary, personal injury, and other liability perils. Insurance companies are controlled by state insurance departments and the statutes of the state in which they operate. The contracts or policies are written, but an agent may place an oral binder on property to obtain immediate coverage.

Insurance records. 1. *Life insurance.* The secretary should keep two classes of life insurance records: a reminder of premium dates and a description of the policies. A premium distribution record might also be desirable.

(a) A tickler card file (see FILING) should be kept as a reminder of premium dates. The card should show (1) due dates of the premiums; (2) amount of premium; (3) to whom the premium is payable (checks are made to the company, agent, or broker who bills the lawyer); (4) where to mail the check; (5) policy number; (6) name of company issuing the policy; (7) name of insured. If dividends are to be applied as part payment of the premium, a note to that effect should be made on the tickler card. If the secretary handles more than one bank account, the tickler card should also show the name of the bank account on which the payment check should be drawn. Some secretaries note on the tickler card the dates the premiums are paid.

(b) The secretary should maintain a record describing the life insurance policies carried by her employer and by each member of his family if she is responsible for those policies. A desirable form for this purpose is a sheet record, which shows at a glance the entire life insurance

POLICY RECORD										
COMPANY	NUMBER	AMOUNT	TYPE	DATE OF ISSUE	AGE AT ISSUE	GROSS YEARLY PREMIUM	DISABILITY		DISABILITY INDEMNITY	BENEFICIARY
							MONTHLY INCOME	PREMIUM WAVER		

Insurance Records: Figure 1.

Sheet record of life insurance policies.

Policy Number	Day of Mo. Due	DISTRIBUTION OF LIFE INSURANCE PREMIUM PAYMENTS												
		Jan.	Feb.	Mar.	Apr.	May	June	July	Aug.	Sept.	Oct.	Nov.	Dec.	Total
397456	6			$100						$100				$200
497653	15						$150							$150
909634	30										$75			$ 75
				$100			$150			$100	$75			$425

Insurance Records: Figure 2.

Life insurance premium distribution record.

program. (See figure 1.) A separate record should be kept of policies carried by each person.

(c) Professional persons and business executives who carry a heavy life insurance program are interested in knowing how the premiums are distributed throughout the year. Figure 2 is a form that may be used for that purpose. The day of the month on which the premium is due is entered in the "Day of Mo. Due" column, and the amount of the premium is entered opposite the policy number in the column for the appropriate month.

The record shows the totals for each month and for the year.

This record may be used in either of two ways: (1) to show the distribution of premiums for the forthcoming year, or (2) to enter payments as they are made, thus providing a running record of all premiums paid in a given year. This record is kept in addition to, and not as a substitute for, the reminder of premium dates and description of the policies.

2. *Insurance other than life.* The records that the secretary should keep for insurance other than life are determined

INSURANCE (OTHER THEN LIFE)												
KIND OF INSURANCE			PROPERTY INSURED					LOCATION OF PROPERTY				
AMOUNT PAID FOR PROPERTY			DATE PROPERTY PURCHASED			PURCHASED FROM			PURCHASED THROUGH			
SUBSEQUENT IMPROVEMENTS												
REMARKS												

DATE OF ISSUE	DATE OF EXPIRATION	NAME OF COMPANY	NAME OF AGENT	POLICY NUMBER	POLICY PAYABLE TO	AMOUNT OF INSURANCE	AMOUNT OF PREMIUM	AMOUNT OF DIVIDEND	RATE OF DIV.	NET PREMIUM	DATE CANCELLED	AMOUNT RETURN PREMIUM
			TOTALS	BROUGHT FORWARD								
			TOTALS	CARRIED FORWARD								

Insurance Records: Figure 3.
Detailed description of policies other than life insurance.
(Courtesy, Trussel Manufacturing Co., Poughkeepsie, N.Y.)

by the extent of the insurance program. A reminder of expiration dates must be kept. The other records described below are desirable.

(a) Whenever a policy or certificate is received, whether as a first contract or as a renewal of an expiring contract, the secretary should make up a 3- by 5-inch tickler card as a reminder of the expiration date. The following are the minimum essentials to be noted: (1) type of coverage and expiration date; (2) identification by company and policy number; (3) agent's name; (4) insured; (5) property covered; (6) amount of premium. There is no need for a tickler card for the premium due date because a bill ordinarily accompanies the new policy.

(b) The form in figure 3 provides for a *detailed description* of policies other than life insurance policies. A separate sheet is kept for each kind of insurance on each piece of property. The entry showing value of the property is particularly useful for reference when market values fluctuate and the insured wants to check on whether he or she is fully insured or overinsured.

(c) A form similar to figure 2 for distribution of life insurance premiums may be used to show a distribution of premiums for general insurance. The premium distribution for all general and life insurance may be kept on the same sheet.

Intangible Property. Property that has no value itself, but that represents valuable things such as bonds, stocks, promissory notes.

Interference Proceeding. A hearing instituted by the Patent Office to determine, from evidence, the prior inventor entitled to the PATENT when two or more applicants claim the same invention. The priority question is determined by a board of three *interference examiners* on the evidence submitted. From the decision of the Board of Patent Interferences, the losing party may appeal to the Court of Customs and Patent

231

Appeals or file a civil action against the winning party in the appropriate United States district court.

Interim. In the meantime.

Interlocking Directorates. Boards of directors of two or more corporations having one or more directors in common. Through this method of control, the will of the common dominant stockholders is executed. See BOARD OF DIRECTORS.

Interlocutory Decree. An intermediate or preliminary finding of a court. It is not conclusive and does not determine the suit, but directs some further proceedings preparatory to the final DECREE. For example, in an action for *partition* (division of property among co-owners), an interlocutory judgment must first declare what is the right, share, or interest of each party in the property. A final decree of partition is thereafter given based on the interlocutory finding. See also JUDGMENT.

Intermediary Appellate Courts. Tribunals to which cases are brought from courts of ORIGINAL JURISDICTION for appeals. They exist in those states where a large volume of cases makes it necessary to relieve the congestion that might develop if all cases for appeal were brought only to the highest appellate court. See COURTS OF INTERMEDIATE REVIEW; APPELLATE COURT; AMERICAN COURT SYSTEM; COURTS OF SPECIAL JURISDICTION.

Internal Revenue Service. A federal agency that administers the nation's tax laws.

Information as to the applicability of internal revenue laws may be obtained from the principal and local offices of district directors of Internal Revenue. Requests for extensions of time for filing returns and requests for information as to cases in their charge, offers in compromise, and claims for abatement, credit, or refund of taxes may be submitted to district directors. See INCOME TAX.

Interpleader. A proceeding whereby a debtor petitions the court to compel parties making the same claim against him or her to litigate the matter among themselves. It is used to avoid multiple liability on the part of the debtor.

Interrogatories. Pretrial inquiry whereby written questions are proposed by one party to the other party. Answers must be written and verified under oath.

Interstate Commerce. Any business transaction conducted directly or indirectly across state boundaries.

The U. S. Constitution gives Congress the power to regulate interstate commerce and forbids the states to regulate, restrict, or interfere with it.

Interstate commerce includes the following:

1. Any interchange of commodities, both tangible and intangible,
2. All facilities of transportation across state lines,
3. Transmission of power and communication—radio, television, telephone, and telegraph,

4. All persons who work in, or in connection with, interstate movements.

The power to regulate interstate commerce also includes the power to regulate any business that "affects" interstate commerce. This means that a business being conducted locally and not across state lines may still be regulated under some circumstances. See INTRASTATE COMMERCE; CONCURRENT POWERS.

Intervenor. See PARTIES TO AN ACTION.

Intervention. A procedure a person uses to become one of the PARTIES TO AN ACTION to protect his or her interests. A person has a right to intervene if that person may be bound by a JUDGMENT in an action where he or she is not represented.

Inter Vivos Trust. See TRUST.

Intestate. Without making a WILL. The word is also often used to designate the person who has died without making a will. See also TESTATOR; LETTERS OF ADMINISTRATION; PROBATE.

Intestate Succession. The method of disposing of the property of a person who has died without a will or who has left a portion of an estate unaccounted for. Disposition is according to the laws of descent and distribution as set out by statute in each state.

Intra. (Latin) Within; inside.

Intrastate Commerce. Business conducted entirely within a state and not part of an interchange or movement of tangible or intangible commodities across state boundaries.

A firm that manufactures, sells, and uses a product entirely within one state is engaged in intrastate commerce. Isolated cases of engaging in INTERSTATE COMMERCE will not affect the standing of an intrastate firm.

A state can prohibit a foreign CORPORATION from doing intrastate business within its borders unless it meets certain qualifying conditions. Of course, these conditions must be reasonable.

It is important to differentiate between intrastate and interstate commerce under most of the federal regulatory laws. Any business (even though intrastate in nature) that "affects" interstate commerce, may be subject to federal regulation. For example, the Wage-Hour Law regulates labor conditions in industries engaged in the production of goods for commerce. Thus, employees of a local linen supply company that services the needs of customers engaged in interstate commerce are rendering services necessary for the production of goods for interstate commerce, and are therefore covered by federal law. See also INTERSTATE COMMERCE; CONCURRENT POWERS.

Invitee. A person on the premises for a purpose of mutual benefit concerning the business of the owner, for example a shopper in a store. A social visitor is not an invitee. The owner of the premises has the legal duty towards the invitee of reasonable care to keep the premises in a safe condition of repair. There is also the duty to give notice of any latent unsafe condition. *See* LICENSEE; TRESPASSER; NEGLIGENCE.

Issue of Execution. When a judgment is obtained by one party against another, the successful party is known as a *judgment creditor* and the other party as a *judgment debtor*. If the judgment debtor does not pay the judgment, the attorney for the judgment creditor may get the CLERK OF THE COURT to issue execution to a designated officer of the law, usually the sheriff, constable, or marshall. The execution is a printed form, easily filled out upon the basis of the information in the file. If the officer to whom the execution is issued can find no property of the judgment debtor against which to levy, the officer returns the execution "unsatisfied." The lawyer may then commence a SUPPLEMENTARY PROCEEDING.

Jason Clause. A clause in a BILL of Lading that requires cargo owners to contribute in GENERAL AVERAGE LOSS in cases of damage resulting from navigation errors or faulty equipment. In order for the Jason clause to operate, the ship owner must have exercised diligence to make the vessel seaworthy and have it properly manned, equipped, and supplied.

Jeopardy. See DOUBLE JEOPARDY.

Jetsam. See JETTISON.

Jettison. The act of throwing part of the cargo overboard to lighten a ship that is in a storm or other emergency. The cargo thrown overboard is called *jetsam*; the loss incurred is a GENERAL AVERAGE LOSS.

Goods that float upon the sea when a ship sinks, or otherwise perishes, are called *flotsam*.

Joinder. Joining of parties as plaintiffs or defendants; also, joining causes of action or defense in a single suit.

Joint Adventure (Venture). An association of two or more persons for a given, limited purpose, without the usual powers, duties, and responsibilities that go with a PARTNERSHIP. Thus, if two people buy a specific piece of real estate for resale at a profit, they become parties to a joint adventure; but if they enter into an agreement whereby each contributes money and services in establishing and carrying on a real estate business, they become members of a partnership.

Joint and Several. An obligation or liability incurred, under contract or otherwise, by two or more parties together and separately is said to be *joint and several*. The parties may be held jointly responsible or severally responsible. Thus a bond may be joint and several, in which case the obligors are liable either individually or together, at the option of the obligee.

Joint Bank Account. A checking, savings, or thrift account opened in the names of two or more people. The deposit agreement and the designation of the account should be specific about whether the depositors are tenants in common or joint tenants.

When two depositors are tenants in common, either party can make deposits, but the signatures of both are required for withdrawal. At the death of

235

one of them, the survivor is entitled to his or her own interest in the account only. The heirs of the deceased are entitled to the decedent's interest. When two depositors are joint tenants, either party can deposit or withdraw. At the death of one of the depositors, the survivor is entitled to the balance of the account. The same principles apply where there are more than two depositors.

Joint Stock Company. A form of business organization created by an agreement of the parties. This agreement is commonly called *articles of association*. This type of company is similar to the CORPORATION in the following respects: (1) the ownership is represented by transferable certificates; (2) management is in the hands of a board of governors or directors elected by the members (shareholders); (3) the business continues for its fixed term notwithstanding the death or disability of one or more of the members. It is unlike the corporation and like the PARTNERSHIP in that each shareholder is personally liable for the company's debts.

Joint Tenancy. An estate held by two or more persons at the same time, under the same TITLE or source of ownership, in which each has the same degree of interest and the same right of possession. The chief characteristic of a joint tenancy is that upon the death of one of the joint tenants, his or her interest automatically passes to the other joint tenants still living. The courts do not favor joint tenancies, and many jurisdictions permit joint tenants to defeat the right of surviving joint tenants in the state

of MORTGAGE or conveyance to other persons.

Some of the states have gone so far as to pass retroactive statutes making existing undivided interests *tenancies in common* unless the survivorship element is expressly provided for in the DEED or WILL that created the interest. See also TENANCY IN COMMON; TENANCY BY THE ENTIRETY.

Joint Tortfeasors. People whose separate wrongs unite in producing a single injury, for example, NEGLIGENCE of two drivers causing a collision. If the defendants are treated as joint tortfeasors, each one is liable for the plaintiff's injuries and either one or both may be sued.

Judge. An officer of the court invested with authority to administer justice. Insofar as power, authority, and duty are concerned, there is no distinction between a judge and a justice. The law in each state specifies whether the members of each court in that state will be designated as judges or justices. In the majority of states, the members of the highest appellate courts are called justices, whereas the members of the trial courts are judges. See AMERICAN COURT SYSTEM, table I, for the technical designation of the various courts listed there.

The lawyer prepares orders and DECREES for the court's approval. It is important to know whether the technically correct designation of the court is *judge* or *justice,* because these papers always contain the court's title, either in the heading or in the signature. Almost all of them begin with a heading similar to the following:

EXAMPLE 1.
Present:
HONORABLE JOHN E. SMITH,
Justice

EXAMPLE 2.
Present:
HONORABLE JOHN E. SMITH,
United States District Judge.

The proper form should always be used in writing or speaking to or about court members. see CORRESPONDENCE, Addressing Officials.

Judgment. An official decision of a court, based on a jury's verdict or, in absence of a jury, on the law and facts as found by the judge. Broadly speaking, any adjudication by a court of law or of equity is considered a judgment, but technically an adjudication by a *court of equity* is a *decree.* The words *judgment* and *decree* are often used synonymously, especially since many courts now combine both law and EQUITY jurisdiction.

A decree usually directs the defendant *to do or not to do some specific thing,* as opposed to a judgment for DAMAGES in a court of law. For example, an owner of real property can obtain an INJUNCTION to prevent a tenant from changing the character of the property, such as by razing a barn and erecting a dwelling house in its place. The injunction is a *decree* of the court.

A decree or judgment is *final* when it disposes of the case, leaving no question to be decided in the future. (See INTER-LOCUTORY DECREE.) The parties, however, may appeal to a higher court from a final judgment or decree. The execution of the judgment is *stayed* pending the higher court's decision.

A judgment is sometimes entered "on the pleadings" upon motion of counsel (see PLEADINGS), before trial of the cause is reached. For example, the plaintiff moves the court to strike the ANSWER of the defendant and direct judgment for the plaintiff (the party who brings a lawsuit). More frequently, however, the judgment is not entered until the case has been tried and FINDINGS OF FACT AND CONCLUSIONS OF LAW have been made.

How to prepare a judgment or decree. In a few jurisdictions, the CLERK OF THE COURT prepares the judgments, but usually the prevailing lawyer does. The lawyer will dictate the judgment or decree. A judgment is similar in style to a court ORDER. Figure 1 illustrates one style of decree.

Number of copies. It might be necessary to prepare extra copies, in addition to the usual original for the court, copy for each opposing counsel, and an office copy. The number of copies will depend upon the following factors:

1. Number of copies to be certified for delivery to the parties,
2. Whether service of copy is made on opposing counsel with notice of entry after judgment is entered, as well as before the judgment is submitted to the court,
3. Kind of action.

Judgment by Default. After a SUMMONS has been served and returned to the court, the court has JURIS-DICTION over the defendant (*see* PARTIES TO AN ACTION). If the defendant fails to defend a civil case by filing proper PLEADINGS, or fails to appear within a definite time, a judgment is given against the defendant in his or her absence. This judgment is called *judgment by default.*

It is important for the secretary to the lawyer for the defendant to remember to enter in the diary (*see* REMINDERS) the *return day of summons.* Failure to do so may lead to a failure to answer by that date resulting in a default judgment.

How to prepare a judgment by default. A printed form is generally available.

1. Make an original and two copies.

2. Calculate the interest at the legal rate, from the date indicated in the summons.

3. Itemize the cost disbursed by the office and include the total in the amount of the judgment.

4. Get the CLERK OF THE COURT to sign the original and file it in court.

5. Conform the two copies. (See CONFORMING DOCUMENTS.)

6. Fill in the notice of entry of judgment in the space provided on the back of the judgment.

7. Mail one copy to the defendant. The other copy is for the office file.

After judgment by default is entered, the plaintiff is known as a *judgment creditor* and the defendant as a *judgment debtor.* If the judgment debtor does not pay the judgment, the attorney for the judgment creditor may ask the Clerk of the Court to issue execution. Should the execution be returned unsatisfied, the attorney will commence supplementary proceedings, if the judgment debtor appears to have any assets out of which the judgment may be collected.

Judgment Creditor. One who has obtained a JUDGMENT against a debtor. For example, when a seller wins a suit against a customer who has failed to pay debts, the seller is given a judgment against the debtor. The judgment officially declares that the debtor owes the seller the amount stated in the judgment, and that the seller shall recover that amount from the debtor. Frequently, however, a debtor refuses to pay a judgment or insists that he or she cannot pay it. The creditor can then instruct an attorney to apply to the court for an order, or WRIT, directing the sheriff to seize the debtor's property. This is called applying for a WRIT of Execution. In some states an attorney can issue the writ without applying to the court. The property is sold and the creditor is paid out of the proceeds of the sale. Only property in the state where the suit is brought can be seized to satisfy the judgment. If the property is located out of the state, another suit, technically known as *suit on the judgment,* must be brought in that state.

Judicial Notice. The knowledge that a judge will officially take of a fact, although no evidence to prove that fact has been introduced on trial. It is a judicial shortcut, a doing away with evidence because there is no real necessity for it. The court will generally take judicial notice of facts that are so notorious that a production of evidence would be unnecessary. It is not necessary, for example,

IN THE DISTRICT COURT IN AND FOR THE CITY AND COUNTY

OF DENVER AND STATE OF COLORADO

CIVIL ACTION NO. 3-504. Div. 7

ANNA R. CARYLE,	)	
	)	
	Plaintiff,	
	)	
-vs-	)	INTERLOCUTORY DECREE IN
	)	DIVORCE.
GEORGE C. CARYLE,	)	
	)	
	Defendant.	

THIS CAUSE, coming on to be heard on this 9th day of January, 19--, upon its merits, the plaintiff being represented by Beale & Beale, attorneys of record, and the defendant appearing by Dow & Sloane, attorneys of record, and the Court having examined the full record herein, finds that it has jurisdiction herein; and having heard the evidence and the statements of counsel, the Court now being fully advised

DOTH FIND that a divorce should be granted to the plaintiff herein upon the statutory grounds of _____

IT IS ORDERED, ADJUDGED and DECREED by the Court, that an absolute divorce should be granted to the plaintiff, and an Interlocutory Decree of Divorce is hereby entered, dissolving the marriage of plaintiff and defendant six months after the date of this Interlocutory Decree.

IT IS EXPRESSLY DECREED by the Court that during such six months period after the signing of this Interlocutory Decree the parties hereto shall not be divorced; shall still be husband and wife, and neither party shall be competent to contract another marriage anywhere during such period, and the Court during all of said period does hereby retain jurisdiction

(continued on following page)

(continued from preceding page)

of the parties and the subject matter of this cause and upon motion of either party; or upon its motion, for good cause shown, after a hearing, may set aside this Interlocutory Decree.

It is further ORDERED, ADJUDGED and DECREED by the Court that defendant shall pay into the Registry of the District Court on the ___

It is further ORDERED, ADJUDGED and DECREED by the Court that the sole care, custody and control of the minor children, Steven Robert Caryle and Marion Linda Caryle, is hereby awarded to the plaintiff as a suitable person to have such care and custody until the further order of the Court, with the defendant to have reasonable visitation rights.

The Court FURTHER DECREES that after six months from the date hereof this Interlocutory Decree shall be and become a Final Decree of Divorce and the parties shall then be divorced, unless this Interlocutory Decree shall have been set aside, or an appeal has been taken, or a writ of error has been issued.

Done in open Court this 9th day of January, 19—.

BY THE COURT,

Judge.

Judgment: Figure 1.
Interlocutory decree of divorce.

to produce evidence to show the laws of the state, international law, historical events, and main geographical features of the community.

Judicial Review. The power of the courts to declare an act of the legislature invalid as a violation of the Constitution.

The United States Supreme Court will refuse to pass upon the validity of a statute unless it is involved in an actual case or controversy presented to it for decision. The Court, in other words, will not render "advisory opinions" upon constitutional questions. A statute that is held to be unconstitutional is as inoperative as though it had never been passed. See AMERICAN COURT SYSTEM; APPELLATE COURT.

Jurat. The clause in an official certificate attesting that the AFFIDAVIT or deposition was sworn to at a stated time before an authorized officer. It is often referred to as the "sworn to" clause. The form of jurat varies slightly in the different states. In a few states, the jurat recites the title of the officer and the state, or state and county, in which he or she is authorized to act. In a few other states, the name of the affiant is repeated in the jurat. The most common form of jurat is:

Subscribed and sworn to before me this . . . .
day of . . . . , 19. . . .
. . . .
Notary Public

Signature of notary. The notary signs immediately beneath the jurat. The notary also affixes the NOTARY'S SEAL and the expiration date of his or her commission.

Jurisdiction. The authority of a court to hear a particular *CAUSE OF ACTION and to render a binding decision.* The laws of our country provide that certain causes of action (lawsuits) must be brought in one court, others in another. It is the lawyer's problem to determine in which court a client's case should be brought—which court has *jurisdiction* over it.

To hear a case, a court must have jurisdiction *in personam* ("of the person") or *in rem* ("of the matter").

1. *In Personam Jurisdiction.* This means that a court must have jurisdiction over litigants (the person or persons bringing the suit and those defending it; see PARTIES TO AN ACTION). For example, if the litigants live in different cities in the same county, the county court, rather than a city or municipal court, has jurisdiction. A New York court does not have jurisdiction over a citizen of Mississippi in a suit brought by a New York citizen.

2. *In Rem Jurisdiction.* This means that the court must have jurisdiction over the subject matter in controversy. *In rem* jurisdiction depends upon the nature of the case, amount involved, location of the property. For example, a magistrate's court has jurisdiction over a traffic violation but cannot try a person for murder. A suit for damages caused by an automobile collision cannot be brought in a probate court (*see* COURTS OF SPECIAL JURISDICTION). Foreclosure actions can be brought only in the county where the property is located. *See also* ORIGINAL JURISDICTION; APPELLATE COURT; AMERICAN COURT SYSTEM.

Jurisdictional Dispute (Labor). A disagreement between two or more labor unions over whose members have the right to do a particular kind of work. This dissension has always been a major problem of organized labor because of the existence of unions whose jurisdictions overlap.

Jury. *In Practice.* A certain number of men or women, selected according to law, and sworn (*jurati*) to inquire of certain matters of fact and declare the truth upon evidence to be laid before them. This definition embraces the various subdivision of juries, as *grand jury, petit jury, common jury, special jury, coroner's jury, sheriff's jury.*

Justice. Broadly speaking, the maintenance or administration of that which is just, or the administration of law according to the rules of law or EQUITY. *See also* JUDGE.

Juvenile Court. See COURTS OF SPECIAL JURISDICTION.

K. Lawyers often use the letter *K* as an abbreviation for contract, a practice that originates during law school note-taking days.

Kidnapping. The act of carrying away a person against the person's will by unlawful force or by FRAUD. Although the kidnapper usually has a further intention, such as holding for RANSOM, the only intent necessary to constitute the crime of kidnapping is the intent to detain the victim against his or her will. Kidnapping may be punishable by death. See also ABDUCTION.

Kin. Relation or relationship by blood or consanguinity. The nearness of *kin* is computed according to the civil law.

Kiting. The unethical and sometimes illegal practice of issuing checks against a bank account in which there are not sufficient collected funds to cover the check, with the expectation that before the check drawn is presented for payment funds will be deposited to make good the withdrawal. A bank may close the account of a depositor who is detected in this practice.

Labor Union. An organization of employees seeking favorable wages, improved labor conditions, better hours of labor, and the righting of grievances against employers.

1. *Craft Union.* Organization of employees engaged in a single occupation. Such a union is based upon skill in the performance of one task or of a number of closely allied tasks or crafts. An example of a craft union is an association of barbers or plumbers.

2. *Industrial Union.* Organized on the basis of the industry rather than the craft. It unites into one group all the workers in a given industry, skilled and unskilled, without regard to craft or occupation. The Amalgamated Clothing Workers of America is an example of an industrial union. See AFL-CIO; AMERICAN FEDERATION OF LABOR; CONGRESS OF INDUSTRIAL ORGANIZATIONS; COLLECTIVE BARGAINING.

Laches. Unreasonable tardiness in bringing suit or seeking remedy in an EQUITY court. To plead *laches* as a defense to a suit, a defendant (see PARTIES TO AN ACTION) must show that he or she suffered from the plaintiff's delay in bringing suit.

Land Description. Identification of a tract of land contained in a DEED, MORTGAGE, LEASE, or other instrument. To avoid dispute and litigation, land should always be described according to one of the following methods, known as a "record description":

1. Rectangular survey system
2. Metes and bounds
3. The plat system

Rectangular survey system. A rectangular system of survey was devised in the eighteenth century. The survey divided the public lands into rectangular tracts, located with reference to base lines running east and west and *prime* or *principal meridians* running north and south. The prime meridians are numbered, as Third Prime Meridian, or named, as San Bernadino Meridian. The rectangular tracts are divided into six-mile squares, known as *townships.* A row of townships running north and south is called a *range,* and the ranges are numbered east and west from the prime meridians. The townships are divided into 36 sections, each one mile square or 640 acres. (See figure 1.) The sections are numbered from 1 to 36, beginning with the section in the northeast corner of the township, proceeding west to boundary of the

245

A SECTION OF LAND = 640 ACRES

A rod is 16½ feet.
A chain is 66 feet or 4 rods.
A mile is 320 rods, 80 chains or 5,280 ft.
A square rod is 272¼ square feet.
An acre contains 43,560 square feet.
" " " 160 square rods.
" " is about 208¼ feet square.
" " is 8 rods wide by 20 rods long,
or any two numbers (of rods) whose
product is 160.
25 x 125 feet equals .0717 of an acre.

80 rods.

10 chains.

330 ft.

5 acres

5 acres
20
rods.

80 acres.

5 ch.

40 rods.

10 acres.

10 chains.

20 acres.

40 acres.

80 rods.

CENTER OF

20 chains.

1,320 feet.

SECTION

660 feet.

Sectional Map of a Township with adjoining sections.

36	31	32	33	34	35	36	31
1	6	5	4	3	2	1	6
12	7	8	9	10	11	12	7
13	18	17	16	15	14	13	18
24	19	20	21	22	23	24	19
25	30	29	28	27	26	25	30
36	31	32	33	34	35	36	31
1	6	5	4	3	2	1	6

160 acres.

40 chains, 160 rods or 2,640 feet.

Land Description: Figure 1.
A section of land.

township; the next row is numbered from west to east, and so on. (See figure 2.) The sections in turn are divided into half and quarter sections, and the quarters into quarter-quarter sections, designated by their direction from the center as northwest, southwest, northeast, and southeast.

The description of a given five acres of land identified by the rectangular survey system might read

The East Half of the Northeast Quarter of the Northeast Quarter of the Northeast

Quarter of Section One, Township 39 North, Range 12 East of the Third Prime Meridian.

The small shaded portion of the diagram in figure 2 represents the parcel described above, assuming that the diagram is Township 39 North, Range 12 East.

Land identification in the 29 public land states in which the rectangular survey description is used is precise and orderly; it is possible to designate any plot of land as small as five acres with perfect accuracy; no two parcels are described in

Land Description: Figure 2.
*Diagram of township
divided into sections.*

exactly the same terms because they are identified with reference to a specific prime meridian.

Metes and bounds description. Before the rectangular survey, the land in the area comprising the 13 colonies (18 states) was held under original grants given by the Crown to the colonists. In these states and in Texas,[1] each parcel of land is different in size and shape and is described by metes and bounds. A

metes and bounds description is not correlated to any system of meridians and base lines, but each tract of land is described by the lines that constitute its boundaries. A natural landmark, such as a tree or river, or an artificial landmark, such as a fence, stake, railroad, or street, often marks the corners and angles. These marks are known as *monuments*. A description by courses and distances constitutes part of a metes and bounds description. The direction from the starting point in which the boundary line runs is a *course;* the length of the line is a *distance.*

---

[1]*The United States never had original title to the land in Texas because it was annexed by the United States as an independent republic.*

The following is an example of a metes and bounds description:

ALL that lot or parcel of land, situate, lying and being in the Town of Oyster Bay, County of Nassau, State of New York, bounded and described as follows:

BEGINNING at a point in the center line of Buena Vista Avenue distant two hundred sixty-one and thirty-one hundredths (261.31) feet southerly from the point of intersection of said line with the center line of Jones Road; running thence along the center line of Buena Vista Avenue South twenty-five (25) degrees thirty-three (33) minutes East four hundred fifty-two and seventy-eight one hundredths (452.78) feet to a point; running thence North sixty-eight (68) degrees thirty-two (32) minutes East three hundred ten and eleven one hundredths (310.11) feet to a point in the center line of a driveway; running thence generally along the center line of said driveway the following courses and distances:

A. North forty-five (45) degrees forty-two (42) minutes West, 50 feet;
B. North thirty-nine (39) degrees two (02) minutes West, 50 feet;
C. North thirty-four (34) degrees sixteen (16) minutes West, 50 feet;
D. North twenty-eight (28) degrees fifty-eight (58) minutes West, 50 feet;
E. North twenty-six (26) degrees seventeen (17) minutes West, 100 feet;
F. North thirty-two (32) degrees six (06) minutes West, 50 feet;
G. North forty-five (45) degrees thirty-four (34) minutes West, 50 feet;
H. North sixty-one (61) degrees thirty-two (32) minutes West, 50 feet;
I. North eighty (80) degrees thirty-three (33) minutes West, 50 feet;
J. South seventy-nine (79) degrees eleven (11) minutes West, 50 feet;
K. South sixty-five (65) degrees thirty-two (32) minutes West, 50 feet; and
L. South sixty-four (64) degrees forty-seven (47) minutes West, 77 feet, to a point in the center line of Buena Vista Avenue, the point or place of beginning; Containing, in area, approximately two and seven hundred seventy-four thousandths (2.774) acres;

Being and intended to be all of Plot No. 5, as shown on a map entitled "Plot Plan, Property of John Doe Estate, Town of Oyster Bay, Nassau County, New York, made by James Brown, Surveyor, November 1, 19..., as revised January 13, 19..., and December 31, 19..."

The plat system. Tracts of land described by metes and bounds or the rectangular survey system may be further divided into streets, blocks, and lots.

Maps or plans of these divisions are called *plats*. A *plat book* is a record maintained showing the location, size, and name of the owners of each plot of real property in a given area. A plat description might read:

Lot ten (10), Block Eight (8) Bay Shore Subdivision, as recorded in Volume 5 of Plats, Page 39, records of Blank County, State of . . . .

Style in preparing descriptions. Descriptions of land to be included in an instrument are usually copied from some earlier document or from a survey or an ABSTRACT OF TITLE. These should be transcribed exactly. It is permissible, however, and sometimes desirable to write out words that have been abbreviated and to correct capitalization. The following general rules should be observed in preparing descriptions for real estate instruments:

1. Single-space, with a double space between paragraphs.

2. Do not abbreviate *Street, Avenue, Road, Boulevard,* in the text.

3. Write the words *North, Northeast, South, West, Southwest,* and the like with initial capitals, but do not capitalize the words *northerly, northeasterly,* and the like.

4. Capitalize *Quarter, Township, Section,* and *Range,* and the name or number of a *Prime Meridian.*

5. Write courses as follows: "South twenty (20) degrees, thirty-three (33) minutes, forty-five (45) seconds West."

6. Write distances as follows: "One hundred thirty-three and twenty-nine one hundredths (133.29) feet."

7. When several courses and distances are given in succession, introduced by a phrase such as " . . . . the

following three courses and distances . . . " each of the courses and distances is written separately, indented and single-spaced, separated one from the other by a double space, and each course and distance is ended with a semicolon. The sentence after the last course and distance is flush with the left-hand margin of the text preceding the itemized courses and distances.

8. It is preferable not to use figures, symbols, and abbreviations, but it is sometimes necessary to use them because of the limited space on a printed form. A description would then be written: "South 20° 33′ 45′′ West, 50 ft." In offices with considerable real estate practice, a special key is placed on the typewriter for the symbol of the word *degrees;* otherwise, the symbol is made by turning the platen back a half space and striking the small *o*.

Checking land descriptions. An error in the description of land can cause a lot of trouble and even result in a lawsuit. The importance of checking the description cannot be overemphasized. It is easy to make an error in copying that is not always discernible merely from reading the description. For example, the section and township description shown earlier contains the phrase "of the Northeast Quarter" three times. It would be easy to omit the phrase once, but difficult to realize the omission in reading over the description; yet the omission would double the amount of land conveyed by the deed. Nor is it advisable for one person to compare the description line by line. The safest method of checking the typographical accuracy of land description is to have one person read aloud to another the original copy, slowly enough to permit him or her to follow the typed copy carefully.

Larceny. The act of wrongfully taking and carrying away the personal goods of another. The physical act of carrying away the property is called *asportation*. Asportation, when done with the intent to steal the thing asported, is the crime of larceny. State laws divide the crime of larceny into degrees, with the severity of punishment depending on the value of the property stolen, whether the act was committed during the night or day, and whether the property was stolen from the victim's person or house. *See also* EMBEZZLEMENT; ROBBERY.

Last Clear Chance. A doctrine that permits a plaintiff to recover in spite of the plaintiff's own CONTRIBUTORY NEGLIGENCE. The doctrine applies when the plaintiff is in a position of peril and the defendant knows that the plaintiff cannot act to save himself or herself. If the defendant has such knowledge in sufficient time to enable him or her to avert the injury by the exercise of reasonable care, but thereafter fails to exercise due care, the plaintiff may recover.

As an example, the last clear chance doctrine would be applied in a case where a boy is trespassing on railroad tracks and the engineer of a train realizes that the boy cannot get out of the way of the moving train. The engineer would be held liable if he or she had sufficient time to stop the train, but did not. The doctrine of last clear chance permits recovery even though the boy was contributorily negligent by being on the tracks.

Last Resort. A court from which there is no appeal is called the "court of last resort."

Latin Terms. The following is an alphabetical list of Latin words and phrases most likely to be used in the law office. (A few French terms that are in legal usage are included also.) Those words or phrases now considered to be a part of everyday English language are in Roman type instead of italics.

a fortiori. With stronger reason; much more.

a mensa et thoro. From bed and board.

a priori. From what goes before; from the cause to the effect.

a rendre. (French; to render, to yield). That which is to be rendered, yielded, or paid. *Profits a rendre* comprehend rents and services.

a vinculo matrimonii. From the bonds of marriage.

ab initio. From the beginning.

Actiones in personam. Personal actions.

ad faciendum. To do.

ad hoc. For this (for this special purpose).

ad infinitum. Indefinitely; forever.

ad litem. For the suit; for the litigation. (A guardian *ad litem* is a person appointed to prosecute or defend a suit for a person incapacitated by infancy or incompetency.)

ad quod damnum. To what damage; what injury. (A phrase used to describe the plaintiff's money loss or the damages he or she claims.)

ad respondendum. To answer.

ad satisfaciendum. To satisfy.

ad valorem. According to value. (See also AD VALOREM TAX.)

aggregatio mentium. Meeting of minds.

alias dictus. Otherwise called.

alibi. In another place; elsewhere.

alii. Others.

aliunde. From another place; from without (as evidence outside the document).

alius. Another.

alter ego. The other self.

alumnus. A foster child.

amicus curiae. Friend of the court.

animo. With intention, disposition, design, will.

animus. Mind; intention.

animus furandi. The intention to steal.

animus revertendi. An intention of returning.

animus revocandi. An intention to revoke.

animus testandi. An intention to make a testament or will.

anno Domini (A.D.). In the year of the Lord.

ante. Before.

ante litem motam. Before suit brought.

arguendo. In the course of the argument.

assumpsit. He undertook; he promised.

Bona fide. In good faith.

bona vacantia. Vacant goods. (Personal property that no one claims, which escheats to the state.)

capias. Take; arrest. (A form of writ directing an arrest.)

capias ad satisfaciendum (ca. sa.). Arrest to satisfy. (A form of writ.)

causa mortis. By reason of death.

caveat. Let him beware; a warning.

caveat emptor. Let the buyer beware.

cepit et asportavit. He took and carried away.

certiorari. To be informed of; to be made certain in regard to something.

cestui que trust. He who benefits by the trust.

cestui que use. He who benefits by the use.

cestui que vie. He whose life measures the duration of the estate.

civiliter mortuus. Civilly dead.

Consensus, non concubitus, facit nuptias, vel matrimonium. Consent, not co-habitation, constitutes nuptials or marriage.

consortium (*pl.* consortia). A union of lots or chances (a lawful marriage).

contra. Against.

contra bonos mores. Against good morals.

contra pacem. Against the peace.

coram non judice. In presence of a person not a judge. (A suit brought and determined in a court having no jurisdiction over the matter is said to be *coram non judice,* and the judgment is void.)

corpus. Body.

corpus delicti. The body of the offense; the essence of crime.

corpus juris. A body of law.

corpus juris civilis. The body of the civil law.

Cujus est solum, ejus est usque ad coelum. Whoever owns the land, owns it up to the sky.

cum testamento annexo (c.t.a.). With the will annexed. (Describes an administrator who operates under a will rather than in intestacy.)

damnum absque injuria. Damage without injury. (Damage without legal wrong.)

datum (*pl.* data). A thing given; a date.

de bonis non administratis. Of the goods not administered. Frequently this is abbreviated to *de bonis non.*

de bono et malo. For good and ill.

de facto. In fact; in deed; actually. (See also DE FACTO CORPORATION.)

De minimis non curat lex. The law does not concern itself with trifles.

de novo. Anew; afresh.

de son tort. Of his own wrong.

dies non. Not a day (on which the business of the courts can be carried on).

doli incapax. Incapable of criminal intention or malice; not of the age of discretion and intelligence to distinguish between right and wrong to the extent of being criminally responsible for his or her action.

donatio mortis causa. A gift by reason of death. (A gift made by a person in sickness, under apprehension of death.)

duces tecum. You bring with you. (A term applied to a writ commanding the person upon whom it is served to bring certain evidence to court. Thus, we speak of a *subpoena duces tecum.*)

dum bene se gesserit. While he shall conduct himnself well; during good behavior.

durante minore aetate. During minority.

durante viduitate. During widowhood.

Eate inde sine die. In criminal practice. Words used on the acquittal of a defendant, or when a prisoner is to be discharged, *that he may go thence without a day,* that is, be dismissed without any further continuance or adjournment.

e converso. Conversely; on the other hand.

enlarger l'estate. A species of release that insures by way of enlarging an estate and consists of a conveyance of the ulterior interest to the particular tenant; as if there be tenant for life or years, remainder to another in *fee,* and the person in remainder releases all his or her right to the particular tenant and the tenant's heirs; this gives the tenant the estate in *fee.*

eo instanti. Upon the instant.

erratum. (*pl.* errata). Error.

et alii (et al.). And others.

et alius (et al.). And another.

et cetera (etc.). And other things.

et non. And not. (Synonymous in use with *absque hoc:* without this.)

et seq. (short for *et sequentes* or *et sequentia*). And the following. (Used most commonly in designating page reference numbers.)

et uxor (et ux.). And wife.

et vir. And husband.

ex cathedra. From the chair.

ex contractu. (Arising) from the contract.

ex delicto. (Arising) from the tort.

ex gratia. As a matter of favor.

ex necessitate legis. From the legal necessity.

ex officio. From the office; by virtue of his office.

ex parte. On one side only; by or for one party.

ex post facto. After the act.

felonice. Feloniously.

feme covert. A married woman.

feme sole. A single woman (including one who has been married but whose marriage has been dissolved by death or divorce).

ferae naturae. Of a wild nature.

fiat. Let it be done. (A short order or warrant of a judge, commanding that something shall be done.)

fieri. To be made up; to become.

fieri facias. Cause to be made. (A writ directed to the sheriff to reduce the judgment debtor's property to money in the amount of the judgment.)

filius nullius. The son of no one; a bastard.

filius populi. A son of the people.

flagrante delicto. In the very act of committing the crime.

habeas corpus. You have the body. (See also HABEAS CORPUS.)

habere facias possessionem. That you cause to have possession. (A writ of ejectment.)

habere facias seisinam. That you cause

to have seisin. (A writ to give possession.)

honorarium (*pl.* honoraria). An honorary fee or gift; compensation from gratitude.

ibid. (short for ibidem). In the same place, at the same time, in the same manner. (It is used in footnotes to avoid repetition of source data when the same reference is immediately preceding.)

id. (short for idem). The same; exactly this; likewise. Also used in footnotes, in place of an author's name in successive references within one note to several works by the same person.)

idem sonans. Having the same sound (as names sounding alike but spelled differently).

Ignorantia legis neminem excusat. Ignorance of the law excuses no one.

illicitum collegium. An unlawful association.

Impotentia excusat legem. Impossibility is an excuse in law.

in bonis. In goods; among possessions.

in camera. In chambers.

in esse. In being; existence.

in extremis. In extremity (in the last illness).

in fraudem legis. In circumvention of law.

in futuro. In the future.

in loco parentis. In the place of a parent.

in pari delicto. In equal fault.

in personam. A remedy where the proceedings are *against the person,* as contradistinguished from those against a specific thing.

in praesenti. At present; at once; now.

in re. In the matter.

in rem. A remedy where the proceedings are *against the thing,* as contradistin-guished from those against the person.

in rerum natura. In nature; in life; in existence.

in specie. In the same, or like, form. (To decree performance *in specie* is to decree specific performance.)

in statu quo. In the condition in which it was. (See *status quo.*)

in terrorem. In terror.

in toto. In the whole; completely.

in transitu. In transit; in course of transfer.

indebitatus assumpsit. Being indebted, be promised, or undertook. (An action in which plaintiff alleges defendant is indebted to plaintiff.)

indicia. Marks; signs.

infra. Below.

innuendo. Meaning.

inter. Among; between.

inter alia. Among other things, as "the statute provides *inter alia . . .* "

inter vivos. Between the living.

interim. In the meantime.

intra. Within; inside.

ipse dixit. He himself said (it). (An assertion made but not proved.)

ipso facto. By the fact itself.

ita est. So it is.

jura personarum. Rights of persons.

jura rerum. Rights of things.

jurat. The clause typed at the end of an affidavit. (See JURAT.)

jure divino. By divine right.

jure uxoris. By his wife's right.

jus (pl. jura). Law; laws collectively.

jus accrescendi. The right of survivorship.

jus ad rem. A right to a thing.

jus civile. Civil law.

jus commune. The common law; the common right.

jus gentium. The law of nations; international law.

jus habendi. The right to have a thing.

jus proprietatis. Right of property.

levari facias. Cause to be levied; a writ of execution.

lex loci. Law of .the place (where the cause of action arose).

lex loci rei sitae. The law of the place where a thing is situated.

lex mercatoria. Mercantile law.

lis pendens. Litigation pending; a pending suit.

locus delicti. The place of the crime or tort.

locus in quo. The place in which.

locus sigilli (L.S.). The place for the seal.

mala fides. Bad faith.

mala in se. Wrongs in themselves (acts morally wrong).

mala praxis. Malpractice.

mala prohibita. Prohibited wrongs or offenses.

malo animo. With evil intent.

malum in se. Evil in itself.

mandamus. We command. (See also MANDAMUS.)

manu forti. With a strong hand (forcible entry).

mens rea. Guilty mind.

modus operandi. The manner of accomplishing an act.

nihil dicit. He says nothing. (Judgment against defendant who does not put in a defense to the complaint.)

nil debet. He owes nothing.

nisi prius. Unless before. (The phrase is used to denote the forum where the trial was held as distinguished from the appellate court.)

nolle prosequi. To be unwilling to follow up, or to prosecute. (A formal entry on the record by the plaintiff or the prosecutor that plaintiff or prosecutor will no further prosecute the case.)

nolo contendere. I will not contest it.

non compos mentis. Not of sound mind.

non est factum. It is not his deed.

non obstante. Not withstanding.

non prosequitur (non pros.). He does not follow up, or pursue, or prosecute. (If the plaintiff fails to take some step that he or she should, the defendant may enter a judgment of *non pros.* against the plaintiff.)

N.O.V. *(non obstante verdicto).* Notwithstanding the verdict. (A type of judgment that reverses the decision of the jury, when it is obvious that the jury decision had no reasonable support in fact or went against the law.)

nudum pactum. A nude pact. (A contract without consideration.)

nul tiel record. No such record.

nul tort. No wrong done.

nulla bona. No goods. (Wording of return to a writ of *fieri facias.*)

nunc pro tunc. Now for then.

obiter dictum. Remark by the way.

onus probandi. The burden of proof.

opus (*pl.* opera). Work; labor.

ore tenus. By word of mouth; orally.

pari delicto. In equal guilt.

particeps criminis. An accomplice in the crime.

paterfamilias. The father (head) of a family.

peculium. Private property.

pendente lite. Pending the suit; during the litigation.

per annum. By the year.

per autre vie. For another's lifetime. (See also *pur autre vie.*)

per capita. By the head; as individuals. (In a distribution of an estate, if the descendants take per capita, they take share and share alike regardless of family lines of descent.)

per centum (percent). By the hundred.

per contra. In opposition.

per curiam. By the court.

per diem. By the day.

per se. By itself; taken alone.

per stirpes. By stems or root; by representation. (In a distribution of an estate, if distribution is *per stirpes,* descendants take by virtue of their representation of an ancestor, not as individuals.)

postmortem. After death.

post obit. To take effect after death.

praecipe or *precipe.* Command. (A written order to the Clerk of the Court to issue a writ.)

prima facie. At first sight; on the face of it.

pro. For.

pro confesso. As confessed.

pro forma. As a matter of form.

pro hac vice. For this occasion.

pro rata. According to the rate or proportion.

pro tanto. For so much; to that extent.

pro tempore (pro tem.). For the time being; temporarily.

prochien ami. Next friend. Also may be spelled *prochien amy, prochain ami* and *prochain amy.*

publici juris. Of public right.

pur autre vie. For, or during the life of another. (See also *per autre vie.)*

quaere. Query; question; doubt. (This word indicates that a particular rule, decision, or statement that follows it is open to question.)

quantum. How much; the amount.

quantum meruit. As much as he deserved.

quantum valebant. As much as they were (reasonably) worth (in absence of agreement as to value).

quare. Wherefore.

quare clausum fregit. Wherefore he broke the close. (A form of trespass on another's land.)

quasi. As if; as it were. (Indicates that one

subject resembles another, but that there are also intrinsic differences between them. Thus we speak of quasi contracts, quasi torts, and so on.)

quid pro quo. What for what; something for something. (A term denoting the consideration for a contract.)

quo warranto. By what right or authority. (See also QUO WARRANTO.)

quoad hoc. As to this.

quod computet. That the account.

reductio ad absurdum. Reduced to the absurd.

res. A thing; an object; the subject matter.

res gestae. Things done; transactions; itself.

res judicata. A matter adjudicated.

respondeat superior. Let the superior reply. (Invoked when there is a master-servant relationship, that is, employer-employee.)

scienter. Knowingly.

scilicet (SS, or ss.) To wit (sc. is not used in legal papers).

scintilla. A spark; the least particle.

scire facias. Cause to know; give notice. (A writ used to revive a judgment that has expired.)

se defendendo. In self-defense; in defending oneself.

semper. Always.

semper paratus. Always ready. (A plea by which the defendant alleges that he or she has always been ready to perform what is demanded.)

seriatim. Severally; separately.

sigillum. A seal.

simplex obligato. A simple obligation.

sine die. Without day. (Without a specified day being assigned for a future meeting or hearing.)

situs. Situation; location.

stare decisis. To stand by that which was decided. (Common law courts hesi-

255

tate to change former decisions and will often uphold them, but they would make a different decision if the issue were new.)

stare judice. To abide by decided cases.

status quo. State in which. (The existing state of things at any given date.) See *in statu quo.*

sub judice. Under a consideration.

sub modo. Under a qualification; in a qualified way.

sub nom. Under the name.

subpoena duces tecum. See SUB-POENA.

sui juris. Of his own right. Having legal capacity to act for himself or herself.)

supersedeas. That you supersede. (A writ commanding a stay of the proceedings.)

supra. Above.

terminus a quo. The starting point.

ultra vires. Without power; beyond the powers of.

venire facias. That you cause to come. (A kind of summons.)

Verba fortius accipiuntur contra proferentem. Words are to be taken most strongly against the one using them.

versus (vs., v.). Against.

vi et armis. By force of arms.

via. A road; a right of way; by way of.

vice versa. On the contrary; on opposite sides.

videlicet (viz.) (contraction of *videre* and *licet*). It is easy to see. (That is to say; namely.)

virtute officii. By virtue of his office.

vis major. A superior force. In law, the term signifies "an inevitable accident—as in common law, "an act of God." (A loss by *vis major* is one that results from some natural cause without the intervention of man, and that could not have been prevented

by the exercise of prudence, diligence, and care.)

viva voce. By the living voice; by word of mouth.

voir dire. To speak the truth. (Denotes a preliminary examination to determine the competency of a witness.)

Law Degree. A rank to which law scholars are admitted by a university, in recognition of their legal attainments. The law degrees obtainable and the abbreviations of them follow. Notice that in some cases the abbreviation of the Latin *juris,* meaning law, is used.

Bachelor of Laws	LL.B.;B.L.
Bachelor of Civil Law	J.C.B.;B.C.L.
Bachelor of Canon Law	B.C.L.
Juris Canonici Bachelor	J.C.B.
Master of Laws	LL.M.;M.L.
Doctor of Laws	LL.D.;J.D.
Doctor of Law	Ju.D.
Doctor of Civil Law	J.C.D.;D.C.L.
Juris Civilis Doctor	J.C.D.
Doctor of Jurisprudence	J.D.
Juris Doctor	Jur.D.;J.D.
Jurum Doctor	J.D.
Doctor of Juridical Science	J.S.D.
Doctor of Juristic Science	J.S.D.
Doctor of Both Laws	J.U.D.
Juris Utrius Doctor	J.U.D.

Law School Reviews. Scholarly publications sponsored by law schools. Law reviews serve as outlets for legal articles by teachers, practitioners, and judges. Editorial work and some writing are done by the best students from the sponsoring school. See CITATION (to Legal Authorities), How to Cite Law Reviews.

Lawyer's Edition. See AMERICAN LAW REPORTS.

Lawyers' Incorporated. The Internal Revenue Service has made provisions for incorporating professional persons with possible large tax advantages to the individual. All 50 states and the District of Columbia have made provision for professional corporations, but the provisions may or may not include lawyers. Following is an example of the mechanics of forming a professional corporation in the state of Ohio. The procedure varies from state to state.

Professional Association Act—in general. Ohio adopted its Professional Association act in 1961 and amended the statute in 1969 and in 1976. Here are some highlights of the statute:

1. *Type of organization.* Ohio calls them professional associations. But the act refers to incorporation and corporation as well as association. The entity is a mixture of corporation and association in concept; there are elements of both.

2. *Statutory purpose.* An Ohio professional association is organized for the sole purpose of rendering one professional service.

3. *What professions are included.* Ohio's professional association act is specific; it names the professions that are involved. These are certified public accountants, licensed public accountants, architects, attorneys, chiropractors, dentists, pharmacists, optometrists, physicians and surgeons, psychologists, professional engineers, veterinarians, and podiatrists.

4. *Incorporators.* One individual or a group of individuals may organize a professional association and may incorporate their practice. Each individual must be licensed to practice the same kind of professional service in Ohio. The organizers become shareholders, so apparently you can't use accommodation parties as incorporators.

5. *Stockholders.* Any number of persons may own stock in an Ohio professional association; there is no specific limitation in the Ohio professional association statute. However, only persons duly licensed to practice the same professional service as the association may be shareholders. A trustee of a qualified pension or profit-sharing plan may hold legal title to stock, as long as the equitable title to the stock is also held by such professionals. Apparently there is no reason why a stockholder in an Ohio professional association must also be an employee of that association.

6. *Directors.* The Ohio professional association statute does not make any mention of directors or governors. It refers to officers and employees and agents but is silent about a board of directors. There apparently is no reason why an Ohio professional association cannot use a board of directors composed of individuals who are not licensed to practice the particular profession and who are not shareholders in the professional association. The incorporating dentist's attorney, for example, could serve as a member of the board of directors. Officers also apparently do not have to be licensed professionals, so the dentist's wife, for example, might serve as an officer of the professional association.

7. *Association name.* The Ohio Professional Association act places no limitations on the name used. The statute is silent concerning the association's name.

However, attorneys must abide by the Supreme Court Rules and one of these rules is that the corporate name must end with the words *Co., L.P.A.* ("legal professional association"). The rules also require that the corporate name must consist only of the surname of one or more of the active shareholders. Most other states do have specific provisions saying, for example, that the name must contain the words *professional association* or similar wording. In Ohio, the association selects a name that is permissible under the rules of the particular profession and without other restrictions.

8. *Certificates and reports.* An Ohio professional association is not obligated by statute to file, in or with the agreement to associate, or the articles of association, any independent evidence that its shareholders are duly licensed professionals. No certificate from regulating boards is required. But, annually, an Ohio professional association must furnish a statement to the secretary of state, certifying that all shareholders are duly licensed to render professional service in Ohio. The form of such annual statement is prescribed by the secretary of state and it must be furnished within 30 days after each June 30th. Failure to do so results in cancellation of the articles of incorporation of the association.

9. *Investments.* Again, the Ohio professional association statute has no direct provision. Many other states' laws do. It seems that an Ohio professional association may invest its funds in all of the usual types of investments, without restriction that these investments be necessary or related to the rendering of professional service.

Other applicable laws. The Ohio General Corporation Law applies to professional corporations, except when its provisions may conflict with the Professional Association Act. In that event the Professional Association Act takes precedence.

For the procedure in your state see your local law library.

Lease. A binding CONTRACT, written or oral, for the possession of lands and improvements on the one side, and the recompense by rent or other compensation on the other side. When the lease is evidenced by a written instrument that binds the parties to fulfill certain covenants or agreements, that instrument is known as a *lease.* It is sometimes called an INDENTURE. Leases range from the letting of an apartment for 1 year to a 99-year lease on vacant property. They may cover REAL PROPERTY, PERSONAL PROPERTY, or both, but a lease of real property is most common. Leases of realty give the lessee a *leasehold estate in the premises.*

Parties to a lease. The parties to a lease are the *lessor,* who owns the property, and the *lessee,* who rents it.

A party to a lease may be a natural person, or a partnership, or a CORPORATION. Leases on behalf of minors or insane persons should be made by a guardian. The officers of a corporation enter into a lease on its behalf pursuant to authorization of the board of directors or stockholders. An administrator cannot make a lease because the administrator's function is to wind up the estate, not to lease real property. An executor or testamentary trustee must receive specific authority from the will to make a lease.

Classification of lease. 1. *Duration.* Leases may be classified according to their duration as *short-term* or *long-term leases.* Although there is no definite duration that takes a lease out of the short-term class and puts it into the long-term class, a lease of ten or more years is generally considered a long-term lease. The fundamental distinctions are in the responsibilities assumed by the lessee and in the bond and security requirements. Under a short-term lease, the lessor usually requires the lessee to deposit with him one, three, or six months' rental at the time the lease is executed, whereas under a long-term lease the lessee is required to furnish a bond or collateral in an amount equal to about three years' rental. The most common practice is for the lessee to deposit with a bank or other financial institution negotiable securities of the required amount.

A special type of long-term lease is the 99-year lease, which has been used extensively for the purpose of developing business districts in large cities. These leases are made on parcels of valuable real estate strategically lcoated for business expansion. They contemplate the erection or improvement of buildings upon the property by the lessee.

2. *Type of property.* Leases may be classified as *commercial* or *residential,* according to the type of property covered by the lease. (See COMMERCIAL LEASE; RESIDENTIAL LEASE.) The secretary in a law office is more likely to prepare commercial leases than residential leases. Short-term leases may be either commercial or residential leases, but long-term leases are almost exclusively commercial leases.

3. *Rental.* The majority of leases call for the payment of a definite amount of rental, which continues at a uniform rate throughout the term of the lease. The amount is called a *flat rental.* Other leases, especially long-term leases, provide that the rental will start at a comparatively low figure and gradually increase. A rental provision of this type is called a *graded rental.* Another method of fixing the amount of rental is to require the tenant to pay a specified percentage of the gross income from sales made upon the premises. A lease with this requirement is called a *percentage lease.* These leases generally cover premises occupied by retail businesses, such as chain stores and department stores. Percentage leases generally run for ten or more years.

Printed forms. Printed forms of leases covering almost any kind of property are available and are frequently used for short-term leases. Many concerns print their own leases, in a form prepared by the lawyer. The lawyer's secretary is more likely to be concerned with the drafting and printing of a form than with filling in the run-of-the-mill lease, such as a lease on an apartment.

Standard lease clauses. Usually the lawyer dictates both the short-term and long-term lease. Although many of the clauses are standard, a variety of other clauses is necessary to express the agreement between the parties, especially in long-term leases. Ninety-nine year leases and many other long-term leases are extremely technical legal instruments, their preparation requiring a lawyer who is a specialist in the field. The secretary will probably have to type several drafts before the lawyer and his client are satisfied.

Here is a list of the standard clauses that appear in almost all commercial leases.

1. Term of duration
2. Rent
3. Water, electricity
4. Alterations
5. Repairs
6. Damage or liability—that is, the provision fixing the liability for injury to persons or property
7. "To let" sign before expiration of the lease
8. Assignment of the lease
9. Surrender of the premises upon expiration of the lease
10. Rules and ordinances
11. Fire—that is, the agreement about the respective rights of the parties if the building should be destroyed by fire or "other action of the elements"
12. Elevators and heat
13. Insurance
14. Default in payment of rent
15. BANKRUPTCY of lessee
16. Peaceful possession or quiet enjoyment of the premises
17. No waiver—that is, the provision that the consent of the lessor to a variation of the terms in one instance is not a waiver of terms and conditions of the lease
18. Subordination to mortgages
19. Sprinkler system
20. Condemnation or eminent domain proceedings—that is, the rights of the respective parties if the city, county, state, or federal authority should condemn or take possession of the premises
21. Security deposited by lessee

22. War—that is, the provision that the lessee is not exempt from payment of rent if lessor, because of shortages caused by war, is unable to supply services or equipment called for by the lease

Execution, acknowledgment, and recording of lease. A lease of land or commerical property is executed with the formalities of a deed. The stage statutes vary, but generally the following apply:

1. Both the lessor and lessee sign the lease.

2. A lease is sealed unless the state statute does not require a deed to be witnessed.

3. A lease is witnessed unless the state statute does not require a deed to be witnessed.

4. If the duration of the lease is more than one year (longer in some states), the lessor and lessee acknowledge it, and the lessee should have it recorded.

5. A lease may be signed by an agent with written authority.

The execution of the run-of-the-mill short-term lease, such as a lease on an apartment, is not so formal. Both the lessor and lessee sign, and usually the signatures are witnessed. Otherwise there are no formal requirements. The directions about acknowledgments and recording apply only to leases that must be recorded. (See RECORDING of Lease.)

Style of typed lease. When a lawyer drafts a lease, he or she simplifies the location of specific provisions by grouping them in a particular order.

In planning the style in which to type the lease, the secretary's object should be to simplify further the location of specific provisions. She can do this by indicating the subject of each provision in the margin. Another style of typing the lease is to make side headings of the subjects and underscore them. Still another style is to center the numbered subjects. Usually the clauses are numbered consecutively throughout the lease. The numbering may be any of the following styles: I, II; FIRST, SECOND; ONE, TWO; 1., 2.; (1), (2).

Preparation of a lease. Unless otherwise instructed you should follow these directions in the preparation of a lease of realty or commercial property. Obviously some of them apply to typed leases, some to printed forms, and some to both.

1. Make four copies—an original for the lessee, a duplicate original for the lessor, a triplicate original for the other attorney, and a copy for the files.

2. Use legal cap or letter-size paper according to preference.

3. Follow carefully the directions for filling in a printed form. (See FORMS.)

4. Don't forget the responsibility and distribution line at the top of the first page. (This goes on the office copy only of a printed form.)

5. Double-space.

6. Number all pages.

7. Type the land description in accordance with directions. (See LAND DESCRIPTION.)

8. If using a printed form, be sure and make the "Z" after the land description. (See FORMS.)

9. Don't forget to have at least two lines of typing on the signature page. (See TESTIMONIUM CLAUSE).

10. Prepare signature lines for the lessor and lessee.

11. If the state statute requires that a deed be sealed, affix seals to the lease in accordance with directions.

12. Type witness lines and ATTESTATION clause if the statute requires that a deed be witnessed. (See SEAL.)

13. Prepare certificate of ACKNOWLEDGMENT for lessor and lessee.

14. Collate. (See TYPING, Collating.)

15. Get someone to compare the LAND DESCRIPTION with you.

16. Check and double-check spelling of names.

17. Endorse legal backs. (If printed forms are used, no LEGAL BACK is necessary.)

18. Staple in backs.

19. Arrange for lessor and lessee to come in and sign.

20. Get lawyer's approval of the lease before it is signed.

21. Have lessor and lessee sign three copies, including broker's copy.

22. Make sure the signatures agree with the names typed in the lease.

23. Have the lease notarized if it is to be recorded. If you are the notary, you should take the acknowledgments. (See NOTARIZE.)

24. After signature and acknowledgment, conform the office copy to the original.

25. *Get the lawyer's approval of the executed lease, and then have the lease recorded.* (See RECORDING of Legal Instruments.) Don't forget to put a notation on the back of the lease asking that it be returned to you. (The secretary to the lawyer for the lessee attends to the recording.)

26. *Make an entry in the diary* (see REMINDERS) to follow the recorder within ten days or two weeks.

27. When the lease is returned, send it to the lessee. (See also RECORDING of DEED.)

Legacy. A testamentary gift of personal property. Legacies (also known as *bequests*) are of three kinds: specific, general, demonstrative.

A *specific legacy* is a bequest of a particular part of a testator's estate, described so as to be distinguished from all other property in the estate. Examples of specific legacies are testamentary gifts of identified bank deposits, or clothing, jewelry and other personal effects. If the subject matter of the gift does not form part of testator's estate at death, the legacy is lost; if it is in existence, the specific legatee has priority over other legatees and is assured of getting his or her share of the estate.

A *general legacy* is a bequest that cannot be traced to a specific source within the estate. Thus a testamentary gift of money, payable out of the testator's general assets and not from a particular bankbook or account, is a general legacy. A general legatee will receive under a WILL only if the specific and demonstrative legatees (see below) have received the specific property designated for them. A general legatee has priority over a residuary legatee (see below).

A *demonstrative legacy* is a bequest of a certain sum of money, stock, or the like, payable out of a particular fund or security. If the fund does not exist at testator's death, the demonstrative legacy is paid from the general estate. Demonstrative legacies are entitled to the same

preference as specific legacies so far as they may be satisfied out of the particular property or fund designated for their payment. However, if this property has disappeared from testator's estate, demonstrative legacies then rank with general legacies for purposes of priority.

A *residuary legacy* is a bequest, general in nature, of all of testator's estate not otherwise effectively disposed of; it is the remainder after other legacies are distributed.

Legal Assistant. (See PARALEGAL.)

Legal Back. A manuscript cover that comprises a backing in which to bind a legal instrument or court paper. It is of thick paper, 8½ or 9 inches by 15 inches. This cover is called a *back* because it covers only the back of the papers that are bound in it. Certain data, referred to as the *endorsement,* are typed on the back cover. The endorsement varies with the instrument and the names of the parties to it; but it must be typed in a definite position on the backing sheet and the sheet must be folded in a special manner so the typing will appear in the proper position.

Court papers usually have a printed panel in which the endorsement is typed; some backs have the name and address of the law firm engraved on them; others are plain. Figure 1 illustrates an endorsed legal back for an Agreement.

To type the endorsement:

1. Lay the backing sheet on the desk as though for reading.

2. Bring the bottom edge up to approximately 1 inch from the top and crease.

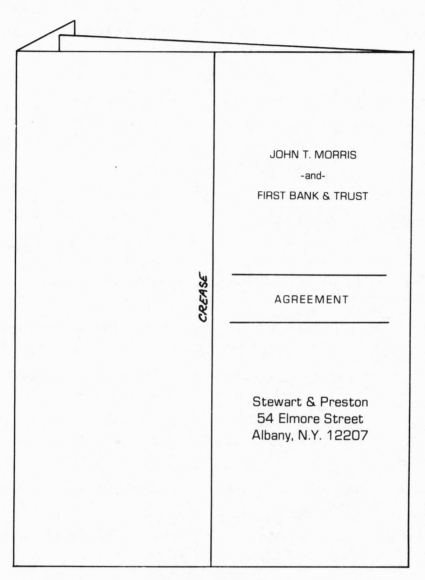

JOHN T. MORRIS

-and-

FIRST BANK & TRUST

AGREEMENT

Stewart & Preston
54 Elmore Street
Albany, N.Y. 12207

CREASE

Legal Back: Figure 1.
Endorsed legal back of agreement.

3. Bring the creased end (which is now at the bottom) up to approximately 1 inch from the top. (There is now a fold with about 1 inch of the top edge of the backing sheet protruding beyond the fold.)

4. The surface of the folded sheet that is uppermost is the surface on which the endorsement is to be typed. (If the backing sheet has a printed panel or the firm's name on it, that portion of the sheet will be the uppermost surface.) Put

a small pencil check in the upper *left*-hand corner of that surface.

5. Partially unfold and insert in typewriter so the pencil mark is on the upper *right*-hand corner of the surface when you type on it.

6. Do not type to the left of the crease (*see* figure 1). After typing the endorsement, turn down the top edge of the backing sheet about an inch (*see* step 3), crease, insert document in the crease, and staple. Fold the document and the backing sheet, creasing the document to fit the creases in the backing sheet.

Legal Cap. The regulation paper used for court papers and for legal instruments such as agreements and contracts. It is white paper, 8 by 13 inches or 8½ by 14 inches, with a wide ruled margin at the left and a narrow ruled margin at the right. Substance 16 is generally preferred for the original or ribbon copy, but substance 20 is preferable for the original wills; substance 13 for the carbon copies. In some states, legal cap has numbers along the left margin.

Bond or onionskin legal cap is used for the carbon copies, substance 13 or 9 if no more than eight copies are made; substance 9 for more than eight copies. Some offices use substance 16 (same as ribbon copy) for the office copy.

The attorney's name and address are sometimes printed on the legal cap in the lower left-hand margin (ending about 1 inch from the bottom) and on the onionskin copy paper. The word *COPY* is printed in large letters down the left margin on the onionskin paper.

Typing should *never* extend beyond the lines marking the margins. See TYPING, Legal Documents.

Legal Dictionaries. A dictionary of legal terms. Most commonly used are *Black's,* or *Ballentine's.*

Legal Instrument. A formal, written document, such as a DEED, BILL (of Sale), LEASE, or WILL. It gives formal expression to a legal act or agreement.

Although both legal instruments and court papers are referred to as *legal documents,* a legal instrument is not to be confused with a court paper. A court paper or *pleading,* as it is called professionally, constitutes a step in bringing or defending a lawsuit and is prepared and filed for the information of the court, whereas a *legal instrument* is designed for the use of the parties who sign it and constitutes evidence of the agreement between them. A legal instrument is not a step in a court action, but it is frequently the basis of one. Copies of a legal instrument are used frequently as exhibits in court actions.

Parties to an instrument. Those who acquire a right or give up a right, as evidenced by a written instrument, are the parties to the instrument. A party may be an individual, a partnership, or a corporation. Almost all instruments have two or more parties, but there are some—for example, assignments and powers of attorney—that have only one party. All parties who have a common interest in the subject matter of the document are grouped together and are usually referred to throughout the instrument by a descriptive identification, instead of by name. An expression occasionally used is "party (parties) of the first part," "party (parties) of the second part." More commonly the term may be a description such as *contractor, seller,* or any other term appropriate to the party's interest in the subject matter of the instrument. There may be more than one party in a group designated by a descriptive term. Notice that the instrument illustrated in figure 1 has two parties of the first part but only one of the second part.

Execution of an instrument. Technically, execution of an instrument is doing that which is required to give effect or validity to the instrument and, therefore, includes signing the delivery. In law office parlance, *execution* more frequently refers merely to the signing of an instrument by the party or parties described in it. Legal instruments must be executed with a certain formality. Some or all of the following formalities attach to the execution of various instruments: sealing, ATTESTATION, ACKNOWLEDGMENT, and notarization. See also ATTESTATION CLAUSE; NOTARY'S SEAL; and TESTIMONIUM CLAUSE.

Signatures on a legal instrument. An instrument recites who will sign it. As a general practice, lines are typed for signatures. Type the first line of signature four spaces below the body of the instrument, beginning it slightly to the right of the center of the page. Type a line for the signature of each person who must sign the instrument. There are no special requirements for the spacing of signature lines, except that sufficient space should be allowed for the average-size handwriting and the lines should be evenly spaced. Three or four spaces between lines are practical.

Frequently the descriptive identification of the parties signing is placed under the signature lines, for example, "First Party," "Parties of the First Part," or whatever identification was used in the instrument. The lawyer usually instructs the secretary as follows: "Two signature lines for parties of the first part, and one for the party of the second part," but the

IN WITNESS WHEREOF, the parties hereto have hereunto set

their hands and seals, the day and year first above written.

In the Presence of:

_____L.S.

_____

_____L.S.
                    Parties of the First Part

_____

_____L.S.
                    Party of the Second Part

Legal Instrument: Figure 1.
*Testimonium clause, signature
and seal for individuals, witnessed.*

secretary knows from the content of the instrument what signature lines are necessary. Figure 1 illustrates signature lines and identification of parties.

When a corporation is a party to an instrument, the instrument is signed in the name of the corporation by the officer or officers authorized to execute it. Type the name of the corporation in solid caps, leaving sufficient space beneath it for signature, and type "By" and a line for signature. Under the signature line, type the title of the corporate officer who is going to sign the instrument. The testimonium clause usually recites the title of the officer who is supposed to sign the instrument. The CORPORATE SEAL is placed at the left margin, parallel to the signature.

When a partnership is a party, type the name of the partnership in solid caps, leaving sufficient space beneath it for signature, and type "By" and a line for signature. Since partnerships do not have officers, there will be no title under the signature line.

Arrange the body, or text, of the instrument so at least two lines appear on the page with the signatures. The signatures must all be on the same page unless there are so many that they require more than a full page.

See also CONTRACT; DEED; BILL (of Sale); WILL; AFFIDAVIT; MORTGAGE.

Legatee. One who is bequeathed a LEGACY.

Lesser-Included Offense. An offense committed in the act of another greater offense. It is proved when the greater offense is proved. With plea bargaining, a defendant can be found guilty of a lesser-included offense rather than the more serious charge.

Letters. See CORRESPONDENCE.

Letters of Administration. The formal instrument of authority and appointment given by the proper court, empowering a person to enter upon the discharge of his or her office as an administrator of an estate. They correspond to letters testamentary granted to an executor. See PROBATE.

When someone dies without leaving a WILL, a person who is over 21, of sound mind, and entitled by law to share in the estate, may ask to be appointed adminstrator of the estate. One does this by applying to the probate court for *letters of administration*.

Parties. The person who files an application for letters of administration is known as the *petitioner.* Letters of administration are granted to persons who are distributees of an estate and who qualify in the following order: (a) the surviving spouse, (b) the children, (c) the grandchildren, (d) the father or mother, (e) the brothers or sisters, and (f) other distributees. All other distributees are necessary parties to the proceeding and are made parties to it either by the service of notice of the application for letters of administration or by the service of a citation, unless they waive citation.

For example, a minor child of the deceased, or a minor child of his prior deceased child, are distributees of the estate and are interested parties. They are not served with citations because they cannot serve as administrators, but they are given notice of the application for letters of administration.

Necessary papers in application for letters of administration. Printed forms of papers that must be prepared by the attorney and filed in an application for letters of administration are usually available, and the courts prefer that they be used. The forms are not uniform, varying even from county to county within a state, but they are similar. In every state, there is a petition for letters of administration, an oath of administrator, and a notice in some form to interested parties. In New York County, the papers consist of the following:

1. Petition for letters of administration (frequently combined with item 2 below),

2. Oath of administrator (frequently combined with item 1 above),

3. Designation of the Clerk of the Court as a person on whom service of process may be made (sometimes combined with petition and oath),

4. Renunciation, if any,

5. Citation,

6. Notice of application for letters of administration, if necessary.

Renunciation. Many states provide that a person who is entitled to letters of administration may renounce this right. An individual does this by signing a simple printed form entitled, "Renunciation of Rights to Letters of Administration and Waiver of Citation." The waiver reads

I, ..., do hereby renounce all rights to letters of administration on the estate of the said deceased and hereby waive the issuance

of a citation in the above-entitled proceeding.

The *I* may be changed to *We* and several distributees may sign the same waiver. It is acknowledged in the presence of a notary. The renunciation makes it unnecessary to serve a ciatation on those who renounced.

Citations. All interested parties must be notified of the application for letters. The method of notifying them varies. In New York State, parties who have a prior or an equal right with the petitioner to letters of administration are made parties to the proceeding by the service of a *citation,* except those who waive citation by renunciation of their right to letters of administration. The writ is signed by the clerk of the probate court (surrogate's court in New York City), but is prepared by the attorney for the petitioner. It cites the person or persons upon whom it is served to appear before the court on a certain date and show cause why letters of administration should not be granted to the petitioner. The person cited does not have to appear in court or reply in any way unless he or she opposes the appointment of the petitioner. Service is had in the same manner as service of citation in a proceeding to prove a will. Printed forms of citations are available. They are similar to, but not the same as, the form used in a proceeding to prove a will. The secretary should be sure of the following points:

1. The citation does not have a caption.

2. Addresss the citation to those distributees who have a right prior or equal to that of the petitioner to letters of administration. The names and addresses

of those to whom the citation is to be addressed are listed in the petition.

3. Make an original for the court, a copy for each person to whom the citation is addressed, and an office copy.

4. Find out the return date of the citation under the court rules. In some jurisdictions, the date is set by the Clerk of the Court when the petition is filed.

5. Get the court clerk to sign the original.

6. Conform the copies and serve.

7. Make affidavit of service.

8. *Enter return date in diary.*

9. Make entry in suit register, and follow the court calendar just as in a contested action.

Notice of application for letters of administration. In New York State, distributees who do not have a right to letters of administration equal to that of the petitioner are not served with a citation but are *notified* of the application. Printed forms are available.

1. Make an original for the court, a copy for each distributee entitled to the notice, and an office copy.

2. Date the notice of application at any time subsequent to the filing of the petition and before the issuance of the letters.

3. Have the petitioner sign the notice.

4. Mail copies of the notice to each distributee entitled to it at the address given in the petition.

5. Make affidavit that notice was mailed.

6. Conform office copy and file original in court.

7. Enter in suit register.

Issuance of letters of administration. If there is no opposition to the appointment of the petition as administrator, the court enters a decree directing that letters

268

of administration issue to the petitioner. The letters of administration serve the same purpose for the administrator as letters testamentary do for the executor. The attorney for the petitioner prepares the decree and the letters in the same manner as when a will is admitted to probate and letters of testamentary are granted.

As soon as letters of administration are granted, notice to creditors must be published. Be sure and make appropriate *diary entries* and suit register entries.

Administrator de boni non. Administrators *de boni non administratis* are, as the term signifies, persons appointed by the court of probate to administer on the effects of a decedent that have not been included in a former administration.

Administrator with the Will Annexed. One appointed administrator of deceased's estate after executors named in the will refused to act.

Letters Testamentary. See PROBATE.

Libel and Slander. That which tends to injure the reputation of a living person or the memory of a deceased person, and to expose that person to public hatred, disgrace, ridicule, or contempt, or to exclude him or her from society, is known as *defamation. Slander* is *oral* defamation of one person by another in the presence of a third person or persons; *libel* is *written* or *printed* defamation of one person by another published before a third person or persons. A corporation is a person in this sense. For a slanderous statement to be actionable, it must be false and must cause injury to the person to whom the statement refers.

In libel actions, no injury need be proved, although, of course, proved injury will affect the amount of damages awarded.

Libelous letter. For a letter to be libelous it must have been read by someone other than the person defamed. The reader may be a stenographer who takes the libelous writing by dictation and transcribes the notes, although some courts have taken the view that publication to a stenographer does not subject the writer to liability unless the letter was prompted by actual malice.

Libel (in admiralty practice). The initial pleading on the part of the complainant in an ADMIRALTY action, corresponding to the COMPLAINT in a COMMON LAW action.

Libelant. The complainant or party who files a LIBEL suit (see LIBEL (In Admiralty Practice) in LIBEL AND SLANDER) in an ADMIRALTY case, corresponding to the plaintiff in an action at law.

License, Business. Federal, state, or city approval and permission are necessary to engage in certain businesses that are of sufficient concern to the public to justify regulation. Permission and approval are issued in the form of a license, for which a fee is charged.

Licensee. One on the premises with the permission of the owner, for a purpose only personally beneficial, such as a passenger in an automobile or a dinner guest. The duty of the owner of the premises is to warn the licensee of a *known* dangerous condition. There is no duty to use reasonable care to keep the premises in a safe condition. See INVITEE; TRESPASSER; NEGLIGENCE.

Lien. A charge imposed on property, by which the property is made security for the discharge of an obligation. (See also ENCUMBRANCE.) The holder of the lien gives notice of his or her claim by recording it in some designated public office.

1. *Landlord's Lien.* In many states, the statute gives the landlord a lien upon the property of the tenant for unpaid rent. The landlord may seize such property, hold it as a security, and sell it within a fixed time to satisfy the tenant's debt. In some states, the lien is enforceable in distraint proceedings; in others it is enforceable in ATTACHMENT proceedings.

2. *Mortgage Lien.* In a majority of the states ("lien theory" states), a MORTGAGE on REAL PROPERTY given as security for a debt is a lien on the property. It becomes a lien upon recording of the mortgage. All persons who thereafter acquire any interest in the property, such as subsequent purchasers or mortgagees, take the property subject to the mortgage lien. Even in "title theory" states, anyone dealing with land on which a mortgage has been given is bound by the mortgage. (See ESTOPPEL certificate.)

Priority as between successive mortgage liens. The general rule is that mortgage liens have priority according to the time they attach to the land. Recording may be required to give the lien effect.

Example:
The owner of land gives a mortgage to X in 1976 and another mortgage on the same property

to Y in 1977. If X's mortgage is valid and properly recorded, it has a lien prior to the lien of Y's mortgage. Even if X's mortgage is not recorded, it may be prior to Y's mortgage if Y has knowledge of the earlier mortgage.

3. *Mechanic's Lien.* A person who furnishes certain kinds of labor or materials in the construction of improvements on land may, on failure of the owner of the land to pay him, acquire a lien on the land and improvements by complying with certain formalities. This is known as a mechanic's lien, and is governed by state statutes. The statutes vary from state to state. In some states, the mechanic must have been hired by the owner of the land or his or her agent to establish the lien; in other states, the consent of the owner is sufficient. The statutes distinguish between a *contractor* hired by the owner to construct an improvement and a *subcontractor* hired by a contractor. In some states, the subcontractor's lien is dependent upon the amount that the owner owes to the contractor (New York system); in other states, the subcontractor's lien is a direct lien independent of the indebtedness from the owner to the contractor (Pennsylvania system). Subcontractors may be required to serve notice of their claim on the owner within a fixed time. Both contractor and subcontractor may be required to file notice of their claims within a specified time after the work is completed. Steps must be taken to enforce the lien by FORECLOSURE within a fixed time after the claim is filed. A mechanic's lien may be released or waived, just like a mortgage.

Priority of mortgage lien over mechanic's lien. The state statutes vary concerning when a mechanic's lien attaches to the land. The time it attaches is most important in determining which has priority, a mortgage lien or a mechanic's lien. In New York, a mortgage recorded before the filing of a mechanic's lien has priority over the lien. However, once recorded, the lien has priority over mortgage money advanced *after* the recordation of the lien. In other states (Illinois and Massachusetts, for example), the mechanic's lien attaches on the date the owner of the land orders the work to be done, and the mechanic's lien has priority over the lien of a mortgage made after the date the work was ordered. In a majority of the states, no mechanic's lien may attach, so far as purchasers and mortgagees are concerned, until actual commencement of the improvements.

When a mortgagee is required to advance funds for *construction* of a building on the land, a different rule prevails. In most states, the mortgage lien is prior to a mechanic's lien for work or materials furnished in constructing the building. To protect the mechanic's lien, however, the mortgagor is required under the terms of the mortgage to apply the advances first to the payment of the cost of improvement before using the funds for any other purpose.

Protection of mortgage against mechanic's liens. To protect themselves against mechanic's liens (particularly on construction loans), owners and mortgagees adopt various measures:

a. The mortgagee may insist that the original construction contract contain a WAIVER of all mechanic's liens. In some states, this is effective and is binding on all subcontractors if the contract is recorded or the subcontractor knows of this provision at the time he furnishes the labor or material. Such a waiver is, in substance, a voluntary release or relinquishment of the lien, the contractor electing to rely solely on the personal responsibility of the party ordering the erection of the building. This arrangement hampers the contractor in obtaining credit from subcontractors.

b. The owner or mortgagee may withhold payout to the contractor of an amount ample to protect against subcontractors' liens until the time for the giving of notice of subcontractors' liens has expired.

c. Under some statutes, an owner or mortgagee is protected in paying out to subcontractors named on a verified list furnished by the contractor. As each payout is made to subcontractors named in the list, each subcontractor is required to furnish a lien waiver. If the general contractor claims that he or she has paid a particular subcontractor and produces the subcontractor's lien waiver, payment may be made to the contractor, although to protect against forged waivers, the check is sometimes made payable to the contractor and subcontractor.

d. When final payment is made to the contractor, he or she is required to furnish a full lien waiver.

e. The arrangement between mortgagor and mortgagee is such that the mortgagee is obligated to pay out the loan as the work progresses.

f. A surety BOND may be required by the mortgagee to protect against mechanic's liens. In some states, the posting of the proper surety bond discharges all mechanic's liens that have attached to the property.

g. For protection when making a loan other than a construction loan, the mortgagee inspects the premises to make sure that no recent repairs or improvements have been made, and requires an AFFIDAVIT from the mortgagor that no such repair or improvements have been made or ordered. If traces of recent work are apparent, lien waivers are required.

h. Since some laws provide that the interest of owners will be subject to liens for any work done with their knowledge (even on the order of a tenant, for example) unless they post in a conspicuous place on the building a notice that they will not be responsible, some owners keep such a notice posted on their buildings at all times.

4. *Judgment Lien.* In most states, a JUDGMENT for money becomes a lien on all the land of the judgment debtor in some other county by filing an official copy of the judgment in the proper office of such county. The judgment may also become a lien on real estate which the judgment debtor acquires after the judgment is entered. The duration of the lien depends upon the governing state statute. The judgment lien is enforced by issuance of EXECUTION and levy. When the judgment is paid, the judgment debtor files a formal declaration known as a *satisfaction.*

Before purchasing property or a mortgage, one should search the judgment records to determine whether there are any judgment liens affecting the property about to be purchased or mortgaged.

See MARITIME LIEN.

Life Estate. An interest in property, real or personal, that lasts only for the duration of the owner's life. A life estate may also be for the duration of another's life or may terminate with the happening of a certain contingency. For example, a life estate may terminate upon the marriage of the owner. This estate may be created by an act of the parties, as by DEED, WILL, or GIFT; or by operation of law, as by dower or curtesy. The owner of a life estate (called the *life tenant*) has the current use of the property and is responsible for its maintenance, including taxes and carrying charges. He or she also gets the income from the property, but cannot ordinarily sell the property or do anything to impair its permanent value. However, the life tenant may be allowed to sell or consume property as a means of support if the deed or will so provides. The life tenant cannot dispose of the property upon death. The person, or persons, to whom the estate passes upon termination of the life estate is determined when the life estate is created. The estate that is left at the termination of the life estate is called a *remainder;* the person to whom it passes is a *remainderman* (plural, *remaindermen*).

Life Insurance. A CONTRACT under which the insuring company agrees, in consideration for the payment of premiums, to pay a stipulated sum of money to a designated beneficiary upon the death of the insured.

The flexibility of the modern life insurance contract makes it possible for insurance to perform a number of useful functions in estate planning. Life insurance gives financial security to dependents. It can serve as a savings program, affording a plan involving the growth of cash value over the years without INCOME TAX liability. Finally, life insurance can assure estate liquidity by making a cash fund available to the insured's legal representatives for the payment of debts, expenses, and taxes, which will eliminate or reduce the need for the forced sale of nonliquid assets.

Limited Partnership. A partnership in which the liability of one or more special partners for debts of the firm is limited to the amount of the partner's investment in the business. Special partners have no voice in the management of the partnership. They merely invest money and receive a certain share of the profits. There must be one or more general partners who manage the business and remain liable for all of its debts.

A limited partnership is organized under state statutes, usually by filing a certificate in a public office and publishing a notice in a newspaper. The statutes, codified in many states as the Uniform Limited Partnership Law, must be strictly observed. A limited partnership is regarded as a general partnership in states other than the state in which it is organized; therefore, it must register and form a limited partnership with the same firm members under the laws of each state in which it wishes to do business.

Liner. A vessel sailing in accordance with a fixed schedule along a line of certain ports at advertised times. See also TRAMP.

Liquidated Damages. An amount that the parties to a contract have agreed upon will be paid in satisfaction of a loss resulting from a BREACH of Contract. The amount must be in proportion to the actual loss; otherwise the agreement is unenforceable.

Lis Pendens. Litigation pending; a pending suit. Whenever a lawsuit involving real property is commenced, a notice of *lis pendens* or "pendency of action" is filed. A notice of *lis pendens* gives constructive notice to the world that the property described therein is involved in a lawsuit. The notice is filed with the proper official, such as the county clerk, recorder, or register of titles under the TORRENS SYSTEM, at the time the COMPLAINT is filed. The filing of the notice of *lis pendens* is a vital step in actions involving REAL PROPERTY, such as foreclosures, actions to quiet title, condemnation proceedings, and partitions. If a defendant disposes of an interest in the property after suit is commenced but before notice is filed, the plaintiff's suit is defective. On the other hand, any claim against, or interest in, the property arising subsequent to the filing of the *lis pendens* is subordinate to the interest of the plaintiff as determined by the lawsuit.

Preparation of notice of lis pendens. As soon as you receive the certification of defendants, or FORECLOSURE report, from the title company (see ABSTRACT COMPANY), you can prepare the notice of pendency without waiting for the lawyer to give you instructions about the complaint. The lawyer will not dictate the notice; you will be expected to follow a form. The only parts that change are the names of the defendants, the description of the mortgage, and the description of the property. Figure 1 illustrates a notice of pendency of action or *lis pendens,* but the wording varies with the state.

1. Use the same kind of paper that is used for any court paper (*see* TYPING Court Papers).

2. Make an original and a file copy. Also make an extra copy for the loose-leaf notebook. Copy of the notice is not served on the defendants.

3. The caption is the same as the caption in the complaint. You may shorten the title by the use of *et al.,* unless the wording of the notice makes this inadvisable. See 6 below.

4. The title of the document is "Notice of Lis Pendens," or "Notice of Pendency of Action."

5. Have someone compare the description with you against the description in the original mortgage. *This is most important.*

6. The notice in figure 1 contains a direction to the county clerk to the effect: "You are hereby directed to index the foregoing notice of pendency against the names. . . ." Insert the name of *every known* defendant as listed in the certification of defendants, but do not include fictitious names. If the form of notice that you follow *refers* to the defendants without listing them, the title of the case must contain the name of *every* known defendant and cannot be shortened by the use of *et al.* A *lis pendens* is not good unless it is indexed against each defendant, insofar as that defendant has an interest in the property.

7. Staple the original in an endorsed LEGAL BACK.

8. The attorney for the plaintiff signs the notice.

Litigants. See PARTIES TO AN ACTION.

IN THE DISTRICT COURT OF THE STATE OF IOWA

IN AND FOR POLK COUNTY

ARNOLD V. SCHOTT and JULIA K.
SCHOTT,

	Plaintiffs,	No. 4896

vs.

NOTICE OF LIS
PENDENS

DAVID C. COOK and MARGARET O. COOK,
husband and wife, PAUL NELSON, DOE ONE,
DOE TWO, DOE THREE, and DOE FOUR,

Defendants

NOTICE IS HEREBY GIVEN, That an action has been commenced and is pending in this Court upon a complaint of the above named plaintiffs against the above named defendants for the foreclosure of a mortgage, bearing date the twenth-first day of September, one thousand nine hundred and ...., executed by David C. Cook and wife, Margaret O. Cook, to Arnold V. Schott and wife, Julia K. Schott, to secure the sum of Five Thousand Dollars ($5,000), and recorded in Liber 2063 of Mortgages, at page 25, in the office of the Recorder of Deeds of the County of Polk, on the twenty-second day of September, one thousand nine hundred and ...... at ten o'clock in the forenoon;

AND NOTICE IS HEREBY GIVEN, That the mortgaged premises affected by the said foreclosure action, were, at the time of the commencement of said action, and at the time of the filing of this notice, situate in the County of Polk in the State of Iowa, and are described in the said mortgage as follows, to wit:

(Insert description that appears in mortgage)

....
Marshall & Foster
Attorneys for Plaintiffs

(continued on following page)

274

(continued from preceding page)

To THE CLERK OF THE DISTRICT COURT OF POLK COUNTY:

You are hereby directed to index the foregoing notice of pendency against the names of each of the following defendants: David C. Cook, Margaret O. Cook, and Paul Nelson.

Dated: May 7, 19—.

....
Marshall & Foster
Attorneys for Plaintiffs

Lis Pendens: Figure 1.
Notice of Lis Pendens.

Litigation Blanks. see FORMS.

Lockout. The refusal of an employer to furnish work to his or her employees. Sometimes there is a tactical advantage for management in closing the plant before employees have a chance to go out on STRIKE. A lockout, like a strike, is a drastic step because it curtails business and thereby stops profits and wages.

Long-Arm Statutes. Statutes that allow local courts to gain the power to hear and determine a case over non-resident defendants when the CAUSE OF ACTION arose locally and affects local plaintiffs.

Long-Term Capital Gain. See CAPITAL, Gain and Loss.

Long-Term Lease. See LEASE, Classification of Leases.

Lot and Block. See LAND DESCRIPTION.

Magistrate's Court. A judicial tribunal that has limited jurisdiction and powers. *See* INFERIOR COURT.

Mail. Postal information that might be needed in the law office can be obtained from the *Postal Manual,* chapters 1 to 6, and the *Directory of International Mail,* which contains domestic and international regulations. These publications are available from the Superintendent of Documents, U.S. Government Printing Office, Washington, D.C. 20013.

1. *Domestic Mail.* There are four classes of mail: first, second, third, and fourth. Each class may involve some special form of handling: priority mail (air mail for items over 10 ounces), special delivery, and the like. *First-class mail* consists of sealed matter and also of certain items that the U.S. Postal Service considers first-class matter whether or not they are sealed. *Second-class mail* consists of newspapers and periodicals; *third-class mail,* of unsealed matter weighing less than 16 ounces; *fourth-class mail,* or parcel post, of packages weighing 16 ounces or more. For details about rate basis, weight limit, preparation for mailing, and postal instructions and regulations, consult your local post office.

2. *International Mail.* Mail deposited for dispatch to points outside continental United States and its territories and possessions. International mail is classified as letters and letter packages, postcards; printed matter, aerogrammes, matter for the blind, small packets, and parcel post. Since rates and regulations vary from country to country, you should consult your local post office for current information.

Majority. Full age; the age at which, by law, a person is entitled to the management of his or her own affairs and to the enjoyment of civic rights.

Majority Vote. The number greater than half of any total.

Malicious Mischief. The intentional destruction of someone's property because of resentment or ill will toward its owner. When the act of destruction is by fire, statutes define the crime as ARSON rather than malicious mischief.

Malicious Prosecution. A lawsuit started out of ill will without reason to believe that the charges would be upheld in court. If the malicious prosecution is a criminal proceeding, suit for DAMAGES may be brought against the prosecuting officer; if a civil action, against the plaintiff. The question of whether there was actual malice is one that a jury answers.

Mandamus. (Latin for "We command.") A writ issued by a court of superior jurisdiction to a public or private corporation, or an official thereof, or an inferior court, commanding the performance of an official act, which the person or body named in the writ had failed or refused to perform. It is an extraordinary WRIT, which is issued in cases where the usual and ordinary procedures do not afford remedies to the party aggrieved. The writ of mandamus is known as a remedy for official inaction. It was introduced to prevent disorder from a failure of public officials to perform their duties and is still an important legal remedy for the protection of the public and of individuals against exploitation and abuse by official inaction. Mandamus is frequently applied for to control the letting of public contracts.

A mandamus may also enforce a private right. It compels the performance by a corporation of a variety of specific acts within the scope of the corporation's duties. For example, a stockholder may institute a mandamus proceeding to compel a corporation to submit to an inspection of its books and records .

The writ is either peremptory or alternate. The *peremptory mandamus* compels the defendant to perform the required act; the *alternate mandamus* compels the defendant to perform the act or show cause on a certain day why he or she should not perform it. The alternate writ is usually issued first.

Manslaughter. The unlawful killing of another without malice. If death is the result of recklessness and NEGLIGENCE, manslaughter would be the crime charged against the offender; for example, death resulting from reckless driving. Killing in the heat of passion amounts to manslaughter. It is the lack of malice that makes a killing manslaughter and not MURDER.

Manuscript. A piece of writing prepared for a printer or compositor. Copy should be typewritten neatly and legibly (see TYPING). Every piece of copy must be checked carefully for errors before it is sent to the printer. Checking saves time and money and contributes to a better finished product. Read your manuscript several times before releasing it and use proofreader's marks in marking your corrections (see PRINTING).

1. *Be consistent.* if a word can be spelled or abbreviated in more than one correct form, choose one and use it consistently. On the first reading, make a list of selections of optional spellings to be a guide toward consistency.

2. Make *short corrections* by crossing out the incorrect word and writing the correction over it, not in the margin. The margin is used for instructions to the printer. To make *lengthy corrections,* cross out the incorrect matter and type the correct matter on a separate sheet of paper. Mark the correction as an insert and show clearly where it is to be inserted.

3. *Circle* anything on the page that the printer should not set in type. Thus any instructions to the printer should be circled.

4. In checking the manuscript, do not indicate corrections to be made in the margins; *make all changes directly on the manuscript.*

5. *To start a new paragraph,* insert a ¶ sign; to run in material typed as a new paragraph, draw a line from the word starting the new paragraph to the last word of the preceding paragraph.

6. *To separate two words* typed as one, draw a vertical line between them.

7. *To make deletions,* use a heavy pencil and ruler and neatly and heavily cross out what is not wanted.

8. *To retain material already crossed out,* insert a row of dots beneath it and write the word *stet* in the margin beside it in a circle. Be sure, however, that the crossed-out material that is to be retained is legible; if there is any doubt, retype it as an insert.

9. *Number the pages* of the manuscript consecutively after all corrections and insertions have been made.

10. Mark your copy for size and style of type (see TYPEFACES), margin width and other desired spacing, and any other instructions you have. You may need to estimate copy length by counting words or characters. Have the printer or compositor help you estimate length accurately and quickly.

11. In the left-hand margin, mark the size and name of the *body type* and the *pica width* of the type area (see TYPE-FACES), for example: 11/13 x 18 Times Roman, which means 11 point Times Roman type, leaded 2 points, and set 18 picas wide.

12. Underline all words or sections to be set in *italics.*

13. Draw a wavy line under the words or sections to be set in *boldface.*

14. Indicate what is to be set in *capital letters* (by inserting three lines under the letters) and what in *small capitals* (two lines under the letters) or a combination of capitals and small capitals.

15. *Mark all headings* in the desired size and style of type.

See PRINTING; TYPING, (Typing Manuscripts); TYPEFACES.

Marital Deduction. Under the Tax Reform Act of 1976, the marital deduction allocable to a decedent's estate is applicable to property belonging to a decedent that passes from the decedent to the decedent's surviving spouse as a result of the decedent's death. The marital deduction in dollar amounts is limited to the fair market value of the property passing from the decedent to the surviving spouse up to but not exceeding one-half of the adjusted gross estate or $250,000, whichever is greater. The amount of the marital deduction is a direct reduction of the taxable estate of the decedent.

Wills that incorporated the marital deduction provision drawn before the 1976 Tax Reform Act should be changed if the adjusted gross estate is less than $500,000. For an adjusted gross estate of $500,000 or more, the wording recommended before the Tax Reform Act of 1976 is still acceptable.

The marital deduction may give substantial tax advantages to the estate of the first married party to die. The marital deduction in the estate tax and gift tax area was enacted to bring about an equalization of taxes between the common law states and the community property states.

Maritime Lien. A right against a vessel arising out of certain maritime contracts and maritime torts. Claims that are subject to maritime liens include the wages of a seaman, a BOTTOMRY

LOAN, a RESPONDENTIA loan, repairs and supplies to vessels, AFFREIGHT-MENT CONTRACTS, TORT and collision claims, TOWAGE, WHARFAGE, stevedore services, SALVAGE, GENERAL AVERAGE LOSS, and pilotage.

One having a maritime lien can sue the ship itself *in rem* and, if successful in the litigation, can cause the ship to be sold and the purchase moneys applied to one's claim. The proceeding *in rem* is begun by the seizure of the vessel by the marshal of the district in which the suit is brought.

Unlike the common law LIEN, the possessor of a maritime lien does not have to retain possession of the object (the vessel or cargo) to retain his or her claim. The lien on a ship and the right to proceed against it will remain even if the ship is sold to another. Only a sale by a United States marshal will strip the vessel of its liens.

Maritime Tort. An injury to an individual or to property that occurs on navigable waters.

Marketable Title. A title that is acceptable to a purchaser. The title need not be perfect but reasonably safe and free from reasonable doubt.

Martindale-Hubbell Law Directory. A seven-volume annual directory of lawyers and a DIGEST of the laws of all the states.

In Volumes I through VI, lawyers' name are listed alphabetically by state and town. If you are looking for the name of a lawyer in Laurel, Montana, for example, search Volume IV covering states alphabetically from Missouri through New York. Within the pages devoted to Montana lawyers, you will find alphabetical breakdowns by city. You will find lawyers in the city of Laurel listed by name with appropriate symbols indicating the date of birth, college and law school graduation, and of admission to the bar, together with membership in the American Bar Association, and a "confidential" rating. A key to the symbols and explanatory notes appears at the beginning of each volume. Ratings are based on the standard of ability for the place where the lawyer practices. Age, practical experience, nature and length of practice, and other relevant qualifications are considered. There might also be a reference to the firm with which the lawyer is associated. Law firms are listed in the second half of these volumes alphabetically by state and city, with the partners' names, bank references, the nature of the practice, and sometimes the names of some clients. In addition, there is a listing of foreign lawyers. A special listing is made of lawyers admitted to practice before the United States Patent Office. Another section is devoted to the American Bar association, its organization, officers, activities, and canons.

Volume VII of the directory contains a digest of the laws of all states and territories of the United States. There are 96 principal subject headings and numerous subheadings all included in the Topical Index at the beginning of the volume. Suppose the lawyer is interested in knowing the usury law in California and instructs you to look it up. Look up *usury* in the Topical Index. Under the term *usury* there is the cross reference, "see Interest." Within the section devoted to the law of California, look under the *I*'s and find a subheading *usury* within the major heading Interest. The uniform arrangement of the material, supported by abundant citations, presents the law in an organized and quickly accessible form. Statutory forms are frequently a part of the text.

Part II of Volume VII is a section confined to digests of United States copyright, patent, tax, and trademark laws. Part III contains digests of the laws of the federal government of Canada and of each of her 10 provinces. Part IV of Volume VII contains digests of the laws of 52 foreign countries. In the case of Australia, there is a digest of the laws of the states of that Commonwealth with the digest of its federal laws. Part V carries the court calendars of the federal judicial system of the United States and of the territories of Puerto Rico and the Virgin Islands. The calendars classify the courts and define their JURISDICTION. In part VI the complete texts of 43 Uniform Acts and 4 Model Acts are presented. Thus the user of this volume has at hand the full texts of these important enactments, which cover so many fields of the statutory law of a large number of the states.

Massachusetts Trust. A business association formed under a DEED OF TRUST, which is really a contract between the trustees and beneficiaries. It is also known as a *business trust* or a common-law trust. Its structure closely resembles that of a CORPORATION. The interests of the beneficiaries are represented by CERTIFICATES, frequently called certificates of stock, which may be divided into several classes of COMMON STOCK and PREFERRED STOCK and may be listed on stock exchanges. The trustees correspond to the directors and the certificate holders to the stockholders. The trustees manage the property and pay dividends out of the profits. They usually appoint and remove the officers. Unlike a corporation, the management is permanent. The trustees are personally liable in dealing with outsiders unless they clearly indicate that they are acting as trustees and that the creditors shall look only to the trust property for all payments.

Massachusetts trusts are regarded as corporations under many taxing statutes and federal acts.

The duration is limited by statute in most states, but the parties interested at the time the trust expires can agree to another trust.

Mechanic's Lien. *See* LIEN.

Mediation. The act of a third person who intervenes between two contending parties with a view towards reconciliation. In a labor dispute, mediation procedures cannot force labor and management to agree. In guiding the parties to mutual agreement, the mediator may only suggest compromises and solutions. *See* ARBITRATION; CONCILIATION.

Memorandum of Law. A document prepared by the attorney before trial to acquaint the judge with the legal theory of the action and the authorities relied upon in support of that theory. The memorandum also presents a general outline of the facts of the case. It should not assist the opposing party by going into details of evidence, the names of witnesses, or a discussion of the admissibility of evidence.

Invariably the judge is gratified to discover that his task has been made lighter at the very outset of the trial by the lawyer who has prepared his case well and has clarified all the issues involved. The lawyer should make his argument clear and unequivocal. Not too many authorities should be cited. An ancient precedent should never be cited if there is anything more recent on the subject. See CITATION (to Legal Authorities).

There is no such thing as a standard memorandum of law. It will vary in accordance with the tastes of the lawyer and the court. Generally, however, it is safe to assume that a brief, concise trial memorandum, which the judge can read in minutes, is preferable to the kind that would require hours to wade through, sometimes with little gain.

Mental Cruelty. A ground for divorce, consisting of behavior of one spouse toward the other, which renders conditions in life intolerable to the other spouse. Examples of such indignities are abuse, contempt, studied neglect, and unmerited reproach, all of which have been habitually and systematically pursued.

Merger. The fusion of one interest into another.

1. *Corporate.* The absorption of one or more corporations by another existing CORPORATION. The latter corporation retains its identity and takes over all the rights, privileges, franchises, and properties of the absorbed companies and assumes their obligations. (See also CONSOLIDATION OF CORPORATIONS.)

2. *Criminal law.* The absorption of a lesser crime into a greater one. As examples, the crime of ATTEMPT disappears once the attempted act is completed; when a person commits a FELONY and also a TORT against someone by the same act, some states merge the tort into the felony and thereby prevent the civil suit.

3. *Contracts.* Oral agreements and proposals merge in a subsequent written CONTRACT that deals with the same subject matter.

Metes and Bounds Description. See LAND DESCRIPTION.

Microfiche. A process by which pages of printed material are reduced and placed on a card that can be read through a viewer. The cards with the reduced images have much greater accessibility through the viewer than the rolls of film used in the microfilm process. Many of the Reporter volumes are now being placed on microfiche to save space.

Microfilming. A process of photographing records on motion picture film (16 or 35mm), thus making it possible to keep the contents of a four-drawer filing cabinet on about three 200-foot rolls of film that require only 48 cubic inches of storage space.

Minute Books. 1. The record books in which the CLERK OF THE

COURT enters abstracts of all court orders. The clerk records them numerically according to index number. He or she might have separate books for law chancery, divorce, and the like.

If you want information about the court's orders in a case, you can get it by consulting the minute book. You must have the index number. Usually the clerk's office will give you the information over the telephone.

2. For corporations, minute books are books that contain records of minutes of shareholders' and directors' meetings, a copy of the incorporation procedures, bylaws, and sometimes a register of stock issued.

Miranda Rule. A requirement that one who is arrested or taken into custody must receive warnings about the right to remain silent so as not to incriminate oneself and the right to have an attorney present before questioning by law enforcement authorities.

Misdemeanor. An offense lower than a FELONY and generally punishable by fine or imprisonment in a place other than a state penitentiary.

Mistrial. A declaration of the COURT that a trial is to be ended because for some reason justice may not be done if the trial continues. Disqualification of the judge or a juror or the inability of the jury to agree upon a verdict may result in a mistrial. The court will declare a mistrial if a matter has been brought to the jury improperly and could possibly prejudice the verdict. The declaration of a mistrial ends the trial, but the action, itself, continues. In other words, the defendant will not be put into DOUBLE JEOPARDY if he or she is again brought to trial on the same charge.

Mitigating Circumstances. Facts or circumstances that reduce or lower the penalty for an offense. By pleading mitigating circumstances, a defendant may thus receive a less severe sentence.

Mitigation of Damages. A rule that the plaintiff must exercise due care to avoid making an injury worse; facts that show that the amount of damages or the size of a claim is more than the plaintiff is entitled to and should be reduced.

M'Naghten Rule. A test to determine if a person is criminally responsible if, as a result of mental disease or defect, the person did not know right from wrong. Such a person is not held responsible for criminal acts and is not guilty by reason of insanity.

Moody's Manuals. A comprehensive source of information on American businesses. The manuals, covering industrial, transportation, public utility, and bank and finance companies, are valuable to the investor, analyst, business executive, and banker. Included in the manuals are financial statements, a listing of the officers, and highlights of outstanding bond and stock issues.

Annual Dividend Yield. A publication by Moody of the annual yield of various stocks, useful in preparing intangible tax returns.

Moot Court. A mock or fictitious court in which students of law argue cases for practice.

Mortgage. A conditional conveyance. A mortgage is given by a borrower or debtor (the *mortgagor*) to secure the payment of a debt, with a provision that the conveyance will become void on the payment of the debt by the date named. In early English times, the debtor actually turned over his property to the lender (the *mortgagee*) who would keep the income and profits from it. The land was "dead" to the owner and gave him no return; hence the word *mort-gage*, meaning "dead pledge." A mortgage may be given on real estate or on personal property, but a mortgage on personal property is referred to as a *chattel mortgage, whereas a mortgage* on real estate is referred to simply as a *mortgage.* . Some mortgages cover both real and personal property, for example, a mortgage on a furnished apartment building.

The word *mortgage* also refers to the instrument used to make the conveyance. The debt is evidenced by promissory notes; the mortgage is the security instrument that secures payment of the notes. In some states, the debt is evidenced by a bond instead of a promissory note. The bond takes the place of the note. Frequently, the bond and mortgage are combined in one instrument, which is referred to as a BOND AND MORTGAGE.

Parties to a mortgage. The parties to a conventional mortgage are the *mortgagor,* who is the debtor or borrower, and the *mortgagee,* who is the lender. The mortgagor owns the property that is being mortgaged and gives a mortgage to the mortgagee, usually in return for a loan; he or she is frequently referred to in the instrument as the "party of the first part." The mortgagee is frequently referred to as the "party of the second part."

The parties to a DEED OF TRUST are the mortgagor, party of the first part, and the trustee, party of the second part. Some states, Colorado for example, have designated officials, known as *public trustees,* to whom the estate is conveyed under a deed of trust.

Designation of the parties. Extreme care should be exercised to see that the name of the mortgagor appears exactly as it appears in the instrument under which he or she claims title to the land; otherwise, the mortgagee's title might be defective if it becomes necessary to foreclose. The mortgagor's name should be exactly the same in the body of the mortgage, in the signature, and in the acknowledgment. If the mortgage is a *purchase money mortgage,* parties should be given precisely as they appear in the deed from the mortgagee to the mortgagor.

The requirements relative to the GRANTOR and the GRANTEE in a DEED apply generally to the mortgagor and mortgagee.

Forms of mortgage. The forms of mortgages most commonly used are the form that might be termed the *conventional mortgage* and the form variously called a *trust deed, deed of trust, trust indenture,* or *trust mortgage.*

A conventional mortgage is essentially a deed from the borrower to the lender, which contains a provision, known as the *defeasance clause,* that the mortgage shall be void on payment of the debt.

The additional provisions, which appear in fine print in the printed form, vary with the state.

A deed of trust conveys the land to a third party instead of directly to the lender. The third party holds the property in trust for the lender until the debt is paid in accordance with the terms of the trust deed. In the District of Columbia and the following states, the deed of trust is more commonly used than the conventional mortgage: Alabama, California, Colorado, Illinois, Mississippi, Missouri, Montana, New Mexico, Tennessee, Texas, Virginia, and West Virginia. In the other states, a deed of trust is seldom used.

Some states have short *statutory* forms of mortgages, which save space when recorded. The brief statutory forms are amplified by statute and therefore are not used outside the state of origin. Many careful conveyancers feel that the short statutory form does not protect the mortgagee sufficiently.

1. *First Mortgage.* The first (in time or right) of a series of two or more mortgages covering the same property and successively attaching as liens upon it; also, in a more particular sense, a mortgage that is a first lien on the property, not only as against other mortgages, but as against any other charges or incumbrances.

2. *Second Mortgage.* One that takes rank immediately after a first mortgage on the same property, without any intervening liens, and is next entitled to satisfaction out of the proceeds of the property.

3. *Purchase Money Mortgage.* A mortgage given in part payment of the purchase price of the property. For ex-

ample, if the purchase price is $40,000, the purchaser might pay $16,000 cash and give the seller a puchase money mortgage for $24,000. The deed and the purchase money mortgage are executed simultaneously. The grantee in the deed is the mortgagor; the grantor in the deed is the mortgagee. All names and descriptions of property in the purchase money mortgage must agree with those in the deed. A purchase money mortgage has certain priorities that other mortgages do not have. It also has priority over existing judgments and other debts of the mortgagor. On the other hand, as a rule, the mortgagee cannot get a deficiency decree against the mortgagor when he or she forecloses a purchase money mortgage, which the mortgagee cannot usually get under other mortgages.

4. *Open End Mortgage.* A mortgage contract (it may be a purchase money mortgage) allowing the borrower to reborrow up to the amount of the original loan. For example, when a loan has been reduced several thousand dollars, at the lender's option, the borrower may reborrow up to the amount that has been paid ahead. See also BLANKET MORTGAGE.

Preparation of mortgage. In preparing a mortgage, you will find the following general directions helpful: (Some of the directions apply only to typed mortgages, some to printed forms, and some to both.)

1. Make an original for the mortgagee, a copy for the mortgagor, and a copy for the lawyer's files.

2. Use LEGAL CAP paper or letter size according to your office or the registry preference.

3. Follow carefully the directions for filling in a printed form. (See FORMS.)

4. Be sure the responsibility and distribution line (see CORRESPOND-ENCE) is at the top of the first page. This goes on the office copy only of printed form.

5. Double-space.

6. Type the LAND DESCRIPTION. Accuracy is essential.

7. If you are using a printed form, be sure to make the "Z" after the land description. See FORMS.

8. Number all pages of a typed mortgage.

9. Have at least two lines of typing on the signature page.

10. Prepare signature line for the mortgagor. The mortgagee does not sign a mortgage.

11. Affix the SEAL when required.

12. Have proper officer affix corporation seal.

13. Type witness lines and ATTESTATION CLAUSE when required.

14. Prepare certificate of ACKNOWLEDGMENT.

15. Collate.

16. Check and double-check spelling of names. If the mortgage is a purchase money mortgage, compare names of mortgagor and mortgagee with names of GRANTOR and GRANTEE. Extreme care should be exercised to see that the name of the mortgagor appears exactly as it appears in the instrument under which he or she claims title to the property; otherwise, the mortgagee's TITLE might be defective if it becomes necessary to foreclose.

17. Endorse back. If the mortgage is typed, prepare LEGAL BACK.

18. Compare LAND DESCRIPTION with someone to insure accuracy.

19. Arrange for the mortgagor to sign the mortgage.

20. Get the lawyer's approval of the instrument before it is signed.

21. Have the mortgagor sign the original only. Be sure that the mortgagor's signature agrees with the name, exactly as it is typed in the mortgage.

22. Have the mortgage notarized. You can take the acknowledgment if you are a notary.

23. After signature and acknowledgment, conform copies to original.

24. Get the lawyer's approval of the executed mortgage and have it recorded. Put a notation on the back to have it returned to the office. (The secretary to the lawyer for the mortgagee attends to the recording.)

25. When the mortgage is returned by the recorder, send it to the mortgagee.

Printed mortgages. Printed forms are used extensively. The forms for the ordinary mortgage and deed of trust usually can be filled in without dictation from the lawyer. He or she will dictate any special clauses needed. Following is a checklist of information needed to fill in a mortgage or deed of trust. (The information can be obtained from the files, the lawyer, or, with permission, from the client.)

1. Full name of mortgagor and mortgagee; also of trustee in the case of a trust deed.

2. County and state of residence of mortgagor and mortgagee; in a large city, their street address; also residence of trustee in the case of a trust deed.

3. Full description of the mortgagor's office and authority if he or she is conveying in a representative capacity.

4. Marital status of mortgagor.

5. Full name of spouse if spouse must join in the conveyance.

6. If purchase money mortgage, is wife to join?

7. Date of mortgage.

8. Amount of mortgage.

9. Period mortgage is to run, as well as its maturity date.

10. Rate of interest and when payable.

11. Description of property.

12. Date and place mortgage is to be acknowledged.

13. If mortgagor is corporation, name and title of officers signing and acknowledging.

14. If mortgage contains power of sale, number of days notice to be given in newspaper (this is determined by statute) and where newspaper is published.

15. If there is to be an AFFIDAVIT OF TITLE, who is to make it?

Typed mortgages; deeds of trust; trust deeds. The lawyer will dictate a mortgage or a DEED OF TRUST or a TRUST DEED when the printed form is inadequate for the special conditions of the transaction. Trust deeds that are given to secure a bond issue are long and involved and are printed especially for a specific bond issue. The secretary follows the general style of the printed form.

Mortgage statement and clauses. The written summation that identifies precisely the debt and all of the conditional terms of a particular mortgage agreement. The statement and clauses set forth:

1. *Description of debt.* A mortgage is given to secure a debt, and the mortgage instrument must describe and identify the debt with preciseness. The descrip-

tion includes the rate and time of payment of interest and clearly states the time of payment of the debt. Some forms call for a copy of the note secured by the mortgage to be copied in the body of the instrument.

Example:

. . . an indebtedness in the sum of fifteen thousand (15,000) dollars, lawful money of the United States, to be paid on the first day of April, 19..., with interest thereon to be computed from April 1, 19..., at the rate of twelve (12) per centum per annum, and to be paid semiannually thereafter, according to a certain note bearing even date herewith . . . .

2. *Defeasance clause.* The provision in the mortgage that if the indebtedness is paid in accordance with the terms of the mortgage agreement, the mortgage shall be null and void.

Example:

Provided always, that said mortgagor, . . . shall pay . . . a certain promissory note, a copy of which is on the reverse side hereof, and shall perform and comply with each and every stipulation, agreement and covenant of said note and of this mortgage, the estate hereby created shall be void, otherwise the same shall remain in full force and virtue.

. . . provided that if I shall punctually pay said notes according to the tenor thereof, then this mortgage shall be void.

3. *Mortgage consideration.* A mortgage recites the consideration for which it was given. Statement of the consideration might name the amount of the indebtedness, or it might recite a nominal consideration.

Examples:
. . . for and in consideration of the aforesaid debt of five thousand dollars ($5,000), and the better securing the payment of the same with interest.

. . .

. . . for the better securing the payment of the sum of money mentioned in the said bond, or obligation, with the interest thereon, and, also, in consideration of One Dollar ($1.) paid by the Second Party, the receipt whereof is hereby acknowledged . . . .

4. *Acceleration clause.* See ACCELERATION CLAUSE.

5. *Description of property.* See LAND DESCRIPTION.

6. *Prepayment privilege.* A clause giving the mortgagor the right to pay off the mortgage, or part of it, before maturity. Mortgages and mortgage notes frequently provide that the debt shall be payable on or before the maturity date, or they contain a specific clause giving the mortgagor the right. A comparable provision in trust deeds securing issues of bonds permits redemption of the bonds before maturity dates. The privilege enables a mortgagor to refinance his or her debt when money is cheaper or to sell the property free and clear of any mortgage. Printed forms do not usually include the prepayment privilege.

Example:
The mortgagor is hereby authorized and permitted to pay the debt hereby secured, or any part of it, not less than . . . . dollars at any one time, whenever and at such time and times as he may choose, and the mortgagee hereby agrees to accept such payment or payments, and thereupon the interest shall cease upon such part of the debt as may be so paid; and upon the full payment of said debt, with all interest up to the date of actual payment, he will discharge this mortgage.

7. *Partial release clause.* This clause permits the mortgagor to sell part of the land, permitting the release of a specified portion of the premises covered by the mortgage upon payment of a specified sum.

Example:
Said mortgagor reserves the right to release all or any part of the said land from the operation of this mortgage, in case said land is subdivided, upon payment to mortgagee of a sum of money to be agreed upon for each lot, the sum to be determined according to the size and location of the lot as soon as the said land is subdivided.

Said mortgagee has agreed to sign a plat of said premises prepared by mortgagor.

Motion. The application for an order addressed to the COURT or to a judge in his or her chambers by the lawyer for a party to a lawsuit. For example, when an attorney wants the court to take a particular action in a pending case, he or she "moves" the court to take that action. Unless a motion is made during a hearing or trial, it is in writing.

Motions are numerous and varied. Some of the motions more frequently addressed to the court include: (1) Motion for Change of Venue (2) Motion to Strike (3) Motion for New Trial (4) Motion for Leave to Amend (5) Motion to set for Trial.

Some jurisdictions have special terms of court at which all motions are heard. In crowded jurisdictions, the contested motions are heard in one part and *ex parte* motions of which opposing counsel has no notice are heard in another part. The secretary must acquaint herself with the part in which they are heard, if there is a distinction in any of the courts in her locality. See also NOTICE of Motion.

Motion to Dismiss. See DEMURRER.

Municipal Court. See COURTS OF SPECIAL JURISDICTION.

Muniments of Title. Written evidence by which title to real property may be defended. The word *muniments* is derived from the Latin verb *munio,* meaning "to fortify." Hence, muniments of title fortify or strengthen rights in property. The expression as generally defined refers to deeds of conveyance, wills, legislative grants and other documents relating to the title land.

Murder. The unlawful killing of someone by deliberate design. In many states, legislative enactments have divided murder into degrees. *First-degree murder* is generally defined as the act of killing another with deliberate and premeditated design, or as killing another while in the act of committing a FELONY (see also FELONY—MURDER). *Second-degree murder* occurs where there is no deliberately formed design to kill; the idea of killing occurs instantaneously with the act. See also MANSLAUGHTER.

Mutiny. An insurrection by military or naval personnel or seamen against the authority of their commanders. Seamen who by force, intimidation, or trick deprive the vessel's captain of his authority, or resist or prevent his exercise of authority, may be guilty of the crime of mutiny.

Nasciturus. Future issue of a marriage.

National Association of Legal Secretaries. Legal secretaries and attorneys recognize that the successful legal secretary must now be more than a proficient stenographer and typist. Not only must she have skills that include a working knowledge of every type of work in either a large or small law office, but she must, in addition, be an expert in human relations, law office ethics and etiquette, and law office procedures and management. The National Association of Legal Secretaries plays a vital role in assisting and educating the legal secretary to attain these goals. Through the association's nationally sponsored program for certifying legal secretaries by special examination, the rating of a Professional Legal Secretary may be earned.

The PLS, as it is known, is awarded to any legal secretary who has at least five years' legal experience and who successfully complete a two-day examination covering seven parts: Part I, Written Communication Skill and Knowledge; Part II, Human Relations and Ethics; Part III, Legal Secretarial Procedures; Part IV, Legal Secretarial Accounting; Part V, Legal Terminology, Techniques, and Procedures; Part VI, Exercise of Judgment; cedures; Part VI, Exercise of Judgment; and Part VII, Legal Secretarial Skills. The examinations are conducted twice a year in various test centers across the country. When the examination is completed and passed, the secretary is given a PLS certificate.

Preparation for the examination can be worth the time and effort, even if it is not passed on the first attempt. Each part passed need not be repeated. Only the parts failed need be taken over, and the subject areas covered are useful to any legal secretary.

For information about the PLS program or about membership in NALS, write to:

National Association of Legal Secretaries
3005 E. Skelly Drive
Tulsa, Oklahoma 74105

National Labor Relations Board (NLRB). A panel appointed by the president with the advice and consent of the Senate. The board is given the power by the National Labor Relations Act (Wagner Act) to establish procedures for the settlement of questions of union representation and to prevent persons from engaging in unfair labor practices.

National Reporter System. The published opinions of the federal courts and the courts of every state, those of several states being published in the same bound volume. This system of reports, published by West Publishing Company, covers the entire country. (See CITATION, table III, for the names of reporters, how they are cited, and the courts covered by each.) Some of the reporters are designated "Second Series." The designation is for numbering purposes and indicates that the numbers of the volume have started over with 1.

These reporters, which are "unofficial" reports of the courts' opinions, are published much sooner than the OFFICIAL REPORTS, especially those in some states. Some states have discontinued the publication of state reports and use the appropriate reporter of the National Reporter System as the official report.

Before the opinions are published in bound volumes of the National Reporter System, they are published in weekly pamphlets known as *Advance Sheets*. (Some official reports also have advance sheets.) Thus the lawyer is informed immediately of the decisions of courts in which he or she is interested. The page numbers in the advance sheets correspond with the page numbers that will appear in the bound volumes.

Necessaries. Articles that a party actually needs, such as food, clothing, and shelter. Infants may be held liable for contracting for necessaries; also mentally incompetent persons. See PROVISION OF NECESSARIES.

Negligence. The failure to use reasonable care to avoid injury to another. The standard of care that should be used is that degree of care that would have been used by a reasonable person in the light of all of the circumstances of the case. For example, a doctor in treating a patient must act with the skill of the average member of the profession.

If the defendant's negligence is the PROXIMATE CAUSE of injury to the plaintiff, and the plaintiff is free from CONTRIBUTORY NEGLIGENCE, he or she is entitled to DAMAGES.

Negotiable Instrument. A written instrument, signed by a maker or drawer, containing an unconditional promise or order to pay a certain sum of money, which can be passed freely from one person to another in a manner that constitutes the transferee as the holder. If payable to bearer, the instrument may be negotiated simply by delivery; if payable to order, it is negotiated by endorsement of the holder, completed by delivery.

The Uniform Commercial Code, which has been adopted by all of the states, governs negotiable instruments. See UNIFORM LAWS. The law states the manner in which a negotiable instrument shall be transferred, and it fixes the rights and duties of the maker, the payee, the holder and the endorser. For example, under the law an endorser of a negotiable instrument vouches for its genuineness. If it is a forgery, the endorser is liable to a HOLDER IN DUE COURSE of the instrument after delivery.

Strictly speaking, documents of title (such as order bills of lading, warehouse receipts, and stock certificates) are not negotiable instruments because they do not contain an order to pay a sum of money. However, various statutes have given certain documents of title the quality of negotiability. These are known as quasi-negotiable instruments.

Negotiation. The transfer of a written instrument in a manner that makes the transferee the holder of the instrument. If payable to order, an instrument is negotiated by endorsement and delivery; if payable to bearer, by delivery alone. An instrument is not negotiated until it is transferred by the person to whom it is issued. Thus *A* make a note payable to *B* and delivers it to him. Subsequently, by negotiation, *B* transfers the note to *C*, and *C* to *D*, and so on. As opposed to transfer by ASSIGNMENT, the innocent transferee by negotiation takes the paper free of defenses that are good against the transferor. See also NEGOTIABLE INSTRUMENT.

New Case Report. A systematically kept record of all of the pertinent information on a new matter received in the law office in which it will act for a client. In any well organized law office, a report is made immediately on every matter received. The lawyer who interviews the client obtains the following information: (1) name, address, and telephone number of the client; (2) name of opposing party, and address and telephone number, if known; (3) attorney for opposing party, if any. Occasionally these data are given to the secretary by the client as he or she leaves the office, but it is usually more diplomatic for the lawyer to make a note of the information during the interview.

What to do. Your job is to get the in-formation from the lawyer as soon as the client leaves the office, so you can make up a new case report. The reports also call for one or more of the following items of information, which the lawyer should indicate.

1. The general nature of the case, whether general litigation, probate, foreclosure, and so on.
2. Whether the case is on an annual retainer basis or is a single case. This affects the bookkeeping.
3. Whether the client is new or old.
4. Whether stenographic services are to be billed separately or included in the overall fee.
5. Name of the junior partner or associate, if any, to be assigned to the case.

Printed forms are provided for new case reports, or they may be mimeographed. Frequently the lawyer makes out the reports, because they call for very little writing. Two types of forms are illustrated in figures 1 and 2. Notice that the form illustrated in figure 2 even has a space in which the attorney indicates whether the client is to be added to the firm's ANNOUNCEMENT CARD list.

When the report is filled out, it is ready to be routed.

Routing of new case report. The routing procedure varies with the office, but the following order of routing is practical and can be adapted to the requirements of any office. When a secretary works in a small office, instead of routing the new case report, she takes the steps indicated by this procedure.

1. File department. File number is assigned and a file opened. File clerk initials. See FILING.

```
┌─────────────────────────────────────────────────────────────┐
│           MORGAN, BURBANK & CHAMBERS                          │
│           REPORT OF NEW CASE OR MATTER                        │
│           MUST BE TYPEWRITTEN                                 │
│                                                               │
│                                    CLASSIFICATION             │
│   Date:                            ☐ General Litigation       │
│   Name of Client:                  ☐ Corporate and            │
│                                      Financial                │
│                                    ☐ Indiv. Pers., Trust      │
│   Address:                         ☐ Estate and Litigation    │
│   Title of Case or Matter:           as to Estate             │
│                                                               │
│                                    REAL ESTATE                │
│                                    ☐ General                  │
│   Court:                           ☐ Certiorari               │
│   Member in Charge:                ☐ Dispossess               │
│   Assistant:                       ☐ Foreclosure             │
│                                                               │
│           (CHECK AND RETURN PROMPTLY)                         │
│   1. Charge Register: ......2. Managing Clerk: ......3. Bookkeepers: ........ │
│           4. Budget Committee: ....5. Files: .......... │
└─────────────────────────────────────────────────────────────┘
```

New Case Report: Figure 1.

2. Accounting department. Ledger sheet for the client and case is opened, after which disbursements may be made for and charged to the case. Bookkeeper initials.

In a large firm, there might be other departments or committees to which the report would be routed.

The new case is then returned to the filing department and filed. The mechanics of processing the case have been completed, and the attorney, paralegal, and secretary are ready to work on it. The matter might consist of drawing an instrument, in which event the file will soon be closed; or it might involve litigation that extends over a period of years; or it might be a matter in a specialized field of law, such as organizing a corpora-

tion. Regardless of the nature of the case, you will have dictation and typing about it and very probably will have contact with the client either in person or by telephone. See also TELEPHONE; SUIT REGISTER.

Next Friend. One acting for the benefit of an infant, or other person not *sui juris,* without being regularly appointed guardian.

Nonage. Under the proper age to be able to do a particular thing. For example, an action for the ANNULMENT OF MARRIAGE may be brought when one or both of the parties have not attained the legal age of consent. Whether the marriage of an infant may be annulled

HALL and DOBB
NEW CASE REPORT

File No.

Received by _____

For Credit of _____ Date _____

Attorney receiving a new case will fill out this blank, sign it, and then send it to Files. Files will assign a file number, index under the names given in 1 to 4; note any instructions as to filing in 5; initial here _____ and send to Assistant Managing Partner.

Assistant Managing Partner will assign attorneys, initial, etc. and send to the Accounting Department.

Accounting Department will see that the report is properly filled out, service ledger cards made, open a service ledger account, and initial here·

| submitted by | verified by |

Accounting Department will list on weekly summary and initial here _____

Estimated Value of Case $ _____

Nature of Case

Add to Firm Announcement List Yes ☐ No ☐

Billing Retainer or Continuing ☐ Single Cases ☐

Client New ☐ Old ☐

1. Name of Client _____

   Address _____

   _____

2. Title of Case _____

   _____

3. Opposing Party _____

   Address _____

   _____

4. Additional Names (if any) _____

   that should be indexed _____

   (Additional names should be given where the name of the person referring the case or the name of a person with whom there is to be much correspondence does not appear in 1, 2, or 3 above.)

5. Filing Instructions (if any) _____

6. Remarks _____

Received by Assistant Managing Partner: _____ Date _____ at _____

Attorney Responsible _____

Assistant Assigned _____

Junior Assigned _____

Will case be litigated?

No ☐

Yes ☐

Doubtful ☐

New Case Report: Figure 2.

for nonage depends upon the age of consent in the place of marriage.

Nonbusiness Expenses. See EXCISE TAXES.

Noncumulative Preferred Stock. A class of stock characterized by the fact that unpaid dividends do not accumulate as arrearages, which must be eliminated before dividends may be paid on COMMON STOCK. See also CUMULATIVE PREFERRED STOCK; PREFERRED STOCK; DIVIDEND.

Nonsuit. A dismissal of the plaintiff's COMPLAINT by the court because he or she failed to establish a good cause of action. Defendant makes a motion for a nonsuit after the close of plaintiff's evidence. Defendant's motion should be specific and should indicate the particular defects or failures in plaintiff's proof. In determining the motion, the court will assume that all plaintiff's evidence is true and will draw every reasonable inference in plaintiff's favor.

Nonsupport. The failure of one spouse to furnish to the other and to their children support consistent with that person's means. Withholding of such support is a ground for SEPARATION in most states and for DIVORCE in some.

No-Par Stock. Stock without any nominal or designated value in money. Such stock may be either COMMON STOCK or PREFERRED STOCK.

It was originally considered necessary for the CERTIFICATE of Stock to show the amount in dollars for which the stock was issued, whether that amount was actually received by the CORPORATION or not. See PAR VALUE STOCK. The actual value of the stock might change from day to day, but the value stated in the stock certificate, the nominal or par value, always remained the same. Thus rather than being a statement of the actual or book value of the stock evidenced by the stock certificate, the statement of par value in the certificate was more often than not no indication at all of the actual or book value of the stock. This fact, in large measure, accounts for the substitution of no-par stock for stock expressing a par value. No-par stock tends to relieve the necessity for, or embarrassment of, explanation of discrepancy between the book or market value and the face value of corporate stocks.

Notarize. To acknowledge or attest a document as a NOTARY PUBLIC. The notary public exercises special care to see that documents he or she notarizes are executed correctly. If the papers are not in conformity with the requirements of the office where they are to be recorded, they will be rejected. The notary does not read an instrument that is notarized but should read the ACKNOWLEDGMENT and also glance over the instrument. The notary observes the following details when taking an acknowledgment.

1. If the instrument recites that it is "under seal," the notary should be sure that the signature to the instrument is followed by "L.S."

2. When a corporation is a party to an instrument, the notary should be sure the CORPORATE SEAL is impressed on

the instrument if required; seals are usually required on corporate instruments.

3. The notary should fill in all blanks in the instrument and in the certificate of ACKNOWLEDGMENT or the JURAT.

4. The notary should show the date of the expiration of his or her commission when required.

5. The notary should be sure to impress the notarial seal on the certificate when required. Some states do not require a notary's seal on papers acknowledged within the state, but all states require a seal on papers acknowledged in another state.

6. The notary should be sure that the rubber stamps make legible imprints. A black stamp pad is preferable because the black ink photostats more distinctly than other inks.

Following the letter of the law when notarizing a paper. A commission as a notary public is a trust; it confers certain powers upon the notary as well as requiring that the notary perform certain duties. In exercising these powers and duties, he or she should observe punctiliously the "letter of the law." In a law office, the principal duty as a notary public will be taking acknowledgments.

Notice that all certificates of acknowledgments illustrated in figures 1 to 4 under ACKNOWLEDGMENT recite that the person making the acknowledgment "personally appeared" before the notary. This is true of all forms of acknowledgments in every state. Therefore, when you act as notary, you should never take an acknowledgment without the actual appearance of the individual making the acknowledgement. In fact, it is illegal to do so.

Acknowledgments also recite that the individual "acknowledged" that he or she signed the instrument. The notary does not administer an oath to a person making an acknowledgment, but asks: "Do you acknowledge that you signed this instrument?" or, "Do you acknowledge that you executed this instrument as attorney-in-fact for R. Stevens?" or a similar question, depending upon whether the acknowledgment is being made by an individual in his or her own behalf, an officer of a corporation, a partnership, or an attorney-in-fact.

Acknowledgments also recite that the notary knows, or has satisfactory evidence, that the person making it is the person "described in and who executed" the instrument. The notary must have satisfactory evidence of the identity of a person whose acknowledgment is taken. Of course, in taking acknowledgments made by clients, the notary is not likely to have difficulty in this respect. A notary who willfully make a false certificate that an instrument was acknowledged by a party to the instrument is guilty of forgery.

A certificate of acknowledgment also shows the date it is signed by the notary. The notary should never postdate or antedate a certificate. To do so constitutes FRAUD and deceit in the exercise of the notary's powers.

Notary Public. (Pl., notaries public.) A commissioned officer of a state, whose powers and duties consist, among others, in administrating oaths, certifying to the genuiness of documents, and taking acknowledgements. In some states, a notary is authorized to act only in the county in which he or she is commissioned; in others, the notary is qualified to act thoughout the state. Almost all law offices have a notary public, and frequently the secretary is the notary. Lawyers in some states have de facto (see LATIN TERMS, de facto) notarial authority, but they must qualify and register and have a notarial seal or stamp (see NOTARY'S SEAL). The eligibility requirements are not stingent, relating primarily to age and residence. If your office wants you to be commissioned as a notary, write to the official in your state who appoints notaries for an application blank. Some states require a bond; stipulate that the notary public must keep a record of all official acts; require that the application be endorsed by a member of the legislature, a judge, or some other designated official. You must meet the requirements of the state in which you reside.

After the commission is received, order a notary's seal and stamp. Register your commission with the CLERK OF THE COURT (or other designated official) in your county, so the officer can authenticate your certificate of ACKNOWLEDGMENT on papers that are to be recorded in another state. The secretary who becomes a notary must follow the letter of the law. Notary commissions are renewable at intervals, except that in some states lawyers are given lifetime commissions. (See NOTARIZE.) Table I describes the requirements for notaries in the various states.

Notary's Seal. The stamp or imprint that is placed upon a legal instrument, certificate, or paper by an authorized NOTARY PUBLIC. The notary's seal (also called the *notarial seal*) is required by some states when acknowledgment is made within the state. *All* states require a seal on papers acknowledged in another state.

Note of Issue. See NOTICING A CASE FOR TRIAL.

Notice. 1. *of Appeal.* Under the rules of a typical state, the filing of a *notice of appeal* with the CLERK OF THE COURT whose order is appealed from gives the appellate court jurisdiction, and an appeal is deemed to have commenced. It is the appellant's notice of intention to appeal a decision rendered by a lower court. (See APPELLATE COURT.) The time usually allowed for filing a notice of appeal is 30 days after receipt of a copy of the judgment with NOTICE of Entry.

You can get the wording of the notice of appeal from the court rules or from FORM books, or the lawyer will dictate it to you or give you a form to follow. Set it up in the same manner and on the same kind of paper as for other court papers. (See TYPING, Legal Documents.) (1) Make an original, a copy for each appellee, and a copy for your own files (but see 5 below); (2) see that the caption is the same as that on the PLEADINGS; (3) bind the notice in a legal back, properly endorsed; (4) see that the attorney for the party who appeals signs the notice of appeal; (5) serve a copy on counsel for appellee, and file the original, with proof of service, with the Clerk of the Court. In some states, the rules do not require service of notice of appeal on opposing counsel. In other states, the rules require that the notice be filed in duplicate, on containing the proof of service.

Service on opposing counsel. Service of all papers and notices required by the

Table I

NOTARIES PUBLIC

State	Appoint- ments made by	Length of term	Notary must affix		Record of acts required	Bond required
			Seal	Date commis- sion expires		
Alabama	Judges of Probate	4	Yes	No	Yes	Yes
Alaska	Secretary of State	4	Yes	Yes	Yes	Yes
Arizona	Secretary of State	4	Yes	Yes	Yes	Yes
Arkansas	Governor	4	Yes	Yes	Yes	Yes
California	Secretary of State	4	Yes	No	Yes	Yes
Colorado	Secretary of State	4	Yes	Yes	Yes	Yes
Connecticut	Secretary of State	5	Yes	No	No	No
Delaware	Governor	2	Yes	No	No	No
District of Columbia	D.C. Com- missioners	5	Yes	No	Yes	Yes
Florida	Governor	4	Yes	Yes	No	Yes
Georgia	Clerks of Superior Court	4	Yes	No	No	No
Hawaii	Atty. Gen.	4	Yes	Yes	Yes	Yes
Idaho	Governor	4	Yes	No	Yes	Yes
Illinois	Secretary of State	4	Yes	No	No[2]	Yes
Indiana	Governor	4	Yes	Yes	No	Yes
Iowa	Secretary of State	3	Yes	No	Yes	Yes
Kansas	Secretary of State	4	Yes	Yes	No	Yes
Kentucky	Secretary of State	4	No	Yes	No[1]	Yes
Louisiana	Governor	Indefinite	No	No	Yes	Yes
Maine	Governor	7	Yes	No	No[3]	No
Maryland	Governor	4	Yes	Yes	Yes	No
Massachusetts ..	Governor	7	No	Yes	No	No
Michigan	Governor	4	No	Yes	No	Yes
Minnesota	Governor	7	Yes	Yes	No[1]	Yes
Mississippi	Governor	4	Yes	Yes	Yes	Yes
Missouri	Secretary of State	4	Yes	Yes	Yes	Yes
Montana	Governor	3	Yes	Yes	No[1]	Yes
Nebraska	Governor	4	Yes	Yes	No	Yes
Nevada	Secretary of State	4	Yes[6]	Yes	No	Yes
New Hampshire	Governor	5	Yes[4]	Yes	No	No
New Jersey	Secretary of State	5	No	No	Yes	No
New Mexico	Governor	4	Yes	Yes	Yes	Yes

(continued on following page)

From the book, *Legal Secretary's Complete Handbook*, 3rd ed., by Besse May Miller, revised by Mary A. DeVries, © 1980 by Prentice-Hall, Inc. Published by Prentice-Hall, Inc., Englewood Cliffs, N.J. 07632.

(continued from preceding page)

| State | Appointments made by | Length of term | Notary must affix | | Record of acts required | Bond required |
			Seal	Date commission expires		
New York	Secretary of State	2	Yes	Yes	No	No
North Carolina ...	Secretary of State	5	Yes	Yes	No	No
North Dakota	Secretary of State	6	Yes	Yes	No[1]	Yes
Ohio	Governor	5	Yes[4]	No	No[1]	Yes
Oklahoma	Secretary of State	4	Yes	Yes	Yes	Yes
Oregon	Governor	4	Yes	Yes	No[1]	Yes
Pennsylvania	Secretary of the Commonwealth	4	Yes	Yes	Yes	Yes
Rhode Island	Governor	5	No	No	No	No
South Carolina ...	Governor	10	Yes	Yes	No	No
South Dakota	Governor	8	Yes	Yes[4]	No[1]	Yes
Tennessee	Governor	4	Yes	Yes	Yes	Yes
Texas	Secretary State	2	Yes	Yes	Yes	Yes
Utah	Governor	4	Yes	Yes	No[1]	Yes
Vermont	Judges of the County Court	2	Yes	No	No	No
Virginia	Governor	4	No	Yes	No	Yes
Washington	Governor	4	Yes	No	No	Yes
West Virginia	Governor	10	No	Yes	No	Yes
Wisconsin	Governor	4	Yes	Yes	No	Yes
Wyoming	Governor	4	Yes	Yes	Yes[5]	Yes

[1]Except with reference to commercial papers.
[2]Except with reference to negotiable instruments.
[3]Except with reference to mercantile and marine protests.
[4]In practice, but not by statute.
[5]For official acts required by law to be recorded.
[6]Stamp, rather than seal.

rules of an appellate court may be made by leaving the same in the office of the opposing counsel during regular office hours with a person in charge of the office. Service may also be made by depositing papers and notices securely sealed and postpaid, in the post office directed to such attorney at his or her usual post office address. *Proof of service* is made by affidavit, when service is had by mail. Placing the properly sealed and addressed document in an "outgoing basket" to be dispatched by the mail clerk in the office is not compliance with the statutes.

You must actually do what the *affidavit of service* says. Figure 1 illustrates an affidavit of service by mail. If the wording of the affidavit used in an office differs, make an extra copy for the office form

IN THE CIRCUIT COURT OF THE ELEVENTH
JUDICIAL CIRCUIT OF FLORIDA, IN AND FOR
DADE COUNTY. IN CHANCERY

———————————————————— x

DAVID HOPE,   :   No. 13,670-C

           Plaintiff,   :

        vs.   : AFFIDAVIT OF SERVICE

JOHN NEVINS,   :

          Defendant.   :

———————————————————— x

STATE OF FLORIDA,)
                  : SS.
DADE COUNTY.   )

      Before the subscriber personally appeared JEANNE NAULT, who, being first duly sworn, deposes and says that she is employed by Stevens and Wyatt and was so employed on January 8, 19—; that on said date she personally placed in an envelope addressed to James Cassidy, Jr., Esq., a true copy of the foregoing Notice to Appeal; that said envelope, having been properly addressed and sealed, with sufficient postage affixed thereto, was deposited by her on said date in the United States Mails at Miami, Florida.

———————————————

Subscribed and Sworn to Before Me
This 8th day of January, 19—.

———————————————————

Notary Public, State of Florida
at Large.
My commission expires: 5/8/—.
(SEAL)

Notice: Figure 1.
Affidavit of service by mail.

book. Notice that the affidavit is preceded by the caption of the case. When this affidavit is copied into the RECORD ON APPEAL, the caption will be omitted, but the recital of venue will be included.

See also AFFIDAVIT.

2. *of Appearance.* A written statement by the attorney for the defendant, *that the defendant appears* in a particular action or jurisdiction. Thereafter, copies of all pleadings will be served on the attorney appearing for the defendant, if such service is required. In some jurisdictions, the notice of appearance is addressed to the attorney for the plaintiff; in others, to the CLERK OF THE COURT. Figures 2 and 3 illustrate notices of appearance in (1) a common law case and (2) in an equity case.

How to prepare a notice of appearance. A printed form of the notice of appearance is available, but the notice may be typed on legal-size paper.

a. Prepare an original for the court, a copy to be served on opposing counsel, and a copy for your office file.

b. The caption is identical with that on the SUMMONS. If the title of the case is long, you may shorten it (see CAPTION).

c. Type signature line for attorney, with his or her address underneath. When a printed form is used, it is advisable to type the attorney's name in parentheses underneath the line for signature so the opposing counsel will have no difficulty in deciphering the signature.

d. Endorse the back. If you type the notice, put a properly ENDORSED LEGAL BACK on it.

What to do about the notice of appearance. A notice of appearance is never verified, because it contains no statements of fact. Otherwise, your responsibilities with respect to the notice of appearance are the same as with respect to the ANSWER. In some jurisdictions, the notice of appearance is not served on opposing counsel; he or she learns from the court record that the appearance has been filed.

3. *of Entry.* Written notification given to opposing counsel by the prevailing attorney, stating that a JUDGMENT is being entered against him or her in the court of record. The right to APPEAL or to make MOTIONS affecting the judgment date from the time notice is given.

4. *of Motion.* A warning in writing to the opposing counsel concerning a particular action that an attorney wants the COURT to take in a pending case.

The notice of motion states the papers and proceedings upon which the motion will be brought and also the grounds of the motion. The supporting papers usually include an affidavit that is attached to the notice of motion.

Return day of motion. All notices of motion give the date the attorney will move the court for entry of the desired order. This date is the *return day* of the motion; the motion is *returnable* on that day. The practice rules provide that the notice shall be served on opposing counsel a specified number of days, or a reasonable time, before the return day of the motion. Some jurisdictions that do not have special terms of courts for motions set aside certain days in the month as motion day, on which days all motions are returnable. You will become familiar with (1) the motion days in the various courts and (2) how many days of notice are required.

SUPREME COURT OF THE STATE OF NEW YORK
COUNTY OF NEW YORK

———————————————————————— x

WALTER LANE,   :

                 Plaintiff,   :
         -against-   :

HENRY MASON,   :

            Defendant.   :

———————————————————————— x

SIR:

      PLEASE TAKE NOTICE that the defendant Henry Mason hereby appears in the above entitled action and that we are retained as attorneys for him therein, and hereby demand that a copy of the complaint and of all other papers in this action be served on us at the office below designated.

Dated, New York, July 25, 19—.

                           Yours very truly,

                           ADAMS & SILLS,
                           Attorneys for Defendant,
                           80 Towers Avenue
                           New York, N.Y. 10017

To:

        CLAYTON BIXBY, ESQ.,
        Attorney for Plaintiff,
        14 Hale Street
        New York, N.Y. 10012

Notice: Figure 2.
Notice of appearance in common law case.

UNITED STATES DISTRICT COURT

EASTERN DISTRICT OF NEW YORK

_____ x

HARVEY DILLON,   :

                Plaintiff,   :

       -against-   : E 87-20

SLOANE, INC.,   :

              Defendant.   :

_____ x

TO THE CLERK OF THE ABOVE COURT:

     We hereby enter our appearance as attorneys and solicitors for the defendant SLOANE, INC. in the above entitled suit.

Dated, New York, July 5, 19—.

                            Yours very truly,

                            KENNEDY & SMITH
                            Attorneys for Defendant
                            Sloane, Inc.
                            36 Mall Street
                            New York, N.Y. 10036

To:

        WILLIAM HILL
         Attorney for Plaintiff
         150 Brown Avenue
         New York, N.Y. 10016

THE CLERK OF THE UNITED STATES DISTRICT COURT
     Eastern District of New York
     Post Office Building
     Brooklyn, N.Y. 11201

Notice: Figure 3.
Notice of appearance in equity case
(Federal Court).

Information needed to prepare a notice of motion. Notices of motion are prepared like other notices. The lawyer will dictate some notices of motions, but you should be able to prepare many of them upon instructions without dictation. You will need the following information:

a. Style of case. Get this from the complaint or other papers in the file.

b. Papers and proceedings upon which the motion will be based. The lawyer usually dictates this.

c. Grounds upon which the motion will be made. The lawyer will dictate these, except when they are standard. For example, a motion to strike is always on the ground that portions of the pleadings are "sham, irrelevant and redundant." (The standard wording of the clause varies with the court.)

d. Return day of motion. If you do not know how to calculate the return day, ask the lawyer.

e. Time motion will be heard. Usually court practice rules set aside a certain hour at which motions will be called. If you are not familiar with this time in the various courts, ask the lawyer or consult the rules. The notice will read "at . . . o'clock in the . . . noon, or as soon thereafter as counsel can be heard."

f. Where the motion will be heard. Motions are usually heard in the court where the case is pending. In some jurisdictions, specific terms, parts, departments, or divisions are set aside for motions.

g. Name of affiant and date of supporting affidavit, if the motion is based on an affidavit, as it usually is. The lawyer will give you this information. Very probably he or she will dictate the affidavit before instructing you about the notice.

What to do about the notice of motion and affidavit. A motion is frequently based upon an affidavit, as appears from the wording of the notice. When this is the case, responsibilities, after preparation of the notice and affidavit, are the following:

a. Endorse a legal back, if one is used, "Affidavit and Notice of Motion" and staple the papers together, placing the notice on top.

b. After approval by the lawyer, see that copy is served on opposing counsel.

c. See that receipt of service is on back of original. If the papers are served by mail, prepare certificate of service by mail.

d. Enter return day of motion in the diary (see REMINDERS).

e. Conform the office copy.

f. File original, with proof of service in court.

g. Make entries in SUIT REGISTER of service and filing.

h. The secretary to the attorney on whom the papers are served makes a notation on back of that copy of date and hour of service. Enter in diary return day of motion. Also make entry in suit register.

5. *of Trial.* See NOTICING A CASE FOR TRIAL.

Noticing a Case for Trial. The procedure by which a case is placed on the trial calendar of the court.

A material point, raised by the PLEADINGS, about which there is a controversy between the parties is an *issue.* The issue may be an *issue of fact* or an *issue of law.* When an issue is raised, it is said to be *joined,* and the case is *at is-*

sue. Issue is deemed joined the date the last pleading is served.

At any time after issue is joined, either party may have the case *noticed for trial.* (In the New York Supreme Court no papers are filed in court until issue is joined—the court does not even know a lawsuit is pending.) In some jurisdictions, a case is noticed for trial by the filing of a *note of issue* or *memorandum setting for trial;* in others, by the filing of a *notice of trial.* Some jurisdictions require both. In still other jurisdictions, a case is set for trial on MOTION of counsel. Regardless of the procedure, or the particular name of the notice used, its purpose is to place the case on the trial calendar.

Noticing a case for trial does not mean that it will be brought up for trial on that date or even at that term of court, but that it will be placed on the trial calendar to await its turn.

When the notice must be served. Note of issue or notice of trial must be served on opposing counsel a designated number of days before the TERM OF COURT at which the case will be placed on the trial calendar. The requirement varies with the jurisdiction. Suppose a new term of court commences on the first Monday of the following month, which, say, is May 5. Practice rules require that the note of issue or notice of trial shall be served 12 days, for example, before the commencement of the term. Therefore, the notice must be served by April 23. Service after that date will not give counsel 12 days notice. Thus if on April 25 the lawyer tells you to prepare a notice of trial, you should know that it will have to be for the June, not the May, term of court.

It is important that you become famil-iar with this particular practice requirement; otherwise, you will not be able to prepare the note of issue or the notice of trial.

Note of issue—preparation. Note of issue is a printed form that can be easily completed without directions from the lawyer. (Figure 1 illustrates a completed form.)

1. Make an original for the court, a copy to serve on each opposing counsel, and a copy for the file.

2. Telephone numbers of attorneys should be included in the note of issue and *must* be included in some jurisdictions.

3. Each sentence is a separate paragraph.

4. Do not staple in legal back, but endorse on printed form.

5. The back of the printed note of issue has forms for affidavit of personal service and of service by mail. After service is made, fill in the appropriate form. Figure 2 illustrates the back of a note of issue with affidavit of service by mail completed.

Notice of trial—preparation. The lawyer does not usually dictate a notice of trial. You can get the wording from a practice manual in the office. (See FORM books.) The wording varies slightly with the jurisdiction, and, in some jurisdictions, notice given by the plaintiff differs from notice given by the defendant. Notice of trial given by the plaintiff recites an intention to take an "inquest," whereas notice by the defendant recites that a motion to dismiss the complaint will be made. Memorize the wording in your jurisdiction to save time in the preparation of notices. (Figure 3 illustrates a notice of trial.)

STATE OF NEW YORK   *File No.* 11660-19--

  SUPREME COURT,   COUNTY OF KINGS

JOHN E. THOMPSON,
> *Plaintiff*

against

SMITH-ROGER, INC.,
> *Defendant*

Action (Proceeding) Commenced   February 4   , 19__.

Issued Joined April 23 *19,—* *Last Pleading Served* April 20
19__ *Issue of* law and fact *Trial by* Court
Nature and Object of Action (Proceeding) _____
Breach of contract.

Note of Issue filed by _____
Note OF ISSUE for next plaintiff. *TERM of this Court, to be*
held _____ November 8 *, 19__*

ELWOOD & ADAMS
Attorneys for Plaintiff
Office & Post Office Address
45 Main Street
Brooklyn, N.Y. 11201

JONES SMITH
AND EDWARDS
Attorneys for Defendant
Office and Post Office Address
14 Congress Street
Brooklyn, N.Y. 11217

Noticing a Case for Trial: Figure 1.
Note of issue.

1. Make an original for the court, a copy to serve on each opposing counsel, and a copy for the office file.

2. Endorse legal backs.

3. Have attorney sign it.

What to do about the notice of trial or note of issue.

1. Prepare the note of issue or notice of trial, as the case may be.

2. After the lawyer approves it, see that it is served on opposing counsel by the required date.

3. Be sure that receipt of service is endorsed on back or that the printed form provided is properly completed.

4. Conform the office copy.

5. File original in court.

6. *Make diary entry.* See REMINDERS.

7. Make appropriate entry in SUIT REGISTER.

8. The secretary to the counsel on whom notice is served notes on her copy the date and hour of service; *makes an appropriate diary entry;* enters it in suit register.

State of New York, County of **Kings**   *ss:*
Elaine Smith,
being duly sworn, deposes and says: that
deponent is **secretary** *to attorney for*
plaintiff *herein; is over 18 years of age; not*
a party to this action; and resides at **216**
East 17 Street, Borough of Brooklyn, New
York, 11217.
On the **25th** *day of* **April** *19-- deponent*
served the within note of issue on **Jones**
Smith and Edwards, *Esqs., attorneys for*
the **defendant** *in the within entitled action,*
by depositing a true and correct copy of the
same properly enclosed in a post-paid
wrapper, in the Post ~~Office a Branch Post~~
~~Office Station Sub-Station Finance Station~~
~~Letter Box~~*-Mail Chute—Official Deposi-*
tory maintained and exclusively controlled
by the United States at **45 Main Street,**
Brooklyn, N.Y. 11201, *that being then the*
Post Office of the attorneys for **plaintiff**
directed to said attorneys for defendant at
No. 14 Congress Street, Brooklyn, N.Y.
11217, *that being the address designated by*
him for that purpose.

Sworn to before me this **25th**
day of **April,**   *19--*

_____

State of New York, County of   *ss.:*

being duly sworn, deposes and says: that
deponent is   *attorney for*
                herein; is over 18 years of
age; not a party to this action; and resides
at

On the   *day of*
19
deponent served within note of issue, on

                        Esq.,
attorney for   *herein, at his office at*

during his absence from said office by then
and there leaving a true copy of the same
with

his partner; his clerk; therein, person
having charge of said office.

Sworn to before me this
day of   *19*

STATE OF NEW YORK
_____ SUPREME _____ COURT
COUNTY OF **KINGS** _____

JOHN E. THOMPSON

                              Plaintiff

            against

SMITH-ROGER, INC.

                              Defendant

𝔑𝔬𝔱𝔢 𝔬𝔣 𝔍𝔰𝔰𝔲𝔢

ELWOOD & ADAMS
Attorneys for Plaintiff
(Office and Post Office Address)
45 Main Street
Brooklyn, N.Y. 11201

Attorney for

Noticing a Case for Trial: Figure 2.
Back of note of issue.

MUNICIPAL COURT OF THE CITY OF NEW YORK

BOROUGH OF MANHATTAN: FIRST DISTRICT

———————————————————————— x

      :

JANE SELIG,   :   No. 7834/—

      :

      :

      Plaintiff,   :

      :   NOTICE OF TRIAL

      -against-   :

      :

      :

WALTER SALES and THE NATIONAL   :

CORPORATION,   :

      :

      Defendants.   :

      :

———————————————————————x

SIRS:

      PLEASE TAKE NOTICE that the issues in this action will be brought to trial and an inquest taken therein at Part II of this Court, to be held at the Court House situated at No. 8 Reade Street, Borough of Manhattan, City of New York, on the 24th day of November 19—, at 10 o'clock in the forenoon of that day or as soon thereafter as counsel can be heard.

Dated, New York, November 8, 19—.

      Yours very truly,

      DONALDSON & STONE
      Attorneys for Plaintiff
      48 Mall Street
      New York, N.Y. 10017

To:

      LINDA WEST,
      Attorney for Defendant
      120 Dew Street
      New York, N.Y. 10036

      CLERK OF THE MUNICIPAL COURT OF
      THE CITY OF NEW YORK—
      Borough of Manhattan,
      First District.

Noticing a Case for Trial: Figure 3.

Notice of trial given by plaintiff.

Novation. An agreement to replace an original party to a contract with a new party. The substitution must be agreed to by all parties. For example, *A* has a contract to repair certain machinery for *B*. *A*, finding himself overloaded with work gets *C* to agree to do the repairs for *B*. Once *B* has agreed to the substitution and released *A* from the contract, a no-vation has been completed and *A* is discharged from liability on the contract.

Nuisance. In tort law, a wrong to another party arising from any unreasonable and annoying inconvenience or damage that is usually recurring and consistent.

Objection to Title. A ground for questioning the validity of a TITLE to REAL PROPERTY. See CLOSING TITLE; CONTRACT OF SALE; TITLE INSURANCE.

Offense. A crime or misdemeanor; a breach of the criminal laws.

Offer and Acceptance. See CONTRACTS, 1.

Officer of a Corporation. A person who has the power and the duty to manage and carry out the business of the CORPORATION. An officer is created by the CERTIFICATE of Incorporation or BYLAWS of the corporation, and the officer is elected by the BOARD OF DIRECTORS.

Most states designate by statute what officers are required. These usually include a president, vice-president, secretary, and treasurer.

In the absence of express provisions in the bylaws, directors of a corporation have the inherent right to remove any officer for cause, even if he or she is employed for a definite term. In the absence of cause, however, directors cannot remove an officer elected for a specified term.

Official Congressional Directory. A listing of the names and addresses of officials associated with the federal government, including members of the press. The directory, published by the U.S. Government Printing Office, also contains biographical data on each member of Congress and maps of congressional districts. The directory is usually issued at least once during each sesssion of Congress.

Official Register of the U.S. Government. A publication that appears approximately annually, listing, by agency, all persons holding administrative or supervisory positions in the legislative branches of the federal government and the District of Columbia. It gives the person's name, title, legal residence, and in most cases, his or her salary. The book is indexed by agency and by name.

Official Reports. The opinions of a court prepared by an appointed reporter and published under authorization of statute. All written U.S. Supreme Court decisions are printed in the official United States Reports. There is also statutory provision for official reporting and publication of judicial appellate decisions in all of the states.

The largest group of *unofficial* reports is the NATIONAL REPORTER SYSTEM. See CITATION, table II.

Official Seal. An authorized stamp by an officer other than a notary public, who has been empowered to authenticate an executed document. See also CORPORATE SEAL; NOTARY'S SEAL; CONFORMING DOCUMENTS.

Olograph. See WILL, Holograph.

Omnibus. A term applied to that which contains two or more independent matters. The term is applied, for example, to a legislative bill that relates to two or more subjects.

Open-End Mortgage. See MORTGAGE.

Opening Statement of Counsel. Outline of anticipated proof.

Open Policy. An insurance agreement where the value of the insured property is not fixed, but is left to be definitely determined after the loss occurs. The term is also used to refer to a "floating" insurance agreement, which covers all goods of the assured as and when acquired. See also VALUED POLICY.

Open Shop. An arrangement whereby the employer is free to hire whomever he or she chooses, but all employees must join the union within a specified period. All employees must remain in good standing of the union

where such an agreement exists. See CLOSED SHOP.

Opinion. A judge's statement, or the reason given for a court's judgment, finding, or conclusion. An opinion is usually written by one judge, but other judges that hear the case may join in the opinion. Also, the conclusions of an attorney about some matter presented to a client.

Opinion Letters. Formal correspondence giving a professional opinion to a client on some legal question. Each law firm has its own method of setting them up, usually in the style that is used for ordinary letters. These letters are generally signed manually with the firm name, because they represent advice from the firm, not merely from the lawyer who dictated the letter. Usually the dictator's initials do not show on the original but do show on the office copies.

See also OPINION OF TITLE.

Opinion of Title. An attorney's written summation of opinion about the validity of TITLE to REAL PROPERTY. When the attorney receives the ABSTRACT OF TITLE, he or she examines it and prepares an *opinion* about the legal strength of the title. If an attorney finds any difficulty, such as a deed that was improperly acknowledged, or a discrepancy in the description of the property, the attorney states the defects. They constitute *clouds* upon the seller's title and must be removed by affidavits, quitclaim deeds, or court procedure to quiet title. The attorney also sets forth in the opinion any LIENS and MORTGAGES on the property, because the title is subject to them. Usually the CONTRACT OF SALE mentions the liens and mortgages and provides for their disposition.

The lawyer dictates the opinion of title, which is usually in the form of a letter. If there are no defects in the title, you might be asked to draft a routine opinion of title letter. Below is a sample of such a letter.

July 21, 19....

Mr. and Mrs. Stephen Felsen
R.R. #1
Hanover, PA 17331

Dear Mr. and Mrs. Felsen:

We have examined the abstract of title continued by the Benton Abstract and Title Company of Benton, Pennsylvania, to date of June 15, 19.. at 8:00 A.M., for the following described premises:

The west three (3) rods of Lots Thirty (30) and Thirty-one (31), Jacob Beeson's Addition to Hanover, York County, Pennsylvania, according to the recorded plat thereof.

From such examination, we find the title thereto to be in Phyllis Franz, subject to the following:

1. There are ancient and minor errors in this title, but we do not consider any of them sufficiently important to affect the merchantability of the title.

2. There are no liens or encumbrances against said premises.

3. The abstract shows no unpaid taxes for 19 . . and prior years. The summer taxes for 19 . . will be due July 1, 19 . . and may be checked with the city treasurer, as may also special assessments.

It is therefore our opinion that a merchantable title exists in said above named title holder, subject to the exceptions above noted. This opinion is based upon the abstract continued as aforesaid and does not cover rights of persons in possession, line fences, location of buildings, or any other matter or thing not contained in said abstract.

Respectfully submitted,

JC:F

Option. An agreement, usually in consideration for the payment of a certain sum of money by the offeree, to hold an offer open for a definite time. The offer ceases to be an offer and becomes a contract of option; it cannot be withdrawn until the option period expires. Although an option is generally based upon a consideration, a few states require no consideration if the contract is in writing. Others recognize an option under seal as binding because a seal, at COMMON LAW, indicates consideration. The consideration for an option is not returnable to the optionee if he or she fails to take up the option; it is however, usually applied to the purchase price if the offer is accepted.

Oral Argument. The spoken presentation by counsel of a client's case before an APPELLATE COURT. In some cases, the lawyer feels that the BRIEF is sufficient and does not choose to argue the case upon APPEAL. If the lawyer does want to appear before the appellate court, he or she makes application for oral argument at the same time the brief is filed. A copy of the application is served on opposing counsel in the same manner that the brief is served.

Ordinance. A law or statute. The word is commonly used to apply to enactments of a municipality.

Original Jurisdiction. An initial authority on the part of a judicial tribunal to hear a particular cause of action in order to render a decision. Some courts have original jurisdiction, whereas others have appellate jurisdiction. See APPELLATE COURT. Suits are commenced and tried first in courts of original jurisdiction, which are usually the lower courts. After a case has been decided in a court of original jurisdiction, it may be brought to a higher court having appellate jurisdiction for another decision. Appellate courts have original jurisdiction over some matters. See also JURISDICTION; COURTS OF SPECIAL JURISDICTION; AMERICAN COURT SYSTEM; INFERIOR COURTS; SUPERIOR COURTS.

P

Pain and Suffering. A result of an injury, for which a person may be compensated when suing for DAMAGES.

Palimony. The term *palimony* has a meaning similar to *alimony*, except that it is given to a partner known to have assumed the status of husband or wife in a "living together" arrangement. Some courts, notably California, will enforce such an express contract between nonmarital partners, unless the contract is founded on the consideration of meretricious sexual services. In the absence of an express contract, the court will inquire into the conduct of the parties to determine whether the conduct demonstrates an implied contract. The court may also apply an equitable remedy such as QUANTUM MERUIT when warranted by the facts of the case.

Paralegals. The paralegal (or legal assistant) assists the attorney in those procedural matters that do not fall within the exclusive, deliberative province of the attorney. Paralegals frequently have a college education, including paralegal studies. Some firms train their most experienced legal secretaries for paralegal duties. Specific duties vary depending on the lawyer's preference, but the following functions are within the general scope of the paralegal's responsibilities:

1. Handling legal research and analyses
2. Drafting and preparing legal documents
3. Conducting preinterviews with clients and witnesses
4. Organizing and maintaining dockets and files
5. Preparing probate inventory
6. Assisting with inheritance, federal, and state tax returns
7. Indexing documents
8. Preparing legal digests

Paralegals may also be assigned to those areas of law that involve litigation, estate administration, corporate law, and real estate law.

Additional information may be secured by writing to:

National Federation of
Paralegal Associations
P.O. Box 14103
Washington, D.C. 20044

Paramour. A lover; someone who takes the place of husband or wife, without the legal rights of a marital relationship.

Pardon. To excuse an offense without penalty. This power is usually vested only in the chief executive, who has few restrictions in using it.

Parent Corporation. See SUB-
SIDIARY CORPORATION.

Parole. The release of a convict from
imprisonment on certain conditions to
be observed by him or her, with the convict's sentence suspended during the
time of his or her liberty.

Parole Evidence Rule. A regulation
that makes a written agreement, when
finally executed, supersede all prior negotiations between the parties. Evidence
of conversations or negotiations before
or at the time of EXECUTION of the instrument may not be admitted to vary its
terms. Courts like to consider a written
CONTRACT as they find it and pass on
its validity in that form. The general rule
protects against FRAUD, PERJURY, in-
firmity of memory, and death of
witnesses.

Partially Disclosed Principal.
See PRINCIPAL.

Partial Release Clause. A clause
in a mortgage agreement that permits
the mortgagor to sell part of his or her
land. See MORTGAGE, Partial Release
Clause.

Particular Average Loss. A property loss borne entirely by the party suffering it. A particular average loss is
distinguished from a GENERAL AVER-
AGE LOSS in that in the latter, there is a
right of contribution from others, so the
party does not bear the loss alone. Unlike the general average loss, the particular average loss is not voluntary and is

not incurred for the common benefit; it is
the result of accident or NEGLIGENCE.
Examples of particular average loss are
damage to a ship by fire, storm, or collision.

Parties to an Action. The principals involved in a particular lawsuit or litigation.

Party bringing a lawsuit. The party
who brings a lawsuit—the one who has a
cause of action—is the *plaintiff,* the one
who complains. (See also COM-
PLAINT.)

Party defending a lawsuit. The party
against whom suit is brought is the *defendant.*

Parties to a cross action. In some
cases, defendant's interests cannot be
defended properly by answering the
plaintiff's complaint or by a counterclaim. For example, an airline and an airplane manufacturer were codefendants
in a wrongful death action. The complaint alleged that the plane was improperly designed and was not safe for its
intended use. The airline claimed that if
defective and hazardous conditions existed in the plane, they were caused by
the failure of the airplane manufacturer
to keep his guarantee that the plane
would be free from defect in design.[1]

Under these circumstances, in almost
all states, the defendant (airline here) is
permitted to *implead* the third party who
becomes a third-party defendant. The
party who is *impled* (airline manufacturer here) is the third-party defendant.

Party intervening. A lawsuit sometimes adversely affects a third party who

[1]Blue et al. v. United Air Lines, Inc., et. al., 98
N.Y.S. (2d) 272 (1950).

is not a party to the litigation. If the court permits, that person may become a party to the action by filing a *complaint in intervention,* and is called an *intervenor,* or in some states, the *third-party plaintiff.* For example, while negotiations for a contract were in progress, the employee who was negotiating the contract as agent for his employer suddenly quit the employer and closed the contract in his own behalf. The former employee later sued to enforce the contract. His former employer claimed that the former employee was his agent, and was permitted to intervene to assert his interest in the contract. He became a party to the actions as an *intervenor.*[2]

Amicus curiae. An *amicus curiae* (Latin for "friend of the court") is not strictly speaking a party to the lawsuit. He or she is a person who has no inherent right to appear in the suit but is allowed to participate to protect his or her own interests. Leave to file a brief as *amicus curiae* is frequently granted to a lawyer who has another case that will be affected by the decision of the Court in the pending case. An *amicus curiae* might also volunteer information for the benefit of the judge. For example, in adoption proceedings the guardian of a child might seek permission to appear as *amicus* for the purpose of presenting evidence about which the court should be informed and that might lead the court to refuse the order of adoption.

Who may be parties to a lawsuit. A party to a lawsuit may be an individual, a partnership, a corporation, or an association.

---

[2]Patterson v. Pollock, et al., 84 N.E. (2d) 606 (1948).

Minors and incompetents. An individual ordinarily sues on his own behalf, but minors (frequently referred to as infants) and incompetents (persons of unsound mind or habitual drunkards) are legally incapable of bringing a legal action. If the minor or incompetent has a legally appointed guardian, the suit is often brought by the guardian. Otherwise, depending upon the state, a suit is brought on behalf of a minor or incompetent by his or her "next friend," or by a guardian *ad litem* appointed by the court for the special purpose of the litigation. The fact that the plaintiff sues by his guardian or next friend is indicated in the caption of the case and is alleged in the pleadings. If a minor or an incompetent is defendant in a suit, he or she answers by a guardian *ad litem* or next friend. In Louisiana a minor is represented by a *Tutor* and a mentally incompetent person, by a *Curator.*

The expressions commonly used follow:

JAMES JONES, a minor, suing by his father and next friend, TOM JONES

JOHN JONES, guardian ad litem of JAMES JONES, an incompetent

MARY ANN JONES by her next friend, GEORGE G. JONES

JOHN BROWN by ROBERT BROWN, guardian by appointment of Orphans' Court of Baltimore City

Executors, administrators, trustees. Often plaintiffs have a cause of action, not for a wrong against them in their individual capacity, but for a wrong against them in their representative capacity as executor, administrator, or trustee. The action is then brought by the plaintiff in that capacity. The capacity in which the action is brought is indicated in the caption and is stated in the introductory sentence of the pleadings. An executor (executrix, if a woman) sues "as executor of the last will and testament of Mary Jones, deceased." An administrator (administratrix, if a woman) sues "as trustee under will of Mary Jones," or "as trustee under trust created by Mary Jones." Actions are also brought against, and defended by executors, administrators, and trustees of estates and trusts.

Husband and wife. In some actions if a married person sues, the spouse joins in the complaint. The caption indicates, and the first paragraph of the pleading declares, the relationship. If the husband has the cause of action, the suit is brought by Thomas W. Jones and Mary R. Jones his wife; if the wife has the cause of action, the suit is brought by Mary R. Jones and Thomas W. Jones, her husband. The same practice is followed when a married person is sued. In the CAPTION of all PLEADINGS, except the complaint, and in the endorsements on the back of a court paper (see LEGAL BACK), the Latin phrase *et uxor,* or *et ux.,* may be substituted for "and Mary R. Jones, his wife"; *et vir* may be substituted for "and Thomas W. Jones, her husband."

Partnerships. When a party to an action is a partnership, that fact is indicated in the caption and declared in the first paragraph of the pleading.

Expressions similar to the following are used in the caption.

JOHN JONES and HENRY A. BROWN, doing business as a partnership

under the name of JONES AND BROWN.
JOHN JONES AND RICHARD ROE d/b/a JONES & ROE, a partnership

See Parties to an APPEAL, DEED, FORECLOSURE action, MORTGAGE, and PROBATE.

Partnership. A business owned by two or more persons, each of whom is legally responsible for the total liabilities of the business, unless this responsibility is limited, as in a LIMITED PARTNERSHIP.

Partnerships are governed by fairly uniform laws, which are codified in many states by the Uniform Partnership Law. A partnership may carry on business in any state without paying greater taxes than residents of the state pay.

Each partner of a general partnership is fully liable personally for all partnership debts regardless of the amount of his or her investment. All types of capital produced or acquired by the partnership become partnership property. Real estate is generally acquired in the individual names of the partners or in the name of one partner who holds the property in trust for the partnership.

In absence of a specific contract, partners share profits and losses equally. It is customary, however, to provide in the partnership agreement that profits and losses shall be distributed pro rata according to the amount of capital contributed by each, or in any other ratio to which they agree. Partners have no right to salaries unless they are agreed upon, even though one partner may devote all of his or her time to the business and another may devote little or none. The agreement may provide for the division of profits after allowing each of the partners an agreed-upon salary.

Partnerships are dissolved without violation of the partnership agreement by (1) withdrawal of one of the members under some circumstances; (2) operation of law through death or bankruptcy of one of the partners or a change in the law that makes the partnership's business illegal; (3) court decree granted because of incapacity or insanity of one of the partners, gross misconduct, or neglect or breach of duty. See also JOINT ADVENTURE (VENTURE).

Party Sheet. A special record of the dates of service on, and appearance by, each defendant in a FORECLOSURE action. This record is not to be confused with the party sheet of paper for the record, with the following heading:

Rule the sheet into vertical columns, with the following columnar headings:

Defendants (specify legal status, such as infant, CORPORATION, trustee)
Interest in premises (owner, tenant, and so on)
Address where served
When served
How served
By whom served
Affidavit of service made before ...(notary's name)
Last day to answer
Appeared by . . .(name of defendant's attorney)
Address and telephone number of attorney
Date appearance entered
Remarks

A glance at the party sheet will tell the lawyer the status of service and appearance of each defendant.

PARTY SHEET

Action No. ... Plaintiffs ... Premises ... (brief description) ... Office No. ...

Par Value Stock. Stock with face or nominal value. No necessary relation exists between the par value and the real value of the stock. The *par value* is an amount predetermined by the corporation and remains the same regardless of how many times the share of stock changes hands or how much is paid for it. The *real or actual value* of stock is the price it can command in the market. Par value is a fixed amount. Emphasis is placed on the distinction because too often the concepts of par value and actual value are confused. See NO-PAR STOCK.

Patent. An exclusive right granted by the federal government for a fixed period, to make, use, and sell an invention. For example, a person who perfects a new machine, process or material or any new and useful improvement of them, or who invents or discovers and reproduces a distinct and new variety of plant, may make application to the government for a patent for it. The person to whom a patent is granted is called the *patentee*. Patent rights are issued in the form of letters and run to the patentee, his or her heirs and assigns, generally for a period of 17 years. A *design patent*, which is an ornamental design to be placed upon an article of manufacture, runs for 3½, 7, or 14 years, according to the application made by the patentee. A patent is not renewable. Anyone using a patented product without the owner's consent may be compelled to pay damages.

How to apply for a patent. When clients want to obtain a patent, they bring or send the details of their invention or discovery to the lawyer in the form of a disclosure. The disclosure may be a picture, sketch, or working model. An idea is not patentable; only the device for carrying out an idea can be patented.

The Patent Office will not respond to inquiries about the novelty of an alleged invention, so the patent lawyer must make a *search* to learn what patent or patents have already been issued on that idea. The copies of other patents issued on an idea are called *prior art,* and they may be inspected at the Patent Office. The patent lawyer studies the art before preparing the application. Copies of patents and trademarks may be obtained from the Patent Office for a small charge.

Various divisions in the United States Patent Office handle applications for certain types of patents. The patent lawyer sends the application to the Commissioner of Patents, who sends it to the appropriate division; the next step will be an *official action.* The official action may be an *allowance,* which means that the Patent Office deems the application ready to issue into a patent. In almost every case, however, the official action is a response by the Patent Office in which the Patent Office Examiner points out the items in the application he or she considers objectionable. Some of the divisions in the Patent Office are so over-

loaded with applications that it may take two years or more to get an official action. After receipt of the official action, the attorney has six months in which to file an amendment. In the amendment, the lawyer takes each point objected to by the examiner and either deletes it from the application or argues for it. The time by which the Patent Office responds to the amendment depends upon the volume of work in the particular division. If the first amendment does not make the application ready for allowance, there must be another amendment and so on until the examiner states that the next amendment must be final. The average number of amendments is three or four. If the patent lawyer does not think the examiner has a clear view of the whole idea, he or she may go to Washington and interview the examiner. Sometimes this facilitates the allowance.

Parts of the application. 1. *Specification.* This is a written description of the invention or discovery and the manner and process of making it.

2. *Claims.* These are the assertions made for the invention. Each individual part of the invention is written up as a claim. A design patent has only one claim, but other patents may have many claims. Some claims will be "stricken" because the claim has been covered by a prior invention.

3. *Drawings of the invention.*

4. *Petition.* This gives the name, residence, and post office address of the inventor and the title of the invention sought to be patented.

5. *Oath or affirmation.* Applicants swear or affirm that they believe themselves to be the first inventor or discov-

erer of the invention sought to be patented.

6. *Power of attorney.* Applicants usually give their lawyer POWER OF ATTORNEY to transact all business in the Patent Office connected with the patent.

What to do. 1. The lawyer will dictate the specification and claims. Make an original, a copy for each inventor, and a file copy on plain legal-size paper.

2. The oath, power of attorney, and petition are printed forms that can be easily filled in. They are frequently combined in one document. Make an original and the same number of copies as were made of the specification and claims.

3. The applications must be signed and verified before a notary public by the inventor(s). When there is more than one inventor, there must be a separate verification for each if the inventors do not sign the application at the same time, or if they are at different locations when signing.

4. Have photoprints made of the drawings of the invention, send one copy to the inventor (or copy to each inventor) and keep one for the files. The originals made by a draftsman accompany the application to the Patent Office for filing.

5. The Patent Office issues rules about how the papers are arranged, the backing, and the like.

6. As soon as the application is typed and assembled, send it to the applicant(s) for signature and verification.

7. Make diary or calendar entries for any transaction that must be taken at a future date. Although an application for a patent is not a legal action, it is advisable to keep a progress record sheet (*see* SUIT REGISTER). The sheet can be kept in the file folder. If litigation develops from the application, the same records are kept as in any litigated matter.

Assignment of application for patent. Frequently an inventor agrees to assign his or her patent rights before applying for the patent. When the inventor does, he or she makes an *assignment of application* simultaneously with the application. A printed form is usually used. Make an original, a copy for each applicant, and a copy for the office file. Send the original to the inventor (or inventors) for signature and acknowledgment before a NOTARY PUBLIC. When the original has been executed by each inventor, forward it to the Patent Office to be recorded. The Patent Office will return the assignment after it has been recorded. It is forwarded to the assignee.

Covering letters that the secretary writes. Whenever the lawyer sends papers to the client or to the Patent Office, you can usually write the covering letters without dictation. Here are three sample letters.

Letter forwarding application to Patent Office

The Commissioner of Patents
United States Patent Office
Washington, D.C. 20013

Sir:

We are enclosing for filing the application of . . . . (inventor or inventors) . . . . for Letters Patent covering an improvement in . . . . (title) . . . ., Case . . . . We are also enclosing our check for $. . . . to cover the first government fee.

Sincerely,

Letter forwarding assignment to Patent Office for recording

The Commissioner of Patents
United States Patent Office
Washington, D.C. 20013

Sir:

We enclose for recording assignment of . . . . . (patentee or patentees) . . . . transferring unto . . . . (assignee) . . . ., a (an) . . . (name of state) corporation, all right title and interest in and to his (their) application for . . (title) . . ., Case . . . ., excuted . . . . and transmitted for filing of even date herewith.

Our check for $. . . . to cover the recording fee is also enclosed.

Sincerely,

Letter sending issued patent to patentee.

Dear Mr./Ms. . . . . :

We are enclosing original United States Letters Patent No. . . . ., issued to you on . . . (date) . . ., covering an improvement in . . . . (title) . . . .

Please acknowledge receipt of the patent.

Thank you.

Sincerely,

Patent Infringement. The act of making, using, or selling, without authority, any patented invention within the United States, while the PATENT is in effect. The legal remedy for patent infringement is INJUNCTION and DAM-AGES. A patent is said to be infringed when "the accused device does the same work in substantially the same way and accomplishes the same result."

Paternity Suit. A suit to establish paternity of a child born out of wedlock and to compel the father to provide support for that child.

Pecuniary. Monetary; relating to money; financial; consisting of money or that which can be valued in money.

Perils of the Sea. Most commonly the risk of damage to a ship or its cargo from unexpectedly violent action of wind and waves, but it also refers to the danger from icebergs, rocks, shoals, and (in former times) pirates. Ocean marine insurance usually covers perils of the sea.

Perjury. The act of deliberately making a false statement under oath. Punishment for perjury, by fine or imprisonment, is provided for by federal and state statutes.

Willful inducement of another to commit perjury is called *subornation of perjury* and is punishable by law.

Personal Property. A right or interest protected by law, in something that is not land or anything permanently attached to land (see REAL PROPERTY). Personal property is movable. It may be tangibles (also called chattels), such as money, gold, merchandise, or any movable object susceptible to physical possession. It may be intangibles, such as contracts, stocks, and the like (see CHOSE IN ACTION). Personal property may be an interest in land: a 99-year lease is personal property. Products of the soil become personal property when severed from the land: trees and crops that are sold while attached to the land constitute real property, but when severed from the land they constitute personal property.

Title to personal property may be acquired by the following methods: (1) appropriation or original possession: although almost all property today belongs to someone, some kinds of property, such as wild game and fish, may be appropriated; (2) discovery: the finder of lost property acquires a title that is good against everyone except the rightful owner; (3) creation: a person is entitled to that which he or she produces by physical or mental labor, unless the product is produced during the course of the person's employment or under some other contract; then it belongs to his or her employer or the party for whom the person is contracted to create the property; (4) gift; (5) sale or exchange; (6) will; (7) operation of law: when a person dies without making a will, his or her property passes by operation of law to certain relatives. Or if a person becomes bankrupt, his or her property, with certain exceptions, passes to a trustee for the benefit of creditors. A person's property may also be taken by legal process (see EXECUTION).

Personal Service. See SERVICE OF SUMMONS.

Petition. A written plea brought before a court so that it may redress some wrong or grant some favor. In some states, the initial pleading is called a "petition" instead of a COMPLAINT.

Petition in Bankruptcy. BANKRUPTCY proceedings are commenced by the filing of a petition, asking that the court declare some person a bankrupt. In *voluntary bankruptcy* the petitioner asks to be adjudged a bankrupt. In *involuntary bankruptcy* the petitioner requests that some person other than the petitioner or petitioners be adjudged a bankrupt.

Petitory Action. A proceeding in which a party seeks to establish his or her title to land or other property in dispute. A petitory action is distinguished from a *possessory* action where the right to the possession is the point in issue. The term is used in ADMIRALTY to describe an action to determine title to a ship.

Petty Cash Fund. An amount of cash on hand used for disbursements that are too small to justify the use of checks. The purpose of the fund is to expedite the payment of any incidental expenses that may arise, such as RECORDING FEES and collect messages. The size of the fund will vary according to the demands made upon it, but it should be large enough to last about a month. Keep the money in a safe place because you usually will be responsible for it. Never mix this money with your own funds; never make change from it unless you can make the exact change; and *never* borrow from it.

Petty cash record. Keep a running record of expenditures made from the fund. As each expenditure is made, no matter how small, enter the date, the amount, purpose for which spent, and the client and case to which it is chargeable. When the petty cash fund gets low, add up the expenditures and write a check, payable to yourself, for the total—that is, the amount necessary to bring the petty cash fund up to its original figure. Attach the record to the check when you give it to your employer for his signature. Mark the record "Paid—(date)—, Ck. No. _____," initial and file it. Then start a new running account for future expenditures from the fund.

A petty cash fund is also called an *imprest fund,* because it is restored periodically to a given level.

Plaintiff. The party who commences a personal action or suit to obtain a remedy for an injury to his rights. See also PARTIES TO AN ACTION.

Plat. A plan or map of land showing its subdivision into smaller parcels or lots, used in LAND DESCRIPTION.

Plea. The answer given to a petition, declaration, or complaint; any one of the common law pleadings; in a criminal procedure, a plea is entered of guilty, not guilty, or, in some jurisdictions, *nolo contendere* ("no contest").

Pleadings. Written statements of the *claims* and *defenses* of parties to a court action.

In almost all states, a legal proceeding is commenced when the *first pleading* is filed with the CLERK OF THE COURT by the person bringing the suit. The plaintiff—the person bringing the suit—makes a written statement in clear and concise language of the facts that caused him or her to bring the suit. The designation of this first pleading varies with the court; it might be called a complaint, a declaration, a libel, or a PETITION. In some states, the first pleading in an EQUITY action is designated as a BILL in Equity or a BILL of Complaint. (See COMPLAINT.) A SUMMONS, or its equivalent, is then issued and served upon the person against whom the action is brought—usually called the DEFENDANT. The defendant answers the summons and complaint, defending himself or herself by raising legal arguments or by denying the facts stated by the plaintiff in the complaint. When the case is finally submitted to the court for a decision, the judge decides controversies about legal points; a jury, or a judge acting in place of a jury, decides questions of fact. See PRACTICE AND PROCEDURE.

Pledge. The placement of personal property by the owner with a lender as security for a debt. Pawned articles and stocks and bonds put up as collateral for a loan are the most common pledges. Essentials of a pledge are (1) a debt or obligation to be secured; (2) the thing pledged; (3) the *pledgor* (the one who gives the pledge) and the *pledgee* (the one who receives the pledge); (4) transfer of possession of the property (if the actual physical possession is practically impossible, the pledgee may acquire CONSTRUCTIVE possession); (5) retention of title in the pledgor; (6) the pledgor's right to redeem the pledge; (7) a contract, express or implied, covering the transaction.

When stock is pledged as collateral, the pledgee has the right and is bound to collect the dividends and apply them to the loan, in the absence of an agreement to the contrary between the pledgor and the pledgee. This is the legal theory. As a matter of practice, the stockholder makes an assignment of the stock in blank and the stock is not transferred on the books of the corporation unless the pledgor defaults; the stockholder-pledgor therefore continues to collect the dividends.

PLS (Professional Legal Secretary). See NATIONAL ASSOCIATION OF LEGAL SECRETARIES.

PLS Certificate. See NATIONAL ASSOCIATION OF LEGAL SECRETARIES.

Police Court. See INFERIOR COURTS.

Police Power. The power that any governmental body has to protect the property, life, health, and well-being of its citizenry by legislation. State minimum wage laws have been held by the United States Supreme Court (see AMERICAN COURT SYSTEM) to be a proper exercise of the states' police powers. Under police powers, states license doctors, lawyers, barbers, beauticians, and the like, and only those who obtain a license are authorized to practice their profession or trade. City ordinances that require certain standards of cleanliness in restaurants, or that impose building restrictions, are regulations issued under police power. The extent of a governing body's police power is limited by the state constitutions and by the Fourteenth Amendment to the Constitution of the United States, which protects personal liberties and freedoms. The power of Congress to regulate and control business activities is not a police power but is a power expressly granted by the Constituition. See also DUE PROCESS OF LAW.

Poor's Register of Directors and Executives. A national listing of corporate executives and directors.

Postal Service. See MAIL.

Power of Appointment. Testamentary authorization to a DONEE to determine to whom testator's property shall be distributed.

If the donee is given an unrestricted power to dispose of property to any person or person he or she may choose, the power is *general*. When the donee's power is restricted in favor of a particular person or class, such as only to members of the family of testator, he or she has a *special* or *particular* power of appointment.

Power of Attorney. A written instrument in which the principal (the person giving the power of attorney) authorizes another to act for him or her. The instrument may be a blanket authorization, as in the case of a person embarking on an extended voyage. More often it authorizes the agent to represent the principal in one specific transaction, as the closing of a real estate deal; or to do a particular act continuously, as the signing of checks or the collecting of money on behalf of the principal or the authority to institute suit or collect dividends.

The appointed person is commonly called an *attorney in fact*. The power of attorney may be revoked at the will of the principal, unless it was given to the agent for a consideration. See also PROXY.

Directions for the preparation of a power of attorney.

1. Make an original for the attorney in fact, a copy for the principal, and a copy for the files.

2. Use legal- or letter-size according to court requirements.

3. Place the responsibility marks on the office copy only.

4. Double-space.

5. Have at least two lines of typing on the signature page.

6. Prepare signature line for principal or principals only.

7. If the powers granted relate to the conveyance of real estate, the instrument must be prepared with the formalities required for a DEED.

8. If the powers granted do not relate to real estate, ask the lawyer if the power of attorney is to be witnessed and acknowledged.

9. Collate (see COLLATING).

10. Endorse LEGAL BACK.

11. Check to see that the principal's signature agrees with the name typed in the instrument.

12. After the instrument is signed, and acknowledged if necessary, conform copies to original. See CONFORMING DOCUMENTS.

13. If a power of attorney relates to real property, it is recorded like any conveyance. However, sometimes it is not recorded until the attorney in fact exercises the power granted. Ask the lawyer for instructions about recording.

14. The lawyer will tell you whether the original of the power of attorney is to be delivered directly to the attorney in fact or to the principal.

15. Make a notation on the office copy of the distribution of the original and copy.

Practice and Procedure. The procedure in law actions is highly technical and is the lawyer's responsibility. The lawyer will dictate many pleadings in their entirety because their wording must be precise to meet statutory requirements. Your responsibilities might consist in (1) keeping an accurate calendar and record of the proceedings; (2) preparing the pleadings in a professional manner; (3) relieving the lawyer of details.

Variations in practice and procedure. The rules of civil practice and procedure vary in detail not only in the various states but, to a lesser extent, in various jurisdictions within a state. A fundamental variation of interest to the secretary is the requirement with respect to the service and filing of pleadings. The jurisdictions may be grouped in respect to service and filing as follows:

A. In the majority of jurisdictions, a copy of every pleading and supporting paper must be served on opposing counsel, and the original filed in court. When a copy of the initial pleading is served with the summons, as is often the case, it is served on the defendant, because there is no counsel of record at that time.

B. In a few jurisdictions, copies of pleadings and supporting papers do not have to be served on opposing counsel, but *a copy as well as the original must be filed in court.* Counsel withdraws the duplicate from court to learn the contents of the papers filed by opposing counsel. (All jurisdictions require service of the summons on the defendant.)

C. In a few jurisdictions, for example in New York Supreme Court, copies of pleadings are served on opposing counsel, but the originals are not filed in court until the case is at issue. The court has no indication that a lawsuit is pending until the case is ready to be set for trial. This procedure does not apply to municipal courts.

D. In some jurisdictions, a copy must be served on opposing counsel, and an original and a copy filed in court. Opposing counsel refers to the counsel for each adverse party. Thus if the rules require service on opposing counsel and there is more than one adverse party, sufficient copies of the paper are prepared to permit service of a copy on counsel for each party.

Practice Manual. See FORMS.

Prayer. See WHEREFORE CLAUSE; COMPLAINT.

Preemptive Rights. In corporation law, the shareholder's right to subscribe pro rata to additional new shares of stock before such new shares are offered to outsiders. A preemptive right, if exercised, will guarantee a shareholder's proportionate interest in the CORPORATION.

Such rights provide a safeguard that operates in favor of the original investor, protecting the investor against the dilu-

tion of voting power and his or her equities in the surplus and earnings of the corporation. A stockholder should determine whether he or she has preemptive rights by examining the CERTIFICATE of Incorporation. If the stockholder has the rights and they are violated, he or she may bring action against the BOARD OF DIRECTORS and may also bring action to cancel the issue if shares are held by persons who took them with knowledge that preemptive rights were being violated.

Preferred Stock. Stock that is given a preference over other stock of the same CORPORATION primarily with respect to DIVIDEND payments, but preferences with respect to asset distribution upon liquidation and other matters, as well as limitations, may also exist.

Preferred stock gives its owner a claim on income either in a fixed amount or at a fixed rate, unlike COMMON STOCK, which entitles its owner to a residual share of the corporate income. In the event of dissolution, the preferred stockholder is entitled to a stipulated sum for his principal claim before anything is paid to common stockholders.

Preferred stock has certain features that are of particular advantage to the issuing corporation. The issuance of preferred stock makes financing possible without sharing profits and control in the unlimited fashion required by common stock. Also, preferred stock has the advantage, generally, of being redeemable at the option of the corporation, thus enabling refinancing with a new security paying a lower dividend.

Preferred stock, like common stock, may have the right to participate in the management of the corporation through its voting power, but ordinarily preferred stock does not carry the general voting privilege. However, preferred stock is frequently given vetoing power or the right to vote as a class on particular questions and the general voting privilege under particular circumstances. *See* also CUMULATIVE PREFERRED STOCK; and NONCUMULATIVE PREFERRED STOCK.

Prentice-Hall Loose-Leaf Services. (For lawyers.) Compilations of *all* pertinent material in specific fields of law. A compilation includes all statutes, administrative regulations, executive orders, rulings, court decisions, and interpretations affecting a specific field of law. In addition, the service gives editorial analysis, comments, and recommendations.

When a court hands down a decision within a field of law covered by a service, a copy of the decision is immediately sent to Prentice-Hall, and the subscriber to the service receives it in his next current supplement. For example, court decisions in the *Prentice-Hall Federal Taxes* are regularly in the hands of subscribers a few days after their issuance by the judges. Accompanying each current supplement is a Report Bulletin that highlights all new laws, decisions, and rulings. In addition, the Report Bulletin gives law notes on important recurring problems on the subject with which it deals.

See FILING (Loose-Leaf Publications).

328

Prepaid Income. See INCOME.

Prepayment Privilege. A clause giving the mortgagor the right to pay off the mortgage, or part of it, *before* maturity. *See* MORTGAGE, Statement and Clauses.

Preponderance of the Evidence. Superior proof, more convincing than the opposing evidence.

Presumption. An inference about the existence of one fact from the existence of some other fact, founded upon a previous experience of their connection.

Presumption of law requires that a particular inference *must* be drawn from an ascertained state of facts. For example, a child of seven is, under the COMMON LAW rule, conclusively presumed to be incapable of committing a crime.

Presumption of fact is a term used to describe a logical inference that the court is authorized, but not required, to draw from the evidence in the case. As an example, it might be inferred that a person in possession of a murder weapon committed the murder.

Prima Facie Evidence. Evidence deemed by law to be sufficient to establish a fact if the evidence is not disputed. For example, the placement of a CORPORATE SEAL on an instrument is prima facie evidence that the instrument was executed by authority of the corporation.

Prime Meridian. See LAND DESCRIPTION, Section and Township.

Primogeniture. An ancient common law of descent in which the oldest son inherits all property of the deceased father.

Principal. 1. A sum loaned, borrowed, or invested; the sum of money on which interest is paid.

2. One who authorizes another, called an agent or broker, to act on one's behalf in dealings with third persons. A *principal* may be an individual, a partnership, or a CORPORATION acting through its authorized officers.

3. When transactions are being handled by an agent for a principal, the principal is *disclosed* if the party has notice of the principal's existence and identity; the principal is *partially disclosed* if the party has notice only of the principal's existence; the principal is *undisclosed* if the party is not aware of the principal's existence or identity.

Principal Meridian. See LAND DESCRIPTION, Section and Township.

Printing. The lawyer's secretary usually helps prepare a wide variety of printed materials. She often gets quotes on typesetting and printing costs; types manuscripts; marks copy for typesetters and printers; coordinates work with editors, artists, compositors, and printers; reads galleys; and checks page proofs and negative proofs.

Photo-offset lithography uses a plate prepared photographically. It is often more economical than the letterpress process, especially when many illustrations are involved, although the quality of the photographs is sometimes inferior.

Many instant printing or fast-copy service establishments use small offset presses for quick, inexpensive reproduction of forms and similar black and white line work.

Letterpress uses a relief principle with type and illustrations on raised surfaces called *cuts.* Letterpress is used for both low-quality work such as newspapers and high-quality work such as magazines with elaborate photographs.

Ozalid is a duplicating process frequently used in law offices for making copies of documents. (A print made by this process is frequently called an "ozalid.") The process makes prints the same size as the original document by passing light through the item to be copied onto sensitized paper. The ozalid is fixed in ammonia fumes so it does not become wet; it also maintains its original dimensions. See also MICROFILMING.

Printers will supply a press or negative proof of the finished product before it is printed. This is your opportunity to check for layout and appearance, although typographical errors should have been caught in the earlier typesetting stage.

Layout refers to the design of the job to be printed, showing, page by page, margins, blocks or columns of type, illustrations, heading, captions, and the like, each drawn to exact size. Every item, even page numbers and credit lines, is carefully identified for size.

Line cuts are made of those illustrations (drawings, charts, graphs, pictographs) that consist only of lines and areas of black and white. A *halftone* must always be used to reproduce gradations or shadings of tone between black and white found in photographs, paints, and wash drawings.

Traditionally, a *galley* is a shallow metal tray into which each line of type is deposted as it comes from the typesetting machine. When a galley is filled (it holds enough lines to make about three pages in an average book) it is removed and another put in its place until the entire book is set. Proof of each galley is pulled on a small proof press. Today, many compositors go directly to film, eliminating the traditional stage of casting metal type. However, proof of such photocomposition is still called a "galley." This galley *proof* contains no illustrations, is not broken up into pages, and contains no running head (the line that runs across the top of a page in a book or magazine). Each footnote appears directly beneath the reference to it in the text. Chapter titles are not necessarily set in the type in which they will finally appear. The paper on which the galley proofs are pulled is no indication of the paper that will actually be used in the book.

A *dummy* refers to blank sheets cut and assembled to look like a proposed book or booklet. Layouts are generally drawn and copy stripped into the dummy to give the general appearance of the finished product. A *cut dummy* consists of plain sheets of paper on which engraver's proofs of cuts have been pasted, one cut to a page. Beneath each proof the corresponding label and credit lines are typed. A *page dummy*, also called a "paste-up," is made by cutting galley proofs to size and pasting them on the blank sheets, allowing spaces at the appropriate places for illustrations, tables, and the like.

A page dummy should contain no type corrections, additions, or deletions. All such changes, even those that are necessary to lengthen or shorten pages to make them come out right, should be made on the master set of galleys.

Long or short pages that face each other must be made equal. There should be at least three lines of type between a center heading and the bottom of a page. A paragraph with a boldface side heading should not begin at the bottom of a page. A page must not begin with a *widow*, a short last line carried over to the top of a page or column.

Proofreaders' marks are standard symbols and abbreviations used for marking errors on printer's proof, for example, on galleys. They save time and are understood by the printer. Figure 1 shows standard proofreaders' marks. Figure 2 shows a page of corrected proof. Here are some guides to follow:

Place all marks in the margin of the proof, left or right, whichever is nearer, on the same line as the error. Separate corrections on the same line (for example, lc/tr) and arrange them in order so they read consecutively from left to right. If the same correction is to be made in two places in the line, with no intervening corrections, write the correction only once and follow it with two slant lines. When material is to be added to a line, place a caret (∧) in the text at the point of insertion and write the addition in the margin. When material is to be deleted and none added in its place, cross out the unwanted characters and place a delete sign in the margin. When material is to be substituted for a deletion, do not use the delete sign; just cross out the unwanted material and write the substitution for it in the margin. Use ink or pencil of a different color from any of the markings already on the proof.

See also MANUSCRIPT, TYPEFACE, and BRIEF, Figure 4.

PROOFREADERS' MARKS

∧	Make correction indicated in margin.	⌐⌐	Raise to proper position.
Stet	Retain crossed-out word or letter; let it stand.	⌐⌐	Lower to proper position.
		////	Hair space letters.
. . . .	Retain words under which dots appear; write "Stet" in margin.	*w.f.*	Wrong font; change to proper font.
Stet		*Qu?*	Is this right?
X	Appears battered; examine.	*l.c.*	Put in lower case (small letters).
≡	Straighten lines.	*s.c.*	Put in small capitals.
√√√	Unevenly spaced; correct spacing.	*Caps*	Put in capitals.
//	Line up; i.e., make lines even with other matter.	*C-sc.*	Put in caps and small caps.
run in	Make no break in the reading; no #	*rom*	Change to Roman.
no ¶	No paragraph; sometimes written "run in."	*ital.*	Change to Italic.
		≡	Under letter or word means caps.
out see copy	Here is an omission; see copy.	=	Under letter or word, small caps.
¶	Make a paragraph here.	—	Under letter or word means Italic.
tr	Transpose words or letters as indicated.	⌇⌇⌇	Under letter or word, bold face.
		?/	Insert comma.
	Take out matter indicated; delete.	;/	Insert semicolon.
	Take out character indicated and close up.	:/	Insert colon.
ℓ	Line drawn through a cap means lower case.	⊙	Insert period.
		/?/	Insert interrogation mark.
ᘒ	Upside down, reverse.	(!)	Insert exclamation mark.
⌒	Close up; no space.	/=/	Insert hyphen.
#	Insert a space here.	✓	Insert apostrophe.
⊥	Push down this space.	᾿᾿	Insert quotation marks.
□	Indent line one em.	ℓ	Insert superior letter or figure.
[	Move this to the left.	⊓	Insert inferior letter or figure.
]	Move this to the right.	[/]	Insert brackets.
		(/)	Insert parentheses.
		1/m	One-em dash.
		2/m	Two-em parallel dash.

Printing: Figure 1.

Privilege Against Self-Incrimination. A provision in the Fifth Amendment stating that no person shall be compelled to be a witness against himself or herself in a criminal case in a federal court. No inference of guilt may be drawn from someone's failure to take the stand or to call witnesses in his or her own behalf. The Supreme Court has held that the due process clause of the Fourteenth Amendment does not require state courts to give accused

HOW TO CORRECT PROOF

It does not appear that the earlist printers had any method of correcting errors before the form was on the press. The learned The learned correctors of the first two centuries of printing were not proof/readers in our sense; they were rather what we should term office editors. Their labors were chiefly to see that the proof corresponded to the copy, but that the printed page was correct in its Latinity that the words were there, and that the sense was right. They cared but little about orthography, bad letters or purely printers errors, and when the text seemed to them wrong they consulted fresh authorities or altered in on their own responsibility. Good proofs, in the modern sense, were impossible until professional readers were employed/men who had first a printer's education, and then spent many years in the correction of proof. The orthography of English, which for the past century has undergone little change, was very fluctuating until after the publication of Johnson's Dictionary, and capitals, which have been used with considerable regularity for the past 80 years, were previously used on the miss or hit plan. The approach to regularity, so far as we have, may be attributed to the growth of a class of professional proof readers, and it is to them that we owe the correctness of modern printing. More errors have been found in the Bible than in any other one work. For many generations it was frequently the case that Bibles were brought out stealthily, from fear of governmental interference. They were frequently printed from imperfect texts, and were often modified to meet the views of those who publised them. The story is related that a certain woman in Germany, who was the wife of a Printer, and had become disgusted with the continual assertions of the superiority of man over woman which she had heard, hurried into the composing room while her husband was at supper and altered a sentence in the Bible, which he was printing, so that it read, Narr instead of Herr, thus making the verse read "And he shall be thy fool" instead of "And he shall be thy lord." The word not was omitted by Barker, the King's printer in England in 1632, in printing the seventh commandment. He was fined £3,000 on this account.

Printing: Figure 2. *A page of corrected proof.*

persons the protection against self-incrimination stated in the Fifth Amendment. Most states, however, do have similar provisions in their own constitutions and statutes.

Privileged Communications. Any information one person derives from another by reason of a confidential relationship existing between the parties. The parties to such communications are, under certain circumstances, not allowed to testify in COURT about what was said. Relationships that most states recognize are those of (1) attorney and client, (2) member of the clergy and penitent, (3) physician and patient, and (4) husband and wife.

When the statute so provides, the attorney-client privilege may be extended to include the attorney's secretary if the communication is spoken to the lawyer in her presence.

Privity. Mutual or successive relationshp to the same right of property, or the power to take advantage of and enforce a promise or WARRANTY. Identity of interest is essential. There must be a connection or bond of union between parties about some particular transaction. Thus privity of contract exists between a lessor and lessee, because the parties are mutually interested in the lease. Privity of contract also exists between a lessor and an assignee of the lease, because the assignee succeeded to the rights of the lessee. Heirs, executors, and assigns succeed to the rights and liabilities of a contract whether or not it so states. They are thus *privies* to the contract.

Privity affects legal rights and duties and, in many cases, determines whether a party may sue or be sued. Thus a privy has the same right to relief against mistake of facts as the original party to a contract. A stranger to a contract has no right to sue for fraud, but a privy does. An injunction extends to all persons in privity with the parties enjoined. Evidence may be admissible or inadmissible because of privity. Privity may be an element in an action for negligence or in the substitution of parties in a legal action.

Probable Cause. Reasonable cause; probable cause is required for a valid search and/or seizure or arrest; that is, a good reason is required for the search and/or seizure or arrest.

Probate. Originally relating to proof; presently relating to the proof of wills, that is, the process of proving a will.

In most jurisdictions, property is deemed to vest in the heir, devisees, or bequeathees at the moment of death. However, it is essential, in order to preserve and protect the property of the estate, to pay the debts of the estate, and to deliver the property to the heirs of the estate, that a personal representative, in the form of an EXECUTOR (when there is a will) or an ADMINISTRATOR (when there is no will), be appointed.

The probate of estates is peculiar within the jurisdiction of each state and the applicable state statutes should be checked to determine whether a probate is required under all circumstances. In some states, if all interested parties will agree, probate may be avoided by contractual family settlement. Many state laws on probates are identical or at least very similar in that many of the states have adopted the Uniform Probate Act. In some states, small estates may be distributed upon affidavit of heirs. Although there is no set definition for a "small estate," under modern statutes, a small estate would probably vary from $3,000 to $30,000.

If a probate proceeding is necessary, the attorney for the estate generally prepares and submits to the executor the necessary papers that need to be filed in the probate proceeding. Not all forms and/or actions are necessary in all states, and you should determine what procedure to follow within the jurisdiction of a particular state by checking the applicable state statutes. In most cases, the statutes are found in the library of the law office. In the states that have adopted the Uniform Probate Code, a full text of the Uniform Probate Code is outlined in the Martindale-Hubbell Law Dictionary.

In New York, the probate proceeding is initiated by the filing of the will itself, together with a copy of it, certified to be a correct and true copy (figure 1 shows entries made in the suit register record in a probate proceeding). A petition for the probate of a will is also filed with the will and the copy. Simultaneously, a transfer tax affidavit is filed (this is not required in most states). The inheritance tax is not based upon the affidavit, but upon a final determination of the value of the estate. A special proceeding must be had to determine the inheritance tax.

Legal notice of the probate proceeding must be served upon all interested parties and an affidavit of service (or each interested party may enter a waiver of service) filed with the court. Sworn depositions of witnesses to the will (or in

some states an affidavit of proof of will) must also be filed. If there are no objections to the admission of the will within the time specified, the will is admitted to probate by a decree of the court.

The person or institution named as executor in the will or the person or institution appointed by the court (in which case they are generally referred to as "administrator") files the bond (unless waived in the will) and an oath, and then the LETTERS TESTAMENTARY as executor are issued to him or her. If a bonded institution is serving as the executor, generally a bond is not required of it. Letters testamentary are not issued until an acceptance is signed and filed. Also, simultaneous with the issuance of the letters testamentary or shortly thereafter, notice will be delivered for publication in a newspaper having general circulation in the area of residence of the decedent notifying all persons who have claims against the estate to file those claims within the statutory specified time.

Parties to a probate proceeding. The proponent of the will, that is, the person or corporation seeking to have the will probated, is the *petitioner.* The petitioner is usually the person or corporation named in the will as executor. There are three groups of interested parties who must be informed of the probate proceeding so they may protect their interests:

1. The surviving spouse and the distributees. These are the heirs-at-law of the deceased who would have inherited if the decedent had died intestate. This group of distributees includes the heirs-at-law who are also named in the will as legatees, because they might take less by the will than they would have inherited if there had been no will.

SURROGATE'S COURT—COUNTY OF NEW YORK   FILE NO. P 1277—19—

x

: PROBATE PROCEEDING

In the Matter

: Date of death: March 28, 19—
:   105 East 37th Street, NYC.

of

: King & Snow, Esqs.,
: Attorneys for Petitioners

Proving the Last Will and Testament of

:   Partner in Charge: Mr. Rey
:   Principal Assistant: Mr. Blank

CHARLES RAY DOE,

Deceased,

As a Will of Real and Personal Property.

x

19—

April 23	Mr. Blank filed original and sworn copy of will dated February 25, 19— and petition of Charles T. Doe, John T. Roe and Barbara S. Roe, and their oaths and designations as executors and trustees and filed waiver of citation executed by Beatrice S. Roe.
24	M. J. Ryan mailed 31 copies of notice of probate to legatees, etc. named therein.
25	Filed original notice of probate with proof of mailing.
25	Depositions of the subscribing witnesses Mary Roeman and Anthony J. Maurman were sworn to before John A. Killoran, Probate Clerk.
25	Decree signed, Collins, S., and filed, admitting will to probate and directing that letters testamentary and letters of trusteeship be issued to the executors and trustees who may qualify thereunder.
25	Letters Testamentary issued to Charles T. Doe, John T. Roe and Barbara S. Roe, Liber 633, Page 434.
26	Letters of Trusteeship issued to Charles T. Doe, John T. Roe and Barbara S. Roe, in Liber 51, Page 842.

Probate of a Will: Figure 1.
Progress record.

335

2. The executors and trustees named in the will who do not sign the petition.

3. Legatees or devisees who are not distributees. These are the legatees or devisees named in the will who would not have inherited if the decedent had died intestate. They are interested in the proceeding because they lose their legacies if the will is not admitted to probate.

Copy of will and affidavit. A copy of the will is filed in the probate court with the original will. In most jurisdictions a photocopy may be filed. In the administration of a large, complicated estate, where numerous copies of the will are needed, the will is sometimes duplicated or printed.

1. Make as many legible copies as can be made in one typing.

2. Copy the will exactly, typing also the signature and data that are written in ink.

3. Have two adults (you may be one of them) compare one copy with the original and make an affidavit to that effect. They must both compare the same copy. Figure 2 illustrates the affidavit.

4. Fill in the blanks on the back of the affidavit. If you do not use a printed form of affidavit, make a legal back endorsed like the printed form in figure 3.

5. Staple the affidavit to the compared copy of the will, placing the affidavit beneath the copy.

Petition for probate of will. The petition sets forth certain factual data about the testator, his or her heirs, legatees, and devisees, and prays that the will be admitted to probate and that letters testamentary be issued to the executor. If trustees are named in the will, the petition also prays for letters of trusteeship.

1. Make an original for the court and a copy for the office file.

2. Be especially careful about names, addresses, and values of legacies and devises.

3. The lawyer will give you a memorandum of (a) the name and address of the petitioner of petitioners; (b) the name of the testator, the testator's residence at the time of death, and the time and place of death; (c) the names, addresses, ages, and degree of kinship to the decedent of the heirs-at-law and of those interested in the will; (d) the addresses of the other legatees and devisees. This memorandum and the copy of the will give you the information necessary to fill in the form, unless the will is complicated. If so, the lawyer will dictate the necessary information.

4. The executors and trustees, if any, named in the will are listed with the distributees.

5. Delete from the form of petition unnecessary allegations. The relationship of the distributees indicates the allegations that should be deleted. A surviving spouse always shares in a decedent's estate. The distributees, other than the surviving spouse, take in the following order:

Children and issue of deceased children
Father, mother
Brothers, sisters, and issue of deceased brothers and sisters
Uncles, aunts, and issue of deceased uncles and aunts

There is no need to make an allegation concerning relatives of a deceased who are not entitled to inherit. Thus in the illustration, surviving children are listed as distributees. There is no need to make an allegation about a surviving

Surrogate's Court
County of New York

In the Matter of Proving the Last Will and
Testament of

EDGAR BROWN

Deceased

Affidavit Proving a Correct Copy
of the Will Filed for Probate

P _____ 19—

County and State of New York, ss:

We, __PAUL BELL__

and __MARY WILLIAMS__ , being duly and severally sworn, say,

each for himself, that he has carefully compared the foregoing papers with the

original thereof dated the ___23rd___ day of ___November___ , 19

about to be filed for probate, and that the same ___are___ in all respects a true

and correct copy of said instrument and of the whole thereof.

Paul Bell
Mary Williams

Sworn to before me this **5th** day of

June , 19—

Leslie Nash

(Notary Stamp)

Probate of a Will: Figure 2.
*Affidavit proving a correct copy of
will filed for probate.*

SURROGATE'S COURT
County of New York

COPY

of the Last Will and
Testament of

EDITH KLINE

Deceased

Affidavit Proving a Correct Copy of
the Will
Filed for Probate

King & Snow

Attorneys and Counsellors at Law

No. ____ 70 Fifth Avenue

New York City

Filed the 5th day of June, 19 —

Probate of a Will: Figure 3.
*Back of affidavit proving a correct
copy of will filed for probate.*

mother or father, or others, because in this case they cannot inherit. If there were no surviving children or issue of a predeceased child, and no surviving mother or father, the brothers and sisters would be listed as distributees. It would then be necessary to allege that there were no surviving children or issue of a deceased child, and no surviving mother or father. It would not be necessary to allege that there were no surviving aunts or uncles and no issue of a deceased aunt or uncle, because they could not inherit, unless specifically named in the will.

6. The petition indicates the kind of legacy, as well as its value. This information can be taken from the will. Thus the testator might leave the residue of his estate in trust for the testator's spouse, the remainder to go to the children upon the death of the spouse. The petition would show that the spouse was the "benefic-

iary of a residuary trust" and that the children were given a "remainder interest in the residuary trust."

If the testator does not place the residue of the estate in trust but leaves it outright to someone, the petition indicates that the person is the "residuary legatee."

When specific personal property, rather than a sum of money, is bequeathed, the bequest is indicated in the petition as a *specific legacy.*

7. Arrange for the petitioners to come in and sign the petition.

8. Have the petitioners verify the petition. When the petitioner, or one of them is a corporation, type a VERIFICATION by a corporation on the form if there is space. If there is no space, type it on plain paper the width of the printed form and attach to the form immediately following the individual verification.

9. Conform the office copy.

10. File the original of the petition, the original and certified copy of the will, and the transfer tax affidavit (see below) in the probate court.

11. Mark on the office copy the date the petition was filed.

12. Make entry in suit register.

Transfer tax affidavit. A *transfer tax affidavit* is filed with the petition. This is a sworn statement about the totals of realty and personalty affected by the will and of the names, amounts of legacies, residences, and relationship of those who receive gifts under the will. The affidavit supplies the state taxing authorities with data to be used by them for taxing purposes. It is typed on a printed form supplied by the taxing commissioner.

Citation and waiver in probate proceeding. Some courts require that the surviving spouse, distributees, and executors and trustees named in the decedent's will be given notice of the petition for probate by service of a *citation.* The citation is a legal writ citing those to whom it is addressed to appear in court on a certain date and show cause why the will should not be admitted to probate. It does not command an appearance as a summons does. Those who do not want to contest the will need not appear in court. A citation is issued by the CLERK OF THE COURT, but is prepared by the petitioner's attorney.

Any person over 18 may serve a citation. Service is made by delivering a copy to the person upon whom it is served. If an infant is a distributee, the citation is addressed to the infant, but is served upon the parent with whom the infant resides or upon the infant's guardian. If an infant is over 14, service is made upon the infant as well as the infant's parent or guardian.

Service of citation by publication and mailing. If any of the distributees live outside the state, or if there are any heirs or next of kin whose names and places of residence are unknown, service is had upon them by publication and mailing. The procedure is similar to that in a civil action. See SERVICE OF SUMMONS.

Adults may waive the issuance and source of a citation in the matter of proving the last will and testament of the deceased, but infants may not. Thus before the citations are prepared, waivers are secured.

How to prepare a waiver of citation. Figure 4 illustrates a properly completed form of waiver.

1. Make an original for the court and an office copy.

2. Have those who waive citation sign the original in the presence of two witnesses.

3. Take the acknowledgment of those signing the waiver.

4. Conform office copy, marking on it the date the original is filed.

5. File original in court.

6. Make entry in suit register.

How to prepare a citation. Figure 5 illustrates a properly completed form of citation in probate proceedings.

1. Make an original for the court, an office copy, and a copy for each person to be served. In the illustrated case 5 copies must be made—an original for the court; an office copy; a copy for service upon Robert Brown, an infant over 14; a copy for service upon his mother in his behalf; a copy for service upon the mother of Irene Brown, an infant under 14. The adult distributees waived citation.

2. Find out the last return date allowed by the court rules.

3. Get the Clerk of the Court to sign the original.

4. Conform copies and give original and copies (except office copy) to person who is to serve the citation.

5. Prepare affidavit of service, which is usually printed on the back of the citation (figure 6), and have the person who served the citation sign and swear to the affidavit in the presence of a notary.

6. Conform office copy, marking on it the date the original is filed in court.

7. File original in court.

8. *Enter in diary* return date of citation.

9. Make entry in suit register.

Preparations for hearing. The hearing in an uncontested probate proceeding is informal. The lawyer for the petitioners

appears before the Clerk of the Court with the witnesses to the will. The date of the hearing is the return day indicated in the citation. (In some jurisdictions, the Clerk of the Court sets the date for hearing at the time the petition is filed.) You will have to make certain preparations before the hearing.

1. Prepare deposition of witnesses.

2. Notify witnesses to the will.

3. Prepare and mail notice of probate.

4. Prepare oath of executor.

5. Prepare decree.

6. Prepare letters testamentary; also letters of trusteeship if the petition prays for them.

Notice of probate. The legatees and devisees who are not heirs-at-law must be given notice that the will has been offered for probate. The printed form of notice calls for the name and address of the proponents (the petitioners) and for a list of the names and addresses of the legatees, devisees, and beneficiaries who have not been cited or have not waived citation.

1. Make an original for the court, an office copy, and a copy for each person listed in the notice.

2. Send the notices by mail if directed to do so by the attorney. The attorney for the petitioners makes affidavit of service by mail on the back of the notice.

3. Notarize the affidavit made by the attorney.

4. Conform the office copy.

5. Place the original with the papers that the lawyer will take to the hearing.

6. Make entry in suit register that the notices were mailed.

Deposition of witnesses to the will. As soon as the date of the hearing is known, notify the witnesses to the will of the time

Surrogate's Court, County of New York

In the Matter of Proving the Last Will and
Testament of

EDGAR BROWN

Deceased,

As a Will of Real and Personal Property

Waiver of Citation in Probate
Proceeding

P 11,235 19-

We, ELIZABETH R. BROWN, JOHN BROWN, and MARY
BROWN,

the undersigned,   being   heirs at law and next
of kin of _____ EDGAR BROWN _____ , deceased, do
hereby _____ appear in person and waive the issuance
and service of a citation in the matter of proving the last will and
testament of said deceased, bearing date   November 23,
and consent that the said instrument be admitted to probate.

Dated New York

    June 6   , 19-

Elizabeth R. Brown
John Brown
Mary Brown

Signed in the presence of

John Blank
Susie White

State of New York

                ss.:

County of New York

    On the   6   day of _____ June _____ 19-, before
me personally came ELIZABETH R. BROWN, JOHN BROWN, and
MARY BROWN, to me known and known to me to be the individuals
described in and who executed the foregoing instrument, and they
duly acknowledged that they executed the same.

Mary Williams

(Notary Stamp)

NOTE—Outside the State of New York see the estimated probate on the reverse page.
(OVER)

Use BLACK ink only, as this sheet will be photographed.

Probate of a Will: Figure 4.

*Waiver of citation in probate
proceeding.*

Form A

CITATION

26416-(C.1)——04

P 11,235 19-

The People of the State of New York

By the Grace of God Free and Independent,

TO

ROBERT BROWN, IRENE BROWN

the above   next of kin and heirs at law of   **EDGAR BROWN**

,deceased, send greeting:

Whereas, Thomas Nelson and The City Trust Company of New York, residing at 52 Gramercy Park, North, New York City and having its principal place of business at 70 Fifth Avenue, New York City, respectively, have lately applied to the Surrogate's Court of our County of New York to have a certain instrument in writing bearing date November 23,   19 , relating to both real and personal property, duly proved as the last will and testament of   **EDGAR BROWN**

, deceased, who was at the time of his death a resident of **214 East 17 Street, New York City**   . the County of New York.

Therefore, you and each of you are cited to show cause before the Surrogate's Court of our County of New York, at the Hall of Records in the County of New York, on the 18th day of June   , one thousand nine hundred and --------, at half-past ten o'clock in the forenoon of that day, why the said will and testament should not be admitted to probate as a will of real and personal property and why letters of testamentary and letters of trusteeship should not be issued to the executors and trustees who may qualify thereunder.

In testimony whereof, we have caused the seal of the Surrogate's Court of the said County of New York to be hereunto affixed.

Witness, Honorable John Doe

Surrogate of our said County of New York, at said county, the

6th   day of   June   in the

year of our Lord one thousand nine hundred and

Richard Roe

Clerk of the Surrogate's Court

NOTE: The original citation must be returned to the Probate Clerk before one p.m. on the day preceding the Return Day, with sworn proof of service.

Probate of a Will: Figure 5.

Citation in probate proceeding.

Surrogate's Court, County of New York

In the Matter of Providing the Last Will and Testament of

EDGAR BROWN

Deceased,

As a Will of Real and Personal Property

AFFIDAVIT OF SERVICE OF CITATION

State of New York

County of _____ **New York** _____ ss.:

Matthew Davis

of _____ **33 West 10 Street, New York City** _____, being duly sworn, says that he is over the age of eighteen years; that he made personal service of the within citation in the above-entitled special proceeding on the persons named below, whom deponent knew to be the persons mentioned and described in said citation, by delivering to and leaving with each of them personally a true copy of said citation, as follows:

On the _____ **7th** _____ day of _____ **June,**
19 _____, at **214 East 17th Street, New York City, on Robert Brown.**

On the _____ **7th** day of _____ **June,**
19- , at **214 East 17th Street, New York City, on Elizabeth R. Brown, in behalf of Robert Brown, an infant.**

On the _____ **7th** _____ day of _____ **June**
19-, at **214 East 17 Street, New York City, On Elizabeth R. Brown, in behalf of Irene Brown, an infant.**

On the _____ day of _____
19 , at _____

Matthew Davis

On the _____ day of _____
19 , at _____
Sworn to before me on the
8th day of June   19—

Mary Williams
(Notary Stamp)

Specify clearly time and place of service of each party served.

Probate of a Will: Figure 6.

Affidavit of service of citation.

and place of the hearing. Their names and addresses can be gotten from the will. If the witnesses are not available, the lawyer will have to take other legal steps to prove the will. Make an entry of the notice in the suit register. In some states, wills no longer have to be proved with deposition of witnesses, except in the case of Contest of Will.

Printed forms of deposition are available.

1. Prepare an original and an office copy for each witness. Thus if there are two witnesses, prepare two sets of depositions.

2. Do not date the depositions. They are signed and sworn to before an officer of the court, who dates them at that time.

3. Place the originals with the papers the lawyer will take to the hearing.

4. Draw checks to witnesses for fee allowed by law. The lawyer will probably take the checks to the hearing and pay the witnesses at that time; otherwise mail the checks after the depositions are taken. In some states, deposition of witnesses is prepared by the probate court, acknowledged by the court, and the fees are paid by the court out of the costs placed on deposit with the court at the time the will is filed.

Oath of executor. In some states, an executor must take an oath to perform faithfully his or her duties as executor. Printed forms are available.

1. Prepare an original and an office copy for each executor. Thus if there are two executors, prepare two sets of oaths.

2. Each executor signs the original of his oath in the presence of a notary.

3. Conform the office copies.

4. Place the originals with the papers the lawyer will take to the hearing.

5. Make an entry in the suit register that the oaths have been executed.

Decree admitting will to probate. A decree in a probate proceeding serves the same purpose as an order or judgment in a civil action. A favorable decree admits the will to probate and directs that letters testamentary be issued to the executor nominated in the will. The probate judge signs the decree, but the petitioner's attorney prepares it. Printed forms are available.

1. Make an original for the court and a copy for the office file.

2. Do not date the decree. It will be dated when the judge signs it.

3. Place the original with the papers that the lawyer will take to the hearing.

4. The decree might not be signed for several days after the hearing. *Make a follow-up entry in the diary* for a few days after the hearing and inquire of the Clerk of the Court if it has been signed.

5. Mark on the office copy the date the decree was signed.

6. Make entry in the suit register.

Letters testamentary. After the judge signs the decree, the Clerk of the Court issues letters testamentary to the executor. In some courts, the attorney for the executor prepares the letters. They are the evidence of the executor's authority to act. Anyone dealing with the executor as the representative of the estate will require a certificate to the effect that letters have been issued and are still in force. Certificates are available from the Clerk of the Court for a small fee.

1. Prepare an original or duplicate original for each executor, an office copy, and a sufficient number of copies to be certified by the Clerk of the Court. Thus if there are two executors, prepare

three copies in addition to the copies that are to be certified. There must be a certified copy for each bank account, each security issue, each safe deposit box, and the like.

2. If there are two or more executors, all of them are named in the letters.

3. Do not date the letters. The Clerk of the Court will date them when he or she issues them.

4. Place the original and duplicate original with the papers the lawyer will take to the hearing. The clerk will sign a copy for each executor named in the letters and return them to the office.

5. Conform the office copy.

6. Deliver a signed copy to each executor. If the lawyer is an executor, he or she will retain one of the signed copies.

7. Make entries in suit register.

Notice to creditors. As soon as letters testamentary are issued, notice to creditors should be published in a local newspaper. Creditors of the decedent are given a certain time in which to file any claims they may have against the decedent. *Enter in diary* the last day the creditors have to present claims.

Newspapers usually have an appropriate printed form of notice to creditors that can be filled in without any difficulty. Within a specified time after the last publication, affidavit of publication is filed with the Clerk of the Court. The publisher makes the affidavit of publication and delivers it to either the Clerk of the Court or the attorney. *Enter in diary* the date by which the affidavit must be filed; also make entries in the suit register.

Probate Court. See COURTS OF SPECIAL JURISDICTION.

Procedural Law. See SUBSTANTIVE LAW.

Procedure. See PRACTICE AND PROCEDURE.

Proctor. The term used to designate an attorney in an ADMIRALTY proceeding.

Progressive Taxes. See GRADUATED TAXES.

Prohibition. The name of a writ issued by a SUPERIOR COURT, directed to the judge and parties to a suit in an INFERIOR COURT, commanding them to cease from the prosecution of the suit, because the original cause of action (or some matter arising from it) belongs to the jurisdiction of another court. See also MANDAMUS; HABEAS CORPUS; STAY; QUO WARRANTO; CERTIORARI.

Promissory Estoppel. If a person (the *promisor*) promises something that he or she knows will induce another person (the *promisee*) to do something, and that does in fact induce that person to act, the court will enforce the promise to prevent injustice. For example, if an employer promises an employee a pension upon retirement but does not honor the promise, the promise may be enforced by the court.

Promissory Note. A written contract or instrument whereby one party promises to pay the other party a certain amount in a certain way.

Promoter of a Corporation. A person who undertakes to form a new CORPORATION, to procure for it the rights and money by which it is to carry out the purposes set forth in its CERTIFI- CATE of Incorporation, and to establish it for the prosecution of its business.

A promoter occupies a FIDUCIARY relationship, or a relationship of trust and confidence toward the corporation that he or she promotes. The utmost good faith is required in the promoter's deal- ings with it. The promoter also occupies a position of trust and confidence toward the persons induced to subscribe for shares to be issued by the corporation. Ordinarily a promotor's activities are over when the corporation is fully formed—that is, when the real stock- holders in interest have elected a perma- nent and independent BOARD OF DIRECTORS that undertakes the man- agement of the corporation.

Proof of Service. See NOTICE (of Appeal).

Property Descriptions. See LAND DESCRIPTION.

Property Exempt. Property ex- empt is property allowed in some states to the surviving spouse of a decedent, which is paid after costs of administration and funeral expenses and before other debts. It may consist of PERSONAL PROPERTY or cash.

Proprietorship, Sole. One of the three most common forms of business organization. Ownership of the business is vested in one proprietor. The other two common forms of business organi- zation are PARTNERSHIP and COR- PORATION.

Prosecutor. One who prepares for and conducts the prosecution of a per- son suspected of or accused of a crime.

Protest. A formal certificate attesting the DISHONOR of a NEGOTI- ABLE INSTRUMENT after NEGOTIA- TION. A protest is usually made by a NOTARY PUBLIC but may be made by a responsible citizen, in the presence of two witnesses. The certificate states that the instrument was duly presented for payment, at the proper time and place, that payment was refused for the reason given, and that the holder intends to hold the drawer and endorser responsible for payment. The protest is attached to the dishonored instrument or copy of it. No- tice of protest is then sent to the parties who are secondarily liable (drawer and endorser). Protest is required only when a bill of exchange or check drawn in one state (or country) and payable in another is dishonored, but as a matter of business practice domestic instruments are often "protested." The word *protest* is loosely applied to the process of presenting an instrument for payment, demanding payment, and giving notice to the drawer or endorser.

Example:
Buyer accepts a trade ac- ceptance drawn by Seller. Seller endorses and discounts the acceptance at Doe Bank, which sends it to Roe Bank for collection. Roe Bank's notary public (usually an employee)

presents the instrument to Buyer for payment, which is refused. The notary then protests (using the term loosely): he makes out the certificate, attaches it to the instrument and sends notice of protest to Seller, who is secondarily liable, through Doe Bank. In this case, Seller is the drawer and the endorser.

Provisional Remedies. Methods provided by law to make judgments more effective. The provisional remedies of arrest, temporary injunction, attachment, and receivership prevent defendants from placing themselves or their property beyond reach or from doing damage to the very property the action was brought to protect.

The provisional remedy of *arrest* insures the court's control over the defendant. Restraining a person's liberty can be effective in coercing the performance of an act to be done, such as the payment of ALIMONY. Defendants may also be arrested, in some actions, where they are nonresidents or there is good reason to believe they are about to depart from the state.

A *temporary injunction* can be granted by a court where there is an action seeking a permanent INJUNCTION, if the applicant will be immediately and irreparably injured unless the defendant is restrained *immediately*. A temporary injunction can also be granted when the defendant in any type of action is about to destroy, damage, or get rid of the subject of the action.

Attachment is a means of security for the plaintiff. The property of defendant that is attached is held by the court to secure payment of any judgment the plaintiff may obtain.

The provisional remedy of *receivership* puts property that is the subject of an action in the hands of a representative of the court, or "receiver." By taking custody of the property, the receiver prevents the defendant from taking it out of the court's JURISDICTION or materially injuring or destroying it.

Provision of Necessaries. The supply of food, clothing, medical services, and household supplies that a husband is legally bound to provide for his wife. If a third person, for example, a doctor or grocer, provides these necessaries, the husband may be sued for their cost if he has failed to provide for them. When the wife has breached her marital obligations, such as by committing ADULTERY, the husband is no longer legally bound to support her.

Proximate Cause. That which, in a natural and continuous sequence, unbroken by any intervening cause, produces an injury, and without which the injury would not have occurred. For example, the failure to repair a faulty brake in an automobile may be the proximate cause of a subsequent collision.

Proxy. An authorization to vote at a meeting in place of an absent stockholder. The term is also applied to the person or persons holding the authority. Although the statutory provisions concerning voting by proxy vary throughout the states, the usual provisions are (1) that the proxy will be in writing; (2) that the person giving it can revoke it at any time; (3) that it will expire after a certain number of months or years from its date unless the stockholder executing the proxy indicates the length of time it is to continue in force; and (4) that the term of the proxy will be limited to a definite period.

As a meeting generally cannot be held unless a QUORUM (a certain portion) of stock is represented, it is usually necessary to get proxies when the stockholders are widely scattered. The Securities and Exchange Commission regulates the solicitation of proxies in respect to registered securities. A proxy need not be in any particular form, as long as it meets statutory requirements and requirements of the SEC. It need not be witnessed, but a witness can prove the authenticity of the signature.

Public and Private Law. *Public law* is the law that relates to the public as a whole, rather than to a specific individual. It involves the authority of the federal and state governments to make laws and of federal and state executives to issue orders, as well as ADMINISTRATIVE LAW and CRIMINAL LAW. *Private law* is that body of the law that pertains to the relationship between individuals as such. It includes laws regulating contracts, sales, agency, NEGOTIABLE INSTRUMENTS, and business organizations.

Publici Juris. Of public right.

Public Utility. A private corporation that renders service to an indefinite public, which has a legal right to demand and receive the service or commodities

of the corporation. Public utilities are subject to special laws that do not apply to other corporations, and they are closely supervised by governmental agencies. They owe a duty to the public that they may be compelled to perform. For example, a railroad company cannot abandon part of its route without authority from the Interstate Commerce Commission. On the other hand, public utilities are given certain powers of a public nature, for example, the power of EMINENT DOMAIN. Public utilities include railroads, bus lines, airlines, gas and electric companies, hydroelectric, water, and irrigation corporations.

Punctuation. In general, punctuation of legal documents should be handled the same way as punctuation in CORRESPONDENCE.

The *apostrophe* is used to show possession (the lawyer's notebook, the Adamses' complaint).

Brackets and parentheses are used to set off or enclose material. If the typewriter has a bracket key, use *brackets* to enclose comments or explanations in quoted material, to rectify mistakes, and to enclose parentheses within parentheses; otherwise, use parentheses for these purposes. If necessary, brackets can be made by using the virgule and dash.

Use *parentheses* to enclose parenthetical or explanatory expressions outside the general structure of the sentence.

The place at which an incorporators' meeting (sometimes called the first meeting of the stockholders) is to be held is determined by statute in most states.

Enclose a figure in parentheses when it follows an amount that has been written out in words, and when the American equivalent of foreign currency is given.

> Under the will he receive £100,000 ($280,000).

> Seven thousand five hundred (7,500) dollars.

> Seven thousand five hundred dollars ($7,500).

NOTE: If the figure is written before the word "dollars," do not use the dollar sign; if the figure is written after the word "dollars," use the dollar sign. This rule also applies to the percent sign.

In testimony (question and answer material) use parentheses to enclose matter describing an action and, also, to indicate a person who has not previously taken part in the questions and answers.

> Q. (By M. Smith) Will you identify this handkerchief? (handing the witness a handkerchief)

Enclose in parentheses letters or numbers if enumerations run into the text.

> Stock may be divided broadly into two kinds: (1) common stock and (2) preferred stock.

Parentheses are usually used in pairs, but a single closing parenthesis may be used instead of a period to follow a letter or small roman numeral in outlines and in lettering and numbering paragraphs.

Commas, periods, and similar punctuation marks belong inside the parentheses if they belong to the parenthetical clause or phrase. They are *outside* the parentheses if they belong to the words of the rest of the sentence.

> The boy ran as if a ghost (and, indeed, he may have been right) were following him.

> He reported the action at once. (He has a strong civil sense of responsibility.)

The *colon* introduces something (lawyers keep two types of accounting records: business and personal).

The *comma* separates words and phrases (she typed one complaint, two confirmations, and four introductions).

A *dash* sets off something with emphasis (it was a long day—too long for most of the guests).

Ditto marks indicate that the material typed directly above the marks should be repeated. Ditto marks are not permissible in a legal document. They may be used in exhibits and schedules but not in the document to which the exhibits and schedules are annexed. Ditto marks may sometimes be used in drafts, to save time, but the language is always repeated in full in the final instrument.

Ellipses are used to indicate omission of words from a quote ("The defendant . . . will plead guilty. His attorney, however, seems unhappy. . . .").

The *exclamation point* should be used—sparingly—for emphasis (what an exciting trial!).

Hyphens are connecting links (two-year lease, anti-American) and indicators of word division at the end of a line.

The *period* is used at the end of sentences, abbreviations, and as a decimal (Ind., $12.50).

Question marks are used after a question and to show doubt (he is from Missouri(?), where he practiced law for twelve years).

Quotation marks are used to show precise quotes ("make two copies," he said), except in question and answer material, where the name precedes the quote, the marks are omitted.

The *semicolon* separates parts of compound sentences where the comma and conjunction are omitted (several people waited outside the courtroom; they seemed to know a verdict was near).

Purchase Money Mortgage. See MORTGAGE

Putative. Alleged; supposed; used in family law. For example, in a paternity suit, the court would speak of the "putative" father.

Quantum Meruit. "As much as he deserved." The law imposes an obligation to pay without regard to the intention of the parties, but based on the law of natural justice and equity. For example, if a doctor renders emergency services to an accident victim, the law assumes the implied consent of the victim and the doctor may bring an action in quantum meruit to recover the reasonable value of his or her services.

Quash. To overthrow; to abate; to vacate; to annul; to make void.

Question of Fact. A disputed factual issue that is left for the jury to decide. (See QUESTION OF LAW.)

Question of Law. A disputed legal issue that is left for the judge to decide. Whether or not an event occurred is a QUESTION OF FACT. The legal significance of that event is a question of law.

Quiet. Adj. Unmolested; tranquil; free from interference or disturbance. Often used in leases.

Quiet Title, Action to. An EQUITY proceeding to establish the plaintiff's title to land by bringing into court an adverse claimant and compelling him either to establish his claim or to be estopped from asserting it. Whenever a deed or other instrument exists that may throw a cloud over the complainant's title or interest, a court of equity will clear the title by directing that the instrument be canceled, or by making other decrees required by the rights of the parties. For example, when a real estate mortgage is valid on its face but has ceased to be a LIEN, it may be canceled as a cloud on the title by an action to quiet title.

Quitclaim Deed. See DEED.

Quorum. The number of persons who must legally be present at a meeting to transact corporate business or the business of any assembly of persons. When the membership of the assembling group or body consists of a *definite* number of persons as required by law—for example, a board of directors or the United States Senate—a majority (more than half) of the members is required to make a quorum, unless the controlling law expressly states that another number constitutes a quorum. At COMMON LAW, when the membership of the assembling body consists of an *indefinite* number of persons (that is, the law requires no definite number)—as the

351

stockholders of a corporation—any number constitutes a quorum; however, the BYLAWS, and frequently the statutes or charter, customarily make an express provision concerning a quorum. In the case of a stockholders' meeting, the designated quorum usually relates to the amount of stock represented at the meeting and not to the number of stockholders.

Quo Warranto. A WRIT of inquiry as to the warrant or authority for doing the act complained of. The writ tests the right of a person to hold an office or franchise or to exercise some right or privilege derived from the state. Quo warranto affirms an existing right to an office, or it sets aside wrongful claims of a pretender. An information in the nature of a quo warranto has replaced the old writ, but the terms *information in the nature of a quo warranto* and *quo warranto* are used interchangeably and synonymously and have substantially the same purpose. The power to file a quo warranto is incident to the office of the attorney general, but the privilege of instituting the proceeding upon the refusal of the attorney general to act has been granted to private individuals in their capacity as taxpayers and citizens.

R

Rand McNally Bankers Directory. A semiannual publication, with a monthly supplement, giving the latest statement, official personnel, transit number, check-routing symbol, and other data on every bank in the United States. Similar, but less inclusive, data are included on every Canadian bank. Latest statements and names of officers are given for all foreign banks of any importance. United States banking and commercial laws are discussed. Directors of all banks are listed geographically, and there is a list of discontinued bank titles for the five years preceding each issue.

Range. 1. In real estate, a row of *townships* (rectangular tracts of land divided into six-mile squares) running north and south. See LAND DESCRIPTION.

2. In stock market parlance, *range* refers to the price fluctuations that occur at the beginning of a trading session (*opening range*); or to the price fluctuations that occur at the *end* of a trading session at the close of the day's market (*closing range*).

Ransom. The money demanded for release of a person from captivity. See KIDNAPPING.

Rape. The carnal knowledge of a woman taken forcibly and against her will. Carnal knowledge has been interpreted by most courts and statutes as physical penetration to any degree. Traditionally, rape was a crime charged against a man who was not the victim's husband. Recently, however, women in some states have brought charges of rape against their husbands.

Most states have created an offense commonly known as *statutory rape* where the crime consists of having sexual intercourse with a female under statutory age. The offense may be either with or without the female's consent.

Ratification. The approval of an act that had not been binding previously; ratification, or *affirmance*, reverts and becomes effective as of the date the act was performed. An infant may ratify, or affirm, contracts after reaching majority; a principal may ratify, or affirm, the unauthorized acts of an agent; a corporation may ratify, or affirm, the unauthorized acts of its officers. A corporation cannot ratify or affirm the acts of its promoters before the corporation was formed because it was not in existence and could not possibly have entered into a contract at that date. It may, however, *adopt* the acts of the promoters.

Real Party in Interest. The party who will be entitled to and will receive the benefits resulting from an action that is successful.

Real Property. The land, appurtenances, and any man-made improvement attached to it. (All other property is PERSONAL PROPERTY.) Thus in addition to the land, real property includes the buildings, natural growth, minerals, and timber, that *have not been separated from the land.* For example, apples on the tree constitute real property, whereas harvested apples become personal property.

Real Property Description. A written representation contained in a LEGAL INSTRUMENT of a particular piece of land, the appurtenances, and any man-made improvement attached to it. Such representation is usually made from other documents or from an ABSTRACT OF TITLE. You must be exceptionally accurate in preparing the instrument that describes REAL PROPERTY. Property is never identified solely by street and number because the names and numbers of streets might change. For details on how to prepare real property descriptions, *see* LAND DESCRIPTION.

Reasonable Doubt. The degree of certainty a juror requires to determine the guilt of a person on trial.

Receiver. In real estate, a court-appointed custodian who holds property for the court and attends to the details of management pending final disposition of the matter before the court. While the receiver holds the property, no person can proceed against it without the consent of the court. Thus a receivership effectively prevents the dissipation of property through haphazard seizures.

The receiver appointed by the court in which the proceeding is instituted has JURISDICTION only within the territorial limits of the court as prescribed by law. An ANCILLARY *receiver* is one appointed in a foreign jurisdiction for the purpose of taking charge of the assets in the jurisdiction where he or she is appointed.

A MORTGAGE may provide that the holder of the mortgage is entitled to the appointment of a receiver in any action for FORECLOSURE on the mortgage. See also DEFAULT.

Receiver of Stolen Property. One who knowingly obtains goods that are stolen. The act of receiving stolen property is an offense that involves a criminal intent as a material element of the crime, such as an intent to aid the thief, or to obtain a reward for returning the goods to the owner, or in some way to derive profit from the act. A person who receives and passes stolen goods is sometimes known as a *fence.*

Receivership. See PROVISIONAL REMEDIES.

Reciprocity. A relationship between persons, corporations, states, or countries, whereby one grants favors or privileges to the other and the other returns the favors or privileges.

Record on Appeal. A copy of the pleadings, exhibits, orders, or decrees filed in a case in the lower court, and a transcript of the testimony taken in the case. The purpose of the record is to inform the APPELLATE COURT of what transpired in the lower court. The rules specify that the record will be abbreviated as much as possible, so the judges will not have to wade through a mass of extraneous material. The appellate court does not need to be informed about matters that are not pertinent to the decision of the questions before it. The larger the record, the more expensive it is.

Assignment of errors and instructions to the clerk. Within a certain number of days after the NOTICE of Appeal is filed, the number being specified by the rules of the reviewing court (see APPEAL), the appellant files assignments of error and directions to the CLERK OF THE COURT for making up the transcript of record on appeal. The assignments of error and directions to the clerk may be combined in one document.

The purposes of the assignment of errors are to apprise the appellate court of the specific questions presented by the appellant for consideration and to inform the opposite party of the matters of error relied on, so discussion may be limited and concentrated on those points.

The directions to the clerk designate the portion of the proceedings and evidence to be included in the transcript of record—those portions pertinent to the questions before the appellate court. The appellee might consider that other portions of the record will throw light on the questions to be reviewed by the court. If so, the appellee files additional directions and cross-assignments.

In lieu of directions to the clerk, the parties may file written stipulations with the clerk designating the contents of the record.

Preparation. The directions for preparing the notice of appeal apply also to assignments of error and instructions to the clerk. The originals are filed with the Clerk of the Court, and copies are served on counsel for the appellee. Proof of service of these documents on opposing counsel is filed with the clerk and included in the transcript of record.

Who prepares the record. The Clerk of the Court or the appellant prepares the record from the directions to the clerk filed by the parties. The common practice is to employ a court reporter to make up the transcript, but sometimes preparation of the record is the task of the secretary to the attorney for the appellant.

How to prepare the record. The instructions to the clerk will indicate to you the documents and evidence that are to be included in the record. Copy them from the papers in the court file, which may be obtained from the Clerk of the Court. The following directions are applicable to the preparation of records in any state:

1. Omit formal parts of documents.
2. Copy pleadings in the order of filing.
3. In the center of the page, just above the pleading, put in solid caps the nature or kind of document, such as "Demurrer to Amended Complaint" (not simply "Demurrer").
4. Do not copy the caption of the pleadings.
5. Indicate the filing date of each pleading by typing "Filed" and the

date at the end of the pleading. This information is usually stamped on the back of the document.

6. The first page in the record is a complete index that gives in chronological order the date of the filing of each instrument in the court below, the name or character of the instrument, and the page of the record where the same may be found. The index is prepared last.

Format and make-up of record. Consult the rules. They provide whether the record will be printed or typewritten, or either. They also specify the kind of paper, size of type, folio size, and the like. Here are the requirements in a typical state that permit a record to be either printed or typewritten. The following requirements also apply to briefs.

1. Black and distinct lettering
2. Type no smaller than small pica
3. Double spaced (this requirement is stated in terms of leading for a printed brief)
4. Margin no less than 1 inch
5. Quoted material indented and single spaced (for a printed record this requirement is stated in terms of ems)
6. Opaque, white, unglossed paper
7. Legal cap if typewritten; 6- by 9-inch folio if printed

Binding, volumes, and title. The record is bound in pamphlets. If typewritten, the pamphlets are securely fastened; if printed, they are stitched. If the record consists of more than 200 pages, it should be bound in two or more volumes. The cover of each volume contains the style of the cause, the title of the appellate court, the title of the court from which the cause is appealed, and the

names and addresses of counsel, and, if more than one volume, the number of the volume.

Certification, filing, and service. The record is certified by the Clerk of the lower Court, and also verified by the clerk if he or she does not prepare it. A copy (or copies) is served on opposing counsel, and the original and required number of copies (see the rules) filed with the Clerk of the appellate Court, together with proof of service. The record must be filed within the time specified by the rules. A filing fee is required at the time the record is filed.

Recording. 1. *of Conditional Sale Contracts.* The official registration with the proper authorities of a written document that establishes the terms and conditions of the CONTRACT made between buyer and seller in a CONDITIONAL SALE.

In some states, such as New Jersey, a conditional sale contract may be filed or recorded in the land records, with a description of the land on which the articles have been installed; subsequent purchasers or mortgagees of the REAL PROPERTY are bound by the recorded conditional sale contract, and the conditional seller may remove the article in the event of nonpayment. If a conditional sale contract is not recorded, subsequent purchasers or mortgagees are not bound by it unless they knew of the conditional sale contract. As in the case of prior recorded chattel mortgages, some states do not require subsequent purchasers or mortgagees to search the records for conditional sales contracts. They are bound only if they know of the prior conditional sale.

2. *of a Deed.* Filing of a DEED in a public office designated by state statute, generally the county or town clerk's office or recorder's office where the property is located. A person waiting to record a deed deposits with the proper official the original signed instrument, properly acknowledged. It is now filed for record and is deemed to be recorded. All persons have CONSTRUCTIVE notice of the existence of the deed. The official copies the document in his record books, indexes it, and returns the original, with suitable notations about recording, to the person who presented it for recording. An unrecorded deed, although valid and effective as between the parties, is ineffective so far as subsequent bona fide purchasers or mortgagees of the same property are concerned.

The usual practice is for the purchaser's attorney to attend to the recording and for the purchaser to pay the recording fees. The attorney also sees that the proper revenue stamps, known as documentary stamps, are affixed to the deed, if required by his or her state. Federal documentary stamps are no longer required. The attorney also sees that the proper transfer tax is withheld from the seller at closing and paid by check or cash to the proper court official, if his state requires no documentary stamps. See TRANSFER TAX. Where there is a TITLE INSURANCE company representative at the closing, he or she may take the deed, attend to the recording, and return it to the attorney. Eventually the recorded deed is returned to the owner of the property by his or her attorney or mailed to the owner directly by the recorder's office.

3. *of Lease.* Filing a copy of the LEASE with the proper official of the county where the leased property is located. State laws differ in the necessity for recording a short-term lease. As a practical matter, regardless of statute, a lease on property or space of any importance should be recorded by the lessee. Recording serves notice to the world that the lessee holds possession of the premises for a specified term; it assures one of possession against another leasing of the premises by the same owner and protects one's possession if the lessor sells the property.

For recording purposes, a skeleton form of lease may be used. This serves the dual purpose of saving recording fees (which are generally based on the number of words, or the number of pages, in the document recorded) and of avoiding publicity as to the terms of the lease.

4. *of Legal Instruments.* The official registration with the proper authorities of written documents for the purpose of establishing legally some act or agreement. The purpose of recording the instrument is to protect the interests of all persons. For example, *A* wants to purchase some property from *B*. He learns from the public record that *C* holds a mortgage on the property. *A* purchases the property, but he makes legal arrangements that will protect not only his own interests but those of *C* as well.

What to do. When the lawyer asks you to have an instrument recorded, you should know not only what official is to record it, but also *where* it is to be recorded. For example, although the lawyer's office is located in Adams County and the client signs the paper there, if the instrument relates to property located in

Brown County, the instrument will be recorded in Brown County, not Adams County. The firm's name and address will probably appear on the legal back in which the instrument is bound. Some recorders require that the attorney's name as preparer and address be typed on the document to be recorded before it will be accepted for recording. Before having the instrument recorded, write immediately above it, "Please record and return to:" If the firm's name and address are not printed on the legal back, type them on it.

If the instrument is to be recorded in a place located near the office, take it in person to the office of the proper official. He or she will receipt for it and return it to the lawyer's office after it has been recorded.

Pay the *recording fee*, which is fixed by state statutes. Unless the photocopy method of recording is used, the fee is usually based on the number of folios (groups of 100 words) in the instrument. Pay the fee out of petty cash, or take a blank check to the recording office and fill in the amount when you are told what the recording fee will be. When the photocopy method is used, the fee is usually charged per page.

When it is necessary to mail the instrument to the recording office, send it by registered mail, return receipt requested with a covering letter. The letter should be addressed to the designated official and should describe the instrument sufficiently to identify it. Enclose a check for the fee or request that a bill be forwarded. The official will not record the instrument until the fee is received. The model below illustrates how such a letter might be worded:

REGISTERED
RETURN RECEIPT REQUESTED

November 14, 19. .
John R. Perle, Esquire
Clerk of the County Court
Worthington, Ohio 43085
Sir:

We are enclosing for recording lease, dated November 14, 19. ., between Edgar S. Norris and Robert T. Ellis.

Please let us know the correct amount of your fee for recording this instrument, so we can promptly forward a check to you.

Sincerely yours,
KOHN & SECOR
By
L.L. Kohn

Enclosure

A blank check may be sent with the words "not over . . . . . Dollars" typed on the check, and the recording official asked to fill in the proper amount and notify the attorney of the amount when he or she returns the instrument.

5. *of Real Estate Instruments.* The official registration with the proper authorities to those written documents that establish ownership or the right to possess and use certain land, appurtenances, and any man-made improvement attached to it. (See REAL PROPERTY.) Real estate instruments are usually recorded in a public office so the record is available to anyone who is interested. The purpose of the record is to protect the interests of all persons concerned.

Recording Fee. The fee fixed by state statutes for recording a legal document in an official recording office. See RECORDING OFFICE.

Recording Office. A public office where legal instruments are officially recorded so they may be available to anyone who is interested. See RECORDING (of Legal Instruments).

Redemption. 1. *of Real Estate.* The recovery of property given as security for a debt by paying off a note, BOND or MORTGAGE. *Equity of redemption* is the right of a mortgagor to recover (redeem) the property and obtain legal TITLE thereto by paying the amount due in full, with interest.

2. *of Securities.* The exchange of corporate stocks or bonds for cash. Common stock is never "redeemed"; preferred stock may be redeemable; bonds are frequently issued subject to redemption.

Reentry. The act of resuming the possession of lands or tenements in pursuance of a right that the party exercising it reserved when quitting his or her former possession. See FORCIBLE ENTRY AND DETAINER.

Referee. An officer of the court who has power to hear testimony and decide certain facts. The officer then reports to the court those facts upon which the court enters judgment.

Register. See CLERK OF THE COURT (Permanent Record Book).

Release. Giving up some claim, right, or interest to the person who owes the claim or against whom it might have been enforced.

Relict. The survivor of a pair of married people; whether the survivor is the husband or the wife; it means the relict of the united pair (or of the marriage union), not the relict of the deceased individual.

Remainder. The remnant of an estate in the land, depending upon a particular prior estate created at the same time and by the same instrument, and limited to arise immediately on the determination of that estate, and not in abridgement of it. For example, a mother deeds her real estate to her daughter, but reserves a life estate for herself. The daughter is the remainderman. Upon the death of her mother, she will hold a FEE SIMPLE in the real estate. See LIFE ESTATE.

Reminders. *How to remind the lawyer of appointments.* In the later afternoon, or the first thing in the morning, place on the lawyer's desk a typed schedule of appointments, giving all pertinent information. Memorandum paper about 6 by 9 inches is desirable for this purpose. Before the time of the appointment give the lawyer the file and other material that he or she will need for it.

Reminders showing appointments for a month. Many lawyers like to see the month's engagements at a glance. There are calendars designed for this purpose, usually on cardboard about 9 by 11 inches.

How to remind the lawyer of things to be done. To remind the lawyer of a task, place the file on the lawyer's desk, with a memorandum. For example, if a real estate closing is scheduled for the 29th and papers must be drawn for it, put the file on the lawyer's desk about the 27th with a memo that the closing is scheduled for the 29th.

Some lawyers make a practice of calling their secretaries into their office the first thing every morning to dispose of the correspondence and to discuss pending matters and things to be done. This is the ideal arrangement. For the discussion, take with you a list of things to be done and any material pertaining to them, as well as a notebook.

How to remind the lawyer of court work. In a large office, a diary of court cases is maintained by the managing clerk under the supervision of the managing attorney. Although each lawyer in charge of a matter is presumed to know its status, it is the duty of the managing clerk to follow the status of the matter, to furnish information regarding the status, and to aid in securing prompt and orderly disposition of court matters. In a comparatively small office, the secretary to the senior partner or to the managing partner will probably have this responsibility.

From diary records, you would send a written notice to the lawyer in charge, sufficiently in advance to permit him or her to make preparations necessary to take the indicated step. Figure 1 is a printed form, filled out, used for this.

Mimeographed or typed slips would serve the purpose. The lawyer in charge of the matter should return the written notice to you with a notation of the action taken.

Another method of reminding the lawyers in the office about pending court work is to type the entries from the diary each week for two weeks in advance, making as many copies as necessary to circulate among the lawyers. In an office with numerous attorneys, the list would be mimeographed. Each lawyer then checks the cases in which he or she is interested. Note that the diary entries include the initials of the interested lawyers.

When the secretary to a lawyer receives a notice from the managing clerk, or from the secretary to the managing partner, she checks her diary and sees that preparations necessary to take the required action are made.

The *diary* is a daily record of what is accomplished and also of future appointments and work to be done. Diaries instead of calendars are usually kept by lawyers because they want a record of time devoted to a specific client so the client may be charged for the time. The diary has a separate page for each day in the year. Many standard yearbooks are satisfactory. The important thing is that they should have space for work performed and the time consumed doing it, as well as space for appointments and matters to be attended to. A diary is prepared originally in the same manner as are calendars. Entries of time consumed on each task are made from day to day after the work is completed.

Diaries you should keep. Two diaries are required, one for the lawyer and one

EDISON & STEVENS
Managing Clerk's Department

To ..... Mr. Olson ....

Reference   Wilson vs. Green

Time: October 22,   19--. at 10 AM.

Place: County Court House, Department B

Action

    Last day to

    Motion for order dismissing complaint

    Settlement of

    Examination of

    Hearing

    Trial

    Argument

....

                  .... ESR ....
                          Managing Clerk

Dated .. October 19, .. 19--

(Please note below disposition of matter and return to Managing Clerk.)

Attended and argued in support of motion. Decision reserved.

                             J.T.E.

Reminders: Figure 1.
Notice of diary entry.

for you, but the entries are not completely duplicated. In the lawyer's diary, you will enter all appointments and important days the lawyer should remember, such as a spouse's birthday. Watch the lawyer's diary closely for appointments he or she makes without telling you.

In your own diary, enter notations of your own business activities and appointments, as well as the lawyer's appointments and the things you will have to remind the lawyer about.

If you are responsible for following court cases for more than one lawyer, as well as being responsible for personal matters for a member of a firm, it will be less confusing to keep all court matters in a separate diary.

How to make up diaries. Keep a list of items that go in the diary year after year. As soon as diaries for the forthcoming year are available, enter all the recurring items, events, and appointments under the appropriate date.

Enter time-consuming tasks that must be done by a certain date sufficiently *in advance* to permit the work to be finished on time. Also make an entry under the date on which the action must be taken. Similarly, enter reminders concerning presents or cards in advance. It is not usually necessary to make advance entries in the lawyer's diary—you can remind the lawyer of work to be done. Underline important due dates and deadlines in red. Also, advance notice of payments of large sums should also be entered in the diary. The lawyer's funds might be low, or the lawyer might want to negotiate a renewal of a loan.

How to make entries about legal work. Under the date upon which a step must be taken, make an entry setting forth (1) the title of the matter, (2) the time and place for the step, and (3) the nature of the act to be performed, fully described. If you keep the diary for more than one lawyer, include the initials of the lawyer or lawyers interested. The third example of entries, below, indicates that a BRIEF must be prepared. This entry should also be made under an advance date (see above), with a notation of the date the briefs must be ready.

Examples of entries:

Joan Wilson Estate—pay on account New York Estate Tax to obtain benefit of 5% discount. RSF

International Jones Co.—Clerk's Office, U. S. Court House, Foley Square—Order to show cause returnable why certain claims should not be compromised. NEL

Richards v. Rogers (both actions)—Last day to serve and file reply briefs. RSF:NEL

How to obtain information for entries.

1. Observe the dates and the places mentioned in papers that the firm prepares and in those served on it by opposing counsel.

2. Observe the date a notice is served on the office, or the office serves a notice on another concern.

3. Calculate the time prescribed by law or rules of law for answering, replying to, or moving to dismiss or correct a pleading when a pleading is served on the office. You can get this information from the practice rules of the court.

4. Calculate the time for taking any

step when the time limit for that step runs from some other act of which there is notice.

It would be impossible to set forth here all of the instances and time limits that affect litigation; not only are they numerous, but they vary with the state. Knowledge of them is gained by experience and study. The lawyer is responsible for knowing them and instructing you accordingly; you are responsible for making notations in the diary in accordance with those instructions and for asking the lawyer to give you those instructions. A few diaries have an appendix of timetables of procedure and court rules for specific states that are very helpful to the legal secretary.

Remise. To remit or give up. A formal word in deeds of release and quitclaim; the usual phrase being "remise, release, and forever quitclaim."

Remittitur. The power of a judge to decrease the amount of an excessive award made by a jury verdict. The award is decreased, with the consent of the plaintiff, as condition for the denial of defendant's motion for a new trial because of the excessiveness.

Remittitur is a means of giving a just award without the expense and trouble of a new trial. See ADDITUR.

Replevin. A court action to recover possession of property unlawfully taken or detained. Title to the property must be in the person bringing the action. Thus if title passes to the buyer and the seller refuses to deliver the goods, the buyer may bring an action in replevin to get posses-

sion of the goods. Or the seller, under a conditional sale contract by which he or she retains title to the goods until payment is made, may recover the goods by an action in replevin if the buyer does not make the payments called for by the contract.

Representative Action. In corporate law, a suit brought to redress injury to the stockholders rather than to the CORPORATION. (See DERIVATIVE ACTION.) Types of injury that would give a stockholder the right to start a representative action would be wrongful deprivation of the right to vote, to transfer stocks, to share in dividends, or to exercise PREEMPTIVE RIGHTS. One stockholder may bring the action on behalf of himself or herself and all other stockholders who may be similarly damaged.

Rescission. An action in equity whereby a court is asked to annul a contract entered into through fraud, misrepresentation, or excusable error. For example, if a person enters into a contract of partnership and then discovers that material facts were misrepresented, he or she brings an action in rescission. Rescission may be absolute or qualified. Thus in rescission of a contract of sale, the seller resumes title and possession of the goods as though he or she had never parted with them, but the seller has no claim for damages. In qualified rescission, the seller resumes title and possession but does not rescind the entire contract because he or she reserves the right to sue for damages. A contract may also be rescinded by mutual consent.

Research. Court opinions are the cornerstone of the law. The purpose of legal research is to locate previous cases (court opinions) that are similar in some way to the case at hand (lawyers would say the "case at issue"). Armed with these cases, which the law terms *precedents*, the lawyer seeks to persuade the court to rule in his or her client's favor. Since there are many thousands of court opinions in a comprehensive law library, the legal researcher must learn how quickly to find the opinions that would help the case. Two major publishing companies have developed comprehensive research systems for lawyers. They are West Publishing Company and The Lawyer's Co-operative Publishing Company. Both of these companies publish helpful and concise pamphlets that tell how to do legal research most effectively. For the secretary training to do legal research, the best place to start would be with a reading of these pamphlets. Contact:

West Publishing Company
P. O. Box 3526
St. Paul, MN 55165
and
The Lawyer's Co-operative
Publishing Company
Aqueduct Building
Rochester, NY 14603

A few books offer basic information to all law office personnel:

Legal Research in a Nutshell, West
Ballentine's Law Dictionary, Lawyers Co-operative
Black's Law Dictionary, West
A Uniform System of Citations, Harvard Law Review
Legal Secretary's Complete Handbook, Prentice-Hall

Some large law firms and major law libraries now use automated legal research systems. WESTLAW involves searching the headnotes of the National Reporter System by computer. LEXIS involves searching the entire text of published judicial opinions.

See also CITATION; CORPUS JURIS SECUNDUM SYSTEM; NATIONAL REPORTER SYSTEM; OFFICIAL REPORTS; RESTATEMENTS OF THE LAW; SHEPARD'S CITATIONS.

Reservation of Corporate Name. Deciding on a corporation's name is a serious matter, to which the incorporators and the lawyer give careful consideration. All of the states require that a corporation's name should indicate that it is a corporation by the use of *company, association, incorporated,* or similar words or abbreviations of them. Also, the majority of the states will not permit the use of the word *bank* or *trust* in a name of a corporation unless it is a banking institution. The chief importance of a name to the incorporators is that, as a business develops, its name acquires a value in itself, representing to a great extent the GOODWILL of the company. The state laws and the courts generally protect the corporation's exclusive right to the use of its name. The state official will not accept for filing a CERTIFICATE of Incorporation, if the name of the proposed corporation so closely resembles that of a corporation existing in the state that deception or confusion might result. Therefore, the lawyer will tell you to find out if the choice of name is available, and, if so, to reserve it.

What to do to clear the name. Write to the designated state official and ask if the chosen name is available. Ascertain if the proposed name is available not only in the STATE OF INCORPORATION, but also in any states in which the corporation expects to qualify. If the organization of the corporation must be completed quickly, you might wire, or at least ask the state official to answer by wire collect.

In some states, the state official will reserve a name for a specified time for the payment of a fee or as a courtesy. In the states that require a fee, enclose a check when asking to have the name reserved. When you wire, send the check to the designated official as soon as you get a reply.

The letter might read as follows:

The Honorable John R. Blank
Secretary of State of Delaware
Dover, Delaware 19901

Sir:
    <u>Joseph A. Smith, Inc.</u>

Will you please advise us whether the above name is available for a domestic corporation, which we are about to organize under the laws of your state.

    If so, please reserve it for us for the statutory period. Enclosed is check for $_____ in payment of reservation fee.
    Please reply by wire, collect.
        Sincerely,
        Hamilton & Jones

If the incorporators expect to qualify as a foreign corporation in another state, the first paragraph will be changed to read: ". . . foreign corporation, which we are about to qualify to transact business in your state."

If you wire, the telegram might read: "Wire collect if Joseph A. Smith, Inc. is available for corporation."

Reserved Powers. See EXCLUSIVE POWERS.

Residence. A particular locality where a person lives. One need not intend to make the residence a fixed and permanent home, which is what distinguishes a residence from a DOMICILE. A person may have only one domicile but many residences.

Residential Lease. A binding CONTRACT for the possession of lands and improvements to be used for dwelling purposes. These may be single-family homes and two- to four-family houses. See also COMMERCIAL LEASE; LEASE.

Residuary Legacy. See LEGACY.

Res Ipsa Loquitur Doctrine. The *res ipsa loquitur* doctrine means that certain occurrences contain within themselves a sufficient basis to infer NEGLIGENCE. Where the instrument causing the accident was in the exclusive control of the defendant, and the accident is one that would not ordinarily happen without negligence, the facts are sufficient to justify an inference of negligence and to force the defendant to explain it. For example, if a building collapses and injures a man passing by, it may be inferred that the injury is a result of negligence. The injured party is not forced to show at the trial the specific negligent act of the defendant that caused the building to fall. It becomes the duty of the defendant to prove that he or she was not negligent.

Resolution. A formal expression of the opinion or will of an official body or a public assembly, adopted by vote, as a legislative resolution.

Respondent. 1. The opposing party in an APPEAL.

2. The defending party in EQUITY and ADMIRALTY cases (corresponding to the DEFENDANT in a case at law).

Respondentia. A loan usually made to the master of a ship in a foreign port in cases of emergency for which the cargo aboard the ship is pledged as security. If the cargo is lost in the course of the voyage, the lender loses his or her money; if the cargo arrives safely at its destination, the borrower pays the sum borrowed plus the agreed interest. Like BOTTOMRY LOAN, respondentia bonds are becoming obsolete.

The term *bottomry loan* is used when the ship, rather than its cargo, is used as security for a loan.

Restatements of the Law. A presentation by the American Law Institute of the "best rules" of law applied in the United States.

While the Restatements are not primary authority of the law, they have proved to be extremely persuasive. The Restatements are presumed by many to state the COMMON LAW rule, and the party opposing them has the burden to prove the contrary. This does not make the Restatements mandatory on the court, but it does indicate that they are becoming accepted as the authoritative statement of the common law in the United States.

Most of the work of compiling the Restatements was done by reporters for each topic, men eminent in their respective fields, helped by staffs of advisers. After each group of specialists determined for itself the proper statement of the "best rule" of law in each case, the tentative draft or parts of it were submitted to the Council of the American Law Institute for debate and final approval.

Restitution. Making good for loss, damage, or injury; indemnification.

Restraint of Princes and Rulers. A clause in a maritime contract that excuses the shipper for delay in delivery of goods when the vessel carrying cargo is captured or detained by the force of a sovereign nation.

Restrictive Covenant. A stipulation in an agreement limiting or restricting the action of one of the parties to an agreement. A deed may contain a covenant restricting the type of building that may be placed upon the property. A restrictive covenant of this type is said to "run with the land"—subsequent purchasers are bound by the covenant whether or not it is expressly set forth in the deed to them.

Retainer. Compensation paid in advance to an attorney for services to be performed in a case.

Return Day of Motion. See NOTICE (of Motion).

Return Day of Summons. The final date that a DEFENDANT must answer a SUMMONS or file a NOTICE of Appearance in accordance with civil practice and procedure codes and statutes. Thus if the defendant is required to answer "within 20 days" from the service of the summons, the 20th day is the *return day*. In some jurisdictions, certain days, designated as *return days* or *rule days*, are set aside for filing papers in court. In these jurisdictions, the rules provide that the defendant shall appear "by the *next rule day*," if the summons is served a certain number of days before rule day; otherwise, the defendant will appear on the following rule day. Thus the return date is always a rule day.

These return dates are very important, and you should always *enter them in your diary*, whether your office is serving the summons or has received a summons for a client.

How to compute the time. The statutes and codes also provide how the time must be computed. The usual method is to *exclude* the date from which the period begins to run, but to *include* the last day of the period of time. If it falls on Sunday or a legal holiday, the next business day is the return date. Intermediate Sundays or holidays are included in the computation, unless the period allowed is less than *seven* days. The period begins to run the day the summons is served, not the day it is dated. This method of computation of time applies to the time for filing all pleadings as well as to the return day of the summons. See also ALIAS SUMMONS.

Reversible Error. Error in a lower court substantial enough to cause a miscarriage of justice and to justify a reversal by a higher court.

Revoke. To recall a power or authority; to vacate an instrument previously made; or to annul, repeal, rescind, or cancel privileges.

Right of Assemblage and Petition. A provision in the First Amendment to the Constitution that says Congress cannot deny the right of the people to assemble peaceably and to petition the government for a redress of grievances. The Fourteenth Amendment has been interpreted by the Supreme Court as placing the same restriction on the states. See CIVIL RIGHTS; BILL (of Rights).

Right-to-Work Laws. Legislation specifying that no person can be denied or excluded from employment because of membership or nonmembership in a labor organization. Proponents of the laws say they are necessary for the maintenance of basic freedoms being challenged by union autocracy. Labor spokespersons contend that the purpose of the laws is to weaken and destroy unions. Legislative popularity of the right-to-work laws has been limited almost exclusively to rural or southern states where union membership is small.

Robbery. The act of taking property in the possession of another, from his or her person or immediate presence, against his or her will by force or threat of injury. An example of robbery is the act of taking a wallet from a person whom the taker has knocked out; taking a sleeping person's watch, however, is LARCENY. The greater the violence that accompanies the robbery, the more severe is the punishment.

Rules of the Reviewing Court. See APPEAL.

Salvage. A reward for saving property at sea. The principle of salvage has been developed by ADMIRALTY. On land, one who goes to the rescue of a neighbor's property receives no remuneration for one's efforts.

Essentially there are three elements to a valid salvage claim:

1. The ship or property must have been so imperiled that without the salvager's aid it could not have been rescued.

2. A voluntary act on the part of the salvager is essential. There must be no preexisting duty to give assistance, as there might be, for example, under a CONTRACT, or as there is between a vessel and its own crew.

3. The salvager must successfully save, or assist in the saving of, the property at risk.

It is interesting to note that salvage is the factor that often compels captains to remain on board their imperiled vessels, for once a ship is abandoned anyone may salvage it. If not under a preexisting duty, the salvager will thus be entitled to a bounty. Remaining on ship, the captain may be able to overcome the peril or negotiate a reasonable salvage contract. The captain may also be awaiting assistance from his or her own company, assistance he or she knows to be on the way.

Savings Bank Trust. See TOTTEN TRUST.

Scrivener. A writer; scribe; conveyancer. One whose occupation is to draw contracts, write deeds and mortgages, and prepare other species of written instruments.

Seal. An impression upon wax or wafer or some other substance capable of being impressed. The practice of affixing a seal to an instrument originated in the days when only a few people could write their names. Written instruments were marked with sealing wax, which was impressed with a ring or other device. This seal was the mark of the person making the instrument and took the place of a signature. Today, any material affixed to an instrument and intended as a seal, or the writing of the word *Seal* or *L.S.* (*locus sigilli*, Latin for "place of the seal") after the signature is considered a seal. The process of affixing the seal is referred to as *sealing* the instrument, and the instrument then becomes a *sealed* instrument. Today, the sealed instrument has a twofold significance: (1) Under the statutes of limitations, the time during which suit may be brought on a sealed instrument is longer than on an unsealed instrument. (2) Suit on a contract cannot be defended on the basis that it was without consideration, because the consideration of a sealed instrument cannot be questioned. If an instrument is to be sealed, the TESTIMONIUM CLAUSE will so indicate. *See also* CORPORATE SEAL.

Search and Seizure. The act of probing for information or evidence on a person or a person's property. The Fourth Amendment to the Constitution guarantees the security of the individual against searches and seizures that are unreasonable and arbitrary. To assure a citizen his or her constitutional rights, the courts will give a police officer a search WARRANT only for a good reason supported by oath and describing the place to be searched and the persons or things to be seized.

Search Warrant. An order issued by a judge that allows certain law enforcement officers to search a specified place for specified things or persons and to bring them before the court.

Second Mortgage. *See* MORT-GAGE.

Section and Township. *See* LAND DESCRIPTION.

Secured Transactions. A transaction secured by an interest in real or personal property. Examples of such security are the mortgage, pledge, and conditional sale.

Securities. Stock certificates, bonds, or other instruments of value that are used in regular channels of commerce. They are evidenced of a secured indebtedness or the right to return of money.

Security Deposit Under Lease. A deposit by a tenant with the landlord of money or securities, at the time a LEASE is signed, to secure the landlord against loss upon failure of the tenant to pay rent due. The lease may contain various provisions with regard to the security deposit:

1. That interest will be paid to the tenant on such deposit.

2. That upon reletting the premises, damages sustained by the landlord may be collected from the security deposit and the balance returned to the ousted tenant.

3. That the security deposit will be retained by the landlord as liquidated damages if the landlord terminates the lease because of the tenant's DEFAULT. Courts in some cases have compelled the landlord to return the deposit to the tenant, less rent due up to the time of termination of lease.

Bonus. In lieu of a security deposit, the tenant may, at the time the lease is signed, pay a sum of money as a "bonus" for receiving the lease. This amount becomes the property of the landlord upon payment, and no part of it is recoverable by the tenant even if default occurs early in the life of the lease.

Advance rental. In lieu of a security deposit, the tenant, at the time of signing the lease, may pay the landlord a sum of money to be applied in payment of the rent for the last months of the lease. Upon default, the landlord is generally allowed to retain the advance. In a few states, the "advance rental" is treated as a "security deposit," and the landlord must return the amount to the tenant, less the amount of delinquent rent.

Effect of assignment of lease. A tenant's right to refund of a security deposit or advance rental does not automatically pass upon an assignment of the lease. It passes to the assignee only if the assignment specifically so provides or if it is assigned by a separate instrument.

Effect of sale of leased property. The landlord is not relieved of liability to return the tenant's deposit by a sale of the leased property. The fact that the landlord turned the deposit over to the purchaser is no excuse.

Seizin. Actual possession of land. A covenant in a WARRANTY DEED that the seller is "seized" of the premises in FEE SIMPLE and has good right to convey means that at the time of execution and delivery of the DEED, the seller is in lawful possession of the fee estate in the property and has lawful TITLE. If the seller does not have lawful title, the purchaser cannot get title; but under the *covenant of seizin,* the seller becomes personally liable to the purchaser for any expenses incurred up to the time of delivery of the deed. A covenant of seizin does not run with the land but is personal to the GRANTEE. A certification of title by a title company that the seller has a good and marketable title to the premises in fee, and that he or she has the right to convey, may furnish better protection to the purchaser than a covenant of seizin. See also COVENANTS (of title).

Separation. A discontinuance of COHABITATION by mutual agreement of a husband and wife or by the DE-CREE of a court. In an action for separation, the complaining party must establish the existence of a valid marriage and then must prove the wrongdoing by the other party that constitutes grounds for separation. In New York State, an action for separation may be maintained by either spouse on the grounds of CRUELTY, conduct making it unsafe to cohabit with the defendant; DESERTION, or ADULTERY. See also SEPARATION AGREEMENT.

Separation Agreement. A CONTRACT between a husband and wife, who are not living together as such, that provides for the division of property, support, and the CUSTODY OF CHILDREN. The agreement can be enforced in the same way as any other contract. To enter into a separation agreement, there does *not* have to be a SEPARATION action pending in court. A separation agreement will become void upon the resumption of COHABITATION with the intent to reconcile or resume marital relationships.

Separation of Powers. The doctrine that forbids one branch of the government from interfering with another by usurping its powers. To maintain the separation of legislative, executive, and judicial functions, the courts at times have had to clarify the extent of each branch's power. For example, it has been held that the separation of powers protects the president in the exercise of power to remove executive officers appointed by him or her, but it also prevents the president from removing officers who are not essentially executive and whose removal has been restricted by Congress.

Sequester. To set apart from; for example, to sequester witnesses during a trial, so they may not hear other witnesses' testimony.

Sequestration. The seizure and maintenance of the property of a defaulting party in a matrimonial action. Sequestration is a method of enforcing the provisions of a JUDGMENT against someone to pay ALIMONY or support.

Service by Publication. See SERVICE OF SUMMONS.

Service of Summons. The manner in which JURISDICTION is given to the courts by the PARTIES TO AN ACTION. A SUMMONS served on the defendants is also a means of giving the defendant notice that an action is being brought against him or her and that failure to appear or answer will cause a JUDGMENT to be entered against the defendant by DEFAULT.

Personal service is the most direct way of letting the defendant know he or she is being sued. The summons must be served personally within the territorial limits of the court's authority.

Substituted service can be used when personal service upon a resident defendant cannot be accomplished. The plaintiff may see that a summons is left with someone at the defendant's home or can attach it to the defendant's door and mail a copy to him or her.

Service by publication is allowed in certain types of actions where neither personal service within the state nor substituted service is possible. Service is made by actual newspaper publication

of the summons or by personal service outside the state.

Service by mail can be made in some states where new civil rules have been adopted to conform to Federal Civil Rules. The attorney signs a statement on the complaint that the service was made by mail on a certain date.

Whether service should be personal, substituted, or by publication depends on the type of action, where the party to be served resides, and ultimately, the rules of the state. Use of the correct means of service is vital for a court to obtain jurisdiction. If a court is to give a judgment affecting the status of property, it must be given jurisdiction over the property (jurisdiction *in rem*); if it is to give a judgment against a person, it must be given jurisdiction over the person (jurisdiction *in personam*). Generally, personal and substituted services gives *in personam* jurisdiction and service by publication gives *in rem* jurisdiction.

Set-Off. When two parties each owe an ascertained amount to the other, the defendant may deduct what the plaintiff owes him or her from the amount the defendant owes the plaintiff.

Settlor. See TRUST.

Severance Damage. The damage that property sustains when a portion of it is taken in condemnation, and the remaining property becomes less valuable owing to change in size, shape, and utility. An award of severance damage is allowable only if there is unity of ownership and unity of use. In some states, contiguity is also a requisite; that is, the remaining parcel must be contiguous (in actual contact or adjoining) with the part taken. When a parcel is totally absorbed in condemnation proceedings, no severance damage exists. Speculative and doubtful DAMAGES are compensable.

In estimating the amount of severance damage, the appraiser must determine the highest and best use to which the property may be put. The damage cannot be greater than the full value of the property. Special and direct benefits to the property are generally considered as an offset against the amount of severance damage.

Shepard's Citations. A service that tells the lawyer whether statutes and cases to be cited as authority are in fact valid for that purpose. The law is constantly changed by legislative or judicial action. The careful lawyer, therefore, checks upon the present value of each authority sought to be used. By far the most complete American citator system,

in both geographical scope and fullness of treatment, is *Shepard's Citations,* covering all states and units of the National Reporter series and a special Labor Law Citator. (See also CITATIONS.)

Purpose of Shepard's Citations. To prove his point, the lawyer cites a decision contained in a published opinion. Before citing the case, the lawyer wants to know something of its history and subsequent treatment. The lawyer is interested in knowing whether the case has been appealed to a higher court; whether it was affirmed or reversed; whether it has been followed in many other cases; and whether it has been overruled in a subsequent case. *Shepard's Citations* is designed to give the lawyer this information. It is quite easy to "Shepardize" a case, and you will probably be asked to assist the lawyer with this research. A lawyer never cites a case as authority without first "Shepardizing" it.

Abbreviations used. The following abbreviations are used by Shepard for the purpose of indicating the "Judicial History of Case."

History of Case

a	(affirmed)	Same case affirmed on appeal.
cc	(connected case)	Different case from case cited but arising out of same subject matter or intimately connected therewith.
D	(dismissed)	Appeal from same case dismissed.
m	(modified)	Same case modified on appeal.
r	(reversed)	Same case reversed on appeal.
s	(same case)	Same case as case cited.
S	(superseded)	Substitution for former opinion.

Treatment of Case

| c | (criticized) | Soundness of decision or reasoning in cited case criticized for reasons given. |

Treatment of Case

d	(distinguished)	Case at bar different either in law or fact from case cited, for reasons given.
e	(explained)	Statement of import of decision in cited case. Not merely a restatement of the facts.
f	(followed)	Cited as controlling.
h	(harmonized)	Apparent inconsistency explained and shown not to exist.
j	(dissenting opinion)	Citation in dissenting opinion.
L	(limited)	Refusal to extend decision of cited case beyond precise issues involved.
o	(overruled)	Ruling in cited case expressly overruled.
p	(parallel)	Citing case substantially alike or on all fours with cited case in its law and facts.
q	(questioned)	Soundness of decision or reasoning in cited case questioned.

How to use Shepard's Citations. An explanation of how to use the Shepard's Federal Reporter Citations will enable you to use the other Shepard's Citations. Figure 1 illustrates a page from the Federal Reporter Citations.

ILLUSTRATIVE CASE

(Acknowledgment is made to Shepard's Citations, Inc., for this explanation.)

Let us assume that by reference to a digest, encyclopedia, textbook or other unit of legal research, you have located the case of Hanover Star Milling Co. v. Allen & Wheller Co., reported in Volume 208 of the Federal Reporter on page 513 dealing among other things with the property right a complaint has in a trademark.

Figure 1 is a reproduction of a page from Shepard's Federal Reporter Citations. Note the volume of reports to which the citations apply, "Vol. 208," in the upper right-hand corner of the page.

An examination of the heavy face type numbers within the page locates the page number "—513—" in the seventh column of citations. This is the initial page of the case under consideration. Following this page number you will find the citation "sLRA1916D136" indicating that the same case "s" is also reported in 1916D Lawyers Reports Annotated 136.

In obtaining the history of this case, you will observe that upon appeal to the United States Supreme Court, it was affirmed "a" in 240 United States Reports "US" 403, 60 Lawyers Edition of United States "LE" 713, 36 Supreme Court Reporter "SC" 357, 1916 Decisions of the Commissioner of Patents "'16 CD" 265. Wherever there are parallel sets of reports covering the same citing case these citations immediately follow each other.

It is also to be observed that

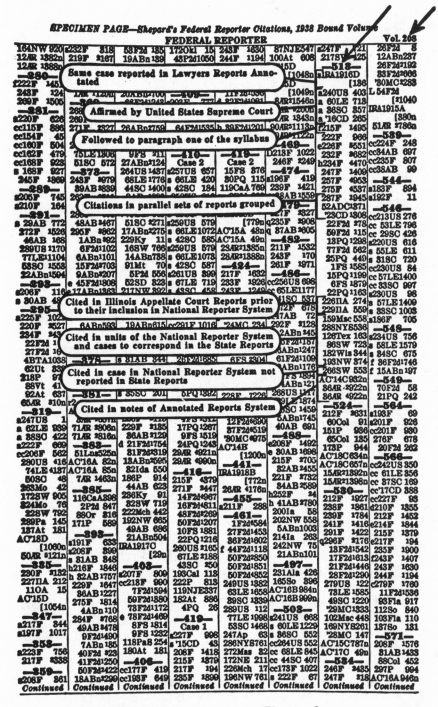

Shepard's Citations: Figure 1.

Page from Shepard's Federal Reporter Citation.
(Courtesy—Shepard's Citations, Inc.)

by examining the abbreviations preceding the citations, this case has been followed "f," explained "e," and harmonized "h" in subsequent cases in the Federal Reporter.

The next citation covers the reference "215F^{1}495." The small superior figure "1" in advance of the citing page number 495, indicates that the principle of law brought out in the first paragraph of the syllabus of the cited case is also dealt with in 215 Federal Reporter 495.

Assuming that you are primarily interested in the principle covered in paragraph one of the syllabus, we find that the additional citations that contain the superior figure "1" in advance of the citing page number include numerous other cases that deal with this particular point of law and that are reported in the Federal Reporter; Federal Reporter, Second Series "F2d"; Federal Supplement "FS"; Appeal Cases District of Columbia "ADC"; Decisions of the Commission of Patents and United States Patent Quarterly "PQ."

In addition to the citations in point with paragraph one of the syllabus, there are several citations to other paragraphs of the syllabus of this case in cases reported in the Federal Reporter, Federal Reporter, Second Series, and in the notes "n" of the American Law Reports "ALR." Thus, the cita-

tions dealing with a point of law in any particular paragraph of the syllabus may be referred to instantly without examining every citation to the case.

It will be noted that this case has been cited by the courts of Illinois, New York, Texas, and Wisconsin. These citations are arranged alphabetically by the state reports with the corresponding reference in the National Reporter System. The citation 266 Southwestern Reporter (SW) 533 is a case decided in the Court of Civil Appeals of Texas and not reported elsewhere. This case has also been cited in the notes of 1914C Annotated Cases 932 (AC'14C932n).

By examining this same volume and page number in the 1953-1961 Bound Supplements, and the latest issue of the Cumulative Supplement, and intervening Advance Sheet, all subsequent citations to this case will be found.

In a similar manner, constructions and references to the statute under consideration may be obtained by referring to the appropriate Shepard edition.

Sheriff's Sale. Where the court orders the sheriff to sell property to satisfy an unpaid judgment debt of the owner.

Short-Term Capital Gain. See CAPITAL (Gain and Loss).

Short-Term Lease. *See* LEASE, Classification of Leases.

Silent Partner. A partner who has no voice in the management of the partnership business. Unless he or she is also a special partner (see LIMITED PARTNERSHIP), a silent partner is equally responsible with the other partners for the debts of the partnership.

Simplex Obligatio. A simple obligation.

Slander. *See* LIBEL AND SLANDER.

Slip Decision. *See* CITATION (to Legal Authorities), How to Cite Slip Decisions.

Slip Laws. The laws enacted by Congress are first published officially as "slip laws." Later they are reprinted in a bound volume of *Statutes at Large.*

Small Claims Court. A court designed to handle claims of a small amount, for example, claims under $300. A citizen may represent himself or herself and does not need to hire a lawyer. The court is designed to relieve the caseload of the larger courts.

Social Security Taxes. Taxes on wages and salaries, as well as on the earnings of self-employed persons, to finance the benefits provided under the Social Security Act. The provisions of the act include old age benefits paid to workers and their families on retirement, survivor benefits paid to the families of deceased workers, and benefits paid to certain disabled workers and their families. The taxing provisions are found in the Federal Insurance Contributions Act and in the Tax on Self-Employment Income section of the Internal Revenue Code.

Both employers and employees are taxed on the employee's salary at the same rate. The employer withholds the employee's contribution and remits it to the government. Self-employed persons are taxed at a rate half again as large because the self-employed person does not have an employer contributing to pay for the benefits.

Participation in a company's private pension plan does not excuse an employee from payment of the tax.

Special Damages. *See* DAMAGES.

Special Partner. *See* LIMITED PARTNERSHIP.

Specific Performance. The performance of a contract according to its exact terms. A court of EQUITY will enforce specific performance, whereas a court of law awards damages to the injured party to a contract. Specific performance is never enforced in contracts for personal services. It is usually confined to sales of REAL PROPERTY and unique personal property, for example an antique.

Spendthrift Trust. *See* TRUST, Spendthrift.

Standing. The legal right of one person to challenge in court the conduct of another person. A person has standing to sue if he or she has a personal stake in the outcome of the case.

Star Page. The line and word at which the pages of a first edition of a law book begin are frequently indicated by a star in differently paginated later editions. The original page number is indicated in the margin. In citing a few well-known works, the edition is left out and the star page is referred to, thus, 1 Bl. Comm. *150.

State of Incorporation. A state in which a CORPORATION is organized. A corporation is not necessarily incorporated under the laws of the state in which its executive office is located, especially if it is to carry on business in more than one state. Each state has a corporation law under which private business corporations for profit are organized. The laws of some states are more favorable to corporations generally than those of other states. The lawyer recommends the state whose laws are most favorable to the proposed corporation. The cost of incorporating and the tax laws in each state are taken into consideration. Therefore, the lawyer might organize a corporation under the laws of a state far removed from his office. Delaware is the leading incorporating state.

In the state of incorporation, a corporation is known as a DOMESTIC CORPORATION; in all other states, as a FOREIGN CORPORATION. (Corporations organized outside the United States are referred to as *alien corporations.*)

Thus a corporation incorporated in Delaware is a domestic corporation there, but in New York and California it is a foreign corporation. A corporation is sometimes incorporated in more than one state, but generally if it wants to carry on its business in another state, it qualifies to do business in that state as a foreign corporation.

States' Rights. A theory of government that advocates more power and independence to the individual states rather than to a strong central government. The conflict between the two points of view when our government was being organized led to the present distribution of power in our federal government. The conflict has continued to this day in the courts and in politics.

Stationery Supplies. The stationery supplies used for various purposes in a typical law office follow.

Legal cap is white paper, 8 by 13 inches or 8½ by 14 inches, with a wide ruled margin at the left and a narrow ruled margin at the right. It is used for court papers and for legal instruments, such as agreements, contracts, and the like. Substance 16 is used for the original or ribbon copy. Legal cap, substance 20, is preferable for the original of wills; substance 13 for the carbon copies. In some states, legal cap has numbers along the left margin. Copies are made by photocopier or on bond or onionskin or with carbon sets.

Legal-size paper, plain without the ruled margins, same substance as the legal cap, is also used for legal instruments of various kinds and for court papers in some jurisdictions.

Short white paper, approximately 8 by 10½ inches, or 8½ by 11, with ruled margins, substance 16, is used for the ribbon copy of briefs and law memoranda; substance 9 or 13 for the carbon copies.

Short white paper, approximately 8 by 10½ inches, or 8½ by 11, plain without ruled margins, is used for legal documents that are not written on long paper. The choice varies with the office.

Manuscript covers are of a heavy colored paper, usually blue, about 25 percent cotton fiber. Legal instruments and court papers can be bound in them.

Legal-size covers, with or without the firm name, are used for binding legal instruments and court papers. Legal-size covers with a printed panel are frequently used for binding court papers. These covers are referred to as *backs,* because they cover only the back of the paper bound in them.

White covers, with or without the firm name engraved on them, are used for binding wills.

Short covers, with or without the firm name, are used for binding briefs, law memoranda, and legal instruments that are typed on short paper. They are double and are bound at the side.

Legal-size yellow manifold is used for drafts.

Legal scratch pads are pads of 8½- by 14-inch yellow paper, with ruled margin and lines. See that there is always one on the lawyer's desk and one in his or her briefcase. The lawyer uses the pads for making notes, writing drafts in longhand, and the like.

Firm letterheads. 8½ by 11 inches, substance 24, 20, or 16, are used for the original of firm correspondence. Some firms also have an 8½ by 7½ inch letterhead for short letters.

Continuation sheets, loosely called second sheets, of the same substance as the letterheads are used for additional pages of a letter. They do not have a letterhead on them but usually have the firm name engraved or printed on them.

Firm letterheads, marked "copy," on unglazed onionskin, substance 9, are used for copies of correspondence. Other copies are made on the office copier.

Colored onionskin or yellow manifold is used for the file copy of correspondence.

Executive letterheads, 6 by 7 inches, engraved with the attorney's name, are used for the attorney's personal correspondence. This paper frequently has a kid finish.

Monarch-size envelopes, 3⅞ by 7½ inches are used with the executive stationery. No. 6¾ (3⅝ by 6½ inches) and No. 10 (4⅛ by 9½ inches) envelopes fit the 8½- by 11-inch letterheads.

Envelopes of heavy manila stock (about 40 pounds), 3½ inches bottom flap, 3½ inches top flap gummed solid, with a ¾ inch scored shoulder also gummed, are used for mailing bulky documents and papers that can be folded.

Statute of Frauds. An ordinance, enacted with variations in all the states, providing that certain contracts cannot be enforced unless they are in writing signed by the party against whom the contract is sought to be enforced. The writing need not be a formal document signed by both parties—a written note or memorandum of the transaction signed by the party to be bound by the agreement is sufficient. The laws in the various states are fairly uniform in requiring the following contracts to be in writing:

1. A special promise to be responsible for the debt, default or miscarriage of a third person.

2. An agreement by an executor or administrator to become liable out of his or her own property for the debts of the estate.

3. A contract, the consideration for which is marriage. Engagement contracts are not included.

4. Contracts for the sale of real estate or any interest therein.

5. Contracts that cannot be performed within one year.

6. Contracts involving the sale of personal property in excess of a certain amount (which varies in the different states), when no part of the property has been delivered and no part of the purchase price has been paid.

In addition, many states require the following contracts to be in writing:

1. An agreement to bequeath property or to make any provision for someone by will.

2. An agreement to pay upon attaining legal majority a debt contracted during infancy.

3. The creation of a trust.

4. The promise to pay a debt that has been outlawed by the STATUTE OF LIMITATIONS or barred by BANKRUPTCY.

5. An assignment of wages to be earned in the future.

6. A mortgage of personal property.

Statute of Limitations. A state ordinance that limits the time within which legal action may be brought, either upon a CONTRACT or TORT. State and federal statutes also limit the time within which certain crimes can be prosecuted. The purpose of the time limitation is to make it impossible to bring suit many years after a cause of action originates, during which time witnesses may have died or important evidence may have been lost. When a debt is involved, it is possible to interrupt (or "toll") the running of the statute—that is, to lengthen the period in which action may be brought—by obtaining a payment on the debt or a promise to pay. A promise to pay a debt that has been barred by the statute of limitations does not require new consideration but many states require such a promise to be in writing. The statutes often differentiate between oral and written contracts. (See table I.)

Statutes and Codes. See CODES AND STATUTES.

Statutes at Large. A bound volume of "slip laws" or laws enacted by Congress. See SLIP LAWS. The *Statutes at Large* have been codified into the *United States Code,* of which there are two unofficial editions—the *U.S. Code Annotated* and the *Federal Code Annotated.*

Statutory Deed. See DEED.

Statutory Law. Rules that have been formulated into law by legislative action. The Constitution of the United States and the constitutions of the various states are the fundamental written law. All other law must be in harmony with the constitutions, which

Table I

STATUTES OF LIMITATIONS IN NUMBER OF YEARS

State	Open Accounts	Notes	Written Contracts	Contracts Under Seal
Alabama	3	6[7]	6[7]	10
Alaska	6[7]	6[7]	6[7]	10
Arizona	3	6[1]	6[7]	6[1]
Arkansas	3	5	5[7]	5
California	4	4[2]	4	4
Colorado	6	6	6[3,7]	6[3,7]
Connecticut	6	6	6[7]	17
Delaware	3	6	3[7]	—
District of Columbia	3[7]	3[7]	3[7]	12
Florida	3	5	5[7]	20
Georgia	4	6	6[7]	20
Hawaii	6[7]	6[7]	6[7]	6
Idaho	4	5	5	5
Illinois	5	10	10[7]	10[4]
Indiana	6	10	10-20	20
Iowa	5	10	10[7]	10
Kansas	3	5	5[7]	5
Kentucky	5	15[5]	15[7]	15
Louisiana	3	5	10	10
Maine	6	6[6]	6[7]	20
Maryland	3[7]	3[7]	3[7]	12
Massachusetts	6	6[6]	6[7]	20
Michigan	6[7]	6[7]	6[7]	6[7]
Minnesota	6	6[7]	6[7]	6
Mississippi	3	6	6	6
Missouri	5	10[7]	10[7]	10[7]
Montana	5	8	8[7]	8
Nebraska	4	5	5[7]	5
Nevada	4	6[7]	6[7]	6[7]
New Hampshire	6[7]	6[7]	6[7]	20
New Jersey	6[7]	6[7]	6[7]	16
New Mexico	4	6	6[7]	6
New York	6[7]	6[7]	6[7]	6[7]
North Carolina	3	3	3	10
North Dakota	6[7]	6[7]	6[1,7]	6[3]
Ohio	15	15	15	15
Oklahoma	3	5	5	5
Oregon	6[7]	6[7]	6[7]	—
Pennsylvania	6	6	6[7]	20
Rhode Island	6[7]	6[7]	6	20
South Carolina	6	6	6	20
South Dakota	6[7]	6[7]	6[7]	20
Tennessee	6[7]	6[7]	6[7]	6[7]
Texas	2	4	4	4
Utah	4	6	6[7]	6
Vermont	6	6[8]	6[7]	8
Virginia	3	5	5[7]	10
Washington	3	6	6[7]	6
West Virginia	5	10	10[7]	10
Wisconsin	6[7]	6[7]	6[7]	10-20
Wyoming	8	10	10[7]	10

[1]Executed without the state, 4 years.
[2]Corporate notes, 6 years.
[3]Contracts affecting real property, 10 years.
[4]Vendor's lien, mortgage, 20 years.
[5]5-year period applies if note is placed on the footing of a bill of exchange.
[6]Witnessed notes, 20 years.
[7]Sales contracts, 4 years (Uniform Commercial Code).
[8]Witnessed notes, 14 years.

From the book, *Legal Secretary's Complete Handbook*, 3rd ed., by Besse May Miller, revised by Mary A. DeVries. ©1980 by Prentice-Hall, Inc. Published by Prentice-Hall, Inc., Englewood Cliffs, N.J. 07632.

define and limit the powers of government. State constitutions must be in harmony with the Constitution of the United States. Congress, cities and towns, and other governmental units find in the constitutions their authority, either express or implied, to enact certain laws. These legislative enactments are called statutes and constitute the greater part of the written or statutory law. Statutory law supplements and supersedes COMMON LAW.

Stay. The legal procedure of stopping a judicial proceeding by the order of a court. The proceeding may be stopped under the authority of the various stay laws that have been enacted by legislation. These stay laws are applicable in legal proceedings in both civil and criminal cases if the situation covered by the legislation exists.

For example, in a criminal case, when a woman is capitally convicted and she is proven to be with child, there will be a stay of execution until after her delivery. In a civil case concerning legal remedies against debtors, a moratorium may grant a term of suspension of certain of these legal remedies during times of financial distress.

Stipulation. Agreements concerning certain phases of a lawsuit made by attorneys for opposing parties by mutual consent. The agreement might be an accommodation to opposing counsel, such as an extension of the time in which to file a pleading; or it might be an agreement that will save time in court, such an agreement admitting certain facts. Usually the stipulation is an agreement among the attorneys for all PARTIES TO

AN ACTION. However, it may be simply an agreement between the attorney for the plaintiff and the attorney for a defendant, the other defendants not being interested in the particular stipulation. Although stipulations are filed in court (except in those few jurisdictions where no papers are filed until note of issue), approval of the court to the stipulation is not usually required.

A stipulation consists of the following parts:

1. Caption
2. Body
3. Dateline
4. Signatures of attorneys for all interested parties.

How to prepare a stipulation. The wording of all stipulations about a particular step in the litigation is substantially the same. The lawyer does not usually dictate the simple stipulations. He or she will say, "Draw up a stipulation in the Jones case extending our time to answer until March 10"; or "Draw up a stipulation in the Smith case to set for trial on March 18." You can get the wording from a practice manual or forms file. Whenever you prepare a stipulation of a different kind, make an extra copy for the forms file. Memorize the short forms to save time in preparing them. The lawyer will dictate some stipulations, such as those admitting certain facts.

It is customary for the attorney seeking the stipulation to prepare it. When typing it, follow the style shown in figure 1.

1. Type on legal-size or regular paper according to court usage.
2. Make an original for the court and a copy for all interested attorneys.

WGR:MH 9/25/— (2)

IN THE COURT OF COMMON PLEAS OF ALLEGHENY COUNTY,
PENNSYLVANIA

JAMES FOSTER and LOLA FOSTER,	:	
Plaintiffs,	:	
vs.	:	No. 223 October Term, 19—
LOWE MANAGEMENT CORPORATION and DELL FASHIONS, INC.,	:	
Defendants.	:	

STIPULATION

IT IS HEREBY STIPULATED AND AGREED by and between the undersigned attorneys that the time for defendant Dell Fashions, Inc. to answer or otherwise plead to the Second Amended Complaint herein, filed the 22nd day of September, 19—, be and the same hereby is extended to and including the 13th day of October, 19—.

_____
(Barnett & McKenzie)
Attorneys for Plaintiff

_____
(Tillman & Queen)
Attorneys for Defendant
Dell Fashions, Inc.

Dated: September 25, 19—.

Stipulation: Figure 1.
Stipulation extending time to answer.

3. Make the caption the same as that on the complaint, except in those cases where the style of the case may be shortened.
4. Type "IT IS HEREBY STIPULATED AND AGREED" in solid caps.
5. When there is more than one stipulation in the same document, type each in a separate paragraph.
6. Type a signature line for each attorney or firm of attorneys who are stipulating. Indicate the party represented by the stipulating attorney, thus: "Attorney for Defendant Richard Brown."
7. Endorse legal back for each copy of stipulation, including the copy for the office, unless instructed to back only the court copy, for purposes of economy.

What to do about stipulations.

1. Prepare the stipulation.
2. Staple original and all copies in endorsed legal backs.
3. Ask the attorney to sign the original and all copies.
4. Deliver them to opposing counsel who is stipulating and ask for his or her signature on the original and your office copy, giving the counsel a copy that was signed in your office.
5. If the stipulation sets a date for future action, *make an entry in the diary.* See REMINDERS.

Stock. See CAPITAL (Stock).

Stock Book. A record of stockholders that contains their names alphabetic-

ally arranged, the residence of each stockholder, and number of shares he or she owns. Also included is the date each stockholder became an owner and the amount paid for the shares.

The stock book must be open for inspection to all stockholders. This right to inspect the stock book is valuable to stockholders who want to change the existing management. They can promptly learn the names and addresses of those entitled to vote for directors and try to influence them into voting for their slate.

Stock Certificate. See CERTIFICATE (of Stock).

Stoppage in Transit. The act of stopping the delivery of goods while they are aboard a carrier.

When a seller, after having shipped goods to a buyer at a distance, learns that the buyer is insolvent, the seller has the right to stop the goods at any time before they reach the buyer. This right is called the right of stoppage *in transitu* ("in transit"). The right continues until the goods are actually delivered to the buyer, or until the carrier tells the buyer that it holds the goods for him. If the seller stops the goods when there is no evidence of the buyer's insolvency, the seller may be compelled to deliver the goods and, in addition, will be held liable for any damage caused to the buyer by the delay.

No special form of notice is necessary to exercise the right of stoppage in transit. The seller simply notifies the carrier of his or her claim, requests it to hold the goods, and forbids their delivery to the purchaser. The seller may sue the carrier for BREACH of Contract or for

DAMAGES if the carrier delivers the goods to the buyer after notice of the seller's claim.

Strike. The act of workmen quitting their employment in a body. The strike and threat of one are the union's most powerful weapons in getting its demands from management.

A *sympathetic strike* is a work stoppage by people not directly involved in the controversy but willing to help another group of workers already on strike.

A *general strike* goes a step further than a sympathetic strike by getting all organized workers within all occupations to go out on strike.

In a *sit-down strike,* the workers remain inside the plant instead of walking out. The continual physical control of the factory by the workers prevents management from hiring replacements.

Subchapter S Corporation. A small corporation that earns limited money and elects to be taxed as an ordinary partnership. Stockholders thereby enjoy limited personal liability and individual taxation.

Subordination. An instrument signed by one having an interest in, or LIEN upon, property declaring that such interest or lien is placed in a lower order or rank than another interest or lien, such as MORTGAGE or LEASE.

Subordination of lease to mortgage. Placing an existing lease in an order or rank lower than that of a new mortgage on a leased property. It sometimes becomes necessary for the owner of leased property to obtain a loan secured by a mortgage on the property. The lender may be unwilling to accept the property as security burdened with the prior lease. The usual procedure is to obtain from the holder of the lease (lessee), for a consideration, a WAIVER of his priority in favor of the new mortgagee. This waiver is known as a "subordination agreement." The agreement may be made between the lessee and the lender (mortgagee); the owner (lessor) is not a necessary party, although in many instances, he or she joins in the agreement as a matter of formality.

Subornation. The crime of procuring another to commit perjury. In legal circles, the expression "*suborning witnesses*" is frequently heard.

Subpoena. The process a COURT uses to assure a person's attendance before it. A subpoena that requires the production of books, papers or documents is called *subpoena duces tecum.* If a person served with a subpoena fails to obey it without reasonable excuse, he or she may be punished for CONTEMPT OF COURT and is liable for the DAMAGES sustained by the aggrieved party.

Subrogation. The substitution of one person in another's place. For example, A's car is insured by an insurance company against collision. A's car is negligently damaged by B. The insurance company pays $550 for repairs to A's car. The insurance company is subrogated to A's position and may prosecute the claim for damages against B. The insurance company would be the *subrogee,* the one who by subrogation acquires the legal rights or claims of another. *A* would be the *subrogor*, the one whose legal rights are acquired by another through subrogation.

Subscribing Witness. See AT-TESTATION.

Subsidiary Corporation. A company in which another CORPORATION (called the *parent corporation*) owns at least a majority of the shares and thus has control.

When a parent corporation appears to have complete control over its subsidiary, the subsidiary is called the parent's *alter ego*. When the *alter ego* doctrine is applied, the dominant corporation may be held liable for the subordinate corporation's NEGLIGENCE.

Substantive Law. The part of the law that creates, defines and regulates rights and duties. Substantive law is opposed to *adjective* or *procedural* law, which provides the method of administering and protecting the rights, duties, and obligations created by substantive law. All statutes of a general nature are substantive law. All CASE LAW, except the decisions interpreting administrative regulations, codes of procedure, and court rules, are substantive law. For example, the right of administration of an estate is substantive; the procedures by which the estate can be administered are adjective law. The line of distinction between the two is narrow and often hard to define.

Substituted Service. See SERV-ICE OF SUMMONS.

Suit on the Judgment. See JUDG-MENT CREDITOR.

Suit Register. The record that a law office keeps of the progress of all of its matters pending in court, whether the matter is a litigated case, a foreclosure, an estate administration proceeding, or a special proceeding. The record saves time that would be required to examine all of the papers in the file. A quick examination of the suit register shows the status of a particular matter, acts as a double check on things to be done in relation to pending cases before term time (see TERM OF COURT).

Physical features of a suit register. The progress record of an action is typed or written on forms designed for the purpose or on plain paper. The form or sheet used depends on where the records are kept. The records are commonly kept in (1) a loose-leaf binder, (2) the file folder, or (3) a portable tray or cabinet.

Loose-leaf binder for the suit register. Either an ordinary three-ring, letter-size binder or a post binder may be used for keeping the suit register. If the record is typed, the former is probably more expedient because the sheets are more easily removed for the purpose of typing the entries. Numerous types of forms for keeping the record are printed by various office supply houses and are on sale at local stationers. These forms are usually designed to fit a special loose-leaf binder, also manufactured by the supply house. Printed forms are not necessary, unless a special binder is used. In an ordinary loose-leaf binder, punched paper of durable quality with reinforced edges is adequate.

File folder used for progress record. Some offices keep progress records in the file folder, either by writing the entries on the folder itself or by typing them on a sheet that is placed in the front of the folder. If the record is kept on a loose sheet, a colored sheet is desirable because it is more easily distinguished from the other papers in the folder. Figure 1 illustrates a sheet appropriate for this purpose.

Portable tray or cabinet for the suit register. A portable cabinet or tray with a visible index is probably the most advantageous facility for keeping the record. The cabinet may be fireproof with a lid that may be locked when the record is not being used. The visible index shows the name of the case, the attorney handling it, and the court index number. (See CLERK OF THE COURT, Index Number.) Celluloid tabs may be used to flag specific cases. The manufacturer of the cabinet or tray also manufactures strips for the index and sheets for typing the record. The sheets are designed for numerous uses and have no printing on them except a ruled space at the left for the dates. They are of heavy stock paper and come in various sizes. Unless a wide carriage machine is available for typing the record, the sheets should be small enough to fit the carriage of a standard machine. The sheets are loose in the pocket provided for them in the cabinet and thus are easily removed for typing entries or for reference. The portable cabinets hold a large number of cases and, therefore, are not appropriate for offices with a light docket unless they are also used to house other records.

How to file the record sheets. The preferable method of filing the record sheets is alphabetically according to the first-named plaintiff, or the decedent in the case of an estate, or the principal corporation or individual named in a special proceeding. In offices with a heavy docket, the estates and special proceedings might be segregated from the litigated cases. Some offices with extremely heavy dockets separate the records according to the court in which the case is pending. When a visible index is used, celluloid tabs of various colors can designate specific courts, if it is desirable to be able to select quickly the cases pending in a particular court.

When and how to open a case in the suit register. A suit register sheet is not opened on every matter in the office—it is opened only on court matters. Therefore, the record is opened when the first paper is filed in court, or when a paper is served on your office, indicating that the case is pending in court. In opening the record, enter on the sheet (1) the court in which the action is pending; (2) the full title of the case, as it appears on the summons and complaint or other first paper filed; (3) nature of the proceeding, that is, "Suit on note," "Divorce," "Petition for letters of administration," and the like, as indicated by the new matter slip (see NEW CASE REPORT); (4) amount, if any, sued for; (5) names, addresses, and telephone numbers of all opposing counsel; (6) name of the attorney in your office who is handling the matter; (7) court index number as soon as available; (8) calendar number, as soon as available. (See DOCKET CALL.)

All of the above information is put at the top of the record sheet. The entries follow, and each entry is dated at the left side of the sheet. Figure 2 illustrates a detailed suit register record.

What to enter. Some offices record

Court _____	HALL and DOBB	OFFICE NAME ____
_____	10 SLATE STREET	_____
DOCKET NO. ____	BOSTON, MASS.	OUR FILE NO ____
SERVICES	_____	ATTACHMENTS
	vs.	

Court _____

DOCKET NO. ____

SERVICES

HALL and DOBB
10 SLATE STREET
BOSTON, MASS.

vs.

OFFICE NAME ____

OUR FILE NO ____

ATTACHMENTS

RESPONSIBLE ATTY. _____
ATTY. TO BE NOTIFIED _____
PLAINTIFFS ATTY. _____,_____,____
DEFENDANT ATTY. _____,_____,____
TRUSTEE ATTY. _____,_____,____

DATE OF WRIT ____
RETURN DAY _____
FORM OF ACTION ____
AD DAMNUM _____
NATURE OF CASE ____
_____

COPY WITHIN	DATE FILED	DESCRIPTION	TRIAL LIST

Suit Register: Figure 1.
Progress record sheet.

	SUPREME COURT—	INDEX NO. 19000-19—

SUPREME COURT—
NEW YORK COUNTY

x ACTION FOR $250,000 FOR BREACH OF

JOHN DOE
CORPORATION,
     Plaintiff,

-against-

RICHARD ROE
CORPORATION,
     Defendant.

: CONTRACT FOR FAILURE TO COMPLETE
: DELIVERY OF JEEPS AND TRUCKS PUR-
: SUANT TO TERMS OF WRITTEN AGREE-
: MENT DATED MAY 26, 19—.
: John Doe, Esq.,   Benson & Benson,
: Attorney for Plaintiff,   Attorneys for Defendant,
: 233 Broadway,   Partner in Charge: Mr. Doe
: New York, N.Y. 10016   Principal Assistant: Mr. Blank
x

19—

July	13	Summons and verified complaint served on defendant.
August	1	Obtained stipulation extending defendant's time to answer or move with respect to complaint to and including August 21, 19—.
	21	Served verified answer to complaint on attorney for plaintiff and obtained "copy received."
	21	Served demand for a verified bill of particulars.
	31	Signed stipulation extending plaintiff's time to serve a verified bill of particulars to and including September 20, 19—.
Sept.	19	Gave "copy received" on plaintiff's verified bill of particulars.
	20	Served note of issue noticing this case for trial for the October 19— Term to be tried by Court with a jury on attorney for plaintiff and obtained "copy received"; filed original with County Clerk of New York County and obtained Index No. 19000-19—; filed copy with Trial Term Calendar Clerk, and obtained Jury Contract Calendar No. 17000.
Oct.,	6	Mr. Blank attended on call of Contract Jury Reserve Calendar and this case was adjourned by consent to the Reserve Calendar of the Contract Jury Calendar for the November 19— Term.
Nov.	10	Mr. Blank attended on call of Contract Jury Reserve Calendar and this case was adjourned by consent to the Reserve Calendar of the Contract Jury Calendar for the February 19— Term.

19—

Feb.	9	Mr. Dee attended on call of Contract Jury Reserve Calendar and requested the Court to set this case down for a day certain because two important witnesses must come from Japan; the Court marked this case for the head of the Ready Day Calendar for trial on March 5, 19—.
March	5	Mr. Dee attended on call of Day Calendar and this case was assigned to Mr. Justice Carter, at Trial Term, Part X.
	5	Mr. Dee reports that a jury was picked and the trial commenced at 2:00 P.M. and is to continue on March 6, 19— at 10:00 A.M.
	6	Mr. Dee reports that the trial went on all day and is to continue on March 7, 19—.
	7	Mr. Dee reports that plaintiff rested, Court reserved decision on motions to dismiss and defendant's case was commenced to be continued on March 8, 19—.
	8	Mr. Dee reports that defendant rested, the usual motions for a directed verdict were made and decisions reserved, both sides summed up to the jury and the Court is to charge the jury on March 9, 19— at 10:00 A.M.
	9	Mr. Dee reports that after the Court's charge, the jury retired, and after four hours deliberation returned a verdict in favor of defendant, the Court denied plaintiff's motions to set the verdict aside and for a new trial, etc.
	12	Entered judgment dismissing plaintiff's complaint with costs as taxed in the sum of $145.00.
	12	Served judgment with notice of entry and copy of bill of costs as taxed on attorney for plaintiff and obtained "copy received."
April	17	Plaintiff paid judgment for costs as taxed amounting to $145.00 and we filed a satisfaction of said judgment.

Suite Register: Figure 2.
Suit register record.

only court papers and orders in the suit register. The office record is then actually a duplicate of the court docket kept by the Clerk of the Court; hence, the name "office docket." Many offices enter all written, formal steps in connection with an action. It is often a matter of practice and judgment about what to enter. You would not enter, "Received phone call from plaintiff's attorney asking when we thought case would would be reached: told him we had no definite estimate." That does not affect the progress of the case. But you would enter, "Served NOTICE OF TRIAL for October 19. . . Term," just as soon as the notice of trial was served on the opposing counsel. The best rule is that you use your own judgment about what actually affects the progress of the action and to enter too much rather than too little. If you are in doubt about the advisability of making an entry, ask the lawyer in charge.

Form and sufficiency of record. In making entries in the suit register, give complete information. Describe the matter entered with particularity, but not in great detail.

1. Date all entries.
2. Avoid abbreviations.
3. When an action is commenced by the service of a summons only, open the record sheet immediately, but the nature and substance of the action cannot be entered until the complaint is received. Enter this information opposite the title as soon as the complaint is received.
4. When an ANSWER or NOTICE of Appearance is served on the office, enter the name of the attorney, his or her address and telephone number, and the party the attorney represents.

5. As soon as the court index number is known, enter it opposite the title. Also enter it on the index tab if a visible index record is kept.

   As a condition precedent to proper filing, the court index or docket number must be placed on every paper that is filed. The individual who files the paper on behalf of the office must get the index number from the Clerk of the Court or from the clerk's docket and give it to you so you can enter it on the record. You should make a practice of checking the suit register weekly for any missing index numbers.

6. Keep the entries opposite the title up to date, including index number, substitutions of attorneys, changes of addresses, office file number, and the like.
7. In describing petitions, orders, and STIPULATIONS, enter a notation about when they were verified, signed, entered, or dated, respectively, and by whom.
8. When entering stipulations, enter, "Obtained stipulation . . ." if the office is granted something by it; enter "Signed stipulation . . ." if the office gives a right. For example, if the office represented the plaintiff, the entry of the stipulation illustrated in figure 1, STIPULATION, would be:

Signed stipulation with Tillman & Owen, dated September 25, 19. . extending time of Dell Fashions, Inc. to answer to October 13, 19. .

If the office represented Dell Fashions, Inc., the entry would read:

Obtained stipulation from Barnett & McKenzie, dated

September 23, 19. ., extending time to answer to October 13, 19.

Some stipulations, for example a stipulation of discontinuance, are both "obtained" and "signed."

9. Enter the name of the attorney from the office who attends motions, calls of calendar at trials, hearings, arguments of appeals, and the like, and the disposition of the respective matters.

10. Enclose in quotation marks any entry from a law journal or similar publication with a reference to the date and page of the publication, because the date of the event is often different from the date upon which the event is announced in the publication.

11. When cases are settled out of court, enter the amounts paid, dates of payment, data concerning exchange of general releases, if any, and the like.

12. When judgment is entered, enter the amount of the judgment, the amount of costs, and payment received, if any.

13. Examine the diary (see REMINDERS) each day for the day just past, to be certain that a report and entry has been made for everything listed there.

Closing the record of a case. Do not close the record of a case in the suit register until you are reasonably certain that no further steps, such as appeal, collecting on a judgment, moving to vacate a judgment, recording a satisfaction, levying execution, and the like, are to be taken by either party. The time to appeal should always have elapsed before the case is closed.

As soon as a case is closed, remove the sheet on that case from the record file and place it in the designated place. This might be another loose-leaf book, or a file cabinet. File the sheets alphabetically according to the first-named plaintiff, or the decedent in the case of an estate, or the principal corporation or individual named in a special proceeding. The closed sheets are kept indefinitely; some law offices have them bound from time to time.

Summary Judgment. An award of victory granted by the COURT to one of the parties without waiting for trial. MOTION for summary judgment must be supported by AFFIDAVIT, a copy of the PLEADINGS, and other available proof to show that there is no issue of fact worthy of trial. The motion for summary judgment will be denied if any party has presented issues that require a trial for settlement. The power to resolve summarily a lawsuit without the expense and trouble of a trial makes summary judgment one of the most practical and useful tools in modern procedure.

Summary Proceeding. A form of legal proceedings in which the established procedure is disregarded, especially in the matter of trial by jury. The term is applied to the process by which a landlord may dispossess a tenant instead of having to resort to eviction, which is a long drawn-out proceeding.

Summons. The first paper that is served on the DEFENDANT, sometimes being served before the preparation of the COMPLAINT. It notifies the person named in the summons that suit is being brought against him or her and commands that person to appear in court or answer the complaint by a certain date. Although the secretary to the plaintiff's attorney prepares the summons, it is generally issued and signed by the CLERK OF THE COURT. The summons consists of the following parts:

1. Caption.
2. Body. This commands the defendant to answer the complaint within the time specified.
3. Signature and seal of the Clerk of the Court. (In New York the plaintiff's attorney signs the summons.)

How to prepare the summons. A printed form of summons (see figure 1) is used, unless there are numerous parties plaintiff or parties defendant.

1. If the name of a court is printed on the form, make certain that it is the court in which the action is being filed.
2. Make an original for the court, a copy for each defendant, and a copy for your file. An extra copy of the summons must be filed in court in those jurisdictions that require an extra copy of pleadings to be filed.
3. The caption is exactly like that of the complaint. List names of all parties in full.
4. If there are numerous parties, type on legal-size paper instead of using a printed form. Copy the printed form exactly, making sure that all punctuation is included, because usually the statutes direct the form of a summons.
5. Put a legal back on a typed summons, so that the affidavit of service can be filled in.

6. Endorse the back of the original summons and of each copy unless the summons is stapled to the complaint. The endorsements need not list all the parties. It is sufficient to show the name of the first plaintiff and the name of the first defendant, with appropriate words indicating that there are others. (See CAPTION.)

What to do about the summons and complaint.

1. Prepare the complaint, and verification when required.
2. Have original complaint signed and verified, after approval by the lawyer.
3. Conform the copies.
4. Prepare summons.
5. Attach copy of summons to each copy of complaint. Place the complaint against the inside of the cover so the VERIFICATION printed on the inside cover will read as a continuation of the complaint. Put the summons on top of the complaint. Do not attach original summons to original complaint.
6. Open case in SUIT REGISTER and make appropriate entry.
7. File original complaint in court, have Clerk of Court issue (sign, seal, and date) original summons, and pay required fee.
8. Conform copies of summons, by filling in date, name of clerk, and seal of court.
9. Make a note of the index number (see CLERK OF THE COURT) assigned by the clerk and put it on all subsequent papers prepared by you in that particular case.
10. Give original of summons, together with copy of summons and copy of

In The Circuit Court of Duval County, Florida At Law

RICHARD JONES AND MARY JONES, his wife,
                                   Plaintiffs____

                    vs.

SMITH & DOUGLAS, INC., a corporation,
                    Defendant_____

Civil Action—
Damages $5,000_____

No. _____ L

Summons at Law

The State of Florida—

To   SMITH & DOUGLAS, INC. _____

_____

You are hereby summoned and required to serve upon ____ Allen S. Brown

_____

plaintiff's attorney, whose address is   321 Main Street, Jacksonville, Florida,

_____

an answer to the complaint which is herewith served upon you within 20 days after service of this summons upon you, exclusive of the day of service. If you fail to do so, judgment by default will be taken against you for the relief demanded in the complaint.

Witness *my hand and the sale of said Court, at Jacksonville, Florida, this*
Sixth   *day of* November *A.D. 19—* _____

Clerk Circuit Court

            BY _____
                Deputy Clerk

_____

Sheriff's Return of Service

Summons: Figure 1.
Printed form of summons.

complaint for each defendant, to process server for service on defendants. (In some jurisdictions, the copies are given to the Clerk of the Court at the time the original summons is issued, and the clerk, in turn, delivers them to the sheriff for service.)

11. The summons illustrated in figure 1 has a space for the sheriff's return, which the sheriff fills in after serving the summons. If a process server is employed to make service, he or she should be instructed to get in touch with the attorney requesting the service as soon as the summons and complaint are served, for the purpose of making affidavit of service. The affidavit should be made on the same day that service is made. If affidavit of service is on a separate sheet, it should have a regular caption, like that on the complaint, but if the affidavit is made on the back of the summons, no caption is necessary.

12. File original summons and proof of service in court. If the summons is not filed within the time permitted by the practice rules, a new summons must be served.

13. Mark on office copy the date service is made and by whom.

14. *Enter in diary* RETURN DAY OF SUMMONS. The period of time begins to run the date the summons is served, not the date it is prepared.

15. The secretary to the lawyer for the defendant must *enter in the diary* the return day of summons. Failure to answer by that date might mean a JUDGMENT BY DEFAULT. See also ALIAS SUMMONS.

Superior Courts. The highest state courts of ORIGINAL JURISDICTION. These courts are usually designated as circuit, district, or superior courts. (In New York the highest court of original jurisdiction is called the Supreme Court.) They have original jurisdiction in the first instance and are the courts where cases not within the jurisdiction of inferior courts are tried originally. They also have appellate jurisdiction over matters arising in inferior courts and, in many states, over probate matters. They control or supervise the lower courts by WRITS of error, appeal, or certiorari.

In some states, superior courts have one or more departments or divisions that have jurisdiction over special matters. For example, the Superior Court of New Jersey has a law division for the trial of actions at law and a chancery division for hearing EQUITY matters; in California, a department of each superior court acts as a probate court. Other states have COURTS OF SPECIAL JURISDICTION to probate matters.

Supplementary Proceeding. When an execution of judgment is returned unsatisfied, the judgment creditor has the right to force the judgment debtor to submit to an examination for the purpose of discovering any assets that may be applied to the payment of the debt. The legal procedure by which the judgment creditor exercises this right is known as a *supplementary proceeding*—it is supplementary to the execution of judgment (see ISSUE OF EXECUTION).

Supreme Appellate Courts. There is only one supreme APPELLATE

COURT in each state. These courts are courts of last resort in their respective states. (In Oklahoma the Criminal Court of Appeals and in Texas the Court of Criminal Appeals are courts of last resort in criminal cases.) The jurisdiction of these courts is appellate (see APPELLATE COURT), their original jurisdiction, if any, being limited to the issuance of writs of MANDAMUS, CERTIORARI, HABEAS CORPUS, and the like.

The highest court in 45 states is designated as the *Supreme Court*. The designations in the other 5 states are as follows:

Maine	Supreme Judicial Court
Maryland	Court of Appeals
Massachusetts	Supreme Judicial Court
New York	Court of Appeals
West Virginia	Supreme Court of Appeals

See AMERICAN COURT SYSTEM; COURTS OF INTERMEDIATE REVIEW; COURTS OF RECORD; COURTS OF SPECIAL JURISDICTION; INFERIOR COURTS; SUPERIOR COURTS; APPEAL (Parties to).

Supreme Court of the United States. The highest judicial tribunal in the government. Every state also has its highest appellate court. For the precise designation of these courts in the 50 states see SUPREME APPELLATE COURTS.

Supreme Court Reports. The opinions of the Supreme Court are published officially in the United States Reports and unofficially in *Supreme Court Reports,* Lawyer's Edition (L.Ed.) and *Supreme Court Reporter.* Supreme Court opinions are also reported in the *United States Law Week.*

Suretyship. See GUARANTY.

Surrender of Lease. An agreement between the landlord and the tenant to terminate the LEASE before its expiration date, followed by delivery of possession of the premises to the landlord. A surrender releases the tenant from liability for rent accruing thereafter. It is the *agreement* between landlord and tenant that distinguishes a surrender from an ABANDONMENT of leased premises by tenant. The agreement need not be in writing, nor need it be in any particular form. No consideration is required to make the agreement binding; the advantage accruing to both parties is sufficient. If the tenant merely abandons the premises, the fact that the landlord accepts the keys does not constitute a surrender.

If the landlord, with tenant's consent, gives a new lease to a stranger during the term of the lease, this is considered a surrender. The making of a new lease between landlord and tenant operates as a surrender of a prior inconsistent lease.

Survey. The process by which the dimensions of a parcel of land are measured and its boundaries, geographical position, and physical details are ascertained. The result is reduced to a pictorial delineation called a map, drawing, or survey. The survey shows the lengths and directions of the boundary lines of the tract surveyed, the location of all buildings and other improvements, and the existence of any encroachment at or above the surface of the land either by or upon adjacent property.

Upon a sale of property, it is always the safer course for the purchaser to obtain a survey. A survey of the land should always be obtained if construction of a building is planned, to make certain that the structure will be built within the lot lines of the property and within the setback lines fixed by ZONING regulations. Even if a previous survey has been made of the property, a new survey is advisable to show conditions existing at the date of sale. A survey may be obtained through a TITLE INSURANCE company.

If a CONTRACT OF SALE provides that the seller may deliver TITLE "subject to survey," or "subject to a state of facts that an accurate survey may show," the purchaser may have to take title even if the survey reveals an encroachment which may render the title unmarketable. A careful purchaser will insist that such a "subject" clause contain the qualifying words "provided the same does not render the title unmarketable." The words "state of facts" refer to any encroachments or projections by or on the property surveyed, such as wall, fences, hedges, cornices, and chimneys, outside of property lines.

A contract of sale may provide that the sale is made subject to a particular survey identified by name of surveyor and date. The purchaser should insist on seeing the survey and have it examined by his or her attorney before accepting the "subject" clause. See also LAND DESCRIPTION.

Sweat Shop. A plant whose employees are overworked and paid low wages in unsanitary or otherwise unfavorable conditions.

"Sworn-To" Clause. See JURAT.

Sympathetic Strike. See STRIKE.

Syndicate. An association of individuals formed to conduct and carry on some particular business transaction, usually of a financial character. A syndicate more nearly resembles a JOINT ADVENTURE than any other business organization. Syndicates in general are temporary associations or firms. They usually terminate automatically when the purpose for which they were formed has been accomplished.

In the securities trade, a *syndicate* is an association of investment bankers formed for the purpose of underwriting the distribution of a new security issue or a block of securities outstanding.

Take-In. In legal work, a dictator will tell the stenographer to "take in" certain material, meaning for her or him to copy it. The "take-in" might be quoted material, from a text or testimony, in which case the take-in is indented and quoted. Or the take-in might be a portion of a printed form or other document, the wording of which is applicable to the document that is being dictated. When the take-in is material of this kind, it follows the rest of the dictation just as if it were original dictation instead of a take-in. See also TYPING, Quotations and Indented Material.

Tax Court Practice. All papers filed with the tax court, including petitions, motions, briefs, and replies, should conform to the "Rules of Practice and Procedure of the United States Tax Court." This pamphlet is sold by the U.S. Government Printing Office, Washington, D.C. 20402. It contains instructions for (1) printed papers, (2) typewritten papers, (3) fastening, (4) captions, (5) signature, and (6) number of copies.

Tax Evasion. The intentional non-payment of taxes. Unlike most crimes, it can be committed wholly by omission. A person is not in DOUBLE JEOPARDY if he or she is tried for committing a crime and later tried for not declaring the profits of the crime as taxable income.

Tax Lien. A claim against REAL PROPERTY that accrues to the taxing agency (municipality, township, city) from taxes that are assessed against the property. If the LIEN is not paid when due, the taxing agency sells the property at a tax sale.

Telegraph. *Domestic Service.* Classes of domestic telegraph service are (1) *fast telegram*—fastest class of service; charge based on minimum of 15 words, with additional charge for each word in excess of 15; (2) *night letter*—delivery made on the morning of the first business day following the day the telegram is sent; charge based on minimum of 100 words with an additional charge for each group of 5 words thereafter, is less than the cost of a 15-word fast telegram; (3) *mailgram*—may consist of 100 words or less, sent at standard Western Union rates plus a special delivery charge. *Automated systems* such as Telex, TWX, and Datagram send messages worldwide, manually or automatically, at low cost. *Money orders,* too, can be transmitted quickly by wire service, nationally and internationally.

How to count charges for domestic messages. No charge is made for the name and address of the addressee or for the name of the sender, but a charge is made for the address of the sender.

The message itself, names of states, counties, and cities are counted according to the number of words they contain. For example, *New York City* is three words; *United States,* two. Running the words together as *Newyork,* does not affect the count. If the names are abbreviated, they count as one word. Thus *NYC* is one word.

Abbreviations that do not contain more than five letters are counted as one word. They should be written without spaces or periods—*COD, UN, FOB.*

If separated by a space, initials are counted as separate words, but if written without spaces, they are counted as one word for each five letters or fraction thereof. Thus *R L* is counted as two words, but *RL* is one word.

Personal names are counted in accordance with the way they are usually written. Thus *Van der Gren* is counted as three words; *Van Dorn,* as two words; and *O'Connell,* as one word.

Mixed groups of letters, figures, affixes, and the characters $, /, &, #, ' (indicating feet or minutes) and " (indicating inches or seconds) are counted at the rate of five characters, or fraction thereof, to the word in messages between points in continental United States and points in Mexico. Thus, "one hundred" is counted as two words, but 100 is counted as one word; $34.50, as one word (the decimal is not counted); 44B42, as one word, but 1000th (six characters) is counted as two words.

In messages sent to Canada and Saint Pierre and Miquelon Islands, each figure, affix, bar, dash, and sign in a group is counted as a word, in determining the charge for the telegram.

Punctuation marks are not charged for, but the words *stop, comma,* and the like are counted.

Compound words that are hyphenated in the dictionary are counted as one word. Thus *son-in-law* is one word.

Paragraphing. Telegrams written in paragraphs are transmitted in paragraphs at no extra cost.

Economies in the use of telegraphic service may be made by considering the urgency of the message and thus the class of service to be used, the time zone in which the addressee is located, and the wording of the message.

How to type a telegram. 1. The number of copies depends upon the requirements of your office. Four is the usual number.

   a. The original for pickup by the telegraph messenger

   b. A carbon copy for confirmation by mail

   c. A carbon copy for the file

   d. A carbon copy for the telegraph account file against which the charges may be checked

2. Check the type of service (e.g., domestic) in the form provided on the telegraph blank. Also type the class of service (e.g., night letter) two spaces above the address.

3. Type the date and hour in the upper right-hand corner.

4. Omit the salutation and complimentary close.

5. Double-space the message.

6. Do not divide a word at the end of a line.

7. Use caps and small letters and punctuate just as you would any other material. Use all caps for code words.

8. In the lower left-hand corner type:

a. The dictator's initials and your initials.

b. Whether the message is to be sent "Charge," "Paid," or "Collect."

c. Address and telephone number of the firm, unless printed on the blank.

9. If the telegram is to be charged, type the name of the charge account in the space provided on the blank.

How to send the same message to multiple addresses. To send the same message to a number of people, type the telegram only once. List the names and addresses on a special sheet obtainable from Western Union (or on a plain sheet). Above the list type, "Please send the attached message to the following 12 (or whatever the number is) addresses."

How to type a telegram when work is in the machine. Always transcribe a telegram as soon as it is dictated. Often a rush telegram will be given when you have other work in the typewriter, but it is not necessary to remove the work to type the telegram. Follow this procedure:

1. Back-feed the paper and carbons that are in the machine until the paper shows a top margin of about 2 inches.

2. Insert the first sheet of the telegram behind the material you are typing, against the paper table, just as if nothing were in the typewriter.

3. To make carbons of the telegram, insert the second sheet of the telegram against the coated side of the carbon paper that is already in the machine. Thus the second sheet of the telegram is between the carbon and the second sheet

of your letter. Do the same for each carbon that is in the typewriter. (A sheet for each carbon in the machine must be inserted to prevent the typing from showing on the carbon copies of the work.) For additional copies, add carbon sheets in the usual manner.

4. Turn the platen knob until the telegram blanks are in position for typing.

5. After typing the message, back-feed until the telegram can be removed from the machine.

6. Forward-feed to the point at which the letter or other work was interrupted and continue with the typing.

International Service. Method of transmitting messages to foreign countries. A message may be sent to any foreign country over either cable or radio facilities by filing the message directly with any of the international telegraph carriers or at any Western Union office. If it is desired that a message go by any specific carrier, the name of the desired route should be typed on the message immediately after the destination. Classes of international messages are (1) *full-rate messages* (FR—standard fast service for messages in plain or secret—code or cipher—language); and (2) *letter telegrams* (LT—sometimes called cable letters or radio letters), an overnight service designed for messages of some length that are not of sufficient urgency to warrant full-rate dispatch. Letter telegrams may be written only in plain language; however, a registered CODE ADDRESS or signature may be used. The charge for a letter-telegram is approximately one-half of the charge per word for a full-rate message.

Code address. An address in code registered with international telegraph carriers to obviate the expense incurred in using full address and signature in international cable or radio messages. Code addresses may be registered with a nearby Central Bureau of Registered Addresses with international carriers such as ITT, RCA, WUI (Western Union International), or French Cable.

Radiophoto. This service covers the transmission of photographs by radio. Among the types of material suitable for transmission are financial statements, machine drawings, production curves, fashion designs, architectural designs, typewritten matter, printed matter, affidavits, contracts, signatures, and business and legal papers of all kinds. Mackay Radio and RCA offer this service.

Overseas Telex service provides teleprinter connections to more than 150 countries. Some rental arrangements such as *leased channel* offer an economical transmission service for large-volume users. Messages can also be sent by Western Union, ITT, or RCA to and from ships by *shore-to-ship* and *ship-to-shore radio.*

How to count charges for international messages. A charge is made for the name and address of the *addressee.* The place of destination, including the name of the country when it is necessary, is counted as one word regardless of the number of letters it contains. The names of persons or of a street may be run together and counted as 15 letters, or fraction thereof, to the word. As an example, STJAMESSTREET is one word, but St. James Street is counted as three words. Registered code address may be used. A charge is made for each word in the signature and address of the *sender,* but the message need not be signed or it may be signed with a code signature.

In *plain-language messages,* each word containing 15 letters or less is counted as one word; each word containing more than 15 letters is counted at the rate of 15 letters to the word. *Secret-language words* (code or cipher) are counted at the rate of 5 characters or fraction thereof, to the word. A *mixed group of figures,* or of figures and letters, is counted at the rate of 5 characters or fraction therof, to the word. A *dollar or cents sign* or a *pound sterling mark* counts as a separate word, but the fraction bar, commas, and decimal points may be grouped with the figures and letters. They then count as 1 character in the group of which they are part. Thus, 8,976, 18.54, or 74/5 are counted as one word each, but $3.25 and 25¢ are counted as two words each. Commercial *abbreviations,* such as *FOB* and *CIF,* are counted at the rate of one word for each 5 figures or letters or fraction thereof. Abbreviations contrary to common usage may not be sent. *Punctuation marks,* hyphens, and apostrophes are not transmitted except when expressly requested, and then they are charged for as one word each. A charge is also made for the telegraph company's code word.

Telephone. *Telephone courtesy.* The following simple rules constitute the basis of courteous and efficient telephone usage:

1. Answer calls promptly.

2. When you leave your desk, arrange for someone to take your calls.

3. Keep pad and pencil handy.

4. In asking a caller to wait, say, "Will you please hold the line while I get the information," and wait for the reply. When you return to the telephone, thank the

caller for waiting. If it will take you some time to get the information, offer to call back.

5. If you have to put down the receiver, do it gently.

6. Do not interrupt and make the caller repeat something because of your inattention.

7. Do not talk while smoking or eating.

8. When you have finished talking, say, "Thank you, Mr. Smith," or "Good-bye" pleasantly and replace the receiver gently. Let the caller hang up first.

Placing calls for the lawyer. Many employers prefer to place their own calls. However, if you place the call, get the person called on the wire before connecting your employer. Assume that you are calling Mr. Wilson for the lawyer, Mr. Rogers. When you get Mr. Wilson's secretary on the wire, ask "Is Mr. Wilson there, for Mr. Rogers?" Mr. Wilson's secretary will put her employer on and trust to your good judgment and care to see that Mr. Rogers comes on the line promptly. (When *she* calls, the courtesy is reciprocated.) When Mr. Wilson comes on the line, say to him, "Here is Mr. Rogers, Mr. Wilson," and establish the connection between the two men at once.

You must be extremely careful not to keep the person called waiting for the lawyer to take the call. On the other hand, it is your job to see that the lawyer does not hold the phone needlessly. When calling a person whose secretary is cooperative and dependable, there is no difficulty because the employers can be connected simultaneously.

There is an exception to this procedure. If you call a close friend or a person to whom deference is due by the lawyer, connect the lawyer as soon as the secretary is reached at the other end of the line. Tell the lawyer that the person he or she is calling will be on the line immediately and let the lawyer receive the call direct. Some secretaries follow this procedure at all times.

Answering calls for the lawyer. If a secretary calls and says that her employer wants to speak with a certain lawyer in the office, ask her to wait a moment and announce the call to the lawyer. Say to the secretary, "One moment, please," and tell the lawyer that "Mr. Wilson of ABC is calling." The lawyer will then pick up the phone and wait until Mr. Wilson is connected with him. Or perhaps the other secretary has learned that you are cooperative and she puts Mr. Wilson on the line simultaneously.

Making notes of incoming calls. It is important that the lawyer be informed of every call that comes in, whether the caller leaves a message or not. Do not depend upon memory for this, but make a note immediately. If the office does not have printed forms for this purpose, you might suggest that some be ordered.

Toll calls. A record must be kept of every long distance or toll call placed from the office. These calls are usually made on behalf of a client and are charged to his account. Always ask the operator to tell the amount of the charge and make a memorandum immediately. Some offices use forms to record such information, showing who was called, regarding what, when, and the amount of the call. After the details are filled in, the lawyer who made the call initials it or the secretary may have the authority to initial it. The form is then sent to the bookkeeper. If you keep the books, have a folder for telephone call memoranda, against which you can check the bill and make the charges to clients' accounts.

Client's telephone calls. Clients frequently ask permission to place telephone calls. Quite often calls are toll calls and the question of payment for them might present an embarrassing situation. The thoughtful client immediately suggests payment, but many excellent clients simply do not think about payment. Keep a record of these calls and bill the client for them, unless special circumstances make it more diplomatic for the law firm to charge the calls to overhead.

Conference calls. Conference telephone service makes it possible for a lawyer to be connected simultaneously with a number of other stations. No special equipment is required. If the lawyer needs to discuss a contract provision, for example, with three other people (or any number up to 10) who are in different cities, by means of a conference call he or she and the other persons can talk back and forth over long-distance as though they were all grouped around a conference table.

The caller asks the operator to be connected with the Conference Operator and explains the setup desired.

Mobile telephone service. This service makes it possible to interconnect mobile units, such as cars, trucks and passenger trains, with the general telephone system. Direct telephone communication with mobile units eliminates mileage and time required by special trips, thus saving operational costs. Radio equipment is installed on the mobile unit. Equipment may be rented from the telephone company or provided by the owner of the mobile unit.

Special services. Large firms may use WATS (wide area telephone service),

402

which provides access lines to customers on a nationwide dialing network. *Tie lines* connect offices in different locations nationally or locally. *Data-Phone Service* permits transmission of information such as photographs over telephone lines. *Teletypewriters* send messages at high speed nationally and internationally. Some firms use switching systems to channel calls throughout the firm, for example, *PBX, Centrex,* and *console.*

Screening calls. A lawyer usually expects the secretary to screen calls. A polite way of asking who is calling is, "May I tell Mr. Rogers who is calling?" Or, "May I ask who is calling?" A legitimate caller seldom objects to giving his or her name.

If the caller does not want to give his name, you have the right to insist, politely but firmly, that he do so. As a matter of fact, you have no right to put through calls without first screening them, when this is expected of you, and without learning that the lawyer is willing to talk. If the caller insists upon withholding his name, you might say, very politely, "I'm very sorry, but Mr. Rogers has someone with him at the moment. If you'd rather not give your name, I'd suggest you write to him and mark your letter 'personal'. I'll be glad to see that he gets it promptly."

Finding the purpose of a call. A secretary is usually expected to find out why a person wants an appointment with her employer. This frequently poses a delicate problem in the law office, because the callers are often reluctant to disclose the nature of their legal business. However, knowledge of what the client wants frequently enables the secretary to save considerable time, not only for the lawyer but also for the prospective client. This situation is illustrated by the following conversation between a secretary and Mr. Wilson, the caller:

Secretary: Rogers & Williams.
(The practice in answering the
telephone varies. In some offices, the practice is to answer
the telephone with the number.)
Mr. Wilson: This is James
Wilson. I'd like an appointment
to see Mr. Rogers, please.
Secretary: I'm Jane Wright,
Mr. Rogers' secretary, and I'll
be happy to arrange an appointment for you. What date and
time would you like to see Mr.
Rogers?

Informing the caller that you are the
lawyer's secretary gives him an opening
to tell the nature of his business. But this
caller did not respond in the manner the
secretary desired.

Mr. Wilson: I would like to see
him on Tuesday afternoon, say
around 2 o'clock.
Secretary: Mr. Rogers will be
busy part of the afternoon on
Tuesday, Mr. Wilson. About
how long will you need for your
appointment?

This gives the caller another opportunity to state the nature of his business,
but Mr. Wilson is rather elusive.

Mr. Wilson: I won't need more
than an hour of his time. How
about two to three?

Now comes the difficult part. The secretary must find out what he wants and
she must do it diplomatically. The "voice
with a smile" is especially important
here.

Secretary: In connection with a
client's visit, Mr. Wilson, it's often necessary for Mr. Rogers
to have certain forms or information available. So I'll have

everything ready for your appointment on Tuesday, could
you give me a general idea about
the nature of your business? I
don't need to know any of the
details, of course, just a brief
statement.

By giving him a good reason for the
inquiry and assuring him of not being interested in details, the secretary has
asked him, in a gracious and courteous
manner, for a statement concerning his
appointment.

Perhaps he says he wants a divorce.
The secretary knows that Mr. Rogers will
not handle the case but that it will be
turned over to a junior member of the
firm.

Secretary: Mr. Davis of this office usually handles those matters and confers with Mr.
Rogers when necessary. It
would really be better for you to
see Mr. Davis on Tuesday. If
that's satisfactory, I'll arrange
the appointment with Mr. Davis
instead of Mr. Rogers.

Or perhaps Mr. Wilson says that he
has a small collection matter he would
like Mr. Rogers to handle. The office
does not handle collections except for retainer clients.

Secretary: I'm sorry, Mr.
Wilson. As much as Mr. Rogers
would like to help you, he
doesn't handle collections.
However, Mr. Robert Ames, a
young member of the Bar located in this building, would be
happy to handle the matter for
you. Would you like his telephone number?

There are innumerable situations, but
by exercising discretion and diplomacy,
you will soon be able to handle them all.

A caller who wants advice. Lawyers seldom handle a legal question in a brief telephone conversation. When a caller asks for advice by telephone, suggest that he or she make an appointment. Explain that the lawyer will need to examine the problem in greater detail to be of help. If the caller asks for *your* advice, explain that you are not able to answer such questions and recommend that the caller consult an attorney. Similarly, leave the matter of quoting fees to the lawyer and, again, recommend to the caller that he or she talk to the lawyer about such matters.

An irate client. Occasionally a client who is annoyed about something telephones while the lawyer is out. It is usually advisable to avoid making explanations. Simple tell the caller that you will ask the lawyer to call as soon as he returns—and make sure you tell the lawyer about the call.

Temporary Alimony. See ALIMONY.

Temporary Injunction. See PROVISIONAL REMEDIES.

Tenancy by the Entirety. An estate held by husband and wife by virtue of TITLE acquired by them jointly after marriage. Upon the death of either spouse, his or her interest automatically passes to the other by survivorship. A tenancy by the entirety cannot be terminated without the consent of both parties. Thus neither spouse can defeat the right of survivorship. A tenancy by the entirety cannot be terminated without the consent of both parties. Thus neither

spouse can defeat the right of survivorship by MORTGAGE or conveyance without the consent of the other. The courts do not look with disfavor upon a tenancy by the entirety as they do upon a JOINT TENANCY. Not all states recognize tenancy by the entirety, or "tenancy by the entireties," as it is sometimes called. *See also* TENANCY IN COMMON.

Tenancy in Common. If two or more persons hold an estate by separate and distinct titles, with unity of possession only, the estate is called *tenancy in common.* The tenants in common may acquire their TITLE at different times, from different sources, and have different degrees of interest in the estate, but their right of possession is common. Upon the death of one of the tenants in common, his or her interest passes to heirs and legatees, and not to the other tenants in common. *See* TENANCY BY THE ENTIRETY; JOINT TENANCY.

Tender. A contract term that refers to an unconditional offer to perform along with the ability to carry out the offer.

Termination of Lease. The dissolution of a LEASE by (1) *performance,* that is, expiration of the lease at the end of its term; (2) *agreement* (see SURRENDER OF LEASE); or (3) *breach* (see EVICTION and FORFEITURE OF LEASE). The tenant usually watches the termination date of the lease so he or she will not be a holdover tenant. The tenant removes all property by the time the lease expires. The landlord, as a rule, makes a careful physical examination of the premises when the lease terminates. The landlord checks to see if the premises have been left in good order, if there has been unusual damage, and if the utilities work. Some leases specifically allow the landlord to inspect the premises before termination and to show the premises to prospective tenants. See also ABANDONMENT.

Term of Court. The designated period prescribed by law during which a court may sit to transact business. This period may also be called *term time.* The periods during the term when the court actually sits are known as *sessions.* The terms are usually designated by the time they commence, for example, *November term.* A term of court is also referred to in various jurisdictions as *general term* or *trial term,* meaning the term during which cases are tried.

Testacy. The state or condition of leaving a WILL at one's death opposed to "intestacy." see INTESTATE.

Testamentary Capacity. The possession of sound mind, disposing memory, and proper age to make a WILL disposing of real and personal property. Each state has its own minimum age requirement to make a will.

Testator. A person who leaves a WILL that is in force at death. Having left a will, the person is said to have died *testate.* See also INTESTATE; PROBATE; LETTERS OF ADMINISTRATION.

Testatrix. Feminine form of TESTATOR.

Testimonium Clause. The closing declaration by the parties to a legal instrument that their signatures are attached in testimony of the preceding part of the instrument. The testimonium clause, which is at the close of the instrument, should not be confused with the ATTESTATION CLAUSE. The testimonium clause relates to the parties themselves, whereas the witness or attestation clause relates to those who sign the paper as witnesses, not as parties to the instrument.

Quite often, the testimonium clause will guide you in setting up the signature lines. It will indicate (1) what parties are to sign the instrument; (2) what officer of a corporation is to sign; (3) whether the instrument is to be sealed; and (4) whether a CORPORATE SEAL is to be attested. For example, from the following clause, which is a form commonly used, it is evident that the president of the corporation is to sign, that the SEAL is to be affixed, and that the secretary of the corporation is to attest the seal.

IN WITNESS WHEREOF, Alvin Corporation has caused its corporate seal to be hereto affixed, and attested by its secretary, and these presents to be signed by its president, the 21st day of September, 19. . . .

On the other hand, from the following clause, also commonly used, it is evident that the instrument is not to be sealed.

IN TESTIMONY WHEREOF, the parties hereto have hereunto set their hands the day and year first above written.

Figure 1 is an illustration of a testimonium clause, signature and seal for individuals, witnessed.

Testimony. Evidence given by a witness under oath. See also DEPOSITION.

Tickler-Card File. See FILING.

Time Charter. See CHARTER-PARTY.

Time Differentials. Variations in standard time in different parts of the world. If one time zone is on daylight savings time, the normal differential that exists between that zone and another when both are on standard time is increased or decreased by one hour.

Time Table on an Appeal. A record that the legal secretary maintains of the dates certain steps must be taken by the lawyer when a case is up on APPEAL. The rules of the APPELLATE COURT require that an appeal must be perfected according to a strict time table. It is your duty to make diary entries (see RE-MINDERS) of the schedule so there will be no slip-up on the part of your office. You should also note the progress of the appeal in the SUIT REGISTER. The rules of some courts provide for return days of appeals, just as they do for PLEADINGS. Other courts consider the date upon which the record on appeal is filed as the date from which the time for filing motions and briefs will run. You can get the appropriate time table from the reviewing court's rules, or the lawyer will give it to you. Dates by which the following steps must be taken should be entered in the diary:

1. Filing notice of appeal by appellant.
2. Assignment of errors and instructions by appellant for making up the transcript of the record.
3. Filing of additional instructions by appellee.
4. Filing of record on appeal in reviewing court.
5. Appellee's motion to quash or dismiss an appeal.
6. Hearing of motions.
7. Filing of appellant's BRIEF.

IN WITNESS WHEREOF, the parties hereto have hereunto set their hands

and seals, the day and year first above written.

In the Presence of:

_____ L.S.

_____

_____ L.S.
Parties of the First Part

_____

_____ L.S.
Party of the Second Part

Testimonium Clause: Figure 1.
Signature and seal for individuals,
witnessed.

8. Filing of appellee's brief.
9. Filing of appellant's reply brief.

Title. All of the elements that prove ownership. Title to REAL PROPERTY is the means whereby a person's right to the property is established, the means whereby the owner has the legal and just possession of his property.

Equitable title. A person's *right* to obtain absolute ownership of property to which another has title under the laws. (See MORTGAGE.)

Evidence of title. Proof that a seller has good title to property to be conveyed may be evidenced in any one of the following ways: (1) TITLE INSURANCE, (2) ABSTRACT OF TITLE, (3) CERTIFICATE of Title, and (4) TORRENS SYSTEM. Local custom generally determines which kind of evidence of title will be required upon a sale of REAL PROPERTY. Title insurance is customary in urban centers. An abstract of title and opinion is widely used in rural areas in the Middle West. The certificate of title is popular in the southern states. The Torrens system is used in a few localities throughout the United states.

Broker's duties with respect to title. In many states (New York included), a broker is under no obligation to ascertain whether his or her PRINCIPAL has good title to the property. When the principal employs the broker to sell some property, it is implied that the principal will furnish a good and marketable title to the property. The broker is entitled to a commission even if the transaction is not consummated because of a defect in title, unless the broker's contract of employment makes the commission dependent upon consummation of the transaction.

A broker may apply for title examination and insurance in behalf of the principal or prospect and direct that the "title report" be delivered to the broker directly. When the report is delivered, the broker should examine it at once and see that the seller clears any OBJECTION TO TITLE disclosed in the report; otherwise CLOSING TITLE may be delayed, or the deal may fall through completely. See also OPINION OF TITLE.

Title Closing. See CLOSING TITLE.

Title Insurance. A CONTRACT by a title insurance company guaranteeing to make good to the beneficiary any loss, up to a fixed amount, sustained through defects in title to real property. Title insurance is also known in some localities as "title insurance policy," "title guaranty policy," and "guaranty title policy." A title company issuing its policy of insurance agrees to indemnify the beneficiary against any loss he or she may sustain by reason of any defects in title not enumerated as "exceptions" in the policy. These defects may be (1) discoverable defects that are disclosed by the public records, or (2) hidden defects, such as forgery of a DEED in the chain of title. Some title insurance also guarantees that the title is marketable, and the title insurance company agrees to defend, at its own expense, any action attacking the title based on a defect in the title insured.

Title Search. A thorough investigation of the documented ownership of property, and liens or encumbrances against the property, as listed in the public records. It is customary to have a title search whenever real property is sold, mortgaged, or involved in litigation. For example, title should be searched between the date of the contract of sale and the date of closing title. This gives the seller enough time before the closing to clear up any objections raised by the title searcher. The seller, for example, may have to clear the record of an old mortgage that had been paid; procure a correction deed to correct an error in a previous deed; prepare an AFFIDAVIT that he or she is not a person with a similar name against whom there is a judgment of record, and so on.

A title search need not go back beyond the previous point of title guarantee, since the title company making the previous search guarantees good title up until that point. See also TITLE INSURANCE; ABSTRACT OF TITLE; CERTIFICATE of Title; TORRENS SYSTEM; TITLE.

Torrens System. A system of registering TITLE to REAL PROPERTY, so called because Sir Robert Torrens devised it. Under the system, a person or persons in whom the FEE SIMPLE is vested, either in law or in EQUITY, may apply to have the land placed on the register of titles. After certain legal formalities are complied with, a certificate of registration is issued, and the registered owner has good title to the property. The object is to have a system of registration that accurately determines the ownership of land and every LIEN and claim upon it; the title registered is absolutely conclusive. It is not necessary to go behind the registry to effect transfer after the first registration. Many states permit registration of title in the Torrens system, but in only a few states is the system used to any extent.

Tort. A civil wrong inflicted otherwise than by a BREACH of Contract. Elements of tort are (1) a wrongful act or omission to obey the law, and (2) an injury to some person. Tort gives the injured party the right to sue for any resulting damage. Persons (including minors) and corporations are liable for torts. Some of the more common torts are NEGLIGENCE, ASSAULT AND BATTERY, CONVERSION, FALSE IMPRISONMENT, and LIBEL AND SLANDER. *Example of tort:* A visitor to a department store (even one having no expressed intention to make a purchase but intending merely to examine the merchandise) can recover damages from the proprietor for injuries caused by the negligent maintenance of the store premises. See also CIVIL LAW; CIVIL COURT.

Tort-Feasor. One who commits a TORT.

Totten Trust. Money deposited in a savings bank "in trust for" another person. A savings bank trust may be revoked by the depositor at will unless he or she acts in a way that clearly shows the intent to make the trust irrevocable. Such an intent will be evidenced by unconditional delivery of the passbook to the beneficiary or by notice to the beneficiary or bank that the trust is absolute. A savings bank trust is also called a *Totten trust,* the name being derived from the precedent-making case *Matter of Totten,* which was decided in New York.

Towage. The pulling or pushing of one vessel by another. Ore and grain are commonly transported in barges pulled, or in some cases, pushed by towboats, also called tug boats.

To Wit. That is to say.

Township, See LAND DESCRIPTION, Section and Township.

Trademark. A mark, symbol, or design that is used to distinguish a particular make of merchandise or an individual service. Registration of a trademark with the United States Patent Office is not obligatory, for a trademark rightfully belongs to the first person who has used it.

Registration does not automatically protect the owner from litigation. Once the trademark has been registered, the Patent Office is empowered to refuse the registration of infringing ideas, but the owner has to bring suit to restrain the use by another who has unlawfully appropriated his trademark.

Certificates of registration covering trademarks remain in force for 20 years, subject to cancellation at the end of 6 years unless the registrant, within 1 year preceding the expiration of such 6-year period, files an AFFIDAVIT showing that the mark is still in use, or showing that the nonuse is due to special circumstances, and not due to any intention to abandon the mark.

Trade Secrets. The formulas, manufacturing processes, and ideas used by a particular business to give it an advantage over its competition. The court reads into every contract of employment an implied term that the employee will not disclose to another, or use for his or her own benefit, trade secrets learned in the course of employment. If the employer feels that trade secrets are in danger of being appropriated, he or she may ask the court to issue an INJUNCTION to forbid the disclosure and use of these trade secrets.

Tramp. A vessel that does not follow a fixed itinerary or schedule and is available to carry cargo to any port. See also LINER.

Transfer Tax. A tax imposed by some states on the conveyance of real estate. The tax is paid by the seller. Some states require documentary stamps to be placed on the warranty deed to show evidence that the tax has been paid. At one time the federal government imposed a revenue tax on real estate conveyances that required that documentary stamps be purchased and placed on the deed. The federal government no longer collects this tax.

Travel. *Travel agency.* Many large firms have an agency make all travel reservations for domestic business trips as well as foreign trips. A firm may open an account with an agency and be billed once a month, thus avoiding the nuisance of paying for numerous tickets throughout the month.

FROM	TO	VIA	EST DATE & TIME	ARRIVE	ACCOMMODATION	HOTEL
N.Y.	Boston	New Haven	5/6—11:30P	5/6—5:15A	Car 106 Room M Train 467	Parker House
Boston	N.Y.	Eastern	5/8—3:30P	5/8—4:45P	Flight #633	Home
N.Y.	Washing.	Eastern	5/13—8:30A	5/13—9:47A	Flight #431	Shoreham
Washing.	Atlanta	Eastern	5/15—2:50P	5/15—7:32P	Flight #565	Atlanta-Biltmore
Atlanta	Cleveland	Eastern	5/19—5:50P	5/19—10:32P	Flight #732	Carter Hotel
Cleveland	Chicago	United	5/22—6:10P CST	5/22—7:10P	Flight #501	Stevens Hotel
Chicago	New York	United	5/28—12:00N	5/28—4:00P	Flight #622	Home

All Standard Time one hour earlier than Daylight Time.

Checking Out Time—3:00 P.M.

Travel: Figure 1. *Travel itinerary.*

The American Society of Travel Agents, Inc. (ASTA) has members in the principal cities of the United States and Canada. There are, of course, many reliable agents who are not members of ASTA, but the code of ethics of this association is high and its members, therefore, are dependable and efficient.

Itinerary. The itinerary of a business trip shows (1) point of departure, (2) points of arrival, (3) name of railway or airline, (4) date and time of departure from each point, (5) date and time of arrival at each point, (6) train or flight number, and (7) hotels at which the traveller is stopping. The itinerary should be prepared similar to figure 1. It should be typed on durable paper in triplicate: a copy for the employer, a copy for the family, and a copy for you. Additional copies should be made if anyone else in the organization needs the information shown by the itinerary.

Credit cards. A credit card allows the holder to be billed for travel arrangements and services, obviating the necessity for payment in cash. The charge for travel tickets, hotel accommodations, car rental, and many other travel services are billed by itemized monthly statement. Where services are involved, the statement is accompanied by a *record of charge* made at the time the service is completed. This record of charge shows the date and items of purchase, the signature of the purchaser, and the name and address of the service establishment.

You should check the items of the record of charge signed by your employer against the itemized monthly statement received. You should also make certain that any travel ticket cancellations have been properly credited to your employer's account.

Hotel reservations. Information necessary to make a hotel reservation includes the name of the person for whom the reservation is to be made, the time of arrival and approximate time of departure, and the type of accommodations required. The reservation can be made by telephone, telegraph, or letter depending upon how soon it is needed. The type of accommodation desired should always be given in the request for a reservation.

Confirmation of a hotel reservation in writing or by wire should always be requested; a confirmation by wire is usually sent collect. The confirmation should be attached to the copy of the itinerary the lawyer takes along.

Plane reservations. A plane reservation may be made by telephoning *Reservations* at the desired airline or through a travel agency. Information necessary to make a reservation includes (1) point of departure and destination, (2) date desired, (3) time of departure, (4) airline and flight number. The secretary to a lawyer does not ordinarily leave the selection of flight, route, and the like to the airline representative or travel agent but might ask for suggestions if it is not possible to get the desired reservation. The airline representative making the reservation at the point of departure will follow through on reservations for the entire trip. In making any reservation, always request confirmation—by wire if time is short.

Goodwill of the transportation companies is kept by the prompt cancellation of any space that is not going to be used. As the reservation is usually made locally, it may be canceled by phone. A reservation for a return flight for stages of an interrupted flight is not held if the traveler does not confirm the reservation within a certain number of hours before his flight is to be resumed.

Train reservations. Train travel can be arranged through travel agents or by telephone with the railroads themselves. Amtrak and other agents need to know (1) name and position of person desiring reservation; (2) accommodation desired; (3) point of departure and destination; (4) date and time; (5) name of train, if known; (6) arrangement for delivery of tickets; (7) confirmation; (8) arrangement for payment. Again, request immediate confirmation of any reservations. If you must cancel, notify the railroad immediately.

Refunds. A brief statement giving the necessary facts is the best way to secure a prompt refund for unused travel tickets. Here is a recommended pattern to follow in returning a ticket, after cancellation has been made by phone.

1. Enclose and describe the ticket, giving ticket number, accommodation, travel points, time, and date.

2. Tell when canceled.

3. Ask for refund, stating amount if it is known.

4. State to whom refund should be made.

If the lawyer is traveling at the firm's expense and wants the refund made to the firm and sent to his or her attention, it is better to write the letter in the lawyer's name.

Foreign travel. When a lawyer plans a business or pleasure trip to a foreign country, it is advisable to make arrangements through an accredited travel service.

A travel agent should be told the number in the party, names, ages, sex, and, if the trip includes a foreign country, citizenship. Also, he or she should be told where the party wants to go, dates of departure and return, mode and class of travel, and, if the expense of the trip is important, the approximate amount that can be spent. The travel agent will be able to advise about the classes of travel and rates on a particular steamship or airline and on the trains in the foreign countries and recommend hotels to conform to a budget.

What the travel service will do. The following is some of the assistance that travel agents are able to give:

1. Prepare and submit tentative itinerary, which can be changed or adjusted.

2. Make all travel, hotel reservations, and sight-seeing arrangements for the entire trip.

3. Tell what documents are necessary, such as passport, health and police certificates, and how to get them. The travel service will get them for a client unless a personal appearance is necessary.

4. Supply, in exchange for dollars, a small amount of currency of the country to be visited, for tips, taxi fares, and the like. It will also help the traveler get a letter of credit or traveler's checks and to arrange insurance.

5. Advise as to all regulations, such as restrictions on currency and customs requirements.

6. Have a foreign correspondent meet the traveler on arrival, take care of his or her baggage, and see him or her through customs.

Passports and visas. An applicant for a passport must appear in person at the nearest agent of the Passport Office, Department of State, or to a clerk of a federal court or a state court authorized by law to naturalize aliens. The travel agent will indicate whether a visa is required, or the lawyer can inquire at the consulates of the countries to be visited. Generally, the passport must be presented at the consulate and a visa form filled out. Sometimes personal appearance of the applicant is required.

Customs information. Anyone going to a foreign country should know in advance what the United States customs laws and regulations are with regard to purchases made in a foreign country and brought into the United States. A competent travel agent will usually supply this information, as well as details about customs requirements in countries to be visited. But whether or not a travel service is used, it is advisable to send for *United States Customs Information for Passengers from Overseas.* If the traveler is going to visit Western Hemisphere nations, he should send for *Customs Hints for Returning Americans—Visitors from Canada, Cuba, Mexico and Other Western Hemisphere Nations.* These pamphlets are available from the United States Treasury Department, Bureau of Customs in Washington, D.C.

Trespasser. One on the premises without the permission of the owner. There is no duty owed to the trespasser to keep the premises safe or to warn the trespasser of defects. Of course, there is a duty to refrain from willful, wanton harm. See INVITEE; LICENSEE; NEGLIGENCE; ATTRACTIVE NUISANCE.

Triplicate Original. See TYPING.

Trust. A holding of property subject to the duty of applying the property, the income from it, or the proceeds for the benefit of another, as directed by the person creating the trust. A trust is created when *A* transfers property to *X*, the trustee, and *X* undertakes to apply the property and income from it for the purposes in the manner directed by *A*. The elements of an ordinary trust are (1) the trustor (also called settlor, donor, or grantor), who furnishes the property to be put in trust; (2) the subject matter or property that is put in trust (called the trust principal, corpus, or res); (3) the trustee, who holds the property and administers the trust; and (4) the beneficiaries, for whose benefit the trust exists. A trust may be created by will (testamentary trust) or by deed (*inter vivos* or living trust). A man may put property in trust, the income to go to his wife while she lives, the principal to go to their children upon the wife's death. In these situations, the wives would be *income beneficiaries* (or "equitable life tenants") and the children would be remaindermen. (See LIFE ESTATE.)

Trust Deed. An agreement (sometimes called "trust agreement" or "trust indenture") between a *corporation* and a *trustee* who serves as a "guardian" of bondholders' interests. It sets forth all the terms and conditions of a bond issue, and the rights, powers, and duties of the parties to the BOND ISSUE. These parties are the corporation that borrows the money, the trustee through whom the corporation deals with the bondholders, and the bondholders. The bond and the deed of trust constitute the bondholders' contract with the corporation. See also INDENTURE; CORPORATE MORTGAGE BOND; DEED OF TRUST.

Trustee. See TRUST: BANKRUPTCY.

Trustee in Bankruptcy. See BANKRUPTCY.

Trust Funds. See ACCOUNTING.

Trust Indenture. See TRUST DEED.

Trust, Spendthrift. A trust created to provide a fund for the maintenance of a beneficiary and at the same time to secure it against his or her improvidence or incapacity.

Typeface. The design of a style of type letter. Typefaces are usually known by the name of the designers, for example, Bodoni and Garamond.

Following are some well-known typefaces and characteristics of type:

This type is BODONI BOOK.
Bodoni Book is an easy-to-read typeface. It is particularly suitable for books. The headline here is set in a bold face. *This sentence is set in a medium italic face.*

This type is CENTURY EXPANDED.
Century Expanded is a broad typeface. Even its medium and italic faces give a bold impression. The headline here is set in a bold face. ***This sentence is set in a bold italic face.***

This type is GARAMOND.
Garamond is one of the older, well-known, and popular typefaces. It has graceful and pleasing characteristics. The headline here is set in a bold face. *This sentence is set in a medium italic face.*

This type is SOUVENIR.
Souvenir is a heavy typeface with strong characteristics. Its clean, bold appearance makes it appealing for a variety of uses. The headline here is set in a bold face. ***This sentence is set in a demibold italic face.***

This type is TIMES ROMAN.

Times Roman is another widely used and popular typeface. It has some of the same pleasing and graceful characteristics found in Garamond type. The headline here is set in a bold face. *This sentence is set in a medium italic face.*

This type is NEWS GOTHIC.

News Gothic is a sans serif typeface. This means it lacks the strokes found at the edges of serif letters, such as those characteristic of Garamond type. The headline here is set in a bold face. This sentence is set in a medium condensed face.

Boldface (b.f.). A heavy-face type, used principally for side and center headings, emphasis, short quotations, display lines, and display headings. **This is boldface type.** A wavy line under the word or words indicates that it is to be set in boldface.

Lightface (l.f.). Any typeface with lines fine enough to give a light impression when printed, in contrast to boldface. Lightface, in which this book is set, is the type seen in print generally.

Leading. The white space between the lines of type.

Point. A type measurement. A point is one-twelfth of a pica. Type and the space between lines (leading) are measured in points.

Pica. 1. A printer's measure. There are approximately 6 picas to an inch and 12 points to a pica.

2. A size of type used on typewriters, slightly larger than elite type. Measured horizontally, 10 spaces of pica type measure 1 inch, whereas 12 spaces of elite type measure 1 inch.

Hot type. This refers to typesetting by use of hot metal. Linotype and monotype are two examples of so-called hot type. Each line of type is cast as a solid metal line by operators who work at a keyboard similar to a typewriter.

Cold type. This refers to typesetting by means other than hot metal, in particular by a form of typewriter composition such as the IBM typewriter and the Vari-Typer. Broadly, cold type also includes machines such as Photon that compose type by a photographic process.

See also PRINTING.

Typesetting. See PRINTING; TYPEFACE.

Typing. *Spacing.* Legal documents are double-spaced with a triple space between numbered articles or items and between paragraphs with side headings. Quoted material (see TAKE-IN) and description of land may be single-spaced. See also Typing Legal Documents, below.

Usage has established the following standard rules for spacing between typewriter characters:

One space:
    After a comma
    After a semicolon
    After a period following an abbreviation or an initial but not between initials forming a single abbreviation
    After an exclamation mark used in the body of a sentence
    Before and after "x" meaning "by," for example, 3 x 5 inch card

Two spaces:
    After a colon
    After every sentence
    After a period following a figure or letter at the beginning of a line in a list of items

No spacing:

Before or after a dash, which is two hyphens

Before or after a hyphen

Between quotation marks and the matter enclosed

Between parentheses and the matter enclosed

Between the initials that make up a single abbreviation—for example, C.O.D.

Before or after an apostrophe, unless it begins or ends a word

Punctuation should never be separated from the word it follows—for example, a dash should never be placed at the beginning of a line.

Underscoring. Underscoring, or underlining, in typed material is equivalent to italics in printed material but is used less freely. Generally, the underlining is continuous and not broken at the spacing between words, but may be broken in report headings and title pages for a decorative effect. The following uses of underscoring are recommended:

1. Underscore for emphasis. The dictator indicates when underscoring is to be used for emphasis.

2. Underscore material that is in italics in the original.

3. Underscore to indicate foreign words and phrases, or abbreviations of them.

Do not underscore foreign words that have become part of the English speech through continuous use. Some words are in Roman when standing alone but are in italics when used in certain phrases. For example, the word "caveat" is not italicized, but the phrase *caveat emptor* is.

Alignment of paper. The "lining up" of a large pack of paper and carbons for insertion in the typewriter in such a way that a uniformity of all the sheets is attained. Many secretaries make a special *feeding device* to assure perfect alignment. Figure 1 shows how to make such a device; figure 2 shows it after completion, with paper inserted.

1. Fold a 5- by 8½-inch strip of flimsy Manila tag (a cheap file folder will do) across the center, lengthwise.

2. Cut three U-shaped slots across the upper half of the folded strip, about one-half inch from the crease.

3. Lift up and bend backward the tongues formed by the slots.

4. Insert the assembled sheets of paper in the folded strip.

5. Feed the tongues from the U-slots into the typewriter. The platen grasps them more readily than it does a thick pack of paper.

6. Remove the folded strip before beginning to type.

Several sheets of paper and carbon may be inserted easily in the typewriter

Typing. Figure 1.
Making a special feeding device.

Typing: Figure 2.
Completed special feeding device.

by placing them beneath the flap of an envelope. The platen, however, does not grasp a large pack as readily, and the alignment is not as perfect as when the device described here is used.

Corrections. To erase, use two erasers—a hard one and a soft one. They may be combined into one eraser. Move the carriage as far to the side as possible so paper and eraser fragments will not fall into the typewriter mechanism. Start with the soft eraser to remove the excess surface ink. Then change to the hard eraser to remove the imbedded ink. Finally, use the soft eraser again, to smooth off the surface. When erasing, rub with short, light strokes. A sharp razor blade may be used on a good grade of paper to remove punctuation marks and the tails of letters.

Insert a steel eraser guard between the carbon paper and the copy. Or use a celluloid eraser shield but do not use pieces of paper.

Corrections on carbon copies are often much fainter than the rest of the typing. To avoid this, make the correction as follows: After the necessary erasure has been made, adjust the ribbon control indicator to stencil position. Put the carriage in the proper position and strike the proper key. This will leave the impression on the carbon copies, but the original will still be blank. Then switch the control indicator back to the ribbon, place the carriage in position, and again strike the proper key. This procedure permits a perfect match of the typing on the carbon copies with an equal density of color.

To erase on a line near the edge of the page, feed the sheet back until the bottom of the paper is free of the platen. Erase, and turn the page back into position for typing.

Corrections can be made on pages that are bound at the top. Insert a blank sheet of paper in the typewriter, as though for typing. When it protrudes about an inch above the platen, insert between it and the platen the unbound edge of the sheet to be corrected. Turn the platen toward you until the typwriter grips the sheet to be corrected. You can then adjust the bound sheet to the proper position for making the correction. Correction cannot be made on pages that are bound at the side without unstapling them.

Other methods of correction are also widely used:

1. An eraser made of glass fibers will permit you to erase on the original without the impression of the erasure going through to the carbon. (The carriage should always be moved to the right or left when using this eraser, and the glass part of the eraser should not be handled.)

2. Some secretaries use a battery-operated electric eraser.

3. An eraser material made of special paper erases a mistake by covering it with a white, chalk-like chemical. All you have to do is backspace to the point of the mistake, whether it is a single letter or a complete word, place the erasing paper in front of the error, and retype the error. This results in a blank space in which the correct word or letter may now be typed. There is also a companion product for erasing carbon copy mistakes. Also on the market is a liquid that paints the error white (or same color) to match the paper. Then the correction can be typed over the error. The most well known of these is "Liquid Paper."

4. Many modern offices use typewriters that have built-in correcting devices, which have almost eliminated the need for erasures, tapes, and fluids.

Duplicate original. A carbon copy that is to be signed and treated in all respects as though it were an original or ribbon copy.

In the law office, an original, an office file copy, and a varying number of carbon copies of all legal documents are necessary. Frequently, one or more of the carbon copies must be used in the same manner as the original.

The dictator tells you how many copies to make. Instructions are usually given in this manner: "Two and four," meaning an original, a duplicate, and four copies; or, "One and five," meaning an original and five copies, no duplicate original being necessary.

Use heavyweight paper for the original or ribbon copy, and lightweight for the carbons, the weight depending on the number of copies. Duplicate and triplicate originals are usually typed on paper of the same substance as the ribbon copy. Some offices follow the practice of making the last carbon copy, which is the office copy, on heavy paper because it is more durable.

The kind of paper used depends upon the document that is being typed and also varies with the office.

Triplicate original. A carbon copy to be signed and treated in all respects as though it were an original or ribbon copy. The term *triplicate original* is used when an original and two copies to be treated as originals are needed.

Chinese copy. A duplicate of an original document, signed letter, quoted material, book extract, and the like (not a reproduction, such as a photocopy or camera copy) that has been copied so it follows the original faithfully. It does not correct errors, but purports to be a "true

> The pertinent part of the opinion rendered by the Copyright Office at our request reads as follows:
>
>> The Copyright Office does not undertake to pass upon his [the author's] rights, leaving the question to the courts in case of dispute. It simply records (italics theirs) his claims, and by this recording gives him certain rights provided his claims can be substantiated.
>>
>> •   •   •   •   •   •   •   •
>>
>> ... this [copyright] is taken out in the name of the publisher rather than of the author, as the contract itself is really a license to sell from the publisher to the auther [sic]. It is also the duty of the publisher to take all necessary steps to effect renewals . . . . .
>>
>> An author should be "guided" by his publisher in all questions of copyright. (Emphasis ours.)
>
> We contend that this opinion strongly supports the contention of the petitioner.

Typing: Figure 3.

Exact (Chinese) copy of quoted material.

and exact" copy, including even the most obvious mistakes.

1. Type the word COPY in the upper left-hand corner.

2. Copy exactly even obvious errors.

3. Indicate obvious errors copied from the original as follows: (a) Underline an incorrect letter or figure. (b) Put "sic" in parentheses or brackets after apparently or obviously incorrect words or phrases. (c) Show an omission by a caret. If the typewriter does not have a caret, use the slanting bar and underscore key (/). Below are some examples:

agreement entered into the 31st day of April . . . upon reciept. . . .

I give, devise and bequest (sic) unto . . . meeting of the United/Assembly in New York. . . .

4. Copy page for page and line for line as far as practicable.

Collating. The process of checking a set of typed pages for correct numerical sequence. When a typing job consisting of more than one page is completed, the material must be separated and arranged in sets consisting of the original of each page, the first carbon of each page, the second carbon of each page, and so on. Each set must be checked for correct sequence of pages. The task of compiling the sets of copies and collating them is made easier by the use of a rubber finger or pencil eraser.

Extract. A printer's term for quoted material or an excerpt that is to be set in a smaller size of type than the rest of the text. The printer uses the term *extract* because the copy that is to be set in smaller type is "extracted" from the other copy and is set on a different typesetting machine. Quotation marks are omitted. Lists, examples, problems, and quotations of over four to eight lines are generally set in smaller type.

I have revised the affidavit that you returned, I hope in accordance with your recommendations. If you find it satisfactory as now drawn, may I ask you

1. To swear to it before a notary and have him affix his seal and notarial stamp

2. To fill in the last column of Schedule B as to the months for which payments are in default on each vehicle

3. To return the affidavit with five forms of the conditional sale contract

Typing: Figure 4.

Tabulated textual material.

Quotations and indented material. Passages (words of another) or recessed material that is typed in such a manner as to be set apart from regular text by the leaving of blank space or margins.

1. *Margins and paragraphs.* The left margin of quotations and other indented material should be about 5 spaces to the right of the principal left margin; the beginning of a paragraph within the material should be indented an additional 5 spaces. If a quotation begins in the middle of a paragraph, the paragraph indentation is omitted.

The right margin of indented material may be even with the principal right margin or about 5 spaces to the left of it.

Short lines of indented material should be indented about 15 spaces, thus:

The American Bar
The Bar Register
Lawyer's List

2. *Line spacing.* Quotations are usually single-spaced, but this does not apply to all indented material. Triple space before and after each quotation or other indented material; double space between paragraphs of single-spaced indented material.

3. *Quotation marks.* For quoted material that is not set off (or indented) from the rest of the text, place double quotation marks at the beginning and end of the quotation. For quoted material set off (indented) as an extract, do not use opening and closing quotes. If there are any single quotation marks *within* the material being copied, change them to double quotation marks within your extract.

4. *Errors.* Copy quotations exactly, even obvious errors. Indicate errors in the same way that you do in making an exact copy of any material. (See Chinese Copy, above.)

5. *Italics.* If words in the original are in italics, underscore them. If words that are not in italics in the original are underscored at the direction of the dictator, the words "Italics ours" in parentheses are added at the end of the quotation. It frequently happens that part of a quoted passage is italicized and that the dictator wishes to emphasize another part of it. In that case, put "Italics theirs" in parentheses immediately following the italicized matter, and add the words "Emphasis ours" in parentheses at the end of the quotation. In figure 3 the word *records*

was italicized in the original. The rest of the underscoring was added by the dictator for emphasis.

6. *Omissions.* Omissions of part of a quotation are indicated by the use of ellipses. They may be points (dots) or asterisks (stars) and are usually in groups of three. There should be a space between asterisks or points.

In using either points or asterisks, simply remember that they take the place of words, and place them accordingly. Thus if a quotation begins in the middle of a sentence, there is no space between the quotation mark and the first ellipsis, but there is a space between the final ellipsis and the following word. If some words are omitted in the middle of a sentence, use three dots with a space on either side of each dot. If the end of a sentence is omitted, use four dots—no space between the last word quoted and the first dot but a space around each of the other three dots. Four dots may be used in the same way to show the omission of an entire sentence or paragraph. You may also indicate omission of one or more entire paragraphs by a line of ellipses, five spaces apart. Some law offices use a single group of three asterisks in the center of the line instead of a full line.

Figure 3 illustrates a quotation with points showing omissions. (It also shows errors that were in the material being copied.) Note that the first paragraph begins in the middle; that there are one or more paragraphs omitted; the next paragraph begins and ends in the middle of a sentence; the last paragraph is quoted in full. Note also in figure 3 that there are four points at the end of the second paragraph. One represents the period, indicating the end of the sentence.

See also TAKE-IN.

Tabulated material. When text is tabulated or itemized in the body of a letter, the items are usually preceded by a number or letter in parentheses or followed by a period. Each line of the tabulated text should begin two spaces to the right of the number. Preferably, the punctuation and capitalization should be the same as if the tabulated material were written without breaks, in regular lines (see figure 4), but this style is not followed in all law offices.

Drafts. A first copy of material that is to be revised. The word *draft* should be written across the top of every page of a draft to avoid mistaking it for the final copy. Drafts should be triple-spaced for convenience in making changes. In retyping a draft, the following should be carefully noted: (1) portion marked for omission, (2) additional material to be inserted, (3) transpositions, and (4) corrections in spelling, punctuation, and the like.

Typing court papers. Pleadings and supporting papers, except those for which printed law blanks are used, are typed on legal size paper or regular 8½-by 11-inch paper, depending on court preference. In some states, legal cap is used for court papers; in others, plain legal-size paper, without ruled margins, is used; in some states, either may be used. In a few states, the legal cap has numbers in the left margin.

All court papers have a heading, or caption, consisting of various parts, which is written on every separate document, although several documents might be bound together. For the proper way to type all parts of the heading, see CAPTION. See also Typing Legal Documents, below.

Typing legal documents. To type legal documents in a professional manner, observe the following general suggestions. However, always observe the specific practices of your office, a particular court, and a given state.

1. *Paper.* Legal documents are typed on legal cap, on legal-size paper 8 or 8½ inches by 13 or 14 inches, or on regular 8½- by 11-inch paper.

2. *Margins.* Documents typed on legal cap or legal-size paper are bound at the top; those on letter-size or short paper, at the left. Therefore it is necessary to leave a margin of at least 1½ inches for binding. Allow for proper margins this way:

a. *Top margin.* Begin typing either five or six double spaces from the top of the paper, but make a habit of always allowing the same number of spaces. By following this practice, you know that every page of a document starts at the same place on the paper and has the same number of typed lines.

b. *Bottom margin.* Leave a margin of approximately one inch at the bottom. With a margin of five double spaces at the top and an inch at the bottom, each legal-size page of typing will have 32 lines double spaced; each letter-size page (8½ by 11 inches), 24 lines.

In a neatly typed legal document, the typing on every page of manuscript ends exactly the same number of spaces from the bottom of the page. Carbon paper with a numbered margin, or a backing sheet with a numbered margin, will insure an even bottom margin. If the carbon paper does not have a numbered margin, or if there are too many copies to use a backing sheet, mark lightly the place where the typing should end, before inserting the paper in the typewriter.

c. *Left margin.* Leave a margin on the left of approximately 1¼ or 1½ inches if the paper is to be bound on the left. On legal cap, begin typing one space to the right of the colored line that indicates the left margin.

d. *Right margin.* Leave a right margin of approximately 1 inch. On legal cap, this will place the margin approximately ⅝ inch to the left of the colored line that indicates the right margin. This allows a leeway of seven spaces between the right margin and the line. Avoid excessive hyphenation and also a ragged right margin.

Under no circumstances should the typing extend beyond the colored lines that indicate the margins.

3. *Spacing.* Legal documents are double-spaced, with a triple space between numbered articles or items and between paragraphs with side headings. Quoted material and description of land may be single spaced.

4. *Paragraphs.* Paragraphs should be indented ten spaces. A legal document should *never* be typed in block style. The margins of indented material should be five or ten spaces from the margins of the document itself, with an indentation of an additional five spaces for paragraphing the intended material. The right margin of an indentation may be flush with the margin of the document instead of being indented.

A paragraph should never end with the last line of the page. At least one or two lines should be carried over to the next page. This is particularly important in typing wills as a check against omission of pages.

5. *Numbering pages.* Pages should be numbered at the bottom of the sheet, in the center, or page 1 of 10.

6. *Signature.* The line for signature should never be on a page by itself. At least one line, preferably two, of the document in addition to the TESTIMONIUM CLAUSE should appear on the page with the signature. An ACKNOWLEDGMENT or an ATTESTATION clause following the signature does not obviate this requirement.

7. *Carbon copies.* Duplicate originals (carbon copies that are signed) are typed on the same kind of paper as the original. Other carbon copies may be made on onionskin paper. After the original and duplicate originals are signed, the carbon copies are conformed (see CONFORMING DOCUMENTS). Follow the practices of your office in the use of photocopies.

8. *Erasures and interlineations.* If an error is made involving more than a few letters of a word, the page should be retyped. The signer of the document must initial interlineations.

9. *Backing.* A legal document should be bound in a LEGAL BACK.

10. *Numbers.* Numbers are written in words and repeated in numerals in parentheses—for example, five thousand (5,000).

11. *Amounts of money.* Amounts of money are spelled out and repeated in parentheses, the figures in parentheses following the word *dollars.* Each word except conjunctions begins with a capital—for example, Eight Hundred Fifty and 80/100 Dollars ($850.80).

12. *Dates.* Dates may be expressed in figures or spelled out. Even if the day of the month is spelled out, the year may be written in figures, thus—the twenty-first day of August 1982.

Typing manuscripts. Manuscripts should be typed neatly and legibly, on sheets of uniform size, preferably 8½- by 11-inch white bond, the sheet commonly used in offices. A carbon copy or photocopy should be made for reference purposes but the original is always sent to the printer.

1. Keep the typewritten line down to six inches.

2. Use double or triple spacing.

3. Keep the right-hand margin as even as possible; this will help you in estimating the length of the copy.

4. Indicate paragraph indentions clearly. Five or six spaces are sufficient, but there should be consistency throughout the manuscript in whatever number of spaces is adopted.

5. Type headings and subheadings in the position they are to occupy on the final printed page, and be uniform in capitalizations.

6. Use one side only of the sheet.

7. Leave a margin of at least 1 inch on all four sides.

8. Keep the pages as nearly uniform in length as possible, to help in estimating the length of the copy.

9. If references are made to material appearing in other parts of the manuscript, instruct the printer (on the manuscript) to carry a query on each successive proof as a reminder to put in the correct page reference numbers when the final page proofs are received.

10. Type any extract or quoted material just like the main text, double spaced, full measure. To indicate that it is to be printed in a smaller size of type, draw a

vertical line in the left margin, beginning exactly where the extract begins and ending where it ends.

11. Indicate that lists, examples, problems, and other material of subordinate importance are to be set in smaller type by drawing a vertical line in the left margin.

12. Draw a double vertical line in the left margin to indicate that material is to be set in a third size of type.

See also BRIEF, Figure 1; CONFORMING DOCUMENTS; TAKE-IN; MANUSCRIPT; TYPEFACE; STATIONERY SUPPLIES; FORMS (Printed Law Blanks).

U

Ultra Vires. Without power; beyond the powers of. A term used to apply to a contract or act beyond the powers of a CORPORATION as expressed or implied in its CERTIFICATE of Incorporation or by statute. For example, if a corporation contracts a debt in excess of the maximum allowed by statute, the CONTRACT is *ultra vires*—beyond the power of the corporation. If neither party to the contract has performed, either the corporation or the other party may declare the contract void. After both parties have performed, the courts will not rescind the contract; the weight of authority is to the effect that after one party has performed the other party cannot repudiate the contract by claiming that it was *ultra vires*. Directors may be held personally liable for loss to the corporation occasioned by an *ultra vires* act.

An *ultra vires* contract made by a municipal corporation is not binding upon the municipality, although the other has performed.

Unauthorized Practice of Law. *Black's Law Dictionary* defines the Practice of Law as follows:

"Not limited to appearing in court, or advising and assisting in the conduct of litigation, but embracing the preparation of pleadings, and other papers incident to actions and special proceedings, conveyancing, the preparation of legal instruments of all kinds, and the giving of all legal advice to clients."

However, the American Bar Association, through the Standing Committee of Professional Ethics, Opinion No. 316, dated January 18, 1967, further clarified the matter:

"A lawyer can employ lay secretaries, lay investigators, lay detectives, lay researchers, accountants, lay scriveners, nonlawyer draftsmen or nonlawyer researchers. In fact, he may employ nonlawyers to do any task for him except counsel clients about law matters, engage directly in the practice of law, appear in court or appear in formal proceedings as a part of the judicial process, so long as it is he who takes the work and vouches for it to the client. In other words, we do not limit the kind of assistants the lawyer can acquire in any way to persons who are admitted to the Bar, so long as the nonlawyers do not do things that lawyers may not do or do the things that lawyers only may do."

Canon 3 of a proposed Code of Professional Responsibility states with regard to the unauthorized practice of law:

"A lawyer often delegates tasks to clerks, secretaries, and other lay persons. Such delegation is proper if the lawyer maintains a direct relationship with his client, supervises the delegated work, and has complete professional responsibility for the work product. This delegation enables a lawyer to render legal service more economically and efficiently."

Actions charging unauthorized practice of law are usually brought by local bar associations.

Guidelines for the secretary to avoid practicing law. 1. The secretary should never give "advice" to a client either over the telephone or in person. She should firmly inform the client that she is not an attorney and thus may not give advice. What constitutes advice? Advice is anything upon which a client might rely, act upon, and be injured as the result.

2. The secretary may be trained by the lawyer to draft documents, such as deeds, without his or her help, to prepare accountings for estates and guardianships, to prepare documents for transferring real estate in an estate, selling personal property in an estate, divorce pleadings from predictated forms, and so on, as long as the documents are supervised and reviewed by the attorney.

3. The secretary should never discuss clients' affairs with persons, such as representatives of Internal Revenue Service or authoritative tax persons of various branches of the government. They may have the right to the information, but it is up to the attorney to decide what to divulge.

4. The secretary should never release documents or copies of information in files to anyone without the direction of the attorney, even though the original documents may be the property of the client. If the client insists on having the documents, the secretary should tell the client that she must have the attorney's permission to release them, as the attorney may be holding them for payment of a fee or other reason.

5. The secretary should never discuss the client's affairs with the opposing counsel. She may reveal something that the attorney does not want revealed at that time.

6. The secretary should never try to advise friends and relatives on legal matters, even though she may "know what she is talking about."

Unemployment Insurance. A form of social security that pays a weekly income to workers while they are unemployed. All states have established unemployment insurance funds, which are supported by a payroll tax. Benefit payments usually start after a fixed "waiting period" and continue for a number of weeks that varies with the state laws. Usually the payee must call at the state unemployment insurance office in person to arrange for the collection of his or her check. The payee is expected to take any job that the state finds, providing that the wages paid by the new employer equal the wages paid on the last job.

Uniform Commercial Code. The compilation of laws governing the handling of commercial transactions. This code has been adopted by the various state legislatures and facilitates interstate cooperation in commercial dealings.

The code had its inception with the National Conference of Commissioners on Uniform State Laws. The commission is made up of commissioners appointed by the governors of the states. This national body has as its purpose (1) the promotion of *uniformity* in state laws on all subjects where uniformity is deemed desirable and practicable; (2) to draft model acts on (a) subjects suitable for interstate compacts, and (b) subjects in which uniformity will make more effective the exercise of state powers and promote interstate co-operation; and (3) to promote uniformity of judicial decisions throughout the United States.

See also UNIFORM LAWS.

Uniform Laws. Conflicting state statutes have led to the adoption, in many fields of business and commercial interest, of similar laws by the various states. The laws are known as *uniform laws.* Some of the more important uniform laws are the Uniform Negotiable Instruments Act, the Uniform Partnership Act, the Uniform Stock Transfer Act, and the Uniform Warehouse Receipt Act.

In all states the uniform laws have been supplemented by the UNIFORM COMMERCIAL CODE.

United States Code. A compilation of all general and permanent laws of the United States, as of January 6, 1959, arranged under general subject headings with a detailed index. Annual supplements are published.

United States Code Annotated is a publication arranged in parallel fashion to United States Code. It gives federal and state decisions pertaining to each law in the code. Revised volumes are is-

sued periodically. See SLIP LAWS and STATUTES AT LARGE.

United States Code Annotated. See UNITED STATES CODE.

Unjust Enrichment. A principle in the law of contracts whereby the law creates an obligation to repay in cases where money, property, or services were obtained by one person at the expense of another person. That one person should not in good conscience be allowed to keep what was obtained at another's expense.

Usury. Contracting for or receiving something in excess of the amount of interest allowed by law for the loan or forbearance of money, as in the sale of goods on credit or under the installment plan. In the majority of states, a lender who charges a usurious rate of interest loses his or her rights to collect any interest, although a few states permit the lender to collect the legal rate. In some states, both principal and interest are forfeited. Service charges, investigation fees, and commissions charged by an agent are not usually considered interest and may be added to the legal rate without usury. In some states, the parties to a contract may agree upon a rate of interest higher than the legal rate but within a statutory limit; in a few states, they may agree on any rate. In some states, loans to corporations, but not to individuals, may be made at more than the legal rate. Certain types of loans, such as small personal loans, are not covered by the usury law but are subject to special laws.

Vagrancy. The conduct of an idle person in wandering from place to place with no visible lawful means of support. The idler subsists on charity and does not work though able to do so. The mere possession of funds will not prevent a person's being a vagrant, however. Professional gamblers and those who live by AIDING AND ABETTING prostitutes have been held as vagrants.

Valued Policy. An insurance agreement where the value of the article insured is settled by agreement between the parties and inserted in the policy. See OPEN POLICY.

Vendee. One who enters into a CONTRACT OF SALE and agrees to purchase the real property of another (VENDOR). Every contract of sale must have a vendee ("purchaser" or "buyer"). If two or more vendees want to take TITLE as joint tenants, the contract of sale must describe them as such tenants. The buyer may be an individual or a CORPORATION. If the lawyer is an individual, he or she must be an adult of sound mind. If the vendee is a corporation, the purchase must have been duly authorized by the corporation's board of directors. A seller who enters into a contract of sale with a corporation as vendee

should make certain that the CORPORATION is actually in existence and that it has power under its charter to purchase the real property. A trustee or an executor seldom has power to purchase real estate.

Vendee's Lien. The LIEN of a purchaser (VENDEE) on land as security for repayment of any monies paid in the event the seller (VENDOR) refuses or is unable to convey good TITLE. In order that the vendee's lien may be effective as against innocent purchasers from the seller, the vendee must file suit to enforce his or her lien.

The CONTRACT OF SALE may specifically provide that all sums paid on account of the CONTRACT and the reasonable expenses of title examination shall be a lien on the property in favor of the purchaser if the seller cannot complete his or her contract, but that such will not continue after DEFAULT by the purchaser under the contract.

Vendor. One who enters into a CONTRACT OF SALE and agrees to sell REAL PROPERTY to another (VENDEE). Every contract of sale must have a vendor or "seller." The vendor may be an individual, a PARTNERSHIP, a CORPORATION, or a representative.

429

The individual may be either an adult or a minor, or the person may enter into the contract in a representative capacity. If the vendor is a minor or an incompetent, the contract of sale should indicate that fact and give the name of the individual's guardian, together with the date of the court order under which he or she was appointed. If the vendee is a representative, such as an agent or an executor, the contract should set forth the source of the representative's authority.

Vendor's Lien. (Real estate.) The LIEN a VENDOR (seller) has on the land sold, to secure payment of any part of the purchase price by the VENDEE (purchaser) remaining unpaid after delivery of the DEED. The lien is subject to FORECLOSURE like a MORTGAGE, and a deficiency JUDGMENT may be obtained by the seller against the purchaser. (The vendor's lien exists whether or not the CONTRACT OF SALE provides for it.) Such a lien is, however, of little value unless specifically provided for in the deed, for an innocent purchaser from the first vendee acquires TITLE free of the vendor's lien.

Where the vendor reserves in his or her deed to the vendee a lien on the land to secure payment of the balance of the purchase price, the lien has priority over (1) prior judgments against the buyer, and (2) any subsequent lien or ENCUMBRANCE on the REAL PROPERTY. The buyer is not personally liable for his or her debt unless the buyer has signed a note or other instrument making him or her personally liable. One who purchases from the buyer is not personally liable to the holder of the vendor's lien unless one assumes and agrees to pay

the debt under one's deed. If the debt is assigned, the assignee may foreclose the lien.

A vendor's lien is used in lieu of a MORTGAGE in Louisiana and some other states, just as a WARRANTY DEED is used in Georgia and other states.

Venue. The county and state where the facts of a case are alleged to have occurred and in which the trial is held. If it can be shown that justice requires trial in another county, the case is removed by *change of venue.* The venue of a case in federal court may be changed to another state.

Venue is also used to refer to the clause in a sworn statement showing the state and county or other political subdivision where the instrument was executed.

The venue always appears in legal instruments such as an AFFIDAVIT or COMPLAINT; or in a part of a legal instrument, such as an ACKNOWLEDGMENT or VERIFICATION; and in court papers such as a FORECLOSURE action, or NOTICE of Motion. The venue does not have to do with the power of the court, but with its right to proceed in a given case by reason of the residence of the parties, the place of performance of the contract or the place of happening of the incident.

How to type the venue. Type the statement of the venue in solid caps, bracket it, and follow with *ss.,* the abbreviation for *scilicet* (sc, though correct, is not used in legal papers). The abbreviation may be in caps or small letters. Like many abbreviations, it is followed by a period. Technically, a colon should also follow because scilicet means "to wit," but few law offices observe this technicality.

Verdict. An opinion rendered by a jury, or a judge when there is no jury, on a question of fact. Trial courts may accept or reject such findings of fact in formulating their JUDGMENT.

Verification. A sworn statement by a qualified person that the allegations contained in a PLEADING are true. The statutes require that many pleadings and supporting papers be verified, and some law firms follow the practice of verifying all pleadings whether or not the statute requires it. Some of the papers commonly verified are complaints, answers, petitions, and bills of particulars.

If the complaint is verified, the answer *must* be verified. The verification always recites the VENUE and always has a jurat, or "sworn to" clause. One of the duties of a NOTARY PUBLIC is to administer the oath to a person verifying a pleading. The proper procedure is for the notary to stand and raise his or her right hand and ask the verifier to do the

---

STATE OF MONTANA   )

                            :   SS.

COUNTY OF RICHLAND   )

        DAVID O. CARTER, being duly sworn, deposes and says: That he is the treasurer of Lambert Mills, Inc., the plaintiff in the above entitled action; that he has read the foregoing complaint and knows the contents thereof; that the same is true of his own knowledge; except as to matters therein stated to be alleged upon information and belief, and as to those matters he believes it to be true.

                                        _____

Given under my hand and seal this day of September, 19—.

_____
              Notary Public
My commission expires

Verification: Figure 1.
Verification of complaint by officer of domestic corporation.

same. Then the notary administers the oath in the following, or similar words: "Do you solemnly swear that the contents of the foregoing instrument subscribed by you are the truth, the whole truth, and nothing but the truth, so help you God?" The verifier should answer "Yes" or "I do." Figure 1 is an illustration of a verification of complaint by an officer of a domestic corporation.

Versus. (vs., v.) Against.

Vested. Fixed or absolute. Commonly refers to the title to real or personal property that is not dependent upon some future event.

Void; Voidable. That which is *void* is of no legal force or effect; that which is *voidable* may be rendered void. For example, a gambling or wagering contract is void (see CONTRACT, Legality of Subject Matter), whereas an infant's contracts are merely voidable at his or her election (see CONTRACT, Competent Parties).

Voting Trust. A method devised for concentrating the control of a company in the hands of a few people. A voting trust is usually organized and operated under a *voting trust agreement.* This is a contract between the stockholders and those who manage the corporation, called the voting trustees. The stockholders transfer their stock to the trustees, giving them the right to vote the stock during the life of the agreement. The trustees in turn issue certificates of beneficial interest, called *voting trust certificates,* to the stockholders, who are entitled to the dividends. All stockholders may become parties to the agreement, which is generally subject to statutory regulation. The trust is usually for a definite period. When it is terminated, the certificateholders are notified to exchange their trust certificates of stock.

Voyage Charter. See CHARTER-PARTY.

W

Waiver. The surrender, either expressed or implied, of a right to which one is entitled by law. Thus a stockholder might sign a waiver of notice of meeting or might impliedly waive that notice by participation in the meeting. The essence of the waiver is conduct that indicates an intention not to enforce certain rights or certain provisions of an agreement. A widow may waive her right to share in the estate of her husband; a buyer may waive delivery on a certain date by accepting the goods at a subsequent date. For *waiver of citation* in a probate proceedings, see PROBATE.

Warrant. A directive from a competent authority in pursuance of law, directing the doing of an act and affording the person protection from damage if he or she does it. See SEARCH AND SEIZURE.

Warranty. Affirmation of a material fact or promise by the seller, which acts as an inducement for the buyer to make a purchase. A warranty may be *express* (a direct statement made by the seller), or *implied* (one that is indicated by the nature of the contract). Warranties relate to many things: fitness of the goods sold for a special purpose; merchantability of goods; title to real or personal property; and quiet enjoyment of premises. All representations made by an applicant for insurance, whether material or not, are deemed warranties. The term *guaranty* is loosely used in the sense of warranty. The common guaranty of a product is, strictly, a warranty and not a guaranty. (See GUARANTY.) Any warranty made by a seller that proves to be false gives the buyer a right of legal action.

Warranty Deed. 1. Upon a sale of REAL PROPERTY, a DEED under which the GRANTOR covenants that he or she will forever warrant TITLE to real property conveyed. A full covenant or *general* warranty deed may enumerate all the COVENANTS of Title. In many states, it is necessary to set forth all of the covenants of title in full in the warranty deed; the usual covenants are implied if the deed contains certain words of conveyance, such as *grant, bargain, and sell,* or *convey and warrant,* or if a phrase such as the following is included after the description: *and grantor warrants the title to the same,* or *with warranty,* or *with warranty covenants.*

A warranty deed does not correct a bad title; nor does it cure defects in former deeds. It merely gives the GRANTEE the right to sue the grantor for breach of warranty if anyone later makes a claim against the property.

2. Upon a loan, an instrument used to secure payment of the debt. In some states, particularly Georgia, a warranty deed to secure a debt is used in lieu of a MORTGAGE. In the event of the death of the mortgagor (borrower), the mortgage, as a claim against his estate, is junior to expenses of administration, to a year's support for the widow and children, and to certain other claims. In all states, a warranty deed that is in fact given to secure a debt is treated as a mortgage. Such an instrument is sometimes used in states where a mortgage does not provide adequate security under the law. A warranty deed to secure a debt usually contains the same provisions as a mortgage.

Waste. Generally, an act by someone in possession of land, but who has less than absolute ownership of it. The act in question decreases the value of the land or the owner's interest in the land.

Watered Stock. Stock issued as fully paid, for which the CORPORATION has received assets worth palpably less than the par or stated value of the stock. Watered stock is created, generally, by an overvaluation of the property given the corporation as consideration for stock.

The term *watered stock* gets its name from the old practice of letting cattle fill themselves up with water just before they were to be weighed in and sold at market. The water could bring up the weight and the buyer would be paying an unfair price for "watered stock." See also CAPITAL (Stock).

Wharfage. Wharfage is the money paid for tying a vessel to a wharf, or landing goods upon, or loading them from, a wharf.

Wherefore Clause. The final paragraph of a COMPLAINT in which formal demand for a judgment against the defendant is made. The *wherefore clause* may demand judgment for a specified sum of money, or in EQUITY actions "pray" for or seek other relief to which the plaintiff believes he or she is entitled. Thus the wherefore clause may also be called the *prayer*. See COMPLAINT; PARTIES TO AN ACTION.

White Slave. A term used in the United States statutes to indicate a female with reference to whom an offense is committed under the so-called Mann White Slave Traffic Act of June 25, 1910 (18 U.S.C.A. Sec. 2421-2424), prohibiting the transportation in interstate and foreign commerce of women and girls for immoral purposes.

Will. An instrument that is an effective expression of its maker's intention about what will be done with property under his or her control at the time of death. Usually it must be in writing and executed in strict conformity with the applicable statutory requirements. A will takes effect only at the maker's death. As long as the maker lives, he or she may revoke the will or make any changes in its terms desired.

A *holographic will* is one written entirely in the handwriting of the maker, even though there is no ATTESTATION by any witness. Before a holographic will is admitted to probate, the handwriting of the maker must be proved. A holographic will is not legal in some states.

A nuncupative will is one that is made orally. Oral wills are allowed in most states under certain limited conditions.

Typing a will. Figures 1 and 2 illustrate the first and last pages of a will. Many wills are short, but many also range from 10 to 50 or more pages, all of which are dictated. The lawyer chooses the words very carefully, and the dictation, therefore, is not rapid. The transcription should cause no difficulty; the challenge lies in the typing of the final copy. There should be no erasures in names or amounts, and no discernible erasures in other parts. PROBATE of a will has been refused when material provisions have been erased, because the courts could not tell whether an alteration was made before or after execution. The typing should begin and end at the same point on every page, except the last, and yet there must be continuity from page to page, which means that no page should end with the close of a paragraph or sentence. The purpose of the continuity is to avoid the omission, or the possible insertion of a page. Some lawyers go so far as to require that the last word on each page be hyphenated. The placement of the signature with reference to the testimonium and ATTESTATION clauses is of prime importance in a will.

Frequently the lawyer will tell the secretary to copy a certain paragraph from another will, or from a skeleton form. She should be on the lookout for differences between the will she is typing and the form she is following, such as a change from singular to plural, or from *his* to *her,* and the like.

Signature page and preceding page of a will. The placement of the signature often presents a problem. Good practice makes the solution obligatory in some respect, permissible in others.

It is obligatory that at least one line of the testimonium clause be on the same page as part of the will (Figure 3). In other words, a new page cannot begin with the testimonium clause, because this arrangement would increase the possibility of the loss of a page or permit the insertion of a page without detection.

It is obligatory that at least one line of the attestation clause be on the page with the signature (Figure 4). The purpose of this requirement is to tie in the witnesses' signatures with that of the testator.

The most desirable setup of the signature page is to have at least three lines of text on the page with the testimonium clause, the signature, and the attestation clause and witnesses' signatures (see figure 2).

It is permissible, though not desirable, to have the signature and attestation clause on a page containing only one line of the testimonium clause.

How to gauge and test the page length. Unless a will is very short and simple, a draft, triple-spaced is always typed.

1. Count the lines, exclusive of the testimonium clause, signature line, attestation clause, and witnesses' signatures.

2. Assume the draft is 15 pages, 25 lines to the page (drafts are triple-spaced), or a total of 375 lines.

3. Plan on a top margin of five double

THE LAST WILL AND TESTAMENT OF
ROY WALLACE

I, ROY WALLACE of Centerville, Center County, State of Florida, do hereby declare this to be my Last Will and Testament, and hereby revoke any and all former wills and codicils made by me.

FIRST: I hereby direct my executors hereinafter named to pay all of my just debts and funeral expenses as soon after my demise as practicable.

SECOND: I give and devise my farm located just outside and to the West of Centerville to my son Richard and his heirs and assigns forever.

THIRD: I give and bequeath to my daughter Anne fifty (50) shares of common stock of United States Steel, Inc.

FOURTH: I give and bequeath the following sums of money to the following persons, to-wit:

(a) The sum of Seven Hundred Fifty Dollars ($750.) to Robert Jones of Allentown, Georgia.

(b) The sum of One Thousand Dollars ($1,000.) to Edna Jones of Ellisville, Florida.

FIFTH: I give and bequeath to the Merchants' Loan and Trust Company, a corporation organized under the laws of

Will: Figure 1. *First page of Will.*

requesting him to appropriate it or so much of it as he shall think proper for presents to servants in our employ at the time of my death.

IN WITNESS WHEREOF, I have signed my name at the end of this my Last Will and Testament and affixed my seal this   day of May, 19—.

_____ [L.S.]

The foregoing instrument, consisting of ten pages, including this page, each page being typewritten only on one side, was at the date thereof by the said ROY WALLACE, signed, published and declared to be his Last Will and Testament in the presence of us, who, at his request, in his presence and in the presence of each other, have subscribed our names as witnesses.

_____ residing at _____

_____ residing at _____

_____ residing at _____

Will: Figure 2. *Last page.*

IN WITNESS WHEREOF, I have signed my name at the

Will: Figure 3.
*One line of testimonium clause on page
with part of text of Will.*

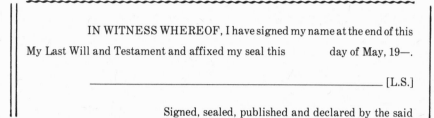

Will: Figure 4.
*One line of attestation clause on page
with signature.*

spaces and an inch margin at the bottom, on a 13-inch paper; this will leave room for 32 lines of typing.

4. Divide the total number of lines by the lines per page. You will have 11 type-written pages with 23 lines left over for the 12th page. A triple space between the text and a three-line testimonium clause, plus three spaces for the signature line places the signature line at the bottom of the page without room for any of the attestation clause. But it is obligatory that at least one line of the attestation clause be on the page with the signature. So you must try another plan.

Plan on a top margin of six double spaces, instead of five, and type 31 lines to the page. This will give 12 typewritten ten pages with three lines remaining for the 13th page. You then have ample room for the testimonium clause, the signature, the attestation clause, and the witnesses' signatures (see figure 2).

Of course, in counting the lines in the draft, you must allow for interlineations and deletions that were made on the draft. If a paragraph is changed considerably, so you cannot tell how many lines it contains, retype it before counting the lines of your draft. You must also take into consideration triple spaces between articles or items, if you plan to use them.

In the illustration in figure 1, there is a triple space between the title and the introductory paragraph; also each article is separated from the preceding one by a triple space, making a total of six extra spaces, which is equivalent to three double spaces, on that page. Although the page length is 32 lines, that page actually has only 28 lines of typing. The extra spaces throughout the will must be added to the total number of lines.

Witnessing a will. The procedure of witnessing a will is rather formal. The practice in most states is for the testator to "publish" the will in the presence of the witnesses by declaring that the document is his or her will. The testator also asks the witnesses to witness the signing of it. The testator not only signs the will but initials the left margin of the other pages. Each witness signs in the presence of the testator and of each other, and no one leaves the room while the will is being signed, witnessed, and sealed. Notice from figure 2 that space for the address of the witness is provided. The address is important because the witness will be called upon to prove the will after the testator's death in states where this is required.

Certifying copies of will. It is customary in many law offices for the secretary to certify the copies of a will. This certification is not for the purpose of the formal affidavit required when the will is probated but is for authentication of the carbon copies made when the will was typed. Type the form of certification on the copies and, after the copies have been conformed to the original, sign the certification. The following is a form of certification to be used when the typist conforms the copies.

I certify that this carbon copy is one that I typed simultaneously with the original will and that after the execution of the original, I conformed this copy to the original by adding the initials, date, signatures, and the addresses of the witnesses.

. . . .

If someone other than the typist of the will conforms it, the form of certification to be signed by the typist should be changed to read:

I certify that this carbon copy is one that I typed simultaneously with the original will and that after the execution of the original, this copy was conformed to the original by the addition of the initials, date, signatures, and the addresses of the witnesses.

. . . .

Some law firms use the following form of certification:

We, the undersigned, hereby certify that we have compared the foregoing copy with the . . . . . . original will of . . . . . dated . . . . . and find it to be a true and accurate copy thereof.

. . . .

This last form of certification requires the reading of the will by three persons, or more if more than two copies are made. One person reads the original will aloud and signs the top line of the certification on each of the copies. Each person who follows a copy signs the second line of the certification on the copy that he or she has followed.

Capitalization and punctuation. Notice from figure 1 that the testator's name is written in solid caps, whereas all other names are underscored (preferably with red ink). The words *last will and testament* are written with initial caps in the will and in the attestation clause. In the phrases *make, publish and declare* and *give, devise and bequeath,* no comma precedes the conjunction *and.* Many lawyers prefer that *executor* and *trustee* be capitalized. Notice from figure 2 that the words *in witness whereof* are written in solid caps and are followed by a comma. These arrangements are arbitrary but are followed extensively in law offices that give considerable attention to these details.

"Dos and don'ts" in preparing a will.

1. Type first in draft form unless the will is only a few pages.

2. In the final typing, make an original and two copies; the original and one copy for the testator and the other copy for your files. (If a bank or other institution is named executor, ask if an extra copy is to be made for it.)

3. Use good quality LEGAL CAP or letter-size bond or specially printed white heavy stock with LAST WILL AND TESTAMENT printed at the top, and white heavy stock backs and matching envelopes.

4. Place the responsibility line at the top of the office copy *only.*

5. Double-space, except the attestation clause.

6. Type the same number of lines on each page.

7. Number each page no more than one double space below the last line, except the last page, which should be numbered one-half inch from the bottom of the page.

8. Don't forget to precede and follow the page number with a hyphen. Type the hyphen preceding the number at 42 on the typewriter scale, if a pica type machine is used, or page 1 of 10, and so on.

9. Triple-space between the text of the will and the testimonium clause.

10. Start the signature line at point 30 on the typewriter scale, if a pica, and continue the line to 67, writing the first bracket in [L.S.] or [SEAL] at point 68. These two scale points are important: the first to accommodate a long signature, and the second to permit a neat application of the seal.

11. If wax seal is used, omit the typed seal. Have wax and ribbon available.

12. Single-space the attestation clause. Start it at the regular left margin, indenting the first line five spaces. Set the right margin stop at 55 on the typewriter scale. (If necessary to conserve space at the end of the will, type the attestation clause all the way over to the right ruled margin of the paper.)

13. Start the first witness line three spaces below the attestation clause, at the left margin, and underscore for 25 spaces; then type "residing at" and underscore for another 25 spaces.

14. Triple-space between the witness lines.

15. Collate.

16. Check and double-check spelling of names.

17. Endorse the back as shown in figure 5 using a back engraved with firm's name. Back the original and first carbon.

18. Have someone compare with you any descriptions of real estate devised by the will.

19. Bind firmly and securely.

Will: Figure 5.
Endorsed back of Will.

After the will is signed and it is witnessed:

20. Conform copies to original.

21. Certify the copies.

22. If your office is to retain the original of the will for safekeeping, give the testator a receipt, signed in the firm's name by one of the lawyers or yourself, reading as follows: "The will of . . . . . . , dated . . . . . . , is in our possession for safekeeping."

23. Enclose the original in an envelope, marked "Last Will and Testament of . . . . , dated . . . . . ."

24. If an institution is named executor, forward conformed copy with covering letter.

25. If a copy of a former will by the testator is in your file, note on it that a later will, of a certain date, has been executed.

Codicil. A CODICIL is written and executed with the same formality as the will. It is not attached to the will, but should be placed in a separate envelope on which is typed, "Codicil to Last Will and Testament of . . . . . . , dated . . . ." A testator may make more than one codicil.

Suggestion for red-inking a will. The usual method of red-inking a will is as follows:

Draw *double* red lines:
    Under the name of the testator in the introductory paragraph and on the cover
    Under each Article number
    Under "IN WITNESS WHEREOF"
Draw *single* red lines:
    Under each name appearing in the will

Under "Executor" and "Trustee"
Under everything appearing on the cover, including the engraved name of the law firm but excepting the name of the testator which has double lines under it.

Will Contest. A proceeding *sui generis,* a suit *in rem,* having for its purpose determination of question whether or not there is a will.

Withholding. Deductions from INCOME as it is earned. The purpose of withholding money from a salary or wage is to cover the recipient's INCOME TAX and other tax liability as required by federal, state, or local laws. The amounts withheld approximate the recipient's tax liability on wages earned.

Withholding for federal income tax. If an employer-employee relationship exists, the responsibility of withholding for federal income taxes rests with the employer. Every employer who is not exempted by statute must withhold from wages regardless of the number of employees or how long each is employed. "Wages" constitutes cash, whether termed vacation pay, bonus, commission, or the like, and other forms of payment such as stocks or other property.

The amount of tax withheld is computed by government withholding tables. The amount is based on the wages earned and the number of exemptions claimed by an employee.

Without Recourse. A phrase used in an ENDORSEMENT that relieves the endorser from assuming liability in the event the maker fails to do something mentioned in the order.

Witness. To subscribe one's name to a deed, will, or other document, for the purpose of attesting its authenticity and proving its execution, if required, by bearing witness thereto.

Witness Clause. See ATTESTATION.

Words and Phrases. A legal dictionary in 73 volumes and supplemented annually that attempts to give every definition appearing in court decisions. See LEGAL DICTIONARIES.

Words of Art. Words having a special meaning in a specific area, such as *last clear chance* in law.

Workmen's Compensation. The name commonly used to designate the method and means created by statutes for giving protection and security to the worker and his or her dependents against injury and death occurring in the course of employment. Workmen's compensation laws generally impose an absolute liability (or liability without fault) on the employer. The employer must compensate employees for injuries sustained in their employment even though the employer takes every precaution to prevent injury and the employee is negligent. See NEGLIGENCE.

Writ. An order issued by a court, or judge, in the name of the state, for the purpose of compelling the defendant to do something mentioned in the order. For specific writs, see MANDAMUS; CERTIORARI; HABEAS CORPUS; QUO WARRANTO; PROHIBITION.

1. *of Error.* A mandatory precept, under seal, issued out of a court of competent jurisdiction. It is directed to the judges of a court of record in which final judgment has been given. The writ commands that the record be examined so some alleged error in the proceedings may be corrected. In some cases, the writ commands the judges to whom it is issued to examine the record; in other cases, it commands them to send the record to another court of appellate jurisdiction.

2. *of Execution.* See JUDGMENT CREDITOR.

Wrongful Death Action. A statutory provision that allows the EXECUTOR of the decedent, for the benefit of the next of kin, to sue one who wrongfully caused the decedent's death. If it were not for this law, a person who injures someone could be sued if the victim lives but would escape suit if the victim dies. In order for the executor to bring a wrongful death action, however, the decedent must have had an enforceable cause of action at the time of death. In other words, there could be no suit by an executor if the decedent could not sue were he or she alive. For example, if the decedent's CONTRIBUTORY NEGLIGENCE is a cause of his or her own injury and death, the executor will not be able to sue. As another example, the executor is barred from suing if the decedent had allowed the STATUTE OF LIMITATIONS to run before the decedent died from the injury.

Yearly Retainer. The fee that a lawyer and client agree upon when the client engages the lawyer on an annual basis. The yearly retainer usually covers certain services, such as professional advice, the drawing up of ordinary business documents, contracts, deeds, mortgages, and the like. When a client is on a yearly retainer, the secretary should know whether a specific matter is covered by the retainer or is to be charged for separately.

Year's Allowance. The amount set by the court or the appraisers in some states for the support of the surviving spouse and/or minor children for one year after decedent's death.

Yellow-Dog Contract. An agreement made by workers, as a condition of employment, not to belong to a union during the period of their employment and not to engage in certain activities, such as collective bargaining or striking. The yellow-dog contract was used effectively by management to keep out unions and preserve the absolute right to employ and discharge workers at will. Legislation has now prohibited the use of anti-union contracts.

York-Antwerp Rules. A set of regulations drafted in 1890 to bring about uniformity in the calculation of GENERAL AVERAGE LOSS claims in the major maritime nations. Although these rules, revised in 1924 and 1950, have never been enacted into law, parties are free to incorporate them into marine insurance policies or other maritime contracts. Today, the York-Antwerp Rules are widely referred to and incorporated into bills of lading (see BILL of Lading) throughout the world.

Z

"Z" Ruling. See FORMS.

Zoning. A regulation, enforced under the police power of municipalities and states and applied to the use of both lands and buildings, whereby land use is restricted to specific purposes and building construction is controlled as to type, intensity, and volume. Most of the larger cities in the United States now have regulatory zoning laws, which exercise powerful influences upon land values.